IMPORTANT NOTE

This book is an A.R.C. (Advanced Readers Copy). It is the second book in the series. It became apparent that the vast amount of previously unpublished historical evidence still hiding in the archives demanded that more than one book to be written. Thus, the various books of the series will be released in paperback before arriving at a final edition. The final edit will be released in hardback once the entire series is finished and edits can be assesseed in relation to the completed series. This new era of on-demand publishing allows for this approach. As such, this initial printing is raw but packed full of previously unpublished research. More importantly, it allows the focus of the project to be the completion of the series.

DEDICATION

For my mother,
Who left this world too young,
And whose guiding hand I perceive to this day.

~ o ~

www.AESamaan.com

H.H. LAUGHLIN: American Scientist. American Progressive. Nazi Collaborator.
Copyright © A.E. Samaan, 2015
Cover design and photography by A.E. Samaan.
Horse swastika deisgn by A.E. Samaan and Mike Rodrigues.
Interior graphics, design, and images by A.E. Samaan.
All rights reserved.

ISBN-13: 978-0-9964163-0-6
ISBN-10: 0-9964163-0-7
Library of Congress Control Number: 2015908772
A.E. SAMAAN*, SAN DIEGO, CA
Samaan, A.E., 1968 -
H.H. LAUGHLIN: American Scientist. American Progressive. Nazi Collaborator.

1. Eugenics - The Holocaust - History - World War II 2. Hitler, Adolf, 1889-1945 - Political and social views. 3. Germany - History - 20th century. 4. Ethics, Evolutionary. 5. National Socialism - philosophy. 6. United States - History - jurisprudence - race laws - anti-miscegenation - segregation. 7. American Civil Rights - History - civil rights legislation. 8. Darwin, Charles, 1809-1882 - Evolutionary theory - Political and social views.

~~~~~

WHY THE SWASTIKA WITH HORSE HEADS?

I am also a photographer and artist in addition to an investigative historian. Having a cover design that is consistent throughout the series was important to me. The design and layout of this cover is an extrapolation of the cover for the first book of the series, "From a 'Race of Masters' to a 'Master Race': 1948 to 1848".

Most importantly, the horse-swastika conveys an important theme about the International eugenics movement and particularly Dr. Laughlin. Most, if not all eugenicists believed human beings to be nothing more than animals. Eugenics was a way of perfecting humanity, and in Laughlin's case, a way of breeding human thoroughbreds. Adolf Hitler called his thoroughbreds a "master race," and every other eugenic-minded zealot had a variation on the theme. Laughlin himself started as an obscure animal breeder in rural Midwest, and would have remained that way if not for his political contacts.

For more information, visit **www.HHLaughlin.com**
For more information on the author, visit **www.AESamaan.com**

H.H. LAUGHLIN

***

American Progressive.
American Scientist.
Nazi Collaborator.

BOOK II
Of a Multi-Part Series

*"No consistent eugenist can be a 'Laisser Faire'
unless he throws up the game in despair.
He must interfere, interfere, interfere!"*
~Sydney Webb~

As quoted on page 117 of Marouf A. Hasain, Jr's 1996 book "The Rhetoric of Eugenics in Anglo-American Thought."

ACKNOWLEDGEMENTS:

This book is the culmination of many years of original research, either by scouring through the various archives or by hunting down old and forgotten books and publications. It would not have been possible without the help and support from the archivists at the following institutions that have preserved the documentation of the eugenics movement. Archives at San Diego State University, University of Southern California, Cold Spring Harbor Laboratory, American Philosophical Society, and our National Archives were of greater use than I initially imagined. However, the following institutions and archivists were truly indispensable:

Truman University – Amanda Langendoerfer
Cal. Tech University – Charlotte (Shelley) Erwin

Certainly, this book would not have been possible without the help and generosity of John Strom. Mr. Strom is the archivist at the Carnegie Institution in Washington D.C. who hunted down the institution's files on the Eugenics Records Office and Harry H. Laughlin. Mr. Strom informs me that these files had not been sourced for decades. He took the time to digitize them and pull them out of obscurity.

Of course, no work of history is possible without help and guidance of those that came before me. The famous bioethicist, Professor Paul Lombardo generously gave his time to answering my questions. This author is particularly thankful to Professor Garland Allen, whom is now retired, but which himself scoured through previously unorganized and forgotten files of the Eugenics Records Office and the Cold Spring Harbor Laboratory both at Truman University and the Carnegie Institution in Washington D.C.

Special thanks go to friends and family, namely George Galatis as he has served as a moral and intellectual backbone that is so necessary when tackling such a controversial subject-matter.

A.E. Samaan
June 2015

H.H. LAUGHLIN

***

American Progressive.
American Scientist.
Nazi Collaborator.

INTRODUCTION	3
EUGENICS PRIMER:	7
A SHORT BIO OF H.H. LAUGHLIN	19
1898 - TIMING IS EVERYTHING	24
1903 - AMERICAN BREEDERS' ASSOCIATION	32
1910 - THE STATION FOR EXPERIMENTAL EVOLUTION	45
1914 - LEGAL ASPECTS OF STERILIZATION	52
1919 - STATISTICAL DIRECTORY OF STATE INSTITUTIONS	60
1920 - BIOLOGICAL ASPECTS OF IMMIGRATION	72
1922 - MODEL EUGENICAL LAW	77
1923 - ANALYSIS OF AMERICA'S MODERN MELTING POT	87
1923 - ERECTING THE GATES ABROAD	95
1924 - IMMIGRATION RESTRICTION ACT	102
1924 - RACIAL INTEGRITY ACT	118
1925 - INT. FEDERATION OF EUGENIC ORGANIZATIONS	132
1927 - BUCK v. BELL	142
1928 - STERILIZING THE "GREATEST GENERATION."	155
1928 - EUGENICAL ASPECTS OF DEPORTATION	164
1932 - ONE-WORLD EUGENIC UTOPIA	171
1933 - A CENTURY OF PROGRESS	183
1933 - EUGENICAL NEWS	191
1933 - TOURING HITLER'S EUGENIC UTOPIA	199
1934 - A REORIENTATION OF THE PROBLEM	218
1934 - PAN AMERICAN CONGRESS	224
1935 - POPULATION CONGRESS IN BERLIN	232
1935 - CARNEGIE'S FIRST ADVISORY COMMITTEE	244
1936 - CONNECTICUT STUDY	248
1936 - HEIDELBERG DEGREE	254
1937 - PIONEER FUND	259
1937 - *ERBKRANK*	273
1938 - THOROUGHBRED STUDY	280
1938 - CONQUEST BY IMMIGRATION	287
1939 - CARNEGIE'S PATIENCE RUNS OUT	304
1944 - *"IN PARI DELICTO"*	311
AMNESIA OR DÉJÀ VU. . . ?	319
FORGETTING OR FOREBODING . . . ?	327

INDEX: Error! Bookmark not defined.

INTRODUCTION

> *"All this my friend, is offered without presuming to anticipate what you alone are qualified to decide for yourself."*
> *- Thomas Jefferson*

Lack of clarity is a direct cause of Holocaust denial. The seeds of Holocaust denial take root and prosper with misinformation. An incomplete history leaves a void. Every question that goes unanswered; every doubt that is left unaddressed; every discrepancy that is not provided an explanation is an opportunity for those that would pervert history. Clarity and transparency are therefore imperative, as they leave no room for denial theories that would deprive the victims of justice, or rob the living of the truth.

Yet, there are critical portions of Holocaust history that remain unaddressed. It seems that the missing pieces of history are typically where that history is politically inconvenient. We rightfully point to the debauchery of the Hitler regime, but have been quite lethargic, or intentionally inactive, in pointing to the aid and support provided by prominent Britons and Americans. The first book of this series, "From a 'Race of Masters' to a 'Master Race': 1948 to 1848," began to piece together the vast amount of support provided by American and British scientists.

However, there is one American scientist that was particularly important in fulfilling Hitler's perverse aspirations: Harry H. Laughlin, the superintendent of the Eugenics Record Office. Laughlin initially became influential throughout the world for his work on eugenics and immigration reform. Later Laughlin had a significant hand in some of the most horrid episodes in human history. His contributions to world history are listed here in order to illustrate just how improbable it is for Laughlin's story to go untold. Laughlin utilized his influence to:

- Draft the "Model Eugenical Law" that was translated by the Germans to create significant portions of Adolf Hitler's eugenic sterilization laws, otherwise known as the Nuremberg racial laws.
- Serve as the "expert" witness for the United States Congress to pass the 1924 Immigration Restriction Act, which would, during World War II, prevent many Jewish refugees from reaching the safety of U.S. shores.
- Provide the "scientific" basis for the 1927 Buck v. Bell Supreme Court case which made "eugenic sterilization" legal inside of the United States, and thus paved the way for 80,000 Americans to be sterilized against their will.
- Defend Hitler's Nuremberg racial laws as "scientifically" sound in order to dispel the mounting international criticism.
- Be granted an honorary degree from Heidelberg University by Hitler's government, specifically for his work on eugenics and immigration control.
- Create the political organization that ensured that the "science" of eugenics would survive the negative taint of The Holocaust in post-WWII America. These political connections would prove instrumental in the Jim Crow era of American racial strife.

Therefore, the history of The Holocaust simply cannot be told with any thoroughness or accuracy without including Harry H. Laughlin, yet that is precisely what has happened. While lesser figures from Holocaust history have several books devoted to them, Laughlin has remained a side topic. As of the writing of this book between 2014 and 2015, no books dedicated to documenting the life of Harry H. Laughlin had been published. Nothing but a single unpublished dissertation and a relative small number of papers in journals were available prior to this book. The unpublished dissertation by Frances Janet Hassencahl was written in 1970 for her Degree of Doctor of Philosophy at Case Western Reserve University. She wrote it primarily as an analysis of Laughlin's effectiveness as a public speaker, but despite its limited scope, has otherwise served as the authoritative work devoted to this pivotal figure. The most thorough academic paper is entitled "The Papers of Harry Hamilton Laughlin." The paper was written by Garland Allen and Randall D. Bird for the Annals of the History of Biology. Professor Allen has dedicated much time and effort to understanding the eugenics movement. Both Hassencahl and Allen will be cited here for guidance.

Scientists like Harry H. Laughlin once enjoyed international fame. Dr. Laughlin should share in the infamy and disrepute of Dr. Mengele, the Nazi scientist known for conducting experiments on concentration camp inmates. However, Dr. Mengele was in truth following Dr. Laughlin's lead. That no books are dedicated to the history of Laughlin or his influential associates, such as Charles B. Davenport, Major Leonard Darwin, Karl Pearson, Alfred Ploetz, Ernst Rüdin, and Otmar von Verschuer, while countless volumes are written about Dr. Mengele, illustrates just how incomplete Holocaust history truly is. Mengele was the subordinate of Ploetz, Rüdin, and Verschuer in the Nazi hierarchy, and in turn, these German eugenicists were very much indebted to Major Darwin, Davenport, Pearson, and Laughlin.

Dr. Laughlin's history goes a long way to explain important questions about The Holocaust, namely how Hitler was able to draft so many laws in such a short period of time, and how Hitler was able to mostly manage international scrutiny of his racial policies in the decade between 1933 and 1943. In addition, Laughlin's efforts significantly impacted both sides of the Atlantic. A full accounting of Laughlin's influence begins to answer pressing questions about U.S. policy during The Holocaust, especially for those of the Jewish faith, whom should be privy to the a full accounting of why their ancestors were denied safe harbor.

Equity also demands a full accounting, as it is only just to expose non-German collaborators. Leading up to The Holocaust, it was quite common to hear American and British eugenicists publicly call for "racial purification" and the systematic sterilization, segregation, or euthanasia of unwanted members of society. Eugenics was in the news frequently. The German, American, and British eugenicists vociferously celebrated the implementation of eugenic legislation (i.e. the infamous

Nuremberg Laws) by National Socialist Germany and these "accomplishments" were broadly documented by the mainline journalism of the time.

More to the point, the newspaper and magazine clippings prior to 1942 would indicate that Laughlin should have been remembered as an indispensable part of Holocaust history, and by extension, equally reviled as Hitler's henchmen. Clearly, this is not what happened. The systematic and intentional distancing of American science from eugenics seems to begin when Hitler's henchmen demonstrated what eugenic utopianism would truly look like in practice. The world winced in disgust, and the politically astute and politically connected eugenicists stopped advertising the parallels and commonalities between themselves and their German associates. Tracing the history from the Nuremberg Trials onwards demonstrates a sinister pattern of evasion; a systematic and seemingly intentional side-stepping of the evidence of the very close relationships between prominent German scientists and their American and British counterparts.

These men were the product of academia, and much of their story remains within the walls of academia. Is it admission by omission for academia to seemingly ignore such pivotal figures? Humanity cannot persist in telling the history of The Holocaust where Mengele's mentors are not made to account for their actions. Academia has done an inordinate amount of hand-wringing for their complicity in creating the atom bomb. Thus, their systematic distancing from eugenics rings uncomfortably hollow by labeling it a "pseudo-science" after the fact. The full history of a figure central to eugenics such as Laughlin will reveal just how entrenched and accepted the "science" truly was.

All previous works on Laughlin depended on the Laughlin Collection held at Truman University's archives. However, none of these works are comprehensive. The Carnegie Institution of Washington D.C. was the organization that funded the Eugenics Record Office where Laughlin worked; what arguably was the epicenter of both the American and international eugenics movement in the 20th century. Professor Allen was writing for journals. Thus the length and scope was limited. Frances Janet Hassencahl was either unaware of, or simply did not source the papers at the Carnegie Institution. However, no analysis of Laughlin or the eugenics movement can be said to be complete without including the internal correspondence of the organization that made his work possible. As such, this is the first book to address Laughlin's history from beginning to end.

The Laughlin files at Carnegie were generously made available to this author. According to the Carnegie archivists, no one has requested these files since they were stored away decades ago. The Carnegie files will serve as the backbone of this work, in order to document for posterity how that otherwise prestigious institution came to be entangled with the likes of Laughlin. These files tell the insider's story of how this organization slowly came to the ghastly realization of precisely what Laughlin's relationship with the Hitler regime truly meant.

A CIVIC BIOLOGY

Presented in Problems

BY

GEORGE WILLIAM HUNTER, A.M.

HEAD OF THE DEPARTMENT OF BIOLOGY, DE WITT CLINTON HIGH SCHOOL, NEW YORK CITY.

AUTHOR OF "ELEMENTS OF BIOLOGY," "ESSENTIALS OF BIOLOGY," ETC.

AMERICAN BOOK COMPANY

NEW YORK   CINCINNATI   CHICAGO

---

196 EVOLUTION

of man upon the earth, we find that a little better than one of the lower an wandering from place to place, feeding u he could kill with his hands. Gradual use weapons, and thus kill his prey, plements for this purpose. As man plements of bronze and of iron were subjugation and domestication of an Man then began to cultivate the field of abode other than a cave. The be long ago, but even to-day the earth i

The Races of Man. — At the present time there exist upon the earth five races or varieties of man, each very different from the other in instincts, social customs, and, to an extent, in structure. These are the Ethiopian or negro type, originating in Africa; the Malay or brown race, from the islands of the Pacific; the American Indian; the Mongolian or yellow race, including the natives of China, Japan, and the Eskimos; and finally, the highest type of all, the Caucasians, represented by the civilized white inhabitants of Europe and America.

REFERENCE BOOKS
ELEMENTARY

Hunter, *Laboratory Problems in Civic Biology*, American Book Company.
Bulletin of U.S. Department of Agriculture, *Division of Biological Survey*, Nos. 1, 6, 13, 17.
Davison, *Practical Zoölogy*. American Book Company.
Ditmars, *The Reptiles of New York*. Guide Leaflet 20. Amer. Mus. of Nat. History.
Sharpe, *A Laboratory Manual in Biology*, pp. 140-150, American Book Company.
Walker, *Our Birds and Their Nestlings*. American Book Company.
Walter, H. E. and H. A., *Wild Birds in City Parks*. Published by authors.

ADVANCED

Apgar, *Birds of the United States*. American Book Company.
Beebe, *The Bird*. Henry Holt and Company.
Ditmars, *The Reptile Book*. Doubleday, Page and Company.
Hegner, *Zoölogy*. The Macmillan Company.

EUGENICS PRIMER:

> "At some future period, not very distant as measured by centuries, the civilised races of man will almost certainly exterminate, and replace, the savage races throughout the world. At the same time the anthropomorphous apes...will no doubt be exterminated. The break between man and his nearest allies will then be wider, for it will intervene between man in a more civilised state, as we may hope, even than the Caucasian, and some ape as low as a baboon, instead of as now between the negro or Australian and the gorilla."
> - Charles Darwin - The Descent of Man (1871), VI, Chap. VI, Pgs. 200-201

So what is eugenics? Even those well-versed in WWII history still misunderstand the ideology that was the impetus behind the "crimes against humanity." A quick primer is in order. The general confusion about the science behind the murders began as American and British academic elites deliberately distanced the eugenics they practiced from the eugenics implemented by the Third Reich. The relationship was further blurred by the Nuremberg Trials. The prosecution at the Nuremberg Trials deliberately described the "crimes" as part of a military conspiracy, and not as the consequence of an ideology, a world-view, or creed that permeated all aspects of Hitler's Third Reich. The Nuremberg Trials were, after all, "military tribunals", and were limited to presiding over crimes of a military nature. Thus, the prosecution at Nuremberg focused disproportionately on those cold water and high-altitude experiments conducted at the concentration camps, as they had been conducted for a military research by the likes of Dr. Mengele. Neither the high altitude nor the cold water experiments had anything to do with Hitler's perverse fascination with breeding a "master race." Despite the horrid nature of these experiments, they were a small handful of incidents compared to the mechanized and industrial scope of eugenic policy in Nazi Germany.

Furthermore, the military tribunal had no jurisdiction to sit in judgment on the German domestic policy that existed prior to the declaration of war, nor did the American military have the jurisdiction to sit in judgment over crimes that occurred in nations where the United States was not actively engaged in the war. This became a distinctly limiting factor after the coalition of nations that presided over the first Nuremberg Trial fell apart and the German territories were divided between East and West along the footprint of what would later be the Berlin Wall.

The above demarcation is of some significance. The peak of Hitler's genocidal campaign came after 1942 or 1943, yet the relevant policies and laws were put in place as soon as the regime came to power a decade earlier in 1933. This is a crucial point to make about the timeline and its relation to the jurisdictional limitations of the Nuremberg Trial. The ethnic cleansing campaign to breed a "master race" began as soon as the National Socialists amassed power in 1933. Thus, much of the early "crimes against humanity" fell outside of the jurisdiction allowed to the military tribunal.

More to the point, one cannot understand The Holocaust without understanding the intentions, ideology, and mechanisms that were put in place in 1933. The eugenics movement may have come to a catastrophic crescendo with the Hitler regime, but the political movement, the world-view, the ideology, and the science that aspired to breed humans like prized horses began almost 100 years earlier. More poignantly, the ideology and those legal and governmental mechanisms of a eugenic world-view inevitably lead back to the British and American counterparts that Hitler's scientists collaborated with. Posterity must gain understanding of the players that made eugenics a respectable scientific and political movement, as Hitler's regime was able to evade wholesale condemnation in those critical years between 1933 and 1943 precisely because eugenics had gained international acceptance. As this book will evidence, Hitler's infamous 1933 laws mimicked those already in place in the United States, Britain, Norway, Sweden, Finland, and Canada.

So what is this scientific and political movement that for 100 years aspired to breed humans like dogs or horses? Eugenics is quite literally, as defined by its principal proponents, an attempt at "directing evolution" by controlling any aspect of human existence that affects human heredity. From its onset, Francis Galton, the cousin of Charles Darwin and the man credited with the creation of the science of eugenics, knew that the cause of eugenics had to be observed with religious fervor and dedication. As the quote on the opening pages of this book illustrates, a eugenicist must "intrude, intrude, intrude." A vigilant control over anything and everything that affects the gene pool is essential to eugenics. The policies could not allow for the individual to enjoy self-government or self-determination any more than a horse breeder can allow the animals to determine whom to breed with. One simply cannot breed humans like horses without imbuing the state with the level of control a farmer has over its livestock, not only controlling procreation, but also the diet, access to medical services, and living conditions. Garland Allen and Randall D. Bird explain how interest in animal breeding turned into an interest in breeding humans like animals:

> Like many eugenicist, Laughlin was fascinated by animal breeding, and for a serious reason. He believed, through analogy, that the eugenicist was to humans what the agricultural breeder was to animals; a scientist using experimental procedures to perfect the species along desired ends. ("The Papers of Harry Hamilton Laughlin", Annals of the History of Biology, Vol. 14, No. 2)

Popular culture has rightfully associated eugenics with ethnic cleansing and dystopian aspirations. However, at one point, it was accepted by the majority of the scientific community as Galton's eugenics had emerged in conjunction with Darwin's Theory of Evolution. Eugenics was exposed as a vile belief system after

The Holocaust. Eugenics now seems to share infamy with other erroneous doctrines such as phrenology, but the general public is yet to understand exactly how pervasive eugenics truly was or how deeply it influenced not just the Third Reich, but comparatively benign governments in Sweden, Denmark, Norway, Canada, England, and the United States.

More to the point of this book, it is important to summarize quickly what the eugenic cause entailed for those that preached its doctrines. Laughlin certainly understood eugenics to imply a nation-wide effort that necessitated the enforcement by an all-powerful state obsessed with the purity of its population. The Laughlin files held at Truman University's archives hold a two-page compendium of the definition of the science of eugenics by several of its key proponents. Much of it was taken from a paper by a "Prof. Dr. Günther Just" entitled "*Bevölkerungspolitische Richtlinien*" which was presented to the International Congress for Population Study that was held in Hitler's Germany in 1935. The first definition is from Otto von Verschuer, the man whom the infamous Dr. Mengele answered to in the Nazi hierarchy:

> O. von Verschuer: "The aim of eugenics (*Rassenhygiene*) is the cultivation of good hereditary qualities, and therefore, the preservation of hereditary soundness in the nation."

Note that Otto von Verschuer's definition is devoid of the overt anti-Semitism Hitler's National Socialist regime is known for. This is what made the movement so dangerous, as it appealed to an otherwise educated group of intellectuals. These were scientists embarking on a project of "directed evolution." Anti-Semitism dovetailed with eugenics because those that wanted to "direct evolution" believed in a racial hierarchy with respects to evolution, and these scientists regarded the Jewish population as being of a lower evolutionary value. Alfred Ploetz, one of the fathers of eugenics in Germany as well as one of the architects of the Third Reich's eugenic legislation, is the next definition Laughlin quotes:

> Alfred Ploetz: "Eugenics (*Rassenhygiene*) is the endeavor to keep the species healthy and to develop its inborn qualities."

Again, these are the seemingly benign words of a true-believer intent on redirecting human evolution. Laughlin's compendium also includes definitions from well-known American and British eugenicists like Havelock Ellis and C.W. Saleeby. Laughlin also provides four different definitions of the science of eugenics from Herman Lundborg. Lundborg was one of the premiere eugenicists from Sweden. In 1922, Lundborg was appointed as the head of Sweden's eugenic governmental agency, the State Institute of Racial Biology. Some of his definitions are telling as to the scope of a nation dedicated to breeding humans like horses, and willing to reorganize society towards this end:

> H. Lundborg: "Its (Racehygiene) aim and endeavor is to prevent the emergence

and spreading of hereditary degeneracy and to organize social conditions so that future generations can best be equipped for their struggle for existence. This can best be achieved by a good mate-selection."

Some of Galton's devoted followers spoke of "positive" and "negative" eugenics in sporadic fashion, and historians of the movement have since tried to split the movement and its proponents down these demarcation lines. Laughlin quotes C.W. Saleeby, who was an associate of Margaret Sanger and an early ideological head of her Birth Control movement. Saleeby provides an interesting dissection of eugenics and is quoted as having "Galton's approval to extend the concept of National Eugenics under three heads":

Positive Eugenics, the encouragement of worthy parenthood.
Negative Eugenics, the discouragement of unworthy parenthood.
Preventive Eugenics, the protection of parenthood from the racial poisons. (according to Saleeby: alcoholism and venereal diseases).

The last point is instrumental in revealing that eugenics was far more than just a human breeding project. It is important as it reveals why Hitler's domestic policy went to the lengths it did to protect its prized gene pool. The Third Reich would implement some of the world's first anti-smoking, anti-alcohol, and the most extensive campaign to stamp out known carcinogens such as food colorants. Controlling human heredity in order to direct evolution in a predetermined path meant vigilantly guarding against anything and everything that would negatively affect the gene pool of a population. Eugenics is not just a tool of totalitarianism. Eugenics, as it was conceived, could not be anything but totalitarian as it desired to control all aspects of society. Hitler's "National Socialist" (*Nationalsozialist*) form of government was amongst the first to put the full force of its government to conduct compulsory health initiatives. It is by no coincidence that the Dachau concentration camp used its slave-labor to run the largest organic produce farm of the era.

This is also what makes the intentions of these scientists relevant today, as the motivation to legislate and micro-manage the lives of the population can hardly be said to be a thing of the past. Many of these compulsory health measures remain part of mainstream collectivist thought. Yet, they are the very mechanisms by which a 'totalitarian' form of government enacts the strangling control over its populace. Dystopias come in the guise of good intentions and are always the inevitable outcome of utopian aspirations. Case in point, before the term "totalitarian" was ever uttered, the young Adolf Hitler was dreaming up an "Ideal State" where everything would be planned for and provided for. These utopian sentiments later informed the expansive domestic policy of a hyper "nationalized" and "socialized" Germany under Hitler's National Socialist German Workers Party. (*Nationalsozialistische Deutsche Arbeiterpartei*)

Thus, Hitler's National Socialism was a centrally-planned society by necessity, as one cannot breed a "master race" without total control over all aspects of society. A eugenic society by necessity is a centrally-planned society, and in many ways centrally-planned economies tempt the necessity for eugenics. Centrally-planned and collectivized societies are focused on the equitable distribution of resources and are, for this reason, easily threatened by a population that either grows beyond the available resources or fails to produce them in the pre-determined quantities. This is why "population control" efforts of the era were synonymous with "eugenics", and why "eugenics" became synonymous with the elimination of "surplus" population. This is also why Hitler's first victims were otherwise "Aryans" and "Nordics" that were simply deemed "useless eaters" or as "lives unworthy of living." This was the "negative" side of eugenics, which aspired to rid society of undesirable, and more importantly, unneeded drains on its resources.

So where does the virulent racism and anti-Semitism come into play into this utopian idea of how to breed humans? All of the leading eugenicists that had influence on the international movement believed in an evolutionary hierarchy which quite literally subscribed to the anthropological view that "whites" were the pinnacle of the evolutionary ladder and that the colored races were closer to apes than to whites. In terms understood by an animal breeder, allowing a superior specimen to breed with an inferior specimen only produced an undesired variation that was considered a "degeneration," an "atavism", or in other words, a step backwards evolutionary speaking. By this measure, anyone deemed lesser than the prized "Aryans" or "Nordics" was a detriment to the population's gene pool. In the case of the Germans, the offending ethnicities were the Jews and the Eastern Europeans. In the case of the American eugenicists, the offending population were the recently arrived Italians, Irish Catholics, Eastern Europeans, and on the West Coast, the Hispanics, and the Orientals.

Frances Janet Hassencahl's unpublished dissertation explains that Charles Darwin's "articulation of the mutability of the species" is what inspired the "idea of man taking active effort to control or change his evolution." (Pg. 20) Thus, it is of no coincidence that the laboratory at Cold Spring Harbor, where Laughlin worked, was named the "Station for Experimental Evolution." Most academics bitterly reject the notion that Charles Darwin had anything to do with the eugenic movement that lead up to The Holocaust. This is a subject that must be broached with equal trepidation as that exercised for the topic of racism. The rhetoric and vitriol that surrounds this conversation reaches theatrical extremes.

The question is not if Charles Darwin would have approved of the tactics of Hitler's SS or Brown Shirts. By all accounts, Charles Darwin was a compassionate man incapable of the violence practiced by Hitler's henchmen. However, what is too easily lost upon those blindly defending Darwin is that the ideology presented by the eugenicists was a biological one.

Charles Darwin is championed for his first book, "On the Origin of Species by Means of Natural Selection, or the Preservation of Favoured Races in the Struggle for Life." However, Darwin would not speak about humans in his first book. To get to the heart of the matter one must ask two questions that touch the core of both what Darwin postulates in his second book, "The Descent of Man," and what Francis Galton and his followers believed to be at the center of the eugenic creed:

- A.) Did Charles Darwin believe that his Theory indicated that some of the "races of man" were closer to apes than to man on the evolutionary ladder he depicted? Or, in the alternative, did Charles Darwin believe that there was a hierarchy of the "races of man" with some of these so-called "races" more evolved than others?
- B.) Did Charles Darwin believe that the interbreeding between a higher evolved and a lower evolved race resulted in a step backward evolutionary speaking?

The answer to both of these questions is unquestionably, yes. There is no version of Darwin's work where he presents the human race as monolithic in evolutionary value. In fact, he says quite the opposite as these are the differences by which "selection" operates per his Theory:

> There is, however, no doubt that the various races, when carefully compared and measured, differ much from each other,—as in the texture of the hair, the relative proportions of all parts of the body, the capacity of the lungs, the form and capacity of the skull, and even in the convolutions of the brain. But, it would be an endless task to specify the numerous points of structural difference. The races differ also in constitution, in acclimatisation, and in liability to certain diseases. Their mental characteristics are likewise very distinct; chiefly as it would appear in their emotional, but partly in their intellectual, faculties. Every one who has had the opportunity of comparison, must have been struck with the contrast between the taciturn, even morose, aborigines of S. America and the light-hearted, talkative negroes. There is a nearly similar contrast between the Malays and the Papuans, who live under the same physical conditions, and are separated from each other only by a narrow space of sea. (Pgs. 216-217, "The Descent of Man," First edition, 1871)

Even the crowned champion of evolutionary science, Stephen Jay Gould concedes this point:

> Biological arguments for racism may have been common before 1859, but they increased by orders of magnitude following the acceptance of evolutionary theory. The litany is familiar: cold, dispassionate, objective, modern science shows us that races can be ranked on a scale of superiority. If this offends Christian morality or a sentimental belief in human unity, so be it: science must be free to proclaim unpleasant truths. (Pg. 127, "Ontogeny and Phylogeny")

It is from this concept that eugenics originates. Those that would follow Darwin, namely Francis Galton, Ernst Haeckel, and other key figures in the eugenics movement believed that the offspring between a white man and one of the "colored races" was a human further down the evolutionary ladder than the white man. This is also where "scientific racism" started to adopt the methods of the animal breeder. Francis Galton picked up on what Darwin postulated and extrapolated it, devising the science of eugenics as the science of directed evolution through better breeding of humans.

This is where academics begin to disregard Darwin's own words, and wrongfully claim that eugenics and its proponents misunderstood, misinterpreted, or perverted Darwin's work. Darwin himself not only praised Galton, but also incorporated Galton's eugenic notions to underscore the foundations of his second book, which addressed precisely how evolution applied to humanity. The introduction to "The Descent of Man, and Selection in Relation to Sex" incorporated both Galton and Haeckel's eugenics and credits both of them generously. More to the point, Darwin himself qualified his "single origins" theory by proposing that there was an evolutionary hierarchy of the various "races of man", and that evolution happened precisely by "sexual selection," with some of the choices between "fittest" and "unfit" being progressive and regressive evolutionary speaking. To deny that "selection" of the more or less "fit" sexual mates was not central to Darwin's "sexual selection" is to deny Darwin's work in its practical entirety.

Laughlin himself would directly quote Darwin as part of his testimony before the United States Congress during the immigration debates of the early 1920's. (Pg. 277, Hassencahl) The eugenicists that labored to advance Laughlin's work described eugenics as "applied biology", or "directed evolution." This was the definition given by Dr. Clarence Campbell, President of the Eugenics Research Association, in a speech delivered before the Social Service Club of Delaware in Wilmington. Laughlin kept a copy of this address in his files:

> Eugenics does not consist, as people have sometimes been led to believe, merely in sporadic attempts to persuade people here and there to produce healthier and better babies. But eugenics is the broad science of human evolution; it is the scientific study of the changes which take place in the evolution of human conditions. Francis Galton who was the first cousin of Charles Darwin, and who originated the science of eugenics and gave it its name, based this science upon the principles of biological evolution which Darwin gave to the world. Galton, who possessed no less genius than Darwin, at once saw the incalculable value of applying the principles of the biological evolution of species to the evolution of humanity. And he devoted the remaining forty odd years of his life to the intensive development of this science. The general principles of eugenic evolution which Galton enunciated in his lifetime, stand today as irrefutable and impregnable. We may well ask why these principles have not been universally accepted and adopted as the basis of our social development. (Laughlin Papers, Box D-2-3:5 Truman Univ., "Race Betterment and Sterilization," Feb. 13th, 1934, Campbell)

Benign as Campbell's definition may sound, this was the essence of "scientific racism," a type of racism which is veiled in intellectual legitimacy because of its scientific foundations. It is a kind of racism that should not be confused with common bigotry. Eugenicists went to great measures to distance themselves from the poor rural whites and the low-brow jingoism of rural bigotry. The most dangerous and influential leaders of the eugenics movement were students and professors from the American Ivy League universities and their European equivalents.

Of equal importance is the need to clarify that scientists like Laughlin and his mentor, Charles B. Davenport, had taken up the cause of eugenics much prior to Adolf Hitler. The international eugenics movement was well entrenched when Adolf Hitler was nothing more than a frustrated artist. The German eugenicists under Hitler, Eugene Fischer, closely collaborated with Charles B. Davenport in a study of blacks of mixed ethnicity decades prior to the National Socialist regime. While German eugenicists had a significant influence in the movement prior to World War I, the devastation in the wake of this war allowed British and American eugenicists to make significant strides while German medicine and science was teetering on the verge of total collapse. Laughlin, Davenport, and Britons like Leonard Darwin, the famous scientist's son, made it a point to bring their German counterparts back up to speed. Thus, the modern and matured version of eugenics that became part of Hitler's repertoire was an American and British export to Germany.

More to the point, Fischer was one of the authors of the eugenics textbook that Hitler was handed while he was writing and researching "Mein Kampf." The insidious nature of Hitler's National Socialism; its obsession with hereditary purity, was an acquired aspect that was not part of Hitler's megalomania prior to him being sent to jail for the failed Beer-Hall Putsch. Hitler would research and write "Mein Kampf" while in jail. As discussed in "From a 'Race of Masters' to a 'Master Race': 1948 to 1848," eugenic notions do not appear in Hitler's speeches until after his brief stint in prison. They are ever present after that, and "racial hygiene" becomes the central concept that permeated all aspects of National Socialism. Robert Proctor, author of the 2001 book "The Nazi War on Cancer," explains the misunderstanding that persists to this day:

> One often hears that National Socialists distorted science, that doctors perhaps cooperated more with the Nazi regime than they should have, but that by 1933, as one émigré said, it was too late, and scientists had no alternative but to cooperate or flee. There is certainly some truth in this, but **I think it misses the more important point that medical scientists were the ones who invented racial hygiene in the first place.** (Pg. 27, "When Medicine Went Mad" – Pg. 58 "From a 'Race of Masters' to a 'Master Race'", emphasis mine)

Hitler would describe his spell in prison as a "free education at the state's expense." J.F. Lehmann, Hitler's publisher, financier, and sympathizer brought Hitler the book titled "*Grundriss der Menschlichen Erblichkeitslehre und Rassenhygiene,*" or in English the "Principles of Human Heredity and Racial Hygiene." The book was first published by J.F. Lehmann in 1923. The book has come to be known by historians as the "Baur-Fischer-Lenz" book. It had been written in conjunction by Eugene Fischer, Fritz Lenz and Erwin Baur. Hitler is widely quoted by historians as stating that he had "studied with great interest the laws of several American states concerning prevention of reproduction by people whose progeny would, in all probability, be of no value or be injurious to the racial stock." We will discuss later why Hitler's reference to "several" States is of historical importance.

There is one important observation to keep in mind. The basic premise that one can breed desirable traits in humans, or breed out undesirable ones, persists to this day. Modern genetics had disproved this claim by the time Harry H. Laughlin and his eugenic-minded counterparts made their concerted effort to radically change American and German law. The Hardy-Weinberg Principle had disproven the claim that eugenics could alter the course of human evolution. The equilibrium model disproved the claim that degenerate families were increasing. Their equation also showed that sterilization of "defective" individuals would never appreciably reduce the percentage of mental defectives in society. In other words, the Hardy-Weinberg Principle proved that the systematic eradication of unwanted people over a thousand years would still fail to "direct evolution" as the eugenicists postulated.

The work by Godfrey Harold "G. H." Hardy and Wilhelm Weinberg was hardly too isolated or obscure to have escaped the eugenic-minded scientific community. According to Daniel Kelves, the author of the book, "In The Name of Eugenics," the principle was used to identify the various blood groups in humans. Felix Bernstein, working with funding from the Rockefeller Institute, used the principle to further refine the work of the Nobel Prize-winning Karl Landsteiner. Landsteiner developed the modern system of classification of blood groups, thus enabling physicians to transfuse blood without endangering the patient's life. This was a major milestone in the advance of science, too important to entertain the notion that the eugenicists could have been unaware of their impact or meaning.

Furthermore, George Shull, who also worked at the Carnegie Station for Experimental Evolution, showed that hybrid corn plants are more vigorous than pure-bred ones. This refuted the notion that racial purity offers any biological advantage or that race mixing leads to "degeneration" of racial types, as the eugenicists contended. We know that Laughlin was aware of Shull's work. Copies of Shull's work and correspondence can still be found at the Laughlin Papers held at the Truman University Archives. (Box: D-5-5:7, D-5-4:13, D-2-1:22)

Furthermore, in spite of the mounting evidence against eugenics, Laughlin himself refused to recognize that economics, culture, and other environmental influences severely affected the individual's ability to be successful members of society. Laughlin, Davenport, and Leonard Darwin stuck to the belief that a heredity determined everything about humans. As Hassencahl points out in her unpublished dissertation, "Laughlin was not trying to avoid the nature-nurture controversy; for him the question did not exist." (Pg. 250, Hassencahl)

So why did it take the rest of the scientific community so long to do an about face on eugenics? The scientific community that had largely supported eugenics didn't dispute the validity of the Hardy-Weinberg Principle; they just seemed to refuse to believe that their previously held convictions that "defectives" should not reproduce was mistaken. After all, it had been no one less than Charles Darwin to propose that humanity could benefit from the animal breeder's hand in "Descent of Man," and at this point in history, it was these Ivy League educated scientists, whom also happened to be heading up most of the influential journals and institutions.

For this reason, it is also important to define what kind of "science" eugenicists practiced. Francis Galton was not a scientist, and Harry H. Laughlin was not a lawyer. Yet, both spent as much time drafting proposals on how government should be run and society organized as they did conducting what we generally understand as scientific endeavors. Also, eugenics did not rely on the type of laboratory science as we know it in the 21st century. Eugenics relied almost exclusively on statistics, and not scientific experimentation as it is typically understood today. It was the science of cranial measurements, family pedigrees, and other statistical methods of gathering information that was utilized to differentiate the different "races" of man. This was the contrast between eugenics and genetics as genetics emerged along with the new technological developments in science.

The internal correspondence of the eugenicists proves that they were keenly aware of what modern genetics was accomplishing. Leonard Darwin bemoans criticism and opines that work being done in laboratories with expensive instrumentation would not make his work obsolete. It had. He just refused to acknowledge it. Karl Pearson, Francis Galton's protégé and founder of the journal *Biometrika*, literally threw tantrums and lashed out at any colleague that even tinkered with any other methodology outside of Biometrics, the other name for the eugenic statistical method. Curiously enough, Charles Darwin's other relatives alluded to as much in the first "Galton Lecture" before the Eugenics Education Society on February 16, 1914:

> The contrast between Galtonism and Mendelism may be illustrated by an example that if not a strict analogy has in it something illuminating, especially for those who do not know too much of the subject. **Galton seems to me like a medieval chemist while Mendel is a modern one.** Galton can observe, or can follow the changes that occur when two compounds are mixed. But the Mendelian is like a modern chemist who calls the chemical elements to his aid, and is able to express the result of the experiment in terms of these elements. This is an enormous advantage, and if my analogy is to be trusted it would seem as though a progressive study of heredity must necessarily be on Mendelian lines. (Francis Darwin, "Galton Lecture", emphasis mine)

Mendel is often said to be the father of genetics, and many historians paint a broad brush and castigate "geneticists" for their relationship to eugenics. Others often point to the institutions that funded eugenics as being the same. This book will evidence that it was the geneticists, many of the ones that worked in the same institutions as Laughlin, which would ultimately be the first to take drastic steps to expose eugenics. The evidence dissected and extrapolated in this book demonstrates that institutions that had at one point been supportive of eugenics shutdown and defunded their eugenic programs prior to any knowledge of the Holocaust crimes. Part of their reasoning was the highly politicized nature of Laughlin's work, which tailored scientific conclusions towards political ends in spite of what the scientific evidence showed.

Therefore, these observations should by no means be construed as an attack on science in general. To the contrary, this is intended to be high-praise for those that practice "pure science," and which place science above the political fray that some scientists are too often caught up in. The truth is that the Hardy-Weinberg Principle was pure science and thus lacked the political and ideological propaganda megaphone that the eugenics movement excelled at. Hardy was a pure mathematician and held applied mathematics in some contempt. He made statements to that effect in his 1940 book "A Mathematician's Apology":

> I have never done anything 'useful'. No discovery of mine has made, or is likely to make, directly or indirectly, for good or ill, the least difference to the amenity of the world. (Pg. 83, "Godfrey Harold Hardy")

As such, this book serves as an indictment of politicized science. It is the political strategies employed by the likes of Laughlin that this book will expose:

> But as Alston Chase put it, "when the search for truth is confused with political advocacy, the pursuit of knowledge is reduced to the quest for power." That is the danger we now face. And this is why the intermixing of science and politics is a bad combination, with a bad history. We must remember the history, and be certain that what we present to the world as knowledge is disinterested and honest. - Michael Crichton "Why Politicized Science is Dangerous" (Excerpted from State of Fear)

Neither politicized science nor the hubris of perfecting humanity can be said to be things of the past. These political strategies and mechanisms are still used in the 21st Century on a regular basis by scientists equally politicized as Harry H. Laughlin. Utopian aspirations may be stronger and more prevalent today than ever. The astute reader will recognize the parallels.

THE
HISTORY OF CREATION:

OR THE DEVELOPMENT OF THE EARTH AND ITS
INHABITANTS BY THE ACTION OF NATURAL CAUSES.

A POPULAR EXPOSITION OF
THE DOCTRINE OF EVOLUTION IN GENERAL, AND OF THAT OF
DARWIN, GOETHE, AND LAMARCK IN PARTICULAR.

FROM THE GERMAN OF
ERNST HAECKEL,
PROFESSOR IN THE UNIVERSITY OF JENA.

THE TRANSLATION REVISED BY
PROFESSOR E. RAY LANKESTER, M.A., F.R.S.
FELLOW OF EXETER COLLEGE, OXFORD.

IN TWO VOLUMES.
VOL. I.

HENRY S. KING & CO., LONDON.
1876.

A SHORT BIO OF H.H. LAUGHLIN

> *"If I can't be great I certainly can do much good. And I intend to do it."*
> – H.H. Laughlin letter to his mother.

Harry Hamilton Laughlin epitomizes the eugenics movement. He exemplifies the jump from animal breeding to human breeding. Every single eugenicist from Francis Galton to Adolf Hitler used the metaphor of the stockyard, the farmer, the gardener, and the breeder to sell their vision. Laughlin was an expert horse breeder, and he routinely compared human breeding to horse breeding and vice versa. While some of his colleagues voiced discomfort with the metaphor as well as the application of the "methods of the stockyard," evidently sensing the obvious moral and ethical concerns, Laughlin voiced no such doubts.

Laughlin was born March 11, 1880 in Oskaloosa, Iowa. He was the son of George Hamilton Laughlin and Deborah Jane Laughlin. His father was a minister of the Christian Church in Kirksville and professor of Romance Languages at the First District Normal School. The Laughlin family was of English, Scottish, Irish, and German ancestry, possibly including President James Madison as an ancestor. He had nine brothers and sisters who called him "Hi Yi." The Laughlin family was politically aware, and the Progressive label perfectly fit the Laughlin family brand of political activism. Frances Janet Hassencahl describes this segment of the American population:

> Most Progressives were from the middle class and well educated, thus eugenics, because it involved a scientific reform, had a particular appeal. Its emphasis upon heredity and good-breeding also appealed to many old-family Protestant reformers, particularly those who were dismayed to find the cities filling up with immigrants whose behavior, appearance and culture was so obviously different from their own. Edward A. Ross, a former Populist, a leading ideologist for the Progressives, and a member of La Follette's brain trust at the University of Wisconsin, in a good example of the Progressives, who lent his name and support to various eugenical causes. (Pg. 35, "Harry H. Laughlin, Expert Eugenics Agent", Frances Janet Hassencahl, 1970, University Microfilms)

Professor Garland Allen, provides a similar assessment:

> It is interesting to note that in this regard eugenics was to the progressive era of the twentieth-century capitalism what social Darwinism had been to the more laissez-faire era of mid-nineteenth-century capitalism. Social Darwinism was an eminently laissez-faire biological theory of society, in an era still dominated by laissez-faire economics. Eugenics was an eminently regulative and scientifically planned biological theory of society, in an era beginning to be dominated by progressive era planners. (Pg. 190, "The Role of Experts in Scientific Controversy," 1987, Cambridge University Press)

Despite the fact that the media has painted the eugenics movement as a phenomenon of the political right, the facts simply do not support that contention. The list of intellectual and cultural elites that vocally supported the eugenics movement is a veritable who's who of Progressive icons. Professor Allen opines:

> It is important to point out that both the expert eugenicists and the leaders of ruling-class interests, such as the Rockefeller and Carnegie philanthropies, saw the eugenics program as forward-looking and progressive. It fitted into the progressivist philosophy of rational and scientific planning (as opposed, for example, to the environmentalist-oriented philosophy of social work, which the ruling class and eugenicists alike described as subjectivist "bleeding heart", and nonscientific). Thus, while today we might describe the overall program espoused by the eugenicists as conservative, even reactionary, in their own day eugenicists regarded themselves as in the forefront of progressive thinking. They saw themselves cutting through irrational sentimentalism and applying the new findings of science to the solution of age-old social problems. For their part some ruling-class leaders, especially those who had been won to the necessity of abandoning laissez-faire for planned capitalism, saw themselves in the same progressive mold. [sic.] (Pg. 193, "The Role of Experts in Scientific Controversy," 1987, Cambridge University Press)

To further underscore Laughlin's credentials as a political Progressive, Laughlin was anti-war as were other eugenicists. They believed war depleted society of its most worthy members and thus its best breeding stocks. Laughlin was also an "internationalist," as were Progressives, socialists, and other collectivists. The League of Nations was the plaything of Progressives and other collectivists of the era. A September 6th, 1934 letter from Laughlin to Walter M. Gilbert, the Administrative Secretary of the Carnegie Institution, reveals that Laughlin "was an original member of the International Committee on Immigration of the Department of Labor of the League of Nations." This is fitting; as this book will document, Laughlin's political inclinations were megalomaniac with global aspirations. Laughlin would spend decades writing and perfecting drafts for world constitutions and structures for one-world governments. Hassencahl notes that Laughlin started this life-long project in college. As will be detailed later in this book, an integral part of Laughlin's one-world government was the abolition of the right to bear arms, yet another aspect of Laughlin's Progressive credentials.

In fact, much of Laughlin's Progressive leanings can be attributed to his mother. Laughlin's mother was a suffragette, and Laughlin admired her political activism. Hassencahl describes the influence his activist mother had on him. Note the reference to "racial poisons":

> Under her influence, young Harry signed a temperance pledge, which he subsequently kept all his life. As an eugenicists he later came to believe that alcohol harmed the precious stuff of heredity, the "germ plasm." (Pg. 46, "Harry H. Laughlin, Expert Eugenics Agent," Frances Janet Hassencahl, 1970, University Microfilms)

The internal correspondence of the Carnegie Institution evidences that Hassencahl was mistaken about Laughlin keeping his temperance pledge. There were various reports to the Carnegie leadership about Laughlin's drinking by concerned employees and townspeople near or at the Station for Experimental Evolution. This is curious as Laughlin did, in fact, consider alcoholism as a "racial poison" and "dysgenic", and the laws he helped draft targeted alcoholics for sterilization. Eugenicists would endeavor to leverage the temperance and purity movement emerging from American Protestantism of the time. Like the rest of his family, Laughlin was a life-long member of the Christian Church, but Laughlin's religious beliefs did not seem to conflict with his scientific endeavors. Interestingly enough, Laughlin saw no conflict between his studies in science and acceptance of evolution. (Pg. 48, Hassenchal)

After a term at the Normal College for Teachers in Kirksville, the young Laughlin took his first teaching job at a school in "white oak timber, 20 miles from any civilized animal." The one-room school house near Livonia, Missouri had fifty-eight pupils in a room made for thirty-two and no supplies save an oaken bucket, a tin cup, a door key, and a chair for the teacher. (Pg. 49, Hassencahl) Laughlin married Pansy Bowen of Kirksville on Sept. 13, 1902, and in 1903, the couple moved to Centerville, Iowa, where Laughlin would work as the high school principal. Laughlin's interest in animal and plant breeding began to become eugenic theories at this time. Ironically, Laughlin, like much of the American eugenics movement, looked down upon the rural population. Hassencahl cites a September 8th, 1896 letter from Laughlin to his mother describing his first job as a teacher in the very rural areas of Missouri. He voiced disgust that the people were "75 years behind the times."

Laughlin would subsequently become the agriculture teacher at the First District Normal School from 1907 until 1910 where he would have likely remained an obscure horse breeder if it not for the vastly influential Charles B. Davenport. Charles B. Davenport was a Harvard University graduate, and later an instructor at Harvard from 1891 until 1899. Prior to Laughlin, Davenport was the undisputed leader of the eugenics movement in the United States. His 1911 book, "Heredity in Relation to Eugenics," was used as a college textbook for many years. Davenport was elected to the National Academy of Sciences the following year. Davenport was president or vice president of ten of the 64 societies and was on the editorial boards of eight scientific journals. Thus, from 1900 until his death in 1944, Davenport was one of the best known and most influential biological scientists in the world. More to the point, the respect Davenport commanded in the scientific world is one of the reasons why eugenics would prove so difficult to discredit or dislodge.

In fact, many of the eugenic institutions that Laughlin would be instrumental in promoting were the product of Ivy League graduates and professors. Laughlin was not a typical Ivy Leaguer of that era. He did not come from a financially privileged family. Laughlin would take a leave of absence from the Eugenics Record Office at Cold Spring Harbor in 1916 to complete his doctorate in biology. Princeton would award him his doctorate on August 9th, 1917 for his thesis "The Duration of the Several Mitotic States in the Dividing Root-tip Cells of the Common Onion." His time at Princeton would only bolster his commitment to eugenics as he studied under the eugenic-minded professor, Edward G. Conklin. Conklin, by the way, was also a former colleague of the pro-eugenics Woodrow Wilson when Wilson was a professor of jurisprudence and political economy at Princeton prior to becoming President. As this book will document, Laughlin would also receive a Doctor of Medicine honorary degree from the University of Heidelberg when the Hitler government decided to recognize Laughlin's contributions to the eugenics movement. Laughlin was at that point in history even surpassing Davenport, and widely recognized as the "expert eugenicist" of international scope.

Interestingly enough, the more successful Laughlin became, the less he spoke to his family about his work on eugenics. Hassencahl interviewed Laughlin's surviving family in the 1970s and had access to their family's correspondence. Hassencahl attests to the obliviousness the family had to the extent of Laughlin's work. (Pg. 44) This is not strange for the members of the eugenics movement. Francis Galton published his first papers unsigned, as he likely foresaw a negative reaction by the British public. Galton would also write a fictional utopian description of a nation governed by eugenics entitled "Kantsaywhere." Galton was shamed and dissuaded from publishing it. He burned copies of it and requested in his will that his niece destroy any surviving copies upon his death, despite having achieved worldwide fame for his other works on eugenics.

In many ways, Laughlin would become the devoted zealot that Galton had prescribed for his eugenic utopia, religiously devoted to his cause. His personality was that of the typical political zealot. A June 19th, 1936 internal memo from the Carnegie Institution states that "Dr. Merriam", the director of the Carnegie Institution, believed "Dr. Laughlin had the reputation of not getting along with people." Hassencahl provides a personality profile of Laughlin that is worth recounting:

> Laughlin tended to be dogmatic about his work and could not tolerate criticism. He dealt with criticism in two ways, either by generating massive amounts of data in a sort of contest to see who would have the largest and most impressive set of graphs and tables, or he ignored criticism completely. (Pg. 64, "Harry H. Laughlin, Expert Eugenics Agent", Frances Janet Hassencahl, University Microfilms, 1970)

Although Laughlin's correspondence certainly indicates the personality of the typical politico that gets flustered by any criticism or dissent, one should not underestimate Laughlin's political skills. Reading the internal communication of the Carnegie Institution and the Eugenics Record Office reveals that Laughlin was the hub of many of the crucial relationships that made the international eugenics movement as successful as it was. The correspondence includes letters from the Secretary of State, the Secretary of Labor, public figures such as Nicola Tesla, Margaret Sanger, and Alexander Graham Bell. Internal memoranda mention Presidents Franklin D. Roosevelt and Herbert Hoover. For example, a June 16th, 1936 letter from Laughlin to Dr. Merriam reveals that Laughlin introduced the leadership of the Carnegie Institution to the surviving members of the famous Darwin family in England. It was also Laughlin that would facilitate the introduction of the infamous Pioneer Fund's patron, Wickliffe Draper, to Hitler's government. The Pioneer Fund would later include several key eugenic-minded individuals that would be instrumental in implementing the rancid Jim Crow legislation throughout the United States.

One last, but important note about Laughlin's personality must be emphasized: Harry H. Laughlin was not the first, and certainly not the last "racist" to walk the earth. What made Laughlin and his eugenic cohorts different is that they mounted a concerted worldwide effort to act on their convictions. Laughlin's career coincided with the golden age of "scientific racism," when sympathetic politicians embarked on enforcing their racial prejudices through legislation. The likes of Laughlin, Davenport, and Leonard Darwin provided the most racially charged legislation a veil of scientific legitimacy. They leveraged their Ivy League pedigrees to make socially acceptable what should otherwise have been received as ethically unthinkable. This made the likes of Laughlin immeasurably more dangerous than the common bigot. To paraphrase the modern environmentalist movement, the petty bigot acted locally, while the eugenicist thought globally.

1898 - TIMING IS EVERYTHING

> *There is, however, no doubt that the various races,*
> *when carefully compared and measured,*
> *differ much from each other, —*
> *Their mental characteristics are likewise very distinct;*
> *chiefly as it would appear in their emotional,*
> *but partly in their intellectual, faculties.*
> *- Charles Darwin, "The Descent of Man," Pgs. 216-217*

Historical context is necessary in order to illustrate just why eugenics commanded such an appeal. The zenith of American eugenics coincided with the great migration of Southern blacks up to the Northern metropolises. Whereas these Northern cities had less than 1% African ethnicity in their populations prior to Reconstruction, the turn-of-the-century saw a drastic increase to about 10%. However, while the eugenics movement coincided with the era of racial strife in the United States, it should not be confused with it. There are important differences between an improvised lynching and systematic genocide. Furthermore, the ex-Confederate South was not alone in enacting Jim Crow laws. It was the ex-Union North that accepted these racial laws as "constitutional" in the Supreme Court they still dominated.

Also, the racial animosities of North and South manifested themselves in different ways. Their actions and ambitions were significantly different. The infamous lynching of the post-Reconstruction South reached its peak in several hundred victims per year. By comparison, the eugenic movement emerging from the North sterilized as many as 10,000 to 15,000 per year, in a single State alone.

The northbound migration of African-Americans also coincided with the immigration of millions from Europe, namely from Eastern Europe, Russia, and Italy. Italian and Irish Catholics were prominent in the public eye with their extravagant and audacious mafias, and the Anarchists and Communists from these countries rounded off the rest of the immigrants. These fears were not altogether unjustified. Historical records prove that over 95% of the Communist and Socialist parties of that era were made up of immigrants. They drew attention to this aspect of their membership by publishing pamphlets and subversive newspapers in foreign languages. The Northeastern cities swelled with unfamiliar faces and cultures. Thus, the Northern elites, many of them the sons and grandsons of ex-Union veterans would go into culture shock as their cities seemed to be overrun by "foreign" elements. This subsequent generation of the Union North that had previously freed the slaves, now embarked on a "scientific" solution to racial tensions. The U.S. Congress and the U.S. Supreme Court, which had been instrumental in securing emancipation, would now be the tools for the most racially charged legislation.

Immigration also was the cause of one of the most powerful eugenic lobbies of the era. Davenport's classmates at Harvard, Prescott Hall and Robert de Courcy Ward founded the Immigration Restriction League. It was the product of members of the Harvard class of 1889. It attracted high-society from the American Northeast, namely members of the exclusive Boone and Crocket Club of New York, whose president was a fellow eugenicist and Harvard graduate, Theodore Roosevelt. The famous racialist authors, Yale's Madison Grant, and Harvard's Lothrop Stoddard were also members of this very select club of elites.

Madison Grant had social and political connections that Laughlin would later leverage. Grant is best known for his wildly famous 1916 book, "The Passing of the Great Race, or the Racial Basis of European History." "The Passing of the Great Race" would give eugenic "racialists" a popular impetus in the United States. Interestingly enough, the introductory pages of the book invoke Darwin's evolutionary theory. Grant's book also gained worldwide acclaim. Adolf Hitler called the book his "bible", and Grant received a personal letter from the *Fuhrer* thanking him for the work. Grant's book had been published in Germany by the publisher of Hitler's "Mein Kampf", and Grant made sure to keep the relationship alive. In turn, Germany's own version of Madison Grant, a "racialist" author by the name of Hans K. Günther would be an important contact for Laughlin.

It should also be noted that the likes of Davenport and Grant were hardly anomalies within the Ivy League institutions. They followed a rich tradition of eugenic thinking at these institutions, with Theodore Roosevelt as its most prominent example. Marouf A. Hasain, Jr's 1996 book "The Rhetoric of Eugenics in Anglo-American Thought" points to the forgotten fact that many Americans learned their lessons about "race suicide" from Theodore Roosevelt. (Pg. 48) "Race suicide" was an invective later used by Nazi propagandists. Roosevelt's eugenic invective has been documented by historians, typically by citing the letter he wrote to Davenport. Note the reference to animal breeding:

> You say that these people are not themselves responsible, that it is "society" that is responsible. I agree with you if you mean, as I suppose you do, that society has no business to permit degenerates to reproduce their kind. It is really extraordinary that our people refuse to apply to human beings such elementary knowledge as every successful farmer is obliged to apply to his own stock breeding. Any group of farmers who permitted their best stock not to breed, and let all the increase come from the worst stock, would be treated as fit inmates for an asylum. (Jan. 3, 1913, "Eugenics Archive," Image #1242, Am. Phy. Soc.)

The Roosevelt family also supported the eugenics movement even after Theodore Roosevelt's death, as the correspondence held at the Laughlin Papers in the Special Collections Department of Truman University proves. The Roosevelt family would lend themselves to Harry H. Laughlin's pedigrees so Laughlin could display them on the floors of Congress and at international symposiums as prime examples of "good breeding."

The prestige Laughlin would gain from his Ivy League colleagues and as an expert for the United States Congress also gained him the financial support and collaboration from eugenic-minded scientists and politicians in the West Coast. What Harvard was to eugenics in the East Coast, Stanford and California State University at Sacramento equaled in the West. Both of these prestigious universities were headed up by like-minded and equally powerful individuals. David Star Jordan, the famous founding president of Stanford University, had been initially inspired by the "racialist" science of Louis Agassiz of Harvard University. Jordan was a leading voice of Darwinian evolution and a prominent political activist with ties to Jane Addams. Jordan gained national notoriety when in 1925, he appeared as an expert witness for the defense in the Scopes Trial. Incidentally, the textbook that was at the center of the Scopes Trial had an entire chapter dedicated to eugenics that had been written by none other than Charles B. Davenport. Jordan also served as a Director of the Sierra Club from 1892 to 1903. Most importantly, he was a member of the initial board of trustees of the Human Betterment Foundation, a eugenics organization established in Pasadena, California in 1928.

C.M. Goethe, the founder of Cal. State, Sacramento would be a financial and philosophical supporter of Laughlin's various ventures and organizations. Goethe was a wealthy land owner and developer. Goethe would dedicate a significant amount of his time to the Human Betterment Foundation, and create his own eugenic-minded institutions as well, namely the Immigration Study Commission, which lobbied for exclusion of the Mexicans, Koreans, Chinese, and Japanese. True to his Progressive leanings, Goethe was also a financier and member of the Sierra Club and the Save the Redwoods Foundation.

Of course, none of this would have been possible without the support and endorsement from prominent British individuals. To begin with, Leonard Darwin fully leveraged his father's fame to make eugenics reputable in England at a time when it was literally laughed at and ridiculed. This is exemplified by the fact that other famous figures had attempted to make eugenics respectable prior to the Darwin-Galton family. Virginia Woodhull was the first woman to start a weekly newspaper, an activist for women's rights and labor reforms, and in 1872, she was the first female candidate for President of the United States. She traveled the world to lecture about eugenics and was outright ridiculed by the British press for doing so. It is not until Francis Galton and Leonard Darwin loaned their family name to the cause that other progressive-minded Britons like Virginia Woolf, Beatrice and Sydney Webb, George Bernard Shaw, John Maynard Keynes, and H.G. Wells provided their support for the movement.

In turn, American eugenicists knew they had to bow to the Darwin-Galton aristocracy in order to gain legitimacy. In 1902, the prominent, Harvard-educated Davenport and his wife traveled to Europe and met Francis Galton and Karl

Pearson. Karl Pearson was Galton's protégé as he, like Galton himself, had a knack for reducing human traits to numbers. The surviving correspondence between Charles Davenport and Francis Galton evidence the deference that Davenport had for the Darwinian origins of eugenics. The October 14th, 1902 letter from Davenport to Galton requesting a reference for his proposal for the Station for Experimental Evolution illustrates how the Darwin-Galton reputation was leveraged in order to commence eugenics movement in the United States:

> Dear Mr. Galton: Word has just reached me that it is possible that some action may be taken by the Carnegie Institution at a Board meeting in November in relation to my application for the Establishment of a station for the Experimental study of Evolution at Cold Spring Harbor, Long Island. The Board would be glad of any testimony relative to (1) the importance of such a station, (2) my qualifications as possible director and (3) the suitability of the locality. Of the last point of course you cannot speak but I feel that it would be a great help to the cause if you could find time to write a short letter concerning the importance of the station proposed [illegible] any thing concerning my equipment for the position that you may care to hazard. The establishment of the station is a thing I have much at heart and for which I am ready to sacrifice a great deal. Trusting that you will not feel my request too bold, I remain, Sincerely yours, Chas. B. Davenport. (Eugenics Record Office, Item #2093)

Alan G. Cock and Donald R. Forsdyke, in their 2008 book "Treasure Your Exceptions: The Science and Life of William Bateson," document that Andrew Carnegie was deeply interested in the science of heredity and had written to Francis Darwin, the other son of the famous biologist, indicating his interest in financially supporting such an effort. (Pg. 225) Timing is everything. Thus, Davenport jumped at this opportunity.

Allan Chase, author of the 1975 book titled, "The Legacy of Malthus: The Social Costs of the New Scientific Racism," documents how The Cold Spring Harbor facility was established upon Davenport's Harvard credentials and Francis Galton's fame. (Pg. 118, "Legacy of Malthus") An Oct. 26th, 1910 letter has Davenport crediting Galton: "My dear Galton: So you see the seed sown by you is still sprouting in distant countries." (Eugenics Record Office, #2094) Davenport's efforts came to fruition in 1904, when the Carnegie Institution established the Station for Experimental Evolution, making Davenport its director.

So how does a teacher from a rural town like Laughlin get to be of such significant influence amongst Ivy League educated scientists and the Darwin-Galton family? Laughlin first met Davenport in 1907, when Laughlin spent a summer at the Brooklyn Institute for Arts and Sciences where he took Davenport's course on human heredity. In 1910, Davenport asked Laughlin to move to New York. Elof Axel Carlson documents this milestone in Laughlin's career in "The Banality of Evil: The Careers of Charles Davenport and Harry Laughlin":

> Laughlin was not as sophisticated as Davenport nor as broadly educated. He adored Davenport, who lifted him from the obscurity of being a country teacher

and gave him a position of responsibility and the credentials to be accepted by the elite. He lived in Davenport's shadow and wanted to impress him by finding a place in eugenics that would meet his limited talents. He found that in several outlets. He was an excellent bureaucrat, and he could amass immense detail and organize it and present it. (Elof Axel Carlson, "The Banality of Evil," 2006, Cold Spring Harbor Laboratory Press)

The correspondence evidences that Davenport would trust Laughlin to be a faithful communicator of Davenport's views even when presenting to prestigious American audiences. A letter from Davenport to Margaret Sanger, the famous American Birth Control activist, demonstrates that Davenport was comfortable using Laughlin as his spokesperson. Laughlin would represent Davenport before a committee of the Sixth International Neo-Malthusian and Birth Control Conference (March 25th - 31st, 1925). Aside from Sanger herself, those attending would include internationally recognized scientists such as Raymond Pearl, C.C. Little, Julian Huxley, Havelock Ellis, and the famous Progressive economist John Maynard Keynes. Note how Davenport felt that his attendance would be redundant as Laughlin was already attending:

> My dear Mrs. Sanger; - If Dr. Laughlin can come on that or some other day I think he could represent me very well. It is hardly necessary for both of us to be present. I will talk over the matter with Dr. Laughlin. (Am. Phil. Soc., E.R.O. Records, Sanger, Sanger folder, letter March 14th, 1925)

Laughlin proved to be much more dangerous than a simple energetic bureaucrat at a laboratory. In fact, it is his penchant for political networking that endeared him to Charles Davenport. This sort of mutual backscratching was typical of the eugenicists. Eugenicists, especially in Laughlin's case, were adept at posing as enthusiastic, but allegedly independent third parties in acquiring appointments and recognition in such manner. While this can be called astute networking, it should be pointed out that Laughlin was supposedly a scientist. Politics has always been a part of the scientific community. Yet, it must be noted that the people Laughlin sought out were not the heads of research institutions, universities, or scientific journals, but rather congressmen, judges, and presidents:

> More important, their correspondence shows how often Laughlin used Grant's contacts to gain special favors or consideration for himself as a representative of the eugenical cause. For example, Laughlin often called upon Grant to recommend him for public positions, such as delegate to the Pan-American Eugenics Congress in 1928, or to commend one of Laughlin's manuscripts to a publisher. Reciprocating, Laughlin in the mid-1930s lobbied officials of Yale University in a vigorous but unsuccessful attempt to persuade them to award Grant (a Yale alumnus, class of 1887) an honorary degree. In Laughlin's mind, that degree would have constituted a significant and prestigious recognition of eugenics at a time when the movement was suffering increased criticism from the scientific and law communities alike. ("The Papers of Harry Hamilton Laughlin", Annals of the History of Biology, Vol. 14, No. 2)

It is precisely through this astute networking that eugenicists found a way to become a coherent international movement in an otherwise disjointed world teetering on world war. For example, Davenport was in touch with German scientists as early as 1910. The American Philosophical Society still holds correspondence between Davenport and Ernst Rüdin. Rüdin was recognized as one of the fathers of National Socialist ideology. In 1933, Ernst Rüdin and Alfred Ploetz were brought together by Reich Interior Minister Wilhelm Frick to form the Expert Committee on Questions of Population and Racial Policy. The committee's eugenic concepts were used as the scientific basis to justify the racialist concepts reflected in the "Law for the Prevention of Genetically Diseased Offspring." Rüdin is credited with authoring the official commentary for the law, and was awarded medals by Adolf Hitler personally. Letters written as early as July 20th, 1910 from Davenport to Rüdin confirm that Davenport would attend the "exhibition for race hygiene" to be held in Dresden that year. Postcards from Rüdin to Davenport from the year 1912 document Rüdin's request for copies of American eugenic publications. (Am. Phil. Soc., TN 26977, Rüdin, Ernst folder) A letter from Davenport to Rüdin demonstrates that Laughlin's work was being fed to the German scientists as early as February 10th, 1911:

> Dear Dr. Ruedin, [sic.] I have started today by mail four packages with items numbered 1 to 25, including a series of charts by Professor H. H. Laughlin, showing inheritance of eye color in map, some books, brochures, blanks, stationery, and an exhibit ... (American Philosophical Society., Eugenics Record Office Records, Rüdin, Ernst folder)

The relationship between Davenport, Rüdin, Ploetz, and the other scientists at the forefront of the Third Reich's racial policies would last into the early 1940s, far into the most violent years of Hitler's regime. A shared utopian vision for the world brought these German, British, and American scientists together into one coherent international movement. All were intent in redirecting human evolution. As documented in the first book of this series, "From a 'Race of Masters' to a 'Master Race': 1948 to 1848," Rüdin and Ploetz had both been part of the utopian socialist movement in Europe prior to dedicating themselves to the eugenic cause. All-in-all, what differentiated the eugenic "scientists" from the actual scientists was a lust for power; a "*Libido Dominandi*" like St. Augustine referred to it; the will to power; the lust to dominate; the desire to sit atop the pyramid of government. As such, Laughlin and company were ready and willing to fill the position of power Progressivism wished to imbue upon the expert and planner. Laughlin's lust for power had no shortage of fountains to replenish itself from. He relished the very close contacts he had at the seats of power in the U.S. and Germany. In turn, Hitler's henchmen equally benefited, and arrogantly fired back at any international criticism by pointing to the support from the likes of Davenport and Laughlin. Case in point, when the German scientists were questioned by the Nuremberg Tribunal at the end of the war, they held up the U.S. Supreme Court's decision that had made eugenics legal in the United States. They filed as evidence the various eugenic laws and statutes passed by the various States in the Union; most of which were directly attributable to Harry H. Laughlin.

American Breeders Magazine

PRICE, SINGLE COPY, 50 CENTS

WASHINGTON, D. C.
1910

Published by the American

The New Magazine
SEC'Y OF AGRICULTURE

Breeding Fat and
DR. L. H. SMITH

Breeding the Arn
CARLOS GUERR

Poultry Breeding
D. F. LAURIE

Imperfection of
DR. C. B. DA

The New Maga

First Quarter
Vol. I

Application for entry as second-class ma

The JOURNAL of HEREDITY

(Formerly the American Breeders' Magazine)

A MONTHLY PUBLICATION DEVOTED
TO PLANT BREEDING, ANIMAL BREEDING AND EUGENICS

PUBLISHED BY THE
AMERICAN GENETIC ASSOCIATION
(Formerly called the American Breeders' Association)

VOLUME V

WASHINGTON, D. C.
1914

1903 - AMERICAN BREEDERS' ASSOCIATION

"To purify the race at all costs is the slogan of eugenics"
H. H. Laughlin, Conference of Race Betterment, Battle Creek, Michigan

The American eugenics movement can be said to have been kick-started by the creation of the American Breeders' Association. This is where Laughlin and Davenport first met. On February 24th of 1909, Laughlin wrote Davenport to thank him for putting him in touch with the American Breeders' Association. They met here once again after the Brooklyn Institute summer program in January of 1909 at the annual meeting of the Breeders' Association in Columbia, Missouri, near Laughlin's family home. Beyond providing the introduction of Davenport and Laughlin, the American Breeders' Association would prove to be of historical importance, as this association was made up of some of the most prominent men and politically connected scientists; precisely what a movement intent on the re-engineering of society needed.

The American Breeders' Association was the brainchild of W.M. Hayes, a professor of plant breeding at the University of Minnesota. The 2012 book by Jon Agar "Science in the 20th Century and Beyond" documents that Willet B. Hays was also assistant secretary of agriculture in Theodore Roosevelt's administration. (Pg. 51) The American Breeders' Association, founded in 1903, was also one of the first scientific organizations in the U.S. to support eugenic research. The association created a Committee on Eugenics in 1906 and pushed its eugenic agenda in its American Breeders' Magazine. In 1912, Hays addressed the National Farmers' Congress on the subject of 'The farm, the home of the race,' outlining a vision in which corn-fed 'genetically efficient people' would be encouraged to breed." (Pg. 54)

The "American Breeders Magazine" advertised as being "Issued Quarterly for Practical and Scientific Breeders of Animals and Plants." It listed as one of its editors "C. B. Davenport." It also seems the activist wing that ultimately spun off into the Eugenics Record Office was always at odds with those members that were only interested in practical agricultural matters. When W.M. Hays died in 1913 the association by itself had little prospect of continuing, and W.E. Castle and David Fairchild, the famous botanist and Director of the Bureau of Plant Industries at the Department of Agriculture, decided to try to save the organization's journal, the American Breeders' Magazine. The new organization was named the American Genetics Association, and the name of its publication was changed to the Journal of Heredity. The first issue published under the new name had Alexander Graham Bell, the famous inventor of the telephone, contributing an article entitled "How to Improve the Race." Incidentally, Bell would serve as the honorary president of the 2nd International Eugenics Congress in 1921.

The journal makes the curious observation that since the Committee on Eugenics "appreciates and insists that eugenics must be investigated before it can be taught", and claims "an assurance" that the work would "proceed cautiously" and with "due regard for all family and general social traditions." It is unclear if such atypical cautiousness was because there were palpable tensions between the commercial animal breeders and the political zealots. Whatever the case, the wishful thinking continues along those lines:

> The group of workers chosen by the membership of this Association to work at this problem will be sane, safe and conservative. It is believed that such a group of chosen leaders will gain an authoritative place in the discussion of the subject which will reduce to a minimum the irrational discussion of the subject by those merely seeking notoriety or by those who might carelessly weaken the morality which is growing up with family life. (Pg. 143, "American Breeders Magazine," No. 1, 1910)

Interestingly enough, at this very early stage of the movement, the so-called "Committee on Eugenics" and the Eugenics Record Office was already targeting institutions for the disabled and infirmed, namely the New Jersey State Village of Epileptics at Skillman, NJ. Notes on a meeting held on Friday, October 14th, 1910 reveal a commitment to mainline eugenics far beyond the demure assertions made in this first edition of the "American Breeders Magazine." In fact, by 1909, when the Association already had 1132 members, the stated goals of the "Eugenics Section" were "investigation, education" and of note, "legislation." Thus, it is safe to say that the goal of race improvement using the power of the state was part of the original inspiration, and not a consequence or afterthought. Hassencahl opines that it was the "beginnings of the eugenics lobby." (Pg. 56, Hassencahl) After all, this was a grouping of some of the most influential and politically connected scientists and academics in the United States. The goal of effecting change through "legislation" was certainly within their grasp, as their members had the clout and the political connections to do so.

Of course, a battery of Ivy League educated scientists accompanied Laughlin and Davenport in their quest. According to the 1910 issue of the "Harvard Graduates' Magazine," the Society had a "Sub-committee on Insanity" under the auspices of its "Committee on Eugenics." The Society was headed up by a prominent eugenicist that would work at Laughlin's and Davenport's Eugenics Record Office, Dr. J.W. Eastabrook. This was also the Harvard class that included Theodore Roosevelt, whom would do more than sympathize with the eugenic cause. (Pg. 569, Vol. 18, "Harvard Graduates' Magazine")

Some analysis of the Ivy League membership of the American Breeders' Association is in order, as the clout of the membership proved to be of more historical importance than the actual work of the association. The fact that both Charles Davenport and President Theodore Roosevelt were so interested in eugenics is no coincidence. They were both products of a generation from Harvard

University intent on perpetuating the eugenics creed. In fact, it is impossible to write the history of eugenics without continually stumbling upon the work of Harvard graduates and professors. It is impossible to disentangle from the history of eugenics, or in other words, it is impossible to imagine a eugenics movement without Charles Benedict Davenport, Madison Grant, Henry Fairfield Osborn, Lothrop Stoddard, or Theodore Roosevelt.

The eugenic creed can be traced back several Harvard generations. According to Thomas G. Dyer, author of "The Racial Education of Theodore Roosevelt," the young Theodore at Harvard came under the influence of Professor Nathaniel Southgate Shaler. Shaler's importance will become evident as this book progresses. Thus, some ink is dedicated to him here.

Shaler was an American paleontologist and geologist who wrote extensively on the theological and scientific implications of the theory of evolution. Shaler, in turn, had studied under Louis Agassiz at the old Harvard College and would go on to become a Harvard fixture in his own right. Shaler was also an apologist for slavery as well as an outspoken believer in the superiority of the Anglo-Saxon race. Even towards the end of his career, Shaler continued to support Agassiz's polygenism, a theory of multiple origins for the different races of humanity that was often used to justify slavery. Shaler served as Harvard's Dean of Sciences and was considered one of the university's most popular teachers. He exemplified Northern racism. Despite his clear prejudice against the black populations, he had served as a Union officer in the American Civil War, ironically fighting for the emancipation of African-Americans.

Shaler's words evidence his racialist views. The Atlantic Monthly published a controversial article by Shaler in Volume 0054 Issue 325 - November 1884. The article was titled "The Negro Problem," pp. 696-709, and was published along with the dissenting and supporting views as side notes. In "The Negro Problem," Shaler voiced grave doubts that men "bred in immemorial savagery and slavery, can blossom out into self-upholding citizens." Shaler, like all eugenicists from Galton onwards, believed heredity was more important than environment. The Northeastern Shaler, like the pro-slavery Southern demagogues of the Civil War era, looked to the examples of emancipated blacks in Haiti and Jamaica as evidence that blacks were not fit for self-government:

> The forecast of the unprejudiced observer was exceedingly unfavorable. Every experiment of freeing blacks on this continent has in the end resulted in even worse conditions than slavery brought to them. The trial in Hayti, where freemen of the third generation from slaves possess the land to the exclusion of all whites, has been utterly disastrous to the best interest of the negro. ---- There is now in Hayti a government that is but a succession of petty plundering despotisms, a tillage that cannot make headway against the constant encroachments of the tropical forests, a people that is without a single trace of promise except that of extinction through the diseases of sloth and vice. ---- In Jamaica the history, though briefer, is almost equally ominous. The

emancipation of the negro was peaceable, and was not attended, as in Hayti, by the murder or expulsion of the whites. Yet that garden land of the tropics, that land which our ancestors hoped to see the Britain of the South, has been settling down toward barbarism, and there is nothing left but the grip of the British rule to keep it from falling to the state of the sister isle. [sic.]

Shaler, like many Northern abolitionists, would blame Southern slave-holders for causing the problem of bringing foreign elements into the gene pool:

I am not deploring the freeing of these Africans of America: that was the least of evils. These people were here in such numbers that any effort for their deportation was futile. It was their presence here that was the evil, and for this none of the men of our century are responsible. – The burden lies on the souls of our dull, greedy ancestors of the seventeenth and eighteenth centuries, who were too stupid to see or too careless to consider anything but immediate gains. There can be no sort of doubt that, judged by the light of all experience, these people are a danger to America greater and more insuperable than any of those that menace the other great civilized states of the world.

Shaler's words are a prime example of the racial tensions growing in the Northeast as the emancipated African-American population moved North, and a precursor of the type of animosities that would only worsen as European immigrants followed:

The real dangers that this African blood brings to our state lie deeper than the labor problem. ---- I have now set forth the fear that must come upon any one who will see what a wonderful thing our modern Teutonic society is; how slowly it has won its treasures, and at what a price of vigilance and toil it must keep them; and therefore how dangerous it must be to have a large part of the state separated in motives from the people who have brought it into existence. ---- The African question is a very serious matter, I should like to propose the following statement of the prime nature of the dangers, and the means whereby they may be minimized, if not avoided. ---- First, I hold it to be clear that the inherited qualities of the negroes to a great degree unfit them to carry the burden of our own civilization; that their present Americanized shape is due in large part to the strong control to which they have been subjected since the enslavement of their blood; that there will naturally be a strong tendency, for many generations to come, for them to revert to their ancestral conditions. ---- Next, I hold it to be almost equally clear that they cannot as a race, for many generations, be brought to the level of our own people. There will always be a danger that by falling to the bottom of society they will form a proletariat class, separated by blood as well as by estate from the superior classes; thus bringing about a measure of the evils of the slavery system, ---- evils that would curse both the races that were brought together in a relation so unfit for modern society."

According to the 1910 book "Theodore Roosevelt as an Undergraduate," by Donald Wilhelm, the young Theodore was more than the usual student at one of Shaler's lectures. He was his prodigy. Much of Shaler's views on race relations became gospel for Roosevelt and remained with him through his years as President of the United States. The line connecting Agassiz, Shaler, and Theodore Roosevelt is crucial to the understanding of American Eugenics, and the deep impact it had on society. Roosevelt's experience was similar to that of Davenport's. The students that Shaler taught at Harvard would all adopt a biological ranking of the races as their core belief system.

E.L. Mark, Hersey Professor of Anatomy and Director of Harvard's zoological laboratory, was one of the professors that caused the transition for Harvard students to accept an evolutionary hierarchy of the races based on the science of anthropology. E.L. Marks was also one of the directors of the zoology department. Theodore Roosevelt took the course entitled "Natural History III – Zoology" taught by Professor E.L. Marks three times a week during his junior year. The pedigree of eugenic-minded zealots follows. Eli Chernin, author of the article, "The 'Harvard System': A Mystery Dispelled," (British Medical Journal, Volume 97, 22 October 1988) describes an amiable relationship between E.L. Marks and Theodore Roosevelt. According to the website, "Lefalophodon: An Informal History of Evolutionary Biology," the list of students E.L. Marks taught include the most prominent of American eugenicists, including Herbert Spencer Jennings, Robert M. Yerkes, and most notably Charles Benedict Davenport.

There is another important aspect in the connection between Harvard, the roster of the American Breeders' Association, and the goal to enact eugenic legislation. There were only 800 students at Harvard at the time Roosevelt and Davenport attended. It was a close-knit community of social clubs and memberships as any other Ivy League of the day. The young Roosevelt was a member of the Phi Beta Kappa honorary society and Alpha Delta Phi along with Oliver Wendell Holmes, the father of the U.S. Supreme Court Justice that would preside over the 1927 landmark case of eugenic sterilization, Buck v. Bell. A 1910 book written about young Roosevelt's undergraduate years at Harvard documents some of Roosevelt's views during this epoch of his life:

> The weakling and the coward are out of place in a strong and free community. In a republic like ours the governing class is composed of the strong men who take the trouble to do the work of government; and if you are too timid or too fastidious or too careless to do your part in this work, the you forfeit your right to be considered one of the governing and you become one of the governed. (Theodore Roosevelt – An Address Delivered at the Harvard Union)

Incidentally, the most notable eugenic accomplishment of the American Breeders' Association was the product of the Committee on Sterilization. This committee was chaired by Bleeker Van Wagenen. Laughlin served as secretary to the committee. The work was done in response to the growing contention in the United States and Europe that "degeneration" was a real threat to modern society. The "unfit" were deemed "Social Menace Number One" by Goddard's study of the so-called "Kallikak Family," one of many studies of the era which claimed to trace the heredity of problem families. Goddard gathered the information on these "degenerate" families using a staff of field workers trained by Laughlin at the Eugenics Record Office. They accumulated the statistics and drafted the pedigrees of those families deemed to have defective hereditary traits.

The American Breeders' Association, via its Committee on Sterilization, finalized its two-part report on 1914 in response to "social menace number one." It was entitled "The Report of the Committee to Study and to Report on the Best Practical Means of Cutting Off the Defective Germ-Plasm in the American Population." The report was widely circulated. A preliminary report was presented at the First International Congress of Eugenics of 1912, which was held in London, England and hosted by Charles Darwin's son, Leonard Darwin. Laughlin himself presented a version of it on January 12th, 1914 at the Frist National Conference on Race Betterment held by Doctor J.H. Kellogg in Battle Creek, Michigan. Laughlin's presentation was taken directly from the committee's work and was entitled "Calculations on the Working Out of a Proposed Program of Sterilization." Hassencahl documents that Dr. Kellogg was a full believer in eugenics himself, and voiced his belief that eugenics could produce "a new and improved race of man" in the same fashion that it was breeding "wonderful new races of horses, cows, and pigs." (Pg. 101, Hassencahl) More than 1500 people attended each lecture at the conference. The conference program delineated the goal of the conference "to assemble evidence as to the extent to which degenerative tendencies are at work in America and to promote agencies for race betterment." (Pg. 102, Hassencahl) Laughlin was invited to speak on the last day of the conference for the part of the program entitled "Eugenics and Immigration." Hassencahl recounts the tone of Laughlin's presentation:

> Dr. Laughlin assumed that his audience was not a critical one and that they, like many reform-minded persons, would tend to see issues in terms of good and evil. He presented a two-valued orientation where ten per cent of the population were worthless and should not propagate their kind and ninety per cent were valuable and useful members of society. Dr. Laughlin did not hesitate to make unqualified judgments about this one-tenth. They were "socially unfit," "totally unfitted for parenthood," "inferior," "anti-social," "the most worthless" and "carriers of hereditary traits of a low and menacing order." He also labeled these people in an uncomplimentary manner and for emphasis continued to repeat these epithets such as "the submerged tenth," "lower tenth," "human 'culls'," and "defective germ-plasm." He was not specific as to what the exact problems of these people were, except that some were insane and feebleminded. (Pg. 107, "Harry H. Laughlin, Expert Eugenics Agent," Frances Janet Hassencahl, University Microfilms, 1970)

The phrase "submerged tenth" is of interest as it is a phrase that permeated through the chattering class of American Progressivism. In typical activist form, Laughlin assured his activist counterparts that science could distinguish between good and bad germ-plasm "in a lawful, just, and humane manner," meanwhile alluding to this portion of the population the way a bureaucrat may refer to the community's stray dog problem. Hassencahl quotes Laughlin:

> The unprotected females of the socially unfit classes bear, in human society, a place comparable to that of the females of mongrel strains of domestic animals. (Pg. 108, "Harry H. Laughlin, Expert Eugenics Agent," Frances Janet Hassencahl, University Microfilms, 1970)

Hassencahl documents that Laughlin repeatedly cited Darwin in proposing that the level of breeding stock be raised in order to arrive at a possible higher or superior form of human. Hassencahl states that "Laughlin might have been looking forward to a race of supermen", and that he cited Darwin in order to "add weight to the proposal." Of course, Charles Darwin is citing his cousin, Francis Galton, in this quote:

> When in any nation the standard of intellect and the number of intellectual men have increased, we may expect from the law of the deviation from the average, as shown by Mr. Galton, that prodigies of genius will appear somewhat more frequently than before. (Pg. 135, "Harry H. Laughlin, Expert Eugenics Agent", Frances Janet Hassencahl, University Microfilms, 1970, Laughlin quoting Darwin)

Laughlin proposed that subjecting the "submerged tenth" to a systematic segregation and sterilization would reduce the number of "unfit" to 2.77% by 1970 and 1.32% by 1985. Laughlin would begin by sterilizing 80 out of 100,000, which represented half of the total population of committed persons at the time. Laughlin calculated that the other half was past the reproductive age, already sterilized naturally or by the state, or near death. After two generations, the rate of sterilization would increase to 150 out of 100,000 of the committed population. All in all this would amount to an astounding 15,000,000 sterilized over several decades. (Pg. 134, Hassencahl) To put this into historical context, Laughlin was proposing that fifteen million people be subjected to the forced mutilation of their bodies thirty years before Hitler. Eradicating the weak and "unfit" was an enduring theme for eugenic-minded zealots, from Galton to Hitler. Hitler's address at the 1929 party convention illustrates this volatile mix of Darwin and Nietzsche:

> The worst danger is that we are interrupting the natural selection process ourselves (by caring for the sick and the weak). ... The most far-sighted racial state in history, Sparta, systematically implemented these racial laws.

Laughlin continues along this theme of comparing the spaying and wasting of unwanted animals to his proposed way in which society should control the human population:

> In the breeding of the higher and more valuable types of animals such as horses and cattle, sterilization of surplus males is one custom universally practiced. The females of these animals are well cared for an protected from free union

with the males, here selected matings are the rule. However, in the case of domestic animals of less value, having mongrel and homeless strains, such as the dog and the cat, the cutting off of their supply is largely effected through the destruction or the unsexing of the females. [sic] (Pg. 126, "Harry H. Laughlin, Expert Eugenics Agent," Frances Janet Hassencahl, University Microfilms, 1970)

One important point must be gleaned from Laughlin's proposal. The eugenicists were under no illusion that eugenics was a quick fix. The various legislative proposals demonstrate that this was a long-term project. It was meant to be a perpetual control of every aspect of society that affected human heredity. They answered their critics in such terms. Though they always presaged the argument with the necessity for drastic measures, they also made sure to follow up this observation with the long-term plans of their mission. Dr. Clarence Campbell, the President of the Eugenics Research Association, would say as much in a 1934 lecture Laughlin kept a copy of in his files:

> The recorded cases of feeble-mindedness and insanity have doubled in a generation, and making every allowance for more complete recording, there can be no doubt of the marked increase of these elements in the population. Contrary to the allegations of the opponents of sterilization, its supporter make no claim that it will immediately eradicate feeble-mindedness and insanity. They only claim that the sterilization of such subjects will diminish its incidence. In the case of feeble-mindedness careful estimates have been made by Leonard Darwin and by Professor R.A. Fischer, going to show that such sterilization will diminish the incidence of feeble-mindedness by something like 15% by generation. [sic] (Laughlin Papers, Box D-2-3:5, Truman Univ., "Race Betterment and Sterilization," Feb. 13th, 1934, Campbell)

The other major accomplishment for the eugenics movement to arise from the American Breeders' Association was the creation of a committee dedicated to immigration. Later in history, this committee would be primarily responsible for the passage of the legislation that would keep Jewish victims from reaching the safety of American shores during The Holocaust. It is important to take note of the fact that the immigration committee within the American Breeders' Association was created by and headed up by Davenport's cohorts at the anti-immigration lobby, the Immigration Restriction League. The fact that the Immigration Restriction League had the influence within the American Breeders' Association to create a committee of their liking further underscores that the eugenic goals of the American Breeders' Association were intended for social engineering from the onset, and not as a consequence of conclusions arrived at scientifically. Frances Janet Hassencahl opines on the relationship between the American Breeders' Association and the Immigration Restriction League:

> In 1911, the American Breeders' Association established a Committee on Immigration, which, unlike Laughlin's sterilization committee, did not just propose legislation, but actively worked for its passage in Congress. The chief reason for such activity was that the Immigration Committee was composed of

men from the Immigration Restriction League, an organization experienced in the art of influencing Congressmen. Laughlin was not well acquainted with the members of the League, because he was of a later generation and did not attend Harvard, however, he did agree with the racist principles they espoused. He concerned himself largely with the sterilization question and left the immigration question to his mentor, Charles B. Davenport, until the 1920's. Davenport was a Harvard man and classmate of the executive secretary of the Immigration Restriction League, Prescott B. Hall. (Pg. 163, "Harry H. Laughlin, Expert Eugenics Agent," Frances Janet Hassencahl, University Microfilms, 1970)

As discussed earlier, the Immigration Restriction League had racial and family pedigree requirements for membership and two men dominated, Harvard's Prescott F. Hall and Robert De Courcy Ward. Hall spent much of his time indulging in Wagnerian music and German philosophy while Ward was a professor of climatology at Harvard. Hassencahl reports on this alliance:

> Despite such initial success, by 1911 the League was groping about for a new propaganda base. The hereditarian ideas of the eugenicists had particular appeal to those who could count back and find the founders of the Republic among their ancestors. The biological fabric of the eugenics movement was soon tailored to clothe the forces of nativism in a fine suit of scientific respectability. Barbara Solomon, in her study of the Immigration Restriction League, wrote that, **"Eugenics transformed the ambiguous xenophobia of Brahmin restrictionists into a formidable racist ideology."** In 1911, Prescott Hall wrote to his old classmate from Harvard, Charles Davenport, asking for information on the work of the Eugenics Record Office and expressing his interest in sterilization and immigration control. From these renewed contacts, Hall and Davenport agreed to organize a Committee on Immigration under the Eugenics Section of the American Breeders' Association." [sic.](Pg. 165, "Harry H. Laughlin, Expert Eugenics Agent," Frances Janet Hassencahl, University Microfilms, 1970, emphasis mine)

The Founders of the great American experiment had divorced themselves from old world aristocracies and monarchies. However, the newly established American elites had found a way to separate and differentiate themselves from the masses, and it is by no surprise that they frequently used the term "natural aristocracy" in describing their eugenics. They could not claim to be part of the Old World aristocracy, as this was an anathema to the creation of the American Republic. However, this did not mean that they shared in the nation's egalitarianism or appreciation for its founding principles. Hassencahl points to an October 1st, 1920 letter from Prescott Hall to Charles Davenport discussing the best means of accomplishing their goals:

> Hall's reply to Davenport was that his scheme "smacks too much of the laboratory." Efforts should be spent on getting a bill through which would "heavily favor the Nordic. ---- After immigration of Asiatics, Alpines, and Meds [Mediterraneans] has been diminished, the Nordic countries would be the easiest in which to apply your plan." In a revealing post-script, he added that he

wished he could share Dr. Davenport's faith that the "United States might establish an efficient system of inspection abroad, but that he doubted a democracy could do anything well. Gone were the good days, when until the 1840's, the United States was practically an aristocracy." (Pg. 170, "Harry H. Laughlin, Expert Eugenics Agent," Hassencahl, Univ. Microfilms, 1970)

This disdain for "democracy" or "*laissez-faire*" limited government, as prescribed by the Founding Fathers, would be a common theme for the "aristocratic" minded eugenicists. Despite their boastful claims of lineage to the Founding generation, they did not have much confidence in its principles. Paul Popenoe, one of the directors of the American Eugenics Society, would mock the Declaration of Independence:

> The self-evidence of the truth that all men are created equal. . . . That phrase has long been a favorite with the demagogue and the utopian. . . . The American educational system is based largely on this dogma, and much of the political system seems to be grounded on it. ---- **Fundamentally, eugenics is anti-individualistic and insofar a socialistic movement, since it seeks a social end involving some degree of individual subordination.** . . . Good government is then an aristo-democracy. In it the final control rests in a democratically chosen legislature, to which only the qualified may be candidates. (Pg. 56, "California's Nazi Eugenics", EIR Investigation, Vol. 22, No. 11, March 10th, 1995, emphasis mine)

Professor Paul Lombardo, author of the 2008 book "Three Generations, No Imbeciles" quotes Dr. Joseph S. DeJarnette. Dr. DeJarnette's disdain for the egalitarian principles, incredibly, were part of the testimony he offered to the U.S. Supreme Court; a court of law sworn to uphold the U.S. Constitution:

> He decried those who constantly invoked "the so-called inalienable rights of man" to oppose surgery and compared accepted rules of stock breeding with the deference paid to "the syphilitic, epileptic, imbecile, drunkard and unfit." In contrast to the political sentimentalists, **DeJarnette believed in a Darwinian scheme where "only the fit survive."** A good farmer, he said, "breeding his hogs, horses, cows, sheep, . . . selects a thoroughbred"; even crops are grown from the "best seed." Yet, "when it came to our own race any sort of seed seems good enough." (Pgs. 121 – 122, "Three Generations," emphasis mine)

Theirs was the type of patriotism voiced by Progressives; supposedly proud of their American heritage, but completely confident the "American Experiment" of self-government had failed. They believed it needed to be superseded by a centrally-planned form of government directed by the elite. Certainly, no eugenic goals could be accomplished if they were left up to the will of the "unfit" and "degenerate" to cooperate of their free will. The hereditarily "unfit" were not regarded as capable of "self-government" after all. This is an important distinction to make. Absolute and total reliance on the intellectual elite for the orchestrating of society was the cornerstone of both Progressivism and eugenics.

Along the same lines, the Theodore Roosevelt Collection at Harvard's Houghton Library holds correspondence between then Police Commissioner Theodore Roosevelt and one of the founders of the Immigration Restriction League, Prescott Hall. The various letters are about mustering up the political support for passing legislation that would restrict undesirable ethnicities from immigrating to the United States.

It also seems that the reliance on the intellectual elite for the passing of legislation started with Theodore Roosevelt. This is noteworthy as it was politicized scientists like Laughlin which would be appointed as "experts" before the United States Congress in order to pass legislation that was wholly based on recommendations of supposedly reliable scientific facts. All of this came full circle when in 1900 President McKinley was assassinated, and Theodore Roosevelt ascended to the Presidency. In 1902 immigration subsequently reached a peak at 1.2 million. According to a memorandum prepared by Oscar Handlin for the Hearings Before the President's Commission on Immigration and Naturalization of 1952, the law passed on Feb. 20th, 1907 called specifically for a commission based on the recommendations and findings of an "expert" fact-finding panel:

> Finally the President had great faith in the efficacy of fact-finding agencies as devices to evade the necessity for clear-cut political decisions. Although the President accepted and supported the idea of such a commission, he subtly modified the conception of what it should be and do. Instead of a Congressional investigating committee, **he proposed a study by a number of experts, appointed by the President**: and confidentially requested Commissioner of Labor Neill, while the question was still being debated in Congress, to proceed at once to "as full an investigation of the whole subject of immigration as the facilities at hand will permit." (Pg. 1841, Oscar Handlin, President's Commission 1952, emphasis mine)

Candice Lewis Bredbenner, author of the 1998 book "A Nationality of Her Own: Women, Marriage, and the Law of Citizenship" further documents the February 1907 Act:

> The basic objective of the Expatriation Act of 1907 was a reduction in the number of Americans who, in the eyes of the federal government, had compromised their citizenship status by maintaining or establishing foreign ties of some type. --- The expatriation statute was Congress's initial response to a series of policy proposals submitted the previous year by a presidential commission appointed to recommend general changes in the country's nationality laws. In 1906, the small group of international-law experts commissioned by President Theodore Roosevelt completed their study of the country's nationality laws, and their report heavily influenced the design of the 1907 law. (Pg. 57, "A Nationality of Her Own")

A true accounting of history reveals that the conclusions came first, and the allegedly independent report by the "experts" followed. The report Candice L. Bredbenner refers to is the Bleecker Report, which was largely drafted by Mr.

Bleecker van Wagenen, who, as we known, was a member of the American Breeders' Association. Considered in the context of the eugenic notions Roosevelt learned at Harvard, his appointment of "experts" to inform national policy can hardly be seen as a gesture towards the "impartial" or "empirical". It can more accurately be characterized as leveraging the scientific credential of his eugenic-minded colleagues to imbue the expert testimony and governmental investigation a veil of scientific legitimacy. Clearly, if Theodore Roosevelt was part of the immigration restriction lobby beforehand, one can only assume that his official actions as President were pre-decided, and not at all the product of serious introspection or debate. The convictions came first, and the hiring of the right-minded "experts" followed.

Carnegie Institution of Washington
DEPARTMENT OF GENETICS
COLD SPRING HARBOR, LONG ISLAND, N.Y.

STATION FOR EXPERIMENTAL EVOLUTION   EUGENICS RECORD OFFICE

July 21, 1928.

MEMORANDUM FOR DR. LAUGHLIN:- Mrs. C. B. S. Hodson is contemplating coming to America to lecture in eugenics. I have suggested patriotic societies. I wonder if you have a list of them at the Eugenics Record Office which you could, perhaps, send her at 20 Grosvenor Gardens, S. W. 1.

D/G

1910 - THE STATION FOR EXPERIMENTAL EVOLUTION

> *"You see what a fire you have kindled!*
> *It is going to be a purifying conflagration some day!"*
> – Letter C.B. Davenport to Mrs. E.H. Harriman

As we have seen, the American Breeders' Association provided a forum where scientists interested in breeding could share information. Its creator, W.M. Hays intended it to be an "amicable union of practical breeders, who used records secured at the feeding trough, at the meat, butter, and wool scales, on the race track, and at the prize ring." (Pg. 232, Allen) The likes of Davenport and Laughlin had their eyes outside of the "race track" and fixed on the human household. Professor Garland Allen documents this point in Cold Spring Harbor's history:

> Although the American Breeders' Association served both to stimulate Davenport's interests in eugenics and to give him a forum for his own ideas on the subject, he soon realized that it would require another organization to develop eugenics on a national scale. The Eugenics Committee was a starting place, but it had neither significant funding nor, especially important in Davenport's eyes, an institutional base. Added to these problems was his growing rift with Hays over including the ABA's businessmen among its members and the society's lack of emphasis on research. Davenport therefore concluded that a separate organization, one devoted exclusively to eugenics investigation and education would be desirable, and he naturally thought of locating any laboratory for the study of human heredity and eugenics in Cold Spring Harbor. As Davenport originally envisioned it, a eugenics institute would be administratively under his control but with the day-to-day supervision of research and operating details given over to a superintendent. (Pg. 234, "The ERO at Cold Spring Harbor")

The Eugenics Record Office was founded at Cold Spring Harbor with initial support from Mary Williamson Averell, wife of the powerful railroad magnate E. H. Harriman. One of Charles B. Davenport's summer students was the daughter of the famously wealthy widow. Davenport was keen on leveraging this contact, and soon thereafter the widow became the enthusiastic supporter of Davenport's eugenic cause. According to Professor Allen, Mrs. Harriman contributed approximately $246,000 towards the overall operating costs of $440,000 between 1910 and 1918, prior to the Carnegie Institution taking charge. Davenport milked the relationship for all it was worth. Davenport made sure to always seek Mrs. Harriman's advice. The eulogy he wrote upon Mrs. Harriman's death is revealing:

> For us at the Eugenics Office [sic.] the things that counted most were her understanding of the needs of the work at a time when it was ridiculed by many and disesteemed by many others. As she often said the fact that she was brought up among well bred race horses helped her to appreciate the importance of a project to study heredity and good breeding in man. (Pg. 236, "The ERO at Cold Spring Harbor")

As documented earlier, Davenport approached Carnegie in 1902. Charitable institutions by the newly dominant industrial elite were a relatively new phenomenon at this time. Thus, the practice of funding scientific laboratories, as opposed to the actual scientist, was also a relatively new practice. Carnegie finally accepted Davenport's proposal, and on December 12th, 1903 Davenport was awarded a grant of $34,250. (Pg. 230, Allen) The name "Station for the Experimental Study of Evolution" was adopted for Cold Spring Harbor, and it was incorporated as the "Department of Experimental Biology of the Carnegie Institution of Washington." This is the organization where the young Harriman would go study for a summer, and which would attract the attention of other like-minded scientists such as Harry H. Laughlin at the American Breeders' Association. Professor Allen explains:

> In the early decades of the century, highly qualified young investigators came to the station for varying periods to work on specific problems relating to heredity and evolution. Davenport himself remained in complete administrative control. It was his kingdom. He administered it scrupulously, autocratically, and sometimes dictatorially, until his retirement in 1934 at the age of sixty-eight. The Carnegie Institution had invested not merely in a facility and a program for research but in one man and his vision of a new direction in biology. (Pg. 231, "The ERO at Cold Spring Harbor")

Frances Janet Hassencahl documents in her dissertation that on January 1st, 1918 the Eugenics Record Office was conjoined with the "Station for Experimental Evolution" under the administration of the Carnegie Institution of Washington, D.C. It was an apt name for the work that would be done in the laboratory under Davenport and Laughlin. Invoking the image of man tinkering with evolution was certainly appropriate, as this was its stated purpose. Davenport envisioned a "campus of a great institution devoted to race and family stock betterment in man" to be erected on the 76.85 acres at Cold Spring Harbor. The lab is still located in the village of Laurel Hollow, New York, on the shores of the harbor. Aside from providing the initial funding, Mrs. Harriman would be joined by John D. Rockefeller in providing scholarships for some of Laughlin's trainees at the Eugenics Record Office. According to Hassencahl, they offered fifty-dollar stipend for graduates in Zoology, psychology, and anthropology whom would work one year as a field worker, collecting eugenical data for Laughlin's family pedigrees. The Eugenics Record Office would in turn use its prestige to ensure that its graduating experts were placed in permanent positions at cooperating institutions across the country.

As mentioned earlier, both Davenport and Carnegie sought out Francis Galton and the Darwin family for guidance and support in creating a new institution. A letter from Charles B. Davenport to Leonard Darwin, the famous biologist's son, and the leader of the British eugenics movement, describes the circumstances:

My dear Darwin;- In response to your letter of April third I am sending you a note that Dr. Laughlin prepared about the history of the Eugenics Record Office. It is very old. The Eugenics Record Office was founded by Mrs. E.H. Harriman, as a result of a conference with her in the autumn '09 and the spring of 1910. As she has often told me her father was interested in breeding race horses and also Mr. Harriman and she appreciated the importance of heredity in horses ad believed the laws equally applicable to man. ---- It was really through Mary Harriman that I was able to approach Mrs. Harriman. Mrs. Harriman financed the work of the Eugenics Record Office for 8 or 9 years and finally in transferring it to the Carnegie Institution of Washington gave it a donation of $300,000. (Am. Phil. Soc., E.R.O. Records, TN 26977, Darwin, Leonard 1850-1943, April 18th, 1931, Folders 1-4)

With the Institution formalized, Laughlin and his wife Pansy moved to Cold Spring Harbor on October 1910, where they stayed for the next 29 years. From its origin in 1910 until 1921 his title was Superintendent in charge of the Eugenics Record Office of the Department of Genetics of the Carnegie Institute of Washington, D. C., and Director from 1921 until 1940. In his first report as superintendent, Laughlin listed his responsibilities as the administrator in a document entitled "Eugenics Record Office, Report No. 1" (Generally from G. Allen's "The ERO at Cold Spring Harbor"):

- To serve Eugenical interests as a repository and clearinghouse. The "Eugenical News" newsletter would be distributed as a non-technical propaganda organ towards these ends.
- To build up an analytical index of traits in American families. The so-called "Trait Book", which Davenport had devised in 1910, listed all the human physical, physiological, and mental traits imaginable, as well as some which evidence the sophistication of the work conducted at the ERO: Amongst the traits listed in this book were a rowdy personality, a penchant for train-wrecking, patriotism, and an ability to play chess. The information was indexed in 3x5 cards and cross-referenced by family name, trait number, and geographical location. By the time the ERO closed in 1939 they had accumulated nearly one million cards.
- To study the forces controlling and hereditary consequences of marriage-matings, differential birth rates, and survival migration.
- To investigate the manner of inheritance of specific human traits. This was done mainly in a Mendelian approach, by charting pedigrees.
- To advise concerning the eugenical fitness of proposed marriages. Prospective couples would visit the ERO for this service.
- To train fieldworker to gather data of eugenical import.
- To encourage new centers for eugenics research and education.
- To publish the results of research and to aid in the dissemination of eugenic "truths."

Per one of the underlying themes of this book, it is important to note how Laughlin extrapolated and expanded on point number three, the study of the "forces controlling and hereditary consequences of marriage." A quote from

Hassencahl makes it clear that the goal was as much about social engineering as it was about scientific research and or biology:

> Man is an animal, and as such is not exempt from the operation of the laws of heredity. Not until a knowledge of the inheritance of specific human traits is obtained can man undertake intelligently to devise plans for cutting off the supply of defectives and **for so modifying the social scheme** that intelligent matings will bring together harmonious hereditary strains. It is the appreciation of these facts and that makes research the passing business of eugenics. [sic.] (Pg. 74, "Harry H. Laughlin, Expert Eugenics Agent," Frances Janet Hassencahl, University Microfilms, 1970, emphasis mine)

Point number six is of consequence for the ability to conduct the all-important Mendelian pedigrees with the rigor and reliability expected of a scientific institution. First, these fieldworkers were the product of a very short summer program conducted by Laughlin. Second, as many historians have pointed out, the pedigree studies conducted could only mimic Mendel's studies. Mendel used peas to study heredity and the geneticists that followed him decided to use fruit flies. There was good reason for this. Studying the pedigrees of peas or fruit flies allows for a distinctly different circumstances than attempting to study the several generations of a human family, specifically when many of the members of that family are long since dead and with no reliable records available. Geneticists, like Mendel before them, specifically chose peas and fruit flies precisely because they reproduce in a relatively short span of time, thus making the observations and proper documentation of those generations feasible. This is an important distinction to make as it proved to be one of several fundamental flaws with eugenics. Laughlin describes his work in these exact terms in a 1939 memorandum written for the Carnegie leadership entitled "Studies on the Archives of the Eugenics Record Office – Purpose, Policy and Nature of the Archives":

> Man being a large animal, slowly reproducing (and not subject to laboratory experimentation for genetic research like drosophila or the white mouse) it is necessary to consider "as experiments" the history already made in migration, mating and size-of-family, and to secure first description of individual persons, their "personal case histories" and records of their blood-kinship. (Laughlin files, Carnegie Inst., Sep. 16th, 1939, Memo Laughlin to Gilbert, emphasis his)

Of relevance to this point is a November 7th, 1925 letter from Laughlin to Dr. Merriam, the president of the Carnegie Institution. In this letter Laughlin pretty much admits to the fact that despite his extensive use of seemingly exact numbers, eugenics was far from an exact science:

> I appreciate the fact that studies in population cannot be so definite as experiments in physics or chemistry. Still there are many important processes which govern the vicissitudes of races which can be analyzed, and for which processes mathematical formulae can be found. (Laughlin files, Carnegie Inst., Nov.7th, 1925, Laughlin to Merriam)

Furthermore, eugenicists were targeting problem families, which by their disorganized and unpredictable nature made historical data difficult to collect. The reports compiled included opinions about an individual's personality traits by the townspeople or surviving family members, many of which were not even alive at the same time that these test subjects were around. Needless to say, one did not need to wait for the science of genetics to mature in order to understand the severe deficiencies in the methods employed by the eugenicists. Geneticists clearly understood the conscious decision to choose fruit flies and peas for the reasons that they did. Thus, any geneticist that took a close look at the studies produced by the ERO's fieldworkers would immediately take note of the subjective and anecdotal nature of the information gathered. Professor Allen, as well as other historians of the eugenics movement, have pointed to the study of a James Dack by fieldworker Anna Wendt Finlayson as emblematic of the quality of information these fieldworkers collected:

> *James Dack* (116) was commonly known as "Rotten Jimmy," the epithet was given because of the diseased condition of his legs, which were covered with chronic ulcers, although the term is said to have been equally applicable to his moral nature. He was a thief and general good-for-nothing, but neither shrewd nor cunning. His conversation quickly revealed his childlike mind. (Pg. 243, "The ERO at Cold Spring Harbor")

Much of the criticism from sober-minded scientists that would inevitably result touched on the unscientific methods of data gathering. However, this is not to say that the sober-minded portion of the scientific community was successful in curtailing the political and practical successes of the ERO. The Davenport, Darwin, Grant, and Stoddard names would give eugenics a veil of legitimacy despite the obvious and somewhat ridiculous aspects of the movement. Less politically influential scientists and critics appear in the newspapers of the epoch poking fun at the methods of the movement, and their more serious peers wrote polite and emotionally detached criticism in journals. Professor Garland E. Allen documents the political importance of creating the E.R.O. in the 1986 paper entitled "The Eugenics Record Office at Cold Spring Harbor, 1910-1940: An Essay in Institutional History":

> The ERO provided both the appearance of sound scientific credentials and the reality of an institutional base from which eugenics work throughout the country, and even in Western Europe, could be coordinated. The ERO became a meeting place for eugenicists, a repository for eugenics records, a clearinghouse for eugenics information and propaganda, a platform from which popular eugenic campaigns could be launched, and a home for several Eugenical publications. ---- Thus the ERO became the nerve center for the eugenics movement as a whole. When it close its doors on 31 December 1939, it was clear that the movement as such no longer existed. (Pg. 226, "The ERO at Cold Spring Harbor")

In other words, the Eugenics Record Office would become the epicenter of the international eugenics movement. The information collected by Laughlin's army of minions would be the basis for the legislation explored in the following chapters; legislation that would directly lead to the segregation, sterilization, and in the end, when followed to its logical and intended lengths, the annihilation of countless numbers of people by Hitler's eugenicists.

würde gut sein, wenn man auch in Californien in erster Linie die Schwachsinnigen sterilisieren würde.

Mit besten Grüssen auch an Dr. Paul Popenoe

Ihr ergebener

F. Lenz

Institut für Rassenhygiene
der Universität Berlin
Prof. Dr. F. Lenz
Fernsprecher: C 1 Jäger Nr. 4544

Berlin NW 7, den 10. Juni 1937
Dorotheenstraße 28a

Mr. E.S. Gosney

Pasadena

Sehr geehrter Herr Gosney!

Sie waren so freundlich, mir mit einem Brief vom 24. Mai neue Informationen über die Sterilisierung in USA, insbesondere in Californien, zu schicken. Diese Erfahrungen sind auch für uns in Deutschland sehr wertvoll, und ich bin Ihnen herzlich dankbar dafür. Mit besonderem Interesse habe ich aus der Mitteilung entnommen, dass von den 12 000 Sterilisierten in Californien zwei Drittel wegen Geisteskrankheit und nur ein Drittel wegen Schwachsinn sterilisiert worden sind. Bei uns in Deutschland ist es umgekehrt. Bei uns machen die Schwachsinnigen die grosse Mehrzahl aller Sterilisierten aus; und wir halten die Sterilisierung der Schwachsinnigen in der Tat für viel wichtiger. Schwachsinnige haben überwiegend auch schwachsinnige Kinder, Geisteskranke dagegen haben nur 10 bis 20% geisteskranke Kinder. Ausserdem kann man die Schwachsinnigen alle vor Beginn der Fortpflanzung erfassen, die Geisteskranken dagegen nur zum Teil. Aus diesen Gründen sind die Aussichten auf schnelle Verminderung des Schwachsinns durch Sterilisierung viel günstiger als die Aussichten auf Verminderung der Geisteskrankheiten. Es mag natürlich sein, dass es bei Ihnen in Californien weniger Schwachsinnige gibt als bei uns; denn Schwachsinnige wandern weniger aus. Immerhin aber glaube ich, es

1914 - LEGAL ASPECTS OF STERILIZATION

"The more the state 'plans' the more difficult planning becomes for the individual."
- Friedrich Hayek

The proverbial "slippery slope" is a well-worn platitude of Holocaust history. Catch phrases like the "slippery slope" fit neatly into the narrative, yet it is their over use that ultimately divorce them of real meaning. The "slippery slope" imagery paints a picture of a slide down a dangerous path once certain political premises are adopted. This imagery alludes to a humanity helplessly pulled down by the weight of fate itself. Of note is that Holocaust historians have begun to describe the path to genocide that can hardly be described as blind or helpless. The history of The Holocaust reveals the formidable labor and effort it took to implement eugenics. Instead, Holocaust historians speak of the "banality" of evil, alluding to the bureaucratic mechanisms that must be deliberated over, enacted, and implemented in order to subvert the will of free individuals to the directives of a eugenic state. It took about 100 years from the first inkling to breed men like horses to its culmination in The Holocaust. In order to provide context one must note that in 1914, when Laughlin was already appearing before the United States Congress, Adolf Hitler was nothing but a young vagrant, struggling to survive while living in a half-way houses.

Also, Laughlin's inroads with the United States Congress should not be underestimated. The United States posed a particular problem for the international eugenics movement during this prolonged endeavor. The nation's legislative emphasis on "individual rights," "equality before the law", and "due process" were significant obstacles for the eugenic notion that the population of a nation was nothing but the biological assets in a glorified plantation. In addition, the United States federalist form of government was not a top-down form of government as those intent on orchestrating all aspects of society would desire. The States and the people supposedly hold equal power to the Federal government, and the directives of the Federal government only apply if the people of each State ratify them. Beyond that, the "separation of powers" doctrine dictates that the Federal and State governments are divided into three "equal" branches. The eugenicists were keenly aware that passing a law in the legislative branch was useless if the judicial branch later deemed it "unconstitutional." This was true at both the State and Federal court levels. In other words, the United States was conceived to be the diametric opposite of the centrally-planned form of government eugenicists needed in order to "direct evolution."

Inevitably, the first step in any attempt to remake the United States into a eugenic nation would be to analyze the existing laws at both the Federal and State level. Understanding how to both propose and pass laws that were deemed "constitutional" at both the State and Federal courts was imperative in the project to reorient the country to a eugenic ethos. Unfortunately, this is precisely what Laughlin excelled at. Laughlin understood what steps needed to be taken to subvert the "checks and balances" designed into the American system of government.

One of the first steps in order to accomplish their goals was convincing the United States government to accommodate its statistics in order to represent the population in ways that served the eugenic cause. Laughlin and company understood that eugenicists needed to define the crisis in order to be able to justify the urgency of their demands. Owning the population statistics meant owning the conclusions to be drawn. Once the politicians were convinced of the urgency and mobilized to act, the second step was drafting ready-made laws that would pass "constitutional" muster. Again, this is where Laughlin became indispensable for the eugenic lobby. Laughlin would appear as an "expert eugenicist" before the United States Congress a total of three times. Both the Eugenics Record Office and the United States Congress would print Laughlin's reports, sometimes under different names. The 1914 Eugenics Record Office "BULLETIN No. 10B: Report of the Committee to Study and to Report on the Best Practical Means of Cutting Off the Defective Germ-Plasm in the American Population" contained Harry H. Laughlin's "LEGAL, LEGISLATIVE AND ADMINISTRATIVE ASPECTS OF STERILIZATION". This was a study of all of the laws that had been passed by State legislatures up till then, as well as a legal analysis of their defects and an opinion on how to modify them to survive attacks on their "constitutionality." Most importantly, it contains Laughlin's first attempt at a ready-made, cookie-cutter law, otherwise known in the legal community as a "model law." For example, the 1914 "Model Law" called for the establishment of a "Eugenics Commission" in each State, which according to Laughlin's wishes would be the all-powerful governmental institutions that would conduct investigations, collect statistical data, and order the sterilization of a citizen. This is but one of the components of the matured version of Laughlin's "Model Eugenic Law" which would later be adopted by Hitler's government.

However, this 1914 version was still too ambiguous. This early version of Laughlin's "Model Eugenic Law" reads more like a wish list than an actual statute to be adopted by the legislature. It could not have been adopted in this form as it provides a list of recommendations, as opposed to rules and procedures that could be copied by the typically lazy legislators seeking out in ready-made law. For example:

> The question may be raised as to the manner of appointment of an eugenics commission, but it seems preferable that responsibility should he centered in the chief executive of the state without the concurrence of any other body. In New York the Governor appoints the commission; in New Jersey the Governor must have the advice of the senate. In some states the whole problem of administering

the affairs of the socially unfit is handled by a State Board of Control. It may be wise in such states to vest the appointment of the Eugenics Commission not in the hands of the Governor, but with the State Board of Control. (Pg. 122, "Bulletin No. 10B")

Laws and statutes need to provide precise descriptions of the acts that either comport or violate them, as the courts that interpret these laws need clear demarcations. Wishlists about the size and scope of departments and institutions do not accomplish this. However, at this point the goal was to gauge if eugenic laws passed "constitutional muster" and more importantly if they would survive the legal attacks that would inevitably come from its victims. The report analyzed where the various States of the Union were in the efforts towards achieving eugenic laws. In this respect "Bulletin No. 10B" was successful and of historical importance. The report pulled together some of the most prestigious "expert" eugenic minds in the United States, including Nobel Prize winner Alexis Carrel, Raymond Pearl, Henry H. Goddard, and Irving Fisher. The inclusion of Carrel is noteworthy. Dr. Alexis Carrel, a French-American Nobel Prize winner, would publish "Man, The Unknown" in 1935 where he advocated killing the "mentally ill and criminals" in "euthanasia" institutions. Carrel's book was a bestseller and highly influential.

Interestingly enough, the "Bulletin" brings together two critical and typically opposing figures in American jurisprudence in order to analyze the "constitutionality" of eugenic sterilization: Judge Warren W. Foster and the famous civil rights attorney Louis Marshall. Judge Warren W. Foster of New York had already published a eugenic tract and was known for believing that criminal behavior was a "hereditary trait." Forster was merciless in believing that the only method of dealing with criminality was to segregate or sterilize the perpetrator as Foster believed that hereditary traits could not be ameliorated by improving the environment or education. In other words, the criminal was a "born criminal", and the state had no other remedy than to exclude both the criminal and their offspring from society. On the other hand, Louis Marshall's inclusion was certainly odd. By stark contrast, Louis Marshall's career indicates that he did not believe that any person was predetermined to be outside of the rights and privileges the Constitution of the United States guaranteed for all. Marshall was the son of German-Jewish immigrants and would later fight directly against Laughlin and his cohorts in their efforts to pass eugenic minded immigration restrictions. Maybe Marshall did not foresee the corrosive effects of eugenics when on April 12th, 1912 Judge Foster requested that Marshall draft an opinion on the constitutionality of eugenic segregation and sterilization. Marshall's opinion appears prominently in Laughlin's "Bulletin" as part of the legal analysis. Marshall opens up his letter by admitting that he rushed the opinion as he did not have the time for a more thorough analysis. Marshall then proceeds to analyze the "constitutionality" of the proposed "Model Law":

Doubtless the state has the power, in the administration of punishment to offenders and in dealing with those who may imperil the safety of the public, to segregate them and to exercise a general supervision over them. The exercise of this function comes strictly within the police power of the state, since it affects the public safety and welfare. In the case of criminals the state has the power to impose more drastic punishment upon second offenders and upon habitual criminals than it sees fit to impose upon first offenders. (Pg. , "Bulletin No. 10")

Marshall goes through the basic legal analysis regarding the prohibition of "cruel and unusual punishment" that limits what the state can do to a "criminal." It is an important contribution as eugenicists henceforth knew they had to distance themselves from any notion that eugenic sterilization was a punishment for a crime. Marshall reveals his reservations, and does so in terms that would have been objectionable to Judge Foster, as they were grounded on the notion that criminals may be a product of their social circumstances, and not their heredity:

I understand that the operation of vasectomy is painless and has no effect upon the person upon whom it is imposed other than to render it impossible for him to have progeny. If it could be said that such a punishment would only be inflicted in the case of confirmed criminals, there would be strong reasons, founded on considerations of the public welfare, which would justify its imposition. The danger, however, is that it might be inflicted upon one who is not an habitual criminal, who **might have been the victim of circumstances** and **who could be reformed**. To deprive such an individual of all hope of progeny would approach closely to the line of **cruel and unusual punishment**. There are many cases where juvenile offenders have been rendered habitual criminals who subsequently became exemplary citizens. It is true that these cases are infrequent, and yet the very fact that they exist would require the exercise of extreme caution in determining whether such a punishment is constitutional. ("Bulletin No. 10," emphasis mine)

Clearly, Marshall's views were in direct opposition to the very core of the eugenic creed. The reference to "circumstances" and the belief that one "could be reformed" indicates that Marshall was a believer that humans were equally a product of their "environment" as opposed to slaves to their "heredity." In the end, Marshall was of the opinion that eugenic sterilization was "unconstitutional" as punishment for a crime, as this violated the Constitution's prohibition on "cruel and unusual punishment":

Although not entirely certain as to this phase of the case, I have no doubt that the imposition of such a penalty by a commission or state board, or by any tribunal other than a court which is to determine the penalty for the offense of which one charged with crime has been convicted, **would be unconstitutional**. The determination that such an operation shall be performed necessarily involves the infliction of a penalty. Unless justified by a conviction for crimes, it would be a wanton and unauthorized act and an unwarranted deprivation of the liberty of the citizen. (emphasis mine)

If those legislators that would blindly adopt Laughlin's legislative proposals had read Marshall's opinion carefully, they would have noted that Marshall pretty much dismissed the very core of Laughlin's proposal. Marshall found the establishment of eugenic courts that operated separate from the rest of the court system as unconstitutional. Marshall states in his opinion that creating the "eugenic court" outside of the traditional court system would violate "due process":

> In order to justify it the person upon whom the operation is to be performed has, therefore, the right to insist upon his right to due process of law. That right is withheld if the vasectomy is directed, not by the court which imposes the penalty for the crime, but by a board or commission, which acts upon its own initiative or which, under a general provision of law, undertakes to determine whether or not the operation shall be performed on a specific individual. ("Bulletin No. 10")

This would turn out to be prophetic on Marshall's part, as it was these "eugenic courts" which were superimposed over the existing court system. German eugenicists would source Laughlin's "Model Eugenic Law" via their participation in the International Federation of Eugenic Organizations and implement it with very little changes, if any at all. At war's end, the Allied prosecution team at Nuremberg would deem both the "people's courts" and the "eugenic courts" part of the "criminal conspiracy" that was deemed to be illegal and against German law.

Interestingly enough, despite discrediting the movement's fundamental tenets in principle, Marshall expressed respect for the eugenics movement as a whole. This may have been diplomacy in practice:

> I fear that the public is not as yet prepared to deal with this problem; it requires education on the subject. **I cannot, however, refrain from expressing the general opinion that the movement is one which is based on sound considerations.** The difficulty is, however, in adopting proper safeguards to adequately protect those who are not hopelessly confirmed criminals, degenerates, or defectives. ("Bulletin No. 10," emphasis mine)

It is highly likely that Louis Marshall knew about Judge Foster's position on heredity and criminality and may have been sympathetic in order to be courteous to the sitting judge. The judge's views were no secret. They were highly publicized at the time. On November 1909, Pearson's Magazine (Vol. 22, No. 5) had published a multi-page piece on the Judge's views, "Hereditary Criminality and its Certain Cure," covering the Judge's views on crime and heredity. Interestingly enough, Foster quotes Dr. Oliver Wendell Holmes, the father of the Supreme Court Justice that would in 1927 write the opinion for the Buck v. Bell case that deemed eugenic sterilization courts constitutional:

> "The best way to train a child is to begin with his grandfather," is a remark attributed to that genial philosopher, Dr. Oliver Wendell Holmes, and its wisdom is apparent to all students of the history of crime and criminals. ---- Whether crime is caused by heredity, environment or just "happens" is a much-

> mooted question. The potency of heredity as a casual factor of crime is doubtful to the casual observer, who is of the opinion that all depends on environment. **But "atavism", or the tendency of nature "to return to type," has come to be recognized generally by scientists, and historical and anthropological search undoubtedly prove its existence.** Lombroso, in "L'Uomo Delinquente," assigns to it a position of preeminence in the etiology of crime. (Pg. 565, "Pearson's Mag.", Nov. 1909, emphasis mine)

It is also interesting to note Foster's reference to Cesare Lombroso, whose belief in "degeneration" to an "atavistic" state was, in essence, Darwin's Theory of Evolution working in reverse. "Degeneration," as eugenicists contend was the potential outcome of poor breeding and poor heredity causing evolution to work backward and have man revert to its "ape" ancestry. Eugenicists like Foster believed this was one of the explanations for a criminal's behavior; that the criminal's poor parentage had resulted in offspring that had reverted back to a savage state. Of note is that one of the most famous eugenic-minded leaders of all time, President Theodore Roosevelt, had written a letter to the editor of the New York Times on October 31st, 1913 voicing his approval of Judge Foster's eugenic views:

> Judge Foster has rendered very great service to the public by the part he has taken in more than one advanced movement for the intelligent treatment of the whole problem offered by the existence of the criminal classes. It was Judge Foster who took the initiative in this city in the administration of the indeterminate sentence law which, with the parole and suspended sentence, also wisely and justly administered by him, constitutes the bases for the new penology, which really does heal and save both society and, where it is possible, the criminal. Peculiar value attaches to the remarkable work the Judge has done in the movement for the sterilization of criminals, one of the most important movements before this country. (Pres. T. Roosevelt, NYT, Oct. 31st, 1913)

In the end, Louis Marshall's input was invaluable to Harry H. Laughlin, as it revealed the importance of having his eugenic courts comporting with "due process" and the importance of side-stepping the charge of "cruel and unusual punishment." Laughlin must have seen the benefit of including this dissenting opinion as he would do so in similar bulletins, reports, and books he would publish thereafter, namely the final version of the "Model Eugenic Law." Eugenicists in both the United States and Hitler's Germany would divorce the eugenic courts from criminal courts and redouble their efforts to sell the measures as medical in nature. Observance of "due process" is what the "constitutionality" of Laughlin's "Model Eugenic Law" would hinge upon once it was deliberated by the United States Supreme Court in the 1927 case of Buck v. Bell. Justice Oliver Wendell Holmes, Jr. would write the opinion and infamously side with the view of his father, President Roosevelt, Judge Foster, and the long line of eugenicists which Laughlin had surveyed in his "Bulletin." This is likely why Laughlin included

Marshall's otherwise dissenting opinion in the "Bulletin," which would be literally sent around the world to scientists, doctors, attorneys, judges, and legislators who sought to implement eugenic laws. It is a lesson that was well learned, as even Hitler's Germany would implement the very legal processes recommended by Laughlin in order to mimic the compliance with "due process." The Third Reich's eugenic courts were substantially similar implementations of those proposed by Laughlin, composed of a three-panel system with an "expert" on the science of eugenics sitting aside the two other judges.

Eugenical Sterilization
in the
United States

By

Harry Hamilton Laughlin, D. Sc.

Assistant Director of the Eugenics Record Office,
Carnegie Institution of Washington,
Cold Spring Harbor, Long Island, New York,
and
Eugenics Associate of the Psychopathic Laboratory
of the Municipal Court of Chicago.

Published by the
Psychopathic Laboratory of the Municipal Court
of Chicago
December, 1922

SCIENTIFIC SOCIAL LEGAL MEDICAL
REDUCE THE BURDEN OF DEFECTIVES BY SELECTIVE STERILIZATION

Buy Home Defence Stamps
IN PADS OF 100
ONE PAD: ONE DOLLAR
FOUR PADS: THREE DOLLARS

SCIENTIFIC SOCIAL LEGAL MEDICAL
REDUCE FEEBLEMINDEDNESS BY SELECTIVE STERILIZATION

Keep Our Cause Before The Public
AND HELP FINANCE THE WORK

SCIENTIFIC SOCIAL LEGAL MEDICAL
SELECTIVE STERILIZATION BENEFITS BOTH PARENTS AND CHILDREN

SELECT YOUR SLOGAN AND
ORDER TODAY FROM THE
Sterilization League of New Jersey
P.O. Box 441, Princeton, N. J.

SCIENTIFIC SOCIAL LEGAL MEDICAL
SELECTIVE STERILIZATION GUARDS THE HEALTH OF HUMANITY

1919 - STATISTICAL DIRECTORY OF STATE INSTITUTIONS

> "How many legs does a dog have if you call the tail a leg?
> Four. Calling a tail a leg doesn't make it a leg."
> - Abraham Lincoln

All manufactured crises heed expertly prepared evidence to justify their political aims. Laughlin's aptitude in compiling and presenting statistical concepts would be the scientific basis for most, if not all, the eugenic legislation passed by Progressive-minded legislatures in the United States. Laughlin's skills were instrumental in molding the nomenclature and terminology to the goals of the eugenics movement. As discussed previously, controlling the statistics was a key part of controlling both the debate and eventually the conclusions that future legislation would be based upon. Laughlin himself would write about these efforts in an article that appeared in the Eugenics Review entitled "The Relation of Eugenics to Other Sciences":

> Thus far the work of the United States Bureau of the Census has been confined largely to the enumeration of individuals, and the tabulation of wealth and its distribution. ---- One thing which is a pressing duty of the eugenicists is to insist that future censuses, both national and state, make serious efforts to evaluate the social adequacy of the individuals whom they count, and to make records of the family relationships. (Pg. 61, "The Relation of Eugenics to Other Sciences," Eugenics Review, July 1919)

The surviving documents reveal that redefining the official terminology used by the government institutions was a goal of the eugenicists from the onset. As early as 1916 the American eugenicists identified the U.S. Census as a vehicle to be commandeered in order to enact legislative change. Laughlin wrote about these convictions in the Journal of Heredity, which, as the reader will recall, was once the organ of the American Breeders' Association:

> EUGENISTS AND GENEOLOGISTS DESIRE AMENDMENT TO POPULATION SCHEDULE – In 1916, Alexander Graham Bell, Chairman of the Board of Scientific Directors of the Eugenics Record Office, proposed a resolution which was unanimously adopted by this body, to the effect that it would be highly desirable in the interests of American family history studies if to the census schedule there were added two items: first, "name of the father of the person enumerated:" and second, "full maiden name of the mother of the person enumerated." The Eugenics Research Association, through its Executive Committee, in following up this purpose, presented on February 21, 1919 . . . to the Director of the Census. (Pg. 208, Journal of Heredity, "Population Schedule For the Census of 1920," Jan. 1919)

Laughlin and his cohorts were keenly aware of the political importance of working with the Census office. The personal correspondence corroborates the real purpose of Laughlin's 1919 "Statistical Directory of State Institutions":

Dear Mr. Goethe: With this letter I am enclosing a copy of the letter which we have prepared, with enclosures, to send to congressmen, committeemen and other persons especially interested in the preparation for the Census of 1940. **Our experience has been that we get a much better hearing from the congressional committees when presenting ideas or propositions to the officers of the Bureau of the Census.** (March 27th, 1939, Laughlin to Goethe, Truman Univ., Special Coll., emphasis mine)

Laughlin and company would not wait for the U.S. Census to heed their demands. The Eugenics Record Office began to collect and catalog statistics of their own. In 1919 Laughlin compiled an impressively thorough directory of all of the state institutions that housed "defective, dependent, and delinquent classes." The Department of Commerce published the work through the Washington Printing Office. Aside from its mundane statistical approach, it was an invaluable accomplishment as it went a long way to establishing the facts and definitions for the coming legislative debates. The report's impressive scope also went a long way towards cementing Laughlin's reputation as the most knowledgeable expert on the subject. Mostly overlooked, Laughlin's 1919 "Statistical Directory" is probably one of his most important works. It provided the eugenicists ownership of the facts to be debated when the manufactured crisis of "racial degeneration" came before the various legislatures.

Aside from listing the facilities, the work contained the geographical location of each institution on maps of each State in the Union. It was a detailed expression of the status of America's incarceration and hospitalization capacity at the time. The statistics covered inmate capacity, percentage of capacity used, state funds appropriated, percentage of those funds utilized, value of institutions, total acreage, total employees, the average number of employees, and just about any other statistical analysis necessary to surmise the status of America's correctional institutions and their human inventory.

Sam L. Rogers provides the only real text. His observation sets the tone by documenting that the census was conducted throughout the years when the country was at war. He alludes to a point made time and time again by various eugenicists in the United States, Britain, and Germany; that the Great War had strained the resources of the nations and that the amount invested in maintaining facilities dedicated to the "defective, dependent, and delinquent classes" had to be reevaluated. Professor Victoria F. Nourse, author of the 2008 book, "In Reckless Hands: Sinner v. Oklahoma and the Near Triumph of American Eugenics" opines:

> Eugenics had always thrived on a sense of doom, that the germ plasm was degenerating, that the numbers of insane or impoverished people were increasing exponentially. (Pg. 22, "In Reckless Hands")

Incidentally, this is a theme that Hitler's government would sound time and time again in propaganda films, speeches, and publications. Hitler's government certainly can be credited with perfecting the art of shaping public opinion. However, the Nazis did not invent this public policy strategy. As Professor Nourse explains, eugenicists consistently sounded the drums of despair. It is how they drummed up impetus behind the legislation they lobbied for as well as the funds for their costly institutions.

Historically speaking, it is important to note that this is a lesson that had been passed down from the beginning of "institutionalization" itself. James W. Trent, Jr., author of the 1994 book, "Inventing the Feeble Mind: A History of Mental Retardation in the United States" thoroughly documents this aspect of the history of the "institutionalization" of the poor and the mentally challenged:

> First, I claim that in the history of mental retardation, state schools became places where care became an effective and integral part of control. Furthermore, superintendents and social welfare agents did not move simply "from care to control," but reshaped the contours of both care and control **to ensure their personal privilege and professional legitimacy.** Second, I hold that the tendency of elites to shape the meaning of mental retardation around technical, particularistic, and usually psycho-medical themes led to a general ignoring of the maldistribution of resources, status, and power so prominent in the lives of intellectually disabled people. Finally, I find that the economic vulnerability of these people and their families, more than the claims made for their intellectual or social limitation, has shaped the kinds of treatment offered them. [sic.](Pg. 5, "Inventing the Feeble Mind," emphasis mine)

As the title of Trent's book suggests, the entire notion of the "feeble-minded" and the need for institutionalization of the less productive or vulnerable members of society was entirely the invention of a like-minded group of people; a group intent on carving out their own field of expertise at a time when society was rapidly professionalizing and specializing. Trent argues quite correctly that the need for professional or specialized institutions had simply not been a part of the human condition. It simply had not existed for all of human history until about the time of the American Revolution:

> All post-revolutionary Americans knew feebleminded people. As members of their families and their communities, feeble minds were an expected part of rural and small-town life. Physically able simpletons found no great obstacle to day-to-day living, and obviously disabled idiots received care from various members of what were usually extended families. When a family broke down, idiots unable to care for themselves were placed with neighbors or in almshouses, and more able simpletons, especially those capable of breaking the law, might find themselves in local jails. Feeble-minded people might be teased, their sometimes atavistic habits might disgust, but unlike the made and the criminal, they were not feared. (Pg. 7, "Inventing the Feeble Mind")

In other words, while their lives certainly were far from ideal, they were not treated as the menace that eugenic diatribes made them out to be. However, the need for funds to run gargantuan institutions more often than not necessitates the fabrication of a crisis, the pervasive classification, demarcation, and delineation of humanity:

> Social problems like mental retardation are in fact social constructs – "modern myths," as James Gusfield (1989) has recently called them – built from a variety of materials: the desire to help and the **need to control**, infatuation with science and technique and **professional status**, responses to social change and economic instability. (Pg. 6, "Inventing the Feeble Mind," emphasis mine)

Trent documents the historical facts behind this claim convincingly. Professional aspirations and ambitions were the impetus behind the abandonment of "outdoor relief," the older term for the community taking care of its own, for "indoor relief", or what we now know as "institutionalization." The feeble mind was "invented" in order to carve out a field of expertise and attract both professional focus and government funds to a previously non-existent profession. Trent cites at least three different sources in documenting the fact that the Association of Medical Officers, for example, had been the fabrication of political necessity and competitiveness as the trend towards professionalization and specialization increased:

> When Kerlin called together in 1876 six fellow superintendents of institutions for feebleminded persons to meet at the Pennsylvania Training School in conjunction with the nation's centennial celebrations, his motives were more professional than patriotic. Previously snubbed by the Association of Medical Officers of American Institutions for the Insane, who insisted that only lunatic-asylum superintendents could enjoy membership, Hervey Wilbur was glad to meet with Kerlin, who had also included Charles Wilbur, Doren, Knight, Brown, and Seguin, in forming an association for their own kind. (PG. 67, "Inventing the Feeble Mind")

In other words, if traditional medicine rejected the findings, then these doctors would manufacture previously non-existent professional associations and institutions. They would print their own publications and journals. This is precisely what the eugenics movement would do at the turn of the century. Both the British and American movements created a handful of journals dedicated to the movement when the leaders of the movement found resistance in the mainstream journals.

This trend towards specialization and professionalization is also documented by Martin S. Pernick, author of the 1996 book, "The Black Stork: Eugenics and the Death of "Defective" Babies in American Medicine and Motion Pictures Since 1915." The book covers the story of Dr. Haiselden, whose eugenic euthanasia of infants born with defects was made a national topic due to his propaganda movie, "The Black Stork." Haiselden starred as the protagonist, and the media magnate William Randolph Hurst backed the effort. Pernick documents two important aspects about eugenic euthanasia. First, he documents that the rivalries amongst the institutions caused only further divisions due to professional jealousies and territorialism. Second, as industrially modernized medicine grew, it embarked in the purging of non-professionalized forms of caregiving:

> Haiselden's crusade coincided with a dramatic expansion of medical authority over many aspects of American cultural life, including such previously private domains as reproduction and the family. In the early decades of this century, obstetricians supplanted midwives, pediatricians professionalized childrearing, and allied professions from psychology to home economics "medicalized" the home from the kitchen to the toilet and the bedroom. In 1915 child care was largely a female responsibility, whereas the medical profession was overwhelmingly male. Thus any growth of medical power over reproduction and childrearing meant an increase in men's authority over what had been women's work. (Pgs. 101-102, "The Black Stork")

The "reshaping" of the meaning of mental retardation "around technical, particularistic" and "psycho-medical themes," as James W. Trent, Jr. describes, is certainly an accurate way of describing what Laughlin and his colleagues were up to. Inventing and reshaping the definitions of the "needy" was a fundamental precursor to any of the legislative changes eugenicists desired. This is what made Laughlin's "Statistical Directory" so important, in the long run. Laughlin would address the peculiar grouping of the "defective, dependent, and delinquents" by referring to them as the "three D's" in his 1921 paper titled "The Socially Inadequate: How Shall We Designate and Sort Them?" that appeared in the July edition, Vol. 27, of the "American Journal of Sociology." Laughlin was looking for a definition that would adequately describe all of its "subclasses." He later added the "deficient" and the "degenerate" to the group of undesirables. Laughlin quotes Professor Franklin H. Giddings's editorial in the September 13th, 1919 issue of the "Independent":

> The Seven Devils are well known and their names are familiar: by the will of God or the whim of man they all begin with "D." They are (1) the Depraved, including the congenitally murderous, cruel, dishonest and obscene; (2) the Deficient, including all the feeble-minded, from idiots to morons; (3) the Deranged, congenitally subject or predisposed to illusion; (4) the Deformed; (5) the Disorderly; (6) the Dirty, habitually unsanitary; and (7) the Devitalized. (Pg. 55, "The Socially Inadequate")

Humorous as this may seem to modern readers, this was a topic of serious discussion. The ability or inability to precisely define, for legal purposes, the people they wanted to sterilize or segregate would be a significant hurdle in courtrooms and halls of parliaments. Professor Allen explains this in the paper entitled "Eugenics and Modern Biology," which appeared in the 2011 issue of Annals of Human Genetics:

> The most generally pervasive criticism of the genetic basis of eugenics, as exemplified by Davenport's interpretation of feeblemindedness, concerned the tendency to oversimplify. One form of oversimplification lay in the definitions of behavioral or personality phenotypes themselves. What is "feeblemindedness", "criminality", or "manic depressive insanity"? A British writer, K.L. Kenrick

claimed as early as 1914 that conditions like "feeblemindedness" are so vague and subjective as to be meaningless. (Pg. 316, "Eugenics and Modern Biology")

Professor Allen goes on to quote various scientists who found the lack of specificity in defining the phenotypes alleged by the eugenicists:

> The term [insanity] designates a wide variety of functional disorders, and not by the widest stretching of the imagination can they all be grouped together and considered as an entity . . . [mathematical ability, musical ability, immorality, alcoholism] are not single definite things, which can be inherited as a unit. They are complex and variable factors, not one of which can ever be thought of as a unit or entity. (Pg. 316, quoting J.B. Eggen, "Eugenics and Modern Biology")

Specifically, the inability to define what "feebleminded" meant became one of the significant reasons why the 1913 Mental Deficiency Act in Britain did not pass with the provisions British eugenicists desired. These definitions had served their purpose and sounded reasonable to the eugenic-minded scientists. However, they did not satisfy the more rigorous requirements of others. For all the invocation of "Mendelism" that the history of eugenics recalls, eugenics was a science that only mimicked Mendelian genetics in a superficial way. Historians of the eugenics movement have pointed to this oversimplification of Mendel's laws by documenting that the eugenicists relied on a "unit character concept" of inherited qualities. Professor Allen explains, that the "unit character concept" is based on the assumption of a one-to-one relationship between an inherited quality and a Mendelian gene. He documents that Herbert Spencer Jennings, a scientist once supportive of eugenics, explained that the assumption originated from the observation that "the 'unit characters' changed when a single gene changed." The eugenicists "concluded that in some ill-defined way, each characteristic was 'represented' or in some way condensed and contained, in one particular gene." Jennings opined in no uncertain terms:

> There is indeed no such thing as a 'unit character', and it would be a step in advance if that expression should disappear . . . . The doctrine is dead. (Pg. 317, "Eugenics and Modern Biology")

The assumptions and oversimplifications were primitive even when compared to the science of genetics in its earliest days:

> That Davenport could, as late in the development of Mendelian genetics as 1919, publish an account of *thalassophilia* (love of the sea) as a Mendelian, sex-linked recessive found in the families of naval officers only underscores the height of oversimplification embodied in the unit-character concept still rampant in American Eugenical thinking. (Pg. 317, "Eugenics and Modern Biology")

However, remember that Laughlin and company had a single-minded focus on political activism. Davenport's and Laughlin's efforts were focused on changing the norms of the lawyers and legislators as opposed to truthfully addressing the fundamental deficiencies their piers pointed out. Instead of redoubling their efforts in the laboratory, they embarked upon enshrining their definitions in the laws and statutes. Note how Laughlin outlines his intentions for the Census:

> The Eugenics Record Office prepared for the Bureau of the Census a study of state institutions covering all types of individuals who require social care or attention of one sort or another, and headed the list, "State Institutions for the Socially Inadequate." The sublist was given as follows: (1) Feeble-minded, (2) Insane, (3) Criminalistic (including the delinquent and wayward), (4) Epileptic, (5) Inebriate (including drug habitués), (6) Diseased (including the tuberculous, the syphilitic, the leprous, and others with chronic infectious segregated diseases), (7) Blind (including those with greatly impaired vision, (8) Deaf (including the crippled), and (10) Dependent (including children and old folks in "homes," ne'er-do-wells, tramps, and paupers). (Pg. 56, "The Socially Inadequate")

A change in nomenclature obviously implied a significant drawback. One of the academics and professionals that responded to "Statistical Directory" understood that a change in terminology inevitably meant an inconsistency in reporting from one generation to the other. Professor Franklin H. Giddings of Columbia University complained:

> The Census Office has, I think, a number of pretty good reasons for wishing to keep the title "defective, dependent, and delinquent classes." For one thing, it insures a unity of classification, and, as you know, one of the things we have most to dread in census administration is the destruction of all possible scientific comparisons by changing classifications from one ten years to another. (Pg. 60, "The Socially Inadequate")

The professor was entirely right, but only if the end goal was consistency in reporting. As history evidences, Laughlin's goal was not consistency in reporting statistics about the "dependent classes." It was quite the opposite; an intentional break with the medical and scientific traditions of the past in order to have government adopt the definitions and *a priori* concepts of the recently conceived science of eugenics.

To take this observation further, one could argue from a historical point-of-view that the concept of "race" is a conceptual "construct" as well. Some historians argue that the entire concept of race is a "modern myth." In 1963, Thomas S. Gossett documented the trajectory of the concept of "race" in his book "Race: The History of an Idea in America." Gossett lists those intellectually concerned with "race" prior to the modern sciences and makes note of the fact that the Catholic Church had decreed any scientific notion that contradicted the single origins of mankind, as depicted in Scripture, a heretical act punishable by death:

> Both astrology and theories of the separate origin of races, however, were in time repudiated by the Roman Catholic church. In 1559, Pope Paul IV places astrology and other methods of divination such as the cult of physiognomy on the Index. The church acted even more strongly against the theory of separate

origin of primitive peoples. Vanini and Bruno were burned at the stake for their various heresies. Peyrére was imprisoned for six months and released only on condition that he retract his heretical beliefs, among them his belief in pre-Adamite races. (Pg. 15, "Race")

"Vanini" was Lucilio Vanini whom in 1619 proposed that Ethiopians must have apes for ancestors because they were the same color as apes. Isaac de la Peyrére was a French Protestant whom in 1655 published a book in which he argued that there had been two separate creations of human beings, since the creation of humans appears before the creation of Adam and Eve; thus, the name for the racialist movement, "pre-Adamite." Interestingly enough, Gossett also surveys the leading thinkers on the topic. Hippocrates, Aristotle, Vitruvius, Augustine, Linnaeus, Blumenbach, Buffon, and even Leonardo da Vinci recognized a single-origin of mankind, with variations being caused by the environment, and not different creations:

> Before the eighteenth century physical differences among peoples were so rarely referred to as a matter of great importance that something of a case can be made for the proposition that race consciousness is largely a modern phenomenon. (Pg. 3, "Race")

What the Church failed to stamp out by force, Charles Darwin did by persuasion. Darwin set out to debunk the notion of separate origins or separate creations. Darwin's evolutionary theory postulated that all life and all "species" had a single "origin." Unfortunately, Darwin's single-origin theory came with a hierarchy of the races as they receded toward that single "origin of the species." Arguably though, these evolutionary gradations we call "races" were conceptual constructs to some extent. It is also important to note that eugenicists never reached a consensus on what the number of gradations or a clear demarcation between the "races." They all disagreed on the number of races present on earth, and all of these constructs predictably fell apart when it came time to pin down the seemingly infinite amount of variations and gray areas. It is no wonder why mixed-ethnicity "hybrids", or "miscegenation", was such a pet peeve for all eugenicists and such a source of scorn for all of them. There was certainly agreement on this point; all eugenicists hated the people that did not fit their neatly subdivided charts.

The correspondence between Laughlin, C.M. Goethe, Madison Grant, and Charles B. Davenport evidences just how persistently eugenics sought to define and reshape the legally accepted understanding of concepts of "feebleminded" as well as "race." Evidently, Laughlin and company knew that changing the legal definition was a fundamental precursor to enacting new legislation.

It is interesting to note that in at least one of the letters from Laughlin to Goethe, Laughlin proposes using the wide reach of the United States Census Department to create a "permanent card-registry" of its citizens, a proposal to keep tabs of the population still popularly debated to this day by politicians of a statist bent. A March 27th, 1939 letter from Laughlin to Goethe evidences Laughlin's intention to leverage the "definitions" about population used by the Census. It was Laughlin's way to conform the state to the a priori views of the eugenicists. This same letter goes on to enumerate the desire to:

1.) Convert the census enumeration into a permanent card-registry of the whole population of the United States.
2.) Include personal identification as an item of enumeration once in the lifetime of each individual.
3.) In the individual enumeration list as formerly name of father and mother and add name of consort and names of children. This would convert the census-registry into a permanent pedigree registry for the entire population. As time goes on and the racial and population problems become more exacting the value of such data will be priceless.

In historical hindsight, this proposal is obviously chilling. Edwin Black's 2001 book, "IBM and the Holocaust," thoroughly documents how Hitler's henchmen used IBM tabulating machinery to harvest information from German censuses in order to pinpoint where the Jewish population was. Black's book documents how these IBM machines were installed in the extermination camps. This is how the Nazis were able to process the census information and cross reference it with the known German-Jewish population. This is how they were able to find Germans with obscure Jewish ancestry, including families that had long since forgotten their Jewish ancestry and lived as Christians since.

It can certainly be argued that the American eugenicists were lobbying for a similar amount of control over the American population. Even after Laughlin and company had succeeded in manipulating the United States Congress into passing the most radical of racially motivated immigration laws, the effort to categorize persisted. For example, as late as July 22nd, 1936 Laughlin was corresponding with Goethe and Grant about these legalistic demarcations:

Dear Mr. Grant --- It seems clear that a categorical definition of the American Race should be available for legal use when an opportunity arises. Doubtless the time will again return when the Senate and the House Committees on Immigration will desire data on and analyses of the racial make-up of the American people, in their anticipated efforts to conserve and improve our foundation racial stocks. I am enclosing a memorandum on the subject of the American Race which I trust you will find time to read and to criticize. I have followed your advice by using the term "Caucasian" instead of "White" throughout because of the definite legal meaning which the word Caucasian has already acquired in this country. (July 22, 1936, Truman Univ. Special Coll., Laughlin Papers)

Another example of this is the June 5th, 1928 letter from Laughlin to C.M. Goethe inquiring about a legal definition for "Mexicans":

I am trying to find out the status of any litigation which may result in a court definition of the Mexicans in reference to color. Of course we have had clean-cut court decisions which exclude the Japanese and the Hindu because they were neither white nor of African descent. If a court decision similar to these (to which I referred on page 721 in the hearing "Immigration from Countries of the Western Hemisphere") were secured for Mexico, legislation would be unnecessary. (June 5, 1928, Laughlin Papers, Truman Univ.)

This preoccupation with the intermixing of ethnicities was not confined to the demarcations that the reader may think obvious. The British eugenicists, for example, viewed the intermixing between the Irish Catholics and British Anglo-Saxon Protestants with the same disdain they had for the other allegedly "interracial" pairings. Likewise, there is a commonplace misunderstanding as to precisely what Hitler regarded as his "Master Race." The famous racialist American author, Lothrop Stoddard, wrote in his book "Into The Darkness" that those from a specific region of Germany were the ideal. Thus, even ethnicities that for the modern reader would be considered "white" were not so for the eugenicists. They took issue with the Italians, Hispanics, Irish, and any Jews from any nationality that they did not want to regard as "Caucasian."

We often hear historians speak of the process of "othering." "Othering" refers to the demarcation between the allegedly acceptable majority and the undesirable minority. It is a term used to describe how the majority portion of a population separates itself from the dissimilar others as a precursor to racial tensions and violence. However, it is important to point out that petty bigotry is a very personal affair. It is typically very localized and confined to the immediate community. The events documented in this book explain how this happens at a legislative level; a level that has a much broader reach than localized bigotry. Lynching and racial riots claim casualties in the single digits. Eugenics segregates and murders in the tens of thousands precisely because it employs the power of the state.

The first step to this process is convincing the state that it has the right to segregate, mutilate, and annihilate significant swaths of its population. Historically speaking, in order to sway the legislative oligarchy, a crisis must first be manufactured. The often heard proclamation that "the numbers do not lie" is often the defense erected by those fully intending to "cook the books." The numbers in of themselves may not lie, but the ways numbers are presented by "experts" have been effectively used to perpetrate major lies throughout human history. Changing the nomenclature and definition of that being studied statistically is one of the time-honored ways to report inflationary trends that would not have been so if the standards were consistent from one report to the other. Specifically, the amount of "dependents" could be made to look like it was a group rapidly expanding by simply expanding the definition of who was included in the group. Thus, artificially depicting a crisis of an undesirable population growing out of control. Laughlin began making his case precisely in this manner in the "Conclusion" of the 1914 "Bulletin No. 10B":

The arithmetic is correct; if one accepts the conditions, he must accept the conclusion also. (Pg. 150, "Bulletin No. 10B")

Marouf A. Hasain, Jr. alludes to the power that scientific documentation has on the layman's legislative efforts in his 1996 book "The Rhetoric of Eugenics in Anglo-American Thought":

> The guise of neutrality may at times involve fraud or deception, but more common is a style of doing science that depends on the mask of neutrality in order to insulate scientific investigators from criticism. Claims of neutrality also legitimate certain modes of inquiry. (Pg. 11, "The Rhetoric of Eugenic Thought")

This was certainly true for a science that applied the methods of the slaughter house to human society. A veil of scientific neutrality allowed them to proceed into what would otherwise have been lambasted as immoral if made by the politicians themselves without the help of "experts" like Laughlin. Eugenics from its earliest days was a "science" that fully relied on statistics. Statistics was Francis Galton's forte, and it is Galton's statistical analysis of Britain's accomplished families that provided the quasi-scientific basis for what were otherwise racial and cultural prejudices. Galton's protégé, Karl Pearson, excelled in the "biometrics" of measuring human beings and statistically analyzing "racial" trends. While craniometric measuring was older than Pearson and Galton, it is their statistical rigor, along with the family and professional link to Charles Darwin, which gave the work a measure of respectability. The eugenics movement legitimized the practice of measuring human skulls and facial features; precisely in the way commonly attributed to Hitler's dogmatic henchmen.

It is of note that Laughlin closes his "Socially Inadequate" article in the American Journal of Sociology by pretty much admitting that what he was doing was in many ways propaganda. The well-worn adage that a lie becomes truth if repeated enough was apparently on Laughlin's mind when he endeavored to change the technical terms:

> Jack London said the way to prove anything is to say it three times. The continued use of a term in a given connection establishes it a language. Newly invented terms, if useful, soon set immovably in the linguistic matrix. "What's in a name," other than a clear-cut designation? (Pg. 69, "The Socially Inadequate," The American Journal of Sociology, Vol. XXVII, No. 1, July 1921)

Even as late as June 22nd, 1936, after all of the highly-publicized victories eugenics had had in both the United States and Germany, Laughlin would write to Madison Grant:

> **Eugenics is gradually establishing itself as a sound science** and our Eugenics Research Association and the Eugenics Record Office, as now organized, stand for the development of eugenics fundamentally as racial and family-stock matters. (Laughlin to Grant, June 22nd, 1936, Truman Univ., Laughlin Papers, Special Coll. Dept., emphasis mine)

Of course, the terms Laughlin was proposing were far from "clear-cut" or even "useful" outside of a eugenic frame of mind, and Laughlin knew it. The terms utilized by the eugenics movement evidenced a severe backwardness when they were juxtaposed against the very technical and scientifically advanced terminology from the emerging science of genetics.

Hassencahl reports in her dissertation that the Eugenics Research Association provided Laughlin fifty dollars to travel to Washington, D.C. in 1920 to present petitions to both the House of Representatives and the Senate committees that had oversight over the Census. (Pg. 174 & 178, Hassencahl) The February 18th, 1919 minutes of the association document that the eugenicists felt an in-person appearance would have a greater effect. They were obviously right as this political networking effort seems to be the beginning of Laughlin's stint as "Expert Eugenics Agent" for the House Committee on Immigration. Laughlin would enjoy franking privileges in this allegedly prestigious governmental institution. Laughlin would remain appointed as the "Expert Eugenics Agent" for the House of Representatives until 1931.

1920 - BIOLOGICAL ASPECTS OF IMMIGRATION

> *"Science commits suicide when it adopts a creed."*
> - T.H. Huxley as Quoted by Herbert Spencer,
> 'The Factors of Organic Evolution' (April/May 1886)

All of the efforts described in the preceding pages finally yielded a victory of significant historical importance in the 1920s. Between April 16th and 17th 1920, the House Committee on Immigration held hearings on the "immigration problem." Harry H. Laughlin had been named the House Committee's "Expert Eugenics Agent of the House Committee on Immigration" on population by Albert Johnson of Washington State, the chair of the committee. Incidentally, Johnson's political career had been significantly bolstered by the financial support of the Immigration Restriction League, which was made up of those powerful eugenic minded Ivy Leaguers from American Breeders' Association.

Laughlin brought to the floor of the United States Congress graphs, pedigree charts, and the results of hundreds of IQ tests as evidence of "the immigrant menace." Of mention were the unflattering photographs of immigrants taken at Ellis Island with a caption that read "Carriers of the Germ Plasm of the Future American Population." The message was clear; Laughlin and company viewed foreign elements in a pathological manner, quite literally as a potential disease upon the social body. Laughlin's opening statement illustrates:

> The character of a nation is determined primarily by its racial qualities; that is, by the hereditary physical, mental, and moral or temperamental traits of its people. (Pg. 3, "Biological Aspects")

This is a statement that merits some introspection. The eugenics movement within the United States consistently stated that it believed that the aptitude for "self-governance" and "democracy" was a racial quality, much in the same way Harvard's Shaler taught his students. They fully subscribed to the view that only Anglo-Saxon Protestants were capable of American-style democracy. They believed that Italian and Irish Catholics were incapable of participating and contributing as valued members of the nation. The above statement says as much. It is the expression of a movement that believes the American experiment to be a "racial" and "ethnic" one, and not an experiment in "self-governance" that stands on its own merits by the values it espouses.

First, and foremost, it is important to gauge this belief against the legislative history of the United States. The notion that the United States was a country solely for White Anglo-Saxon Protestants had, by this time, already been vigorously debated. The debates leading up to and through the American Civil War addressed this claim, and the results of the Civil War and its subsequent legislation thoroughly rejected it. However, the rise of eugenics coincided with a period of massive influx of immigrants as well as the integration of the ex-slave population. These two phenomena revived racial and ethnic tensions. In many ways, American eugenics was an attempt to reverse the legislative accomplishments of the Reconstruction by providing the concept of racial superiority the 'scientific' justification it lacked in the debates preceding the Civil War. As such, Laughlin's "expert" testimony was that of a scientist arguing medical and biological "realities." For Laughlin and his cohorts, "science" had returned the question of racial integration back to the floor of the United States Congress:

> The immigrants ought to be made out of such stock that when they come to this country and are given the best of American opportunities and their children are given still better opportunities, their natural, physical, mental, moral qualities would respond to the democratic environment of equality and opportunity and that the possessors of those traits would develop into desirable citizens. (Pg. 4, "Biological Aspects")

Laughlin proposed to the House Committee that this be accomplished by two general policies:

> To the biologist interested primarily in the practical working out of the eugenical or family-stock ideal in our immigration policy the two things now desired are: (1) That an examination of immigrants be made in their home towns, and that "immigration passports" be issued by the American consuls to individual would-be immigrants who pass the required physical, moral, sanitary, mental, and family-stock tests. (2) The second point is that every alien in America be required to register at least annually until he becomes naturalized, or until he dies, leaves the country, or is deported. The registration tax might well be differential in favor of those aliens who have made the greatest progress toward Americanization, but the total tax should be sufficient to make the registry service self-supporting. (Pgs. 8-9, "Biological Aspects")

Point number one illustrates the pseudo-scientific nature of eugenic statistics. Note that the information gathered about the potential immigrants does not utilize microscopes, centrifuges, or any of the instrumentation necessary to arrive at empirical assessments about an individual's hereditary factors. Even if one would assume this to be a desirable test for citizenship, one must also concede that Laughlin's statistical methods were gathering hearsay and subjective opinions, rather than empirical scientific facts. Laughlin was looking for the rumors, innuendo, and gossip that could only be harvested from the townspeople that knew his subjects:

> The first point that I made was that in order properly to select immigrants on the basis of natural hereditary worth it was necessary to make examinations in their home territories, because when attempted examinations are made in this country we lack the information concerning the environment of the candidate, and such examinations are perfunctory and in most cases a farce. Experience in our field studies in this country has proven that the only way in which adequate information concerning the social and hereditary worth, or the racial or family

worth, of an individual can be obtained is to study him in the community in which he has resided for some time and in which he has become a part of the citizenry. (Pg. 6, "Biological Aspects")

The correspondence also evidences that Laughlin also made sure to leverage his Ivy League contacts to the fullest. He was in direct contact with Davenport's Ivy League brethren, namely Madison Grant. A July 28th, 1936 letter from Grant, the infamous racialist author and leading member of the Immigration Restriction League, illustrates who was to be included and who was to be excluded per the proposed legislation:

> I entirely agree with you, of course, that the use of the word "Caucasian" is better than that of "White". The Jews can and do claim that they are White, but they can hardly claim that they are "Caucasian", although, perhaps, they do claim it. ---- We should say that all ancestors of true Americans should be born in the thirteen colonies of the territory east of the Mississippi prior to Independence, namely 1783. I had suggested a later date, namely 1800, before the Louisiana Purchase, but I think perhaps your date is to be preferred as it equally well leaves out the New Orleans French. ---- As to race, the population was overwhelmingly Nordic, as the Dutch, the few Huguenots and the Palatine Germans in Pennsylvania and New York were thoroughly Nordic. The colonists were overwhelmingly Nordic. ---- When I return, if you remind me, I will get you a statement of Archbishop Carroll of Baltimore that the Catholics in Maryland only numbered about 35,000 at the time of the first census. Perhaps you can check this. It is most important if true. (BOX C-2-2:15, Grant to Laughlin, July 28th, 1936, Special Coll. – Truman Univ.)

While historians have adequately documented the influence of the Immigration Restriction League, it must be noted that Laughlin was supported financially by other like-minded xenophobic institutions. The Special Collections Department at Truman University houses Laughlin's papers. The correspondence with C.M. Goethe, the founder of California State, Sacramento demonstrates that Goethe was in the habit of sending Laughlin a monthly stipend for what he called the "Goethe Fund." For just one of many examples, see the May 25th, 1926 letter from Laughlin thanking Goethe for his contribution:

> The Eugenics Research Association is very glad to have your letter and your check for $19.25, which we have put in the Goethe Fund to be used, as you suggest, for furthering the current studies in immigration. Let me say that I have just returned from Washington, where I had another hearing before the House Committee on Immigration and Naturalization. (BOX C-4-1:2, May 25th, 1926, Goethe to Laughlin, Special Coll. – Truman Univ.)

Much of Goethe's correspondence was written on the letterhead of the Immigration Study Commission of Sacramento, California, the anti-immigration organization he and other prominent members of the California community created. A February 18th, 1926 letter from C.M. Goethe to Dr. H.R. Hunt of the

Department of Zoology and Geology in Michigan Agricultural College was apparently copied to Laughlin, and it reiterates much of the same sentiment:

> I will say very frankly that we did develop opposition in Australia from the Jesuit group. In an editorial in one of their organs my suggestions that the ideal of a "White Australia" was not enough, that it should be changed to a "Nordic Australia," was branded as being most insolent. (BOX C-4-1:2, Goethe to Hunt, February 18th, 1926, Special Coll. – Truman Univ.)

Why is the work of C.M. Goethe's Immigration Study Commission of relevance to the Congressional proceedings? Goethe's Immigration Study Commission is important as it actually embarked on testing Laughlin's theory that all immigrants should be judged in the country of their birth, within their familiar surroundings. A March 15th, 1926 letter from C.M. Goethe to Laughlin documents the work being done on foreign lands by agents hired by the Immigration Study Commission:

> The Immigration Study Commission has been quietly making overseas field studies of migration for a long while. ---- We wanted accuracy. We have now reached the conclusion that the Mediterranean-Alpine elements do not measure up, either in intelligence or in their ability to absorb democracy, with the Nordics. (BOX C-4-1:2, Goethe to Laughlin, March 15th, 1926, Special Coll. – Truman Univ.)

The term "Mediterranean Europe" was a clear reference to Italian immigrants. Italians were just as undesirable to them as Eastern European Jews, Chinese, Japanese, or Hispanic immigrants. A January 26th, 1929, letter from C.M. Goethe to Laughlin regarding his testimony in the U.S. Congress clarifies this point:

> Gangster rule in our great cities is only one phase of America's increasing urban problem. Gangster influence at Washington is powerful in a way few citizens understand. Their methods, being those of Mediterranean Europe, are basically un-American. (BOX C-4-1:2, Goethe to Laughlin, January 26th, 1929, Special Coll. – Truman Univ.)

Goethe was a wealthy landowner in the West Coast. A window into what these men were thinking is preserved in correspondence about whom Goethe considered to be desirable customers for his real estate:

> We have now reached the conclusion that the Mediterranean-Alpine elements do not measure up, either in intelligence or in their ability to absorb democracy, with the Nordics. Since the Johnson-Reed Acts are in force we are no longer getting any considerable Mediterranean customers. We are now receiving European Nordics, and, in much larger numbers, the spill-over from the high rural birth rate of the Middle-west states. Unfortunately we are also now getting a very undesirable class of installment purchasers, the Mexican. (BOX C-4-1:2, Goethe to Laughlin, March 15th, 1926, Special Coll. – Truman Univ.)

In a similar letter of October 22nd, 1928, Goethe proclaims Italian Catholics as a danger to the United States. Curiously enough, Goethe deemed Italians as "dangerous" because of their similarities to "Caucasians," as opposed to their differences:

> The danger to our American wage standard is not in the immigration from the Orient. The color difference there is so great that Americans react vigorously to such coolie immigration. The real menace to our living standards lies in countries like Italy. With a heavy excess of births over deaths, Italian wages are low compared with the United States. If America wishes to hold its present living standard, it must vigorously protest against the present beginnings of a movement to amend to death the Johnson Immigration Restriction Act. (BOX C-4-1:2, Goethe to Laughlin, Oct. 22nd, 1928, Special Coll. – Truman Univ.)

American eugenicists would correspond at length about immigration restrictions based on authoritative definitions of what constituted an "American Race." A July 22nd, 1936, letter from Madison Grant to Harry H. Laughlin continues along these lines:

> It seems clear that a categorical definition of the American Race should be available for legal use when an opportunity arises. Doubtless the time will again return when the Senate and the House Committees on Immigration will desire data on and analyses of the racial make-up of the American people, in their anticipated efforts to conserve and improve our foundation racial stocks. --- I have followed your advice by using the term "Caucasian" instead of "White" throughout because of the definite legal meaning which the word Caucasian has already acquired in this country. (BOX C-2-2:15, Grant to Laughlin, July 22nd, 1936, Special Coll. – Truman Univ.)

All of this correspondence would remain insulting but otherwise innocuous if its goal were not the enacting of law. This is what differentiated the eugenicists from the common bigot. The common bigot mostly persecuted those directly around them. Even in groups like the Ku Klux Klan, the lynching of racial minorities happened in small handfuls compared to the millions targeted by the eugenicists. Recall that Laughlin had a target goal of 15 million to be segregated, sterilized, or otherwise removed from society. His counterparts in the international eugenics movement shared his goals, demanding that between 10 and 25 million be systematically eradicated from the gene pool. In order to remove such vast numbers from the population, these eugenicists could not work under white cloaks or under the cover of night. They needed the legitimacy afforded by white lab coats, business suits, and parliamentary hearings. The vast numbers necessitated that the machinery of government be employed in a systematic eradication of people at industrialized pace and efficiency.

1922 - MODEL EUGENICAL LAW

> *"America, in particular, needs to protect herself against indiscriminate immigration, criminal degenerates, and race suicide."*
> – Introduction to Eugenical Sterilization in the U.S.A.

Harry H. Laughlin collected every piece of information about eugenical sterilization while working at the Eugenics Record Office. He had surveyed more than 60 institutions in order to compile the comprehensive history of eugenic sterilization and segregation in the United States. He had become internationally renowned for his knowledge of the subject, and now looked to formalize his knowledge in a book that clearly delineated a ready-made "Model Eugenical Law." Laughlin contacted the Rockefeller-funded Bureau of Social Hygiene with his intentions to publish. The estimated cost of the printing would be around $7,000, which was too much for the Bureau, so Laughlin wrote to John D. Rockefeller personally, only to have Rockefeller attorney reject the proposal. Laughlin also asked Davenport to help him pitch the idea to Carnegie. Davenport agreed to have the Eugenics Record Office help but communicated that Carnegie would likely not be interested. Laughlin would also seek support from like-minded colleagues during the Second International Eugenics Congress that was held in New York in 1921. Despite leveraging his preferential position, no real interest materialized. The one person that was interested was Judge Harry Olson of the Municipal Court in Chicago. The 494-page volume entitled "Eugenical Sterilization in the United States" was published under the Psychopathic Laboratory imprint:

> Unlike Laughlin's critics, Olson embraced the possibilities of using sterilization as a powerful weapon in the long-term war on crime. In 1922, the year when eugenicists celebrated the centenary of both Mendel and Galton, Olson thought Laughlin's message was exactly what the public needed to hear. He had contacts in the highest echelons of the legal community to ensure that *Eugenical Sterilization* would not be ignored. (Pg. 81, Lombardo, "Three Generations No Imbeciles")

It is worth mentioning that this is a scenario that is repeated enough to evidence a pattern. Many of Laughlin's and Davenport's principal supporters were from the legal community. This would also include Judge Foster, Madison Grant and E.S. Gosney, as well as many of the directors of the infamous Pioneer Fund. The dedicated involvement of several eugenic-minded attorneys certainly played a key role in maneuvering and successfully gaining the approval of eugenic sterilization laws. Professor Lombardo describes this aspect of Laughlin's book:

> The [book] laid out an extensive argument in favor of the state powers to "limit human reproduction in the interests of race betterment." Eugenical sterilization, Laughlin asserted, was like other uses of the state's inherent "police power" to protect the common good. States regularly executed criminals for this reason,

and governments used military conscription to raise armies, sending soldiers to their death to preserve a nation's safety. Limits on reproduction in the name of "common benefit" require a smaller sacrifice from citizens drafted from the ranks of "irresponsible members" than did wartime service; surely the "interests of the common welfare" justified such a restriction of liberties. ---- Sterilization was also a public health measure like compulsory vaccination, designed to prevent the public at large from infection by a diseased individual. Both involved seizing people and subjecting them to intrusive operations. In fact, vaccination was more dangerous and vasectomy, said Laughlin. Moreover, vaccination had been approved as a proper use of state power by the U.S. Supreme Court in the 1905 case of *Jacobson v. Massachusetts*. (Pgs. 85-86 "Three Generations No Imbeciles", Lombardo)

The above analysis would echo and resound through history, as this would also be the legal opinion Justice Oliver Wendell Holmes, Jr. would provide in the 1927 Supreme Court case that would deem Laughlin's "Model Law" constitutional. It would also be a justification given by the Third Reich and the doctors and scientists responsible for Germany's eugenic legislation during Hitler's reign. Laughlin's animal breeder theme was also a consistent theme:

> The final page in the book carried a quotation from the father of social Darwinism, Herbert Spencer: "To be a good animal is the first requisite to success in life, and to be a Nation of good animals is the first condition of National prosperity." (Pg. 84, "Three Generations No Imbeciles", Lombardo)

The Municipal Court funded the publication of 3,000 copies and became the owner of the copyright of Laughlin's work. The complete title would be "Eugenical Sterilization in The United States: A Report of the Psychopathic Laboratory of The Municipal Court of Chicago." Olson would send books to dozens of people from his privileged mailing list. Professor Lombardo describes this list as a "virtual who's who of the U.S. legal world." This included prominent figures such as Secretary of State Evans Hughes and the former President William Howard Taft. This later recipient would prove to be important, as Taft would also become a Supreme Court Justice and preside over the court that would hear the 1927 <u>Buck v. Bell</u> case along with Oliver Wendell Holmes, Jr.

The fact that a judge and a municipal court funded the venture should be regarded as only natural, as at its core, eugenics is about control and regulation, leveraging the coercive might of the state. Chief Justice Olson makes this amply clear in the introduction:

> As a product of scientific research the book will have permanent value. The importance and usefulness of the work is not to be gauged by the extent of its circulation. Enough copies will be published to reach the leaders of medical, legal and clerical professions, the press and members of legislative bodies. (Intro. "Eugenical Sterilization")

And then again in the Preface:

> This volume is intended primarily for practical use. It is designed to be of particular service to four classes of persons. First, to law-makers who have to decide upon matters of policy to be worked out in legislation regulating eugenical sterilization; second, to judges of the courts, upon whom, in most of the states having sterilization statutes, devolves the duty of deciding upon the constitutionality of the new statutes, and of determining cacogenic individuals of ordering their sexual sterilization; third, to administrative officers who represent the state in locating, and in eugenically analyzing persons alleged to be cacogenic, and who are responsible for carrying out orders of the courts; and fourth, to **individual citizens who, in the exercise of their civic rights and duties, desire to take the initiative in reporting the official determination and action, specific cases of obvious family degeneracy.** (Preface, "Eugenical Sterilization", emphasis mine)

Clearly, this is a perspective of government as the care-taker and "breeder" of its populace. It is at odds with the Libertarian underpinnings of the founding documents of the United States, which elevate the rights of the individual to "life, liberty, and pursuit of happiness" to a level that supersedes the prerogative of society or the state.

The reader will recall that Louis Marshall provided a legal analysis of the constitutionality of eugenic sterilization by the decree of the state. One of Marshall's main points was that the medical reasons needed to be considered separately from the punitive measures, such as castration, since such measures would be prohibited by their "cruel and unusual" nature. It is of note that Laughlin insisted on including Louis Marshall's opinion on the "constitutionality" of the proposed eugenical law. Chief Justice Olson would pick up on this legal analysis that separated the medical from the punitive. He made the important observation that compulsory vaccination was deemed constitutional by prior court opinions. Thus, providing a 'theraputic' taint to the analysis. This would turn out to be the central concept in the U.S. Supreme Court's opinion in 1927. Note Justice Oliver Wendell Holmes, Jr.'s final analysis in the 1927 <u>Buck v. Bell</u> case. Note the reference to compulsory vaccination:

> **The principle that sustains compulsory vaccination is broad enough to cover cutting the Fallopian tubes.** Jacobson v. Massachusetts, 197 U.S. 11. Three generations of imbeciles are enough. (BUCK v. BELL, SUPERINTENDENT. No. 292. Supreme Court of United States. -- Argued April 22, 1927. Decided May 2, 1927, emphasis mine)

Interestingly enough, Judge Olson begins his opinion by stating that he has very little to add to Laughlin's exhaustively cataloging of all the laws in the various States as well as any hurdles they encountered in the courts. Laughlin's "Model Eugenical Law" was designed to address those grievances, after all:

> I believe the model law, which you propose, will be held constitutional by the courts. It meets objections which have been made by the courts to legislation

enacted by several states. **Such legislation has often violated the bill of rights, which guarantees to all citizens and equal protection of the laws, "the due process of law" clause, the provision against cruel and unusual punishment,** the bill of attainder clause, the *ex post facto* and the twice in jeopardy provisions of the constitution. The model law applies the law to the population generally, outside of institutions, as well as inmates thereof. --- **The model act has no element of punishment in it, and thus the question of constitutional inhibition against cruel and unusual punishment will not arise.** (Pg. 322, "Eugenical Sterilization," emphasis mine)

Narrowly speaking, Olson was right, but only if all other aspects of the Bill of Rights and the U.S. Constitution are omitted from the analysis. Laughlin's "Model Law" in fact does address all of the legal concerns Olson enumerates, and the United States Supreme Court adopted this very narrow legal analysis. However, one does not need to be a lawyer or a judge to know that the Bill of Rights guarantee to each citizen a much broader definition of civil rights than what Judge Olson admits to. The entire notion of "limited government" where the citizens are free from government intervention in their pursuit of life, liberty, and happiness has been defined to include the rights of parent and child. More poignantly, no honest reading of the intentions of the Founding Fathers includes giving the U.S. government the powers of a monarch over its populace, and certainly not after the abolition of slavery. The right to individual autonomy and bodily integrity are considered fundamental even by the most radical interpretations of what is "constitutional" and what is not. It is by no surprise that the <u>Buck v. Bell</u> decision is generally condemned as one of the lowest points that the United States Supreme Court ever descended to.

However, Laughlin's attempt to significantly alter American jurisprudence was fully within the tradition of "Model Laws." Institutions like the American Bar Association routinely propose "model laws" in order to implement new legal concepts, or like Laughlin, to bring harmony and consistency between the various laws from the different States in the Union. The model law proposed in Laughlin's 1922 book follows the format of the 1914 "Bulletin No. 10B," dissecting the laws implemented in a State by State basis, as well as including attorney Louis Marshall's legal opinion. However, the 1922 book is the matured and complete version. It is ready-made law. It is also about two to three times the length of the 1914 "Bulletin." The substantive difference is that the 1922 version reads like a real statute, outlining specific procedures and providing legalistic definitions, as opposed to the more theoretical "recommendations."

The 1922 book was essential to the goals of the international eugenics movement as it accomplished precisely what Laughlin wanted: a ready-made law that any government could copy verbatim and implement without further deliberation. In this respect, the effort was a brilliant, or really, a catastrophic success; catastrophic in the sense that a nuclear bomb is successful if it accomplishes the annihilation of its target. This is exactly what happened. The law was implemented without change in Virginia, and later translated verbatim in Hitler's Germany; both times wreaking havoc on the targeted "defectives" and "degenerates".

After "Eugenical Sterilization in the United States" was finally published in 1922, Laughlin's eugenic-minded counterparts in Virginia began to prepare a "test case" that would ultimately be decided by the United States Supreme Court in the 1927 case of Buck v. Bell. The test subject for this "test case" had to be carefully chosen. The "Model Law" provided the guidelines for the test subject:

> **Persons Subject.** All persons in the State who, because of degenerate or defective hereditary qualities are potential parents of socially inadequate offspring, regardless of whether such persons be in the population at large or inmates of custodial institutions, regardless also of the personality, sex, age, marital condition, race, or possessions of such person. Standards established and terms defined by the statute.

The types of individuals included in Laughlin's definition of people dangerous to the future prosperity of the State perfectly explain why Germany's doctors changed from curing individual patients to "healing" the collective by riding it of undesirable patients:

> (a) A socially inadequate person is one who by his or her own effort, regardless of etiology or prognosis, fails chronically in comparison with normal persons, to maintain himself or herself as a useful member of the organized social life of the state; provided that the term socially inadequate shall not be applied to any person whose individual or social ineffectiveness is due to the normally expected exigencies of youth, old age, curable injuries, or temporary physical or mental illness, in case such ineffectiveness is adequately taken care of by the particular family in which it occurs.
> (b) The socially inadequate classes, regardless of etiology or prognosis, are the following: (1) **Feeble-minded**; (2) **Insane**, (including the psychopathic); (3) **Criminalistic** (including the delinquent and wayward); (4) **Epileptic**; (5) **Inebriate** (including drug-habitués); (6) **Diseased** (including the tuberculosis, the syphilitic, the leprous, and others with chronic, infectious and legally segregable diseases); (7) **Blind** (including those with seriously impaired vision); (8) **Deaf** (including those with seriously impaired hearing); (9) **Deformed** (including the crippled); and (10) **Dependent** (including orphans, ne'er-do-wells, the homeless, tramps and paupers).
> (emphasis mine)

The salient paragraphs of Laughlin's "Model Law" are quoted here at length in order to provide an example of how proposed legislation need not sound overtly jingoistic in order to pose a direct danger to minorities. Also, it is important to note that the targeted individual need not fall into any of the above-mentioned categories to be in danger of falling into this eugenic dragnet. It was enough to be deemed to be a "carrier" of potential defects. This is made amply clear by the section entitled "Heredity":

> (c) **Heredity** in the human species is the transmission, through spermatozoön and ovum, of physical, physiological and psychological qualities, from parents to offspring; by extension it shall be interpreted in this Act to include also the transmission post-conceptionally and ante-natally of physiological weakness, poisons or infections from parent or parents to offspring.
> (d) A potential parent is a person who now, or in the future course of development, may reasonably be expected to be able to procreate offspring.
> (e) To procreate means to beget or to conceive offspring, and applies equally to males and females.
> (f) A potential parent of socially inadequate offspring is a person who, regardless of his or her own physical, physiological or psychological personality, and of the nature of the germ-plasm of such person's co-parent, is a potential parent at least one-fourth of whose possible offspring, because of the certain inheritance from said parent of one or more inferior or degenerate physical, physiological or psychological qualities would, on the average, according to the demonstrated laws of heredity, most probably function as socially inadequate persons; or at least one-half of whose possible offspring would receive from said parent, and would carry in the germ-plasm but would not necessarily show in the personality, the genes or genes-complex for one or more inferior or degenerate physical, physiological or psychological qualities, the appearance of which quality or qualities in the personality would cause the possessor thereof to function as a socially inadequate person, under the normal environment of the state.
> (g) The term cacogenic person, as herein used, is a purely legal expression, and shall be applied only to persons declared, under the legal procedure provided by this Act, to be potential parents of socially inadequate offspring.

As discussed in the 1914 "Bulletin," the States would be responsible for devising whole eugenic courts and departments that would operate independently of the ordinary courts and bureaucracies already in place. Laughlin proposed that a government official, a "State Eugenicist," would "devote his entire time" with the help of "an ample corps of assistants," to providing the service of making the legal determinations of an individual's eugenic worth:

> **Basis of Selection: Procedure.** 1. Investigation by State Eugenicist upon his own initiative or upon complaints lodged or information given by an official, an organization or a citizen. 2. Opinion concerning a particular individual in reference to "potential parenthood of socially inadequate offspring" rendered after scientific investigation, by State Eugenicist to Court of Record. 3. Early date set by court for hearing case. 4. Court to notify and summon interested parties. 5. Due provision for legal counsel for the defendant and for trial by jury. 6. Judgment: Order for eugenical sterilization if the contention of the State Eugenicist is upheld 7. Execution of the order under the supervision and responsibility of the State Eugenicist. 8. In case of inmates of institutions, execution of order may be suspended until inmate is about to be released, allowing ample time for convalescence. 9. Provision for the study of mental, moral, physiological, social and economic effects of different types of sterilization.

Point #4 is precisely what the United States Supreme Court clung to in order to justify its claim that the law met "due process." The provisions for notification in order to "perfect jurisdiction" over the subject, the provision of legal counsel, as well as access to an appellate court are the token niceties that the U.S. Supreme Court clung to as proof that the persons in question were afforded "due process" before the State deprived them of "life, liberty," or "property."

One other crucial element deemed to be important by eugenicists in the United States and Europe was to make the State representatives immune from any legal consequences of their actions:

> Section 19. Liability. Neither the State Eugenicist, nor any other person legally participating in the execution of the provisions of this Act, shall be liable either civilly or criminally on account of said participation.

One could argue that the mechanisms of totalitarianism are written into the American version of the law. Laughlin's "Model Eugenic Law" makes State functionaries liable for failure to perform their duties, in case they released anyone who had been slotted for compulsory sterilization. Laughlin and his eugenic counterparts were Progressives who had a particular disdain for any form of limited government that would allow any individual to escape the dictates of the central planning body:

> Section 21. Punishment of Responsible Head of Institution for Dereliction. The responsible head of any public or private custodial institution in the State who shall discharge, release or parole from his or her custody or care any inmate who has been duly ordered by a court of this State to be eugenically sterilized, before due consummation of such order as herein contemplated, unless, as herein provided, such particular inmate be discharged, released or paroled into the custody of the State Eugenicist, shall be guilty of a misdemeanor, and shall be punished by not less than — months imprisonment or — dollars fine, or both; or by not more than — months imprisonment or — dollars fine, or both.

Laughlin leverages the "supremacy" of Federal over State law. Ultimately, it is the "supremacy clause" of the Federal constitution which maintains the 1927 Buck v. Bell decision as what attorneys call "valid controlling precedent." The U.S. Supreme Court's upheld the law, and only the U.S. Supreme Court or the U.S. Congress can deem it "unconstitutional." The need for eugenic measures at the Federal level was important to the eugenicists for other reasons as well. The section "Principles Suggested for a Federal Statute" extend the legislation to individuals that fall outside of a strict reading of a single state's jurisdiction, namely immigrants and Native Americans living in reservations, as well as "soldiers and sailors" living within Federal jurisdiction. This section suggests that the model law become a Federal law to allow the "segregation," "sterilization" or "otherwise rendering non-productive" those that the Federal government deemed a danger to the eugenic future of the Nation. This book will later explore how devestating this would be to the Native American population in the years following the <u>Buck v. Bell</u> case:

> **Persons Subject.** 1. Immigrants who are personally eligible to admission but who by the standards recommended in the model state law are potential parents of socially inadequate offspring. 2. All persons below the standards of parenthood set in the model state law who are beyond the jurisdiction of state laws, including the inhabitants of the District of Columbia, unorganized and outlying territories, Indian reservations, inmates of federal institutions, and soldiers and sailors.
>
> CONTINUES.....
>
> Up to the present time, the Federal Government has not enacted any legislation bearing either directly or indirectly upon eugenical sterilization. The matter of segregating, sterilizing, or otherwise rendering non-reproductive the degenerate human strains in America is, in accordance with the spirit of our institutions, fundamentally a matter for each state to decide for itself. There is, however, a specialized field in which the Federal Government must cooperate with the several states, if the human breeding stock in our population is to be purged of its defective parenthood.

It is these passages that indicate precisely what Laughlin wanted to accomplish: a total control and micro-managing of the personal reproductive decisions that had previously been the sole prerogative of the individual. Laughlin's "Model Sterilization Law" would certainly have a direct impact around the world. As discussed, key provisions of the law were translated verbatim and implemented by governments around the world, namely Hitler's government:

> Laughlin stayed in touch with Olson's staff, asking that copies of the sterilization volume be sent to other dignitaries following the judge's death in 1935. For example, Laughlin wanted one copy mailed to the head of the U.S. Attorney's Advisory Committee on Crime and another to Professor Eugen Fischer, rector at the University of Berlin and director of the Kaiser Wilhelm Institute of Anthropology, Human Heredity, and Eugenics. Laughlin's contact with Fischer was timely, occurring when sterilizations under the German eugenics law accelerated dramatically. (Pg. 198, "Three Generations No Imbeciles")

To put this into historical context, the reader should know that Eugen Fischer was one of the three authors of the infamous "Baur-Fischer-Lenz" book. Recall that Hitler's publisher gave him a copy while Hitler was writing and researching "Mein Kampf." All of Laughlin's work would be made available to German eugenicists through the auspices of the International Federation of Eugenic Organizations, which was headed up by Charles Davenport, Leonard Darwin, and other key figures of the movement. Eugenic notions would begin to appear frequently in Hitler's speeches after the publication of "Mein Kampf." It is of note that the German Jewish population afterwards were characterized as a formidable enemy of the

"Aryans." Prior to "Mein Kampf" Hitler depicted them as manipulative and cunning. After "Mein Kampf" Hitler's speeches referred to the German-Jewish population as rodents, vermin, and incapable of civilization. The change from formidable enemies to ineffective pathogens can hardly be said to be a minor conceptual turn. It is noteworthy that this subtle but crucial change coincided with Hitler being handed a copy of the "Baur-Fischer-Lenz" book.

Once in power, Hitler would place German eugenicists like Fischer, Rüdin, and Ploetz, all members of the International Federation of Eugenic Organizations, in charge of drafting and implementing the infamous Nuremberg racial decrees. In fact, it is hardly surprising that the work of the Eugenics Record Office would find a sympathetic ear in Adolf Hitler. The white supremacist underpinnings of Laughlin's "Model Eugenical Law" were readily apparent in Judge Olson's closing:

> **"The Rising Tide of Color," by Lothrop Stoddard, warns us of danger to the white race**, but this book of yours warns humanity of the menace to all races --- to the entire human race --- of racial degeneracy. (Pg. 323, "Eugenical Sterilization," emphasis mine)

Of course, the full title to Lothrop Stoddard's book is "The Rising Tide of Color Against White World Supremacy," another book that Adolf Hitler found particularly insightful and inspiring. Incidentally, Lothrop Stoddard would travel to Hitler's Germany and be given the honor of sitting in as a judge in one of the eugenical courts created in the fashion recommended by Laughlin's "Model Law." Stoddard was given the opportunity to decide along with the regular German judges the fate of those deemed "defective" and "degenerate" by Hitler's government. This book will touch on this event later. By any measure, Laughlin and Olson accomplished precisely what they delineated in the introduction of their book. The law significantly altered the relationship between the government and the governed at home and abroad. It became the tool of those that desired to control their fellow humans, precisely how despots like Hitler desired.

THE
MELTING-POT MISTAKE

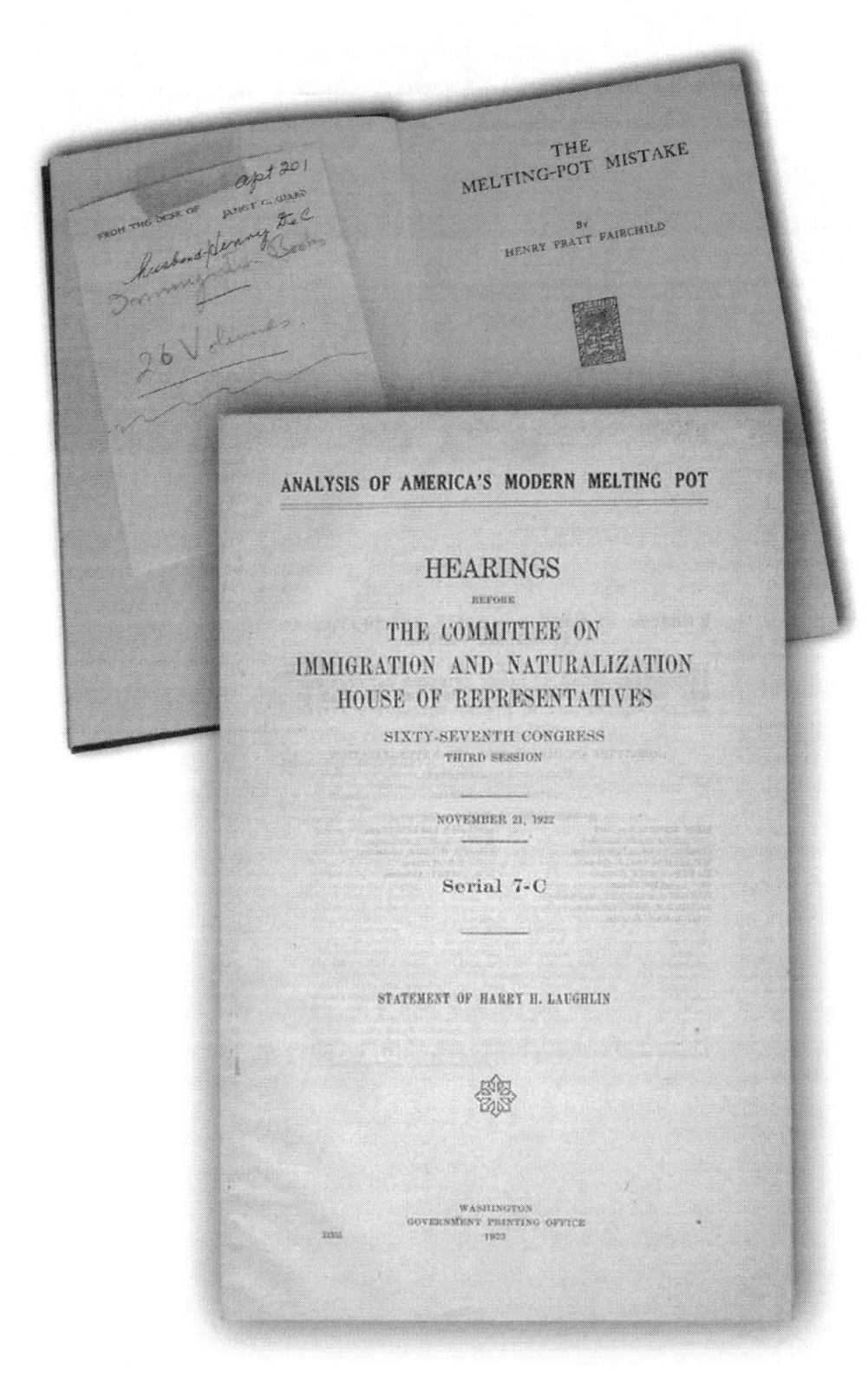

By
HENRY PRATT FAIRCHILD

FROM THE DESK OF JANET C. GIANO

husband Henry Pratt C
Immigration Books

26 Volumes

ANALYSIS OF AMERICA'S MODERN MELTING POT

HEARINGS
BEFORE
THE COMMITTEE ON
IMMIGRATION AND NATURALIZATION
HOUSE OF REPRESENTATIVES

SIXTY-SEVENTH CONGRESS
THIRD SESSION

NOVEMBER 21, 1922

Serial 7-C

STATEMENT OF HARRY H. LAUGHLIN

WASHINGTON
GOVERNMENT PRINTING OFFICE
1923

1923 - ANALYSIS OF AMERICA'S MODERN MELTING POT

"Facts do not cease to exist because they are ignored."
– Aldous Huxley

What had previously been a miniscule single-digit percentage of American blacks in the North swelled to significant numbers in the industrial metropolis. As mentioned in prior chapters, this massive population shift coincided with hordes of Europeans emigrating to the United States, most conspicuously the Eastern European Jews, the Irish Catholics, and the Italians, the later which became synonymous with organized crime in the fashion of Al Capone and the Italian Mafia. The combination of these two waves revealed the racism that had otherwise hidden behind abolitionism in the Northeast, much which was in truth fueled by a dislike for the African slave being brought into white society. As it would turn out, much of the era's race riots and gang related activity was concentrated in the Northeast and Midwest. Nathaniel Shaler's and Davenport's lectures to Harvard students were but one of a multitude of Northeastern voices bemoaning the injection of Africans into society, while equally voicing disdain for the actual institution of slavery itself.

The notion that America's "melting pot" ethos was flawed was consistent throughout the American eugenics movement. A New York Times article from 1921 quotes Davenport as "an authority on evolution." The article is aptly titled "Eugenicists Dread Tainted Aliens: Believe Immigration Restriction Essential to Prevent Deterioration of Race Here":

> The "melting pot" theory is a complete fallacy according to eugenists, because it suggests that impurities and lesser qualities are eliminated by the intermingling of the races, whereas they are as likely to be increased. [sic.] (NYT, Sept. 25th, 1921, "Eugenists Dread Tainted Aliens")

The article has various subtitles including "Melting Pot False Theory" and "The Lesson of Evolution." It quotes Davenport calling the concept of American egalitarianism a "sophistry." In a telling fashion, it quotes Henry Fairfield Osborn attacking the founding values of the American experiment in the subsection "Sees Peril in Individualism":

> "The closing decades of the nineteenth century and the opening decades of the twentieth have witnessed what may be called a rampant individualism – not only in art and literature, but in all our social institutions – an individualism which threatens the very existence of the family: this is the motto of individualism, let each individual enjoy his own rights and privileges – for tomorrow, the race dies." (NYT, Sept. 25th, 1921, "Eugenists Dread Tainted Aliens")

Laughlin's "Analysis of America's Melting Pot Hearings Before the Committee on Immigration and Naturalization House of Representatives" was one of the key documents upon which the Congressmen based their definition of "American homogeneity." (Sixty-Seventh Congress, Third Session of November 21, 1922, Serial 7-C Washington Government Printing Office 1923) The report would significantly influence the passing of the 1924 Immigration Restriction Act, which in turn would deny Jewish refugees entry into the United States during The Holocaust. The section titled "V. THE LAUGHLIN REPORT" documents that Laughlin's report "was designed to correct the inability of the Dillingham Commission report to demonstrate conclusively the social inferiority of the "new" immigrants." Laughlin's report was originally requested in an April 16th, 1920 hearing of the House Immigration Committee, which asked him to study the relations of biology to immigration particularly as they bore on the problems of social degeneracy. The 1952 Congressional report of the sessions that finaly dismantled the 1924 Johnson-Reed Act recalls just how influential Laughlin's "Melting Pot" document was:

> Laughlin's report was presented to the committee in November 1922. The Honorable Albert Johnson, chairman of the committee, examined the report and certified: "I have examined Dr. Laughlin's data and charts and find that they are both biologically and statistically thorough, and apparently sound." ----
> Whatever the chairman's competence to pass upon these matters, he was satisfied that the investigation had proved the inferiority of the new immigrants. The opinions that were before long to be reflected in legislation were summarized by Dr. Laughlin: "The outstanding conclusion is that, making all logical allowances for environmental conditions, which may be unfavorable to the immigrant, the recent immigrants as a whole, present a higher percentage of inborn socially inadequate qualities than do the older stocks." (Pgs. 1853-1854, "Hearings Before the President's Commission")

Incredibly enough, Laughlin had indulged in a rant that directly attacked the concepts upon which the United States Congress was founded, and more specifically, had sworn to uphold:

> We in this country have been so imbued with the idea of democracy, or the equality of all men, that we have left out of consideration the matter of blood or natural inborn hereditary mental and moral differences. No man who breeds pedigreed plants and animals can afford to neglect this thing. (Pgs. 1853-1854, "Hearings Before the President's Commission")

Laughlin's testimony before the House of Representatives heavily relied on the mental and eugenic tests the United States Army had been conducting since World War I. Amongst the many eugenicists that amassed study after study was the eugenicist Carl C. Brigham in his 1923 "Study of American Intelligence." Similar tests were conducted on immigrants passing through Ellis Island. The inspectors checked for blindness, deafness, took physical measurements, and even had a quick questionnaire to discern mental abilities. The language barrier obviously hampered the ability of many to impress the inspectors positively. Frances Janet Hassencahl documents the fervor upon which these tests were being conducted. An inspector by the name of Frank Martocci recalled that in 1907, he examined from four to five hundred immigrants per day, working from 9 A.M. to 9 P.M.:

> I thought it was a stream that would never end. Every twenty-four hours from three to five thousand people came before us, and I myself examined from four to five hundred a day. We were simply swamped by that human tide. (Pg. 266, "Harry H. Laughlin, Expert Eugenics Agent," Frances Janet Hassencahl, University Microfilms, 1970)

The only scientist to dispute Laughlin's findings, Herbert Spencer Jennings, was ignored. When Jennings, a biologist, told the Committee that Laughlin's statistical analysis was flawed, his testimony was cut short by Chairman Alfred Johnson, the Representative that was in the pocket of the Immigration Restriction League. Jennings's was allowed only a few minutes while Laughlin's testimony before Congress amounted to several days,.

Laughlin saw nothing wrong with the way these metrics and statistics were collected. He believed in the eugenic cause strongly enough to deem these methods as passing scientific muster. Interestingly enough, Laughlin utilizes the logic of what modern day Progressives call the "Precautionary Principle" in his "Melting Pot" presentation. Note that Laughlin does not defend the absolute reliability of the mental tests. Rather, he insists that some action must be taken even if the science has not matured to the level that the critics require:

> In his Melting Pot testimony (First Hearing, 1920), Laughlin presented the findings of the Army tests as gospel. Laughlin usually did not qualify data in the face of criticism, but he did so in this instance because the Army tests had come under intensive criticism as being contaminated by environmental factors such as being English both in language and concept. He took care to point out that the tests were the best available, were administered by competent men to a large and representative sample, charging: "Until better and more accurate records are secured these must be accepted as the most nearly approximating the truth, and infinitely superior to the unsupported opinion of the critic." (Pg. 259, "Harry H. Laughlin, Expert Eugenics Agent", Frances Janet Hassencahl, University Microfilms, 1970)

As mentioned earlier, Laughlin simply didn't recognize the "nature-nurture" argument. He simply did not believe personal worth was affected by anything else other than hereditary or racial influences. However, he was aware that the mental tests had come under serious scrutiny. Laughlin addressed this criticism in one of his appearances before the House of Representatives. This is important for more reasons than one. Laughlin's use of the "Precautionary Principle" is a debate tactic still used today to defend legislation based on immature or debatable science. The modern day "Precautionary Principle" states that steps must be taken to avert an impending catastrophe even if the science justifying it is incomplete or of doubtful reliability. This "precautionary" creed would play an important role throughout the life-span of the eugenics movement, namely with German eugenicists. The reliance on "prevention" as the goal behind all of the compulsory health laws during Hitler's National Socialism has strong parallels with the "precautionary principle" of today's environmentalists and naturalists. In fact, the term *"Vorsorgeprinzip"* or "precautionary principle," originated in Germany during the National Socialist era according to Stephanie Joan Mead, author of an article titled "The Precautionary Principle: A Discussion on the Principles Meaning & Status in an Attempt to Further Define and Understand the Principle," for the "New Zealand journal of Environment," Vol. 8, 2004 (Pg. 137-176):

> The precautionary principle emerged out of the German socio-legal tradition in the 1930's and implies that in the face of scientific uncertainty, action to prevent potential harm is favored over non-action. ("New Zealand Journal of Environment," Vol. 8, 2004, Pg. 137-176)

The "Implementing Ecological Integrity: Restoring Regional and Global Environmental and Human Health" report prepared by P. Crabbè for the Scientific Affairs Division of the North Atlantic Treaty Organization (NATO) also states that the "precautionary principle" can be traced back to German legislation of the 1930's. (Pg. 429) The Wingspread Conference defined the "precautionary principle" as such:

> When an activity raises threat of harm to the environment or human health, precautionary measures should be taken even if some cause and effect relationships are not fully established scientifically.

The paper also gives an alternative definition for the "Precautionary Principle":

When the health of humans and the environment is at stake, it may not be necessary to wait for the scientific certainty to take protective action.

This was state policy in the Third Reich's eugenic program. The precautionary principle's application by the Third Reich is documented by the famous Holocaust historian, Robert Proctor:

> The ideology of prevention merged with the ideology of "one for all and all for one" (*Gemeinnutz geht vor Eigennutz*) that was yet another hallmark of Nazi thought: as one anti-tobacco activist put it, nicotine damages not just the individual but the population as a whole. (Pg. 26, "Nazi War on Cancer")

However, it must be noted that Stephanie Joan Mead is incorrect in placing the first use of the principle in 1930s Germany. A survey of the eugenic literature reveals that the precautionary principle was part of eugenic dogma a decade prior to Hitler's Third Reich. The most prominent of eugenicists to defend eugenics by utilizing the "precautionary principle" concept was Leonard Darwin. Leonard Darwin was lobbying for adopting the principle as early as 1924 or 1926 heavily relying on the urgency of taking "precautionary" measures prior to the science being settled. Leonard Darwin's 1926 book, "The Need for Eugenic Reform" frequently addresses the need to take precautionary action or "condemn our own nation to disaster":

> Our admitted ignorance concerning the ways of nature affords no excuse for altogether neglecting to promote eugenic reform, because inaction may leave us at the mercy of unperceived retrograde tendencies, and because evolution is not always progressive. Risks must be run; for to wait for perfect knowledge would be to wait forever. A purely conservative policy on the part of the wise may place the steering of the ship in the hands of the foolish. (Pg. 10, "The Need for Eugenic Reform")

Vorsorgeprinzip then, as it is today, was meant as the legalistic justification for taking action prior to a full accounting of the facts. The catastrophic and apocalyptic predictions of the "race hygienists" demanded that precautions be taken even if there was no consensus on the truth of their predictions. This was the political strategy of a group of scientists that spent just as much time drafting legislation as they did practicing actual science.

The organization called Facing History and Ourselves of Brookline, Massachusetts has excerpts of the debate in Congress posted in their website (www.FacingHistory.org). Facing History quotes several members of Congress, beginning with Representative Clarence F. Lea of California. Lea attended Stanford University, yet another eugenic stronghold of American academia. He was elected as a Democrat to the Sixty-fifth as well as to the fifteen succeeding Congresses (March 4, 1917-January 3, 1949). Representative Clarence F. Lea of California would tell his fellow lawmakers:

> What is that assimilation that we demand of a naturalized citizen? Assimilation requires adaptability, a compatibility to our Government, its institutions, and its customs; an assumption of the duties and an acceptance of the rights of an American citizen; a merger of alienism into Americanism. --- True assimilation requires racial compatibility.

Note that the congressman agrees with the general premise that it is the government's duty to design or farm the type of society it wants:

> But to avoid further racial antipathies and incompatibility is the duty and opportunity of this Congress. The first great rule of exclusion should prohibit those non-assimilable. Our own interests, as well as the ultimate welfare of those we admit, justify us in prescribing a strict rule as to whom shall be assimilable. We should require physical, moral, and mental qualities, capable of contributing to the welfare and advancement of our citizenship. Without these qualities it would be better for America that they should not come.

Lea and the California Legislature had themselves been busy making sure undesirable racial elements were barred from entry into the United States. Their policies are also preserved in a 1921 document by the Japanese Exclusion League of California titled "Japanese Immigration and Colonization" by the U.S. Government

Printing Office. On July 18th, 1921, Lea and several other congressmen from California presented Secretary of State Charles E. Hughes a "skeleton brief" by Valentine Stuart McClatchy, a member of the Japanese Exclusion League of California. The brief claimed that such legislation was necessary for the "protection and preservation of our own." (Pg. 5) The brief was presented along with Senate Resolution No. 26 of the California Legislature which in April 12th, 1921 had "unanimously" endorsed the position of the Japanese Exclusion League.

Of note is that the lines between the eugenicists and its opponents seemed to fall along the political lines that Prohibition created. This was more than a theoretical demarcation. According to Professor Paul Lombardo, author of the 2008 book, "Three Generations, No Imbeciles," Dr. Joseph S. DeJarnette, the man whom would testify as an "expert witness" in the 1927 <u>Buck v. Bell</u> case, was "an advocate for the prohibition of alcohol his entire career." As we know, Laughlin and his activist-minded mother were also in favor of Prohibition.

The opposition sometimes, but not always, came from Congressmen that were ethnic minorities. Adolph Joachim Sabath (April 4, 1866 – November 6, 1952) was a Jewish-American politician. He served as a member of the U.S. House of Representatives from Chicago, Illinois, from 1907 until his death. He immigrated to America at age 15. His support fell along the political lines created by Prohibition. He denounced the Prohibition factions, the Anti-Saloon League (ASL) "and their allied forces and co-workers, the Ku Klux Klan fanatics." He consistently submitted bills in the House of Representatives to allow commerce in beer and wine every year from 1925 to 1933. In 1929, he came to the defense of his large immigrant constituency by challenging the claims of "expert" eugenicists like Laughlin. Eugenicists had always had a significant number of professionals related to correctional institutions ready to claim that immigrants of the era were equated with the organized crime. Representative Sabath saw assimilation from a different perspective. He is quoted here at length as his rebuttal is on point:

> What is meant by assimilation is difficult of definition. ---- The children of these foreign parents brought up in American public schools grow up without even an ability to read the foreign press. --- The majority in its report . . . unjustifiably charged and contended that there is in this country an undigested mass of alien thought, alien sympathy, and alien purpose which creates alarm and apprehension and breeds racial hatreds. This, like most figures of speech, can not bear analysis. What is meant by alien thought and alien purpose as applied to immigrants? Does it mean that they are opposed to the land in which they live, in which they earn their livelihood, where they have established a permanent home for themselves and their children? Does it mean that they would invite conquest by foreign nations, and having to a great extent left the lands of their birth because deprived of liberty and that freedom which they enjoy in this country, that they would be willing to forego the blessings that have come to them under our benign institutions? Have they not by coming here severed their political relations with foreign lands? --- **It is not the immigrants who are breeding racial hatreds. They are not the inventors of the new**

anthropology. Nor do they stimulate controversy. It would rather appear, in fact is clearly shown, to be those who are seeking to restrict or to prohibit immigration who entertain such sentiments and who are now attempting to formulate a policy which is, indeed, alien to the thought, the sympathy, and the purpose of the founders of the Republic and of that America which has become the greatest power for good on earth. (emphasis mine)

Meyer Jacobstein of New York was born on Henry Street on the Lower East Side of Manhattan to Polish Jews who had only weeks earlier immigrated to New York via Stockholm, Sweden. Note the newly arrived immigrant educating his fellow Americans on the dangers the likes of Laughlin posed to a constitutional republic:

> The committee has unquestionably been influenced by the **conclusions drawn from a study made by Dr. Laughlin.** ---- The trouble is that the committee is suffering from a delusion. It is carried away with the belief that there is such a thing as a Nordic race which possesses all the virtues, and in like manner creates the fiction of an inferior group of peoples, for which no name has been invented. --- Nothing is more un-American. Nothing could be more dangerous, in a land the Constitution of which says that all men are created equal, than to write into our law a theory which puts one race above another, which stamps one group of people as superior and another as inferior. The fact that it is camouflaged in a maze of statistics will not protect this Nation from the evil consequences of such an unscientific, un-American, wicked philosophy. (emphasis mine)

Representative Grant M. Hudson of Michigan took issue with the idea that immigrants could change their customs and their behavior if exposed to American values. His argument before the Congress is evidence that the propaganda efforts of the eugenicists had reached much of its intended audience:

> The "melting pot" has proved to be a myth. **We are slowly awakening to the consciousness that education and environment do not fundamentally alter racial values.** ---- Today we face the serious problem of the maintenance of our historic republican institutions. Now, what do we find in all our large cities? Entire sections containing a population incapable of understanding our institutions, with no comprehension of our national ideals, and for the most part incapable of speaking the English language. (emphasis mine)

More than a few shared racial views with the eugenicists. Ira Hersey of Maine was elected as a Republican to the Sixty-fifth as well as to the five succeeding Congresses, serving from March 4, 1917 to March 3, 1929. Hersey offered his view of the nation's history:

> Mr. Chairman, the New World was settled by the white race. --- America! The United States! Bounded on the north by an English colony, on the south by the Tropics, and on the east and west by two great oceans, was, God-intended, I believe, to be the home of a great people. English speaking—a white race with great ideals, the Christian religion, one race, one country, and one destiny. [Applause.] It was a mighty land settled by northern Europe from the United

Kingdom, the Norsemen, and the Saxon, the peoples of a mixed blood. The African, the Orientals, the Mongolians, and all the yellow races of Europe, Asia and Africa should never have been allowed to people this great land.

One of the most tangible consequences of the "Melting Pot" report was that the Carnegie Institution was made to feel the political backlash, and, as a result, it began to temper and reign in Laughlin. Dr. Merriam supported the eugenics cause, and seemingly was not fazed by the poorly veiled racism in the work being produced under the Institution's name. However, he would be embarrassed when visiting Mexico, where the local press pointed out that their guest had put forth plans before the U.S. Congress to halt the entry of Mexicans into the United States. Merriam was hosted by the Ambassador of the United States, so the negative press did not go unnoticed and apparently became a hurdle in the negotiations the Institute was involved in while visiting Mexico. Merriam contacted Davenport and complained about the devaluing of the eugenics research by overreaching with conclusions that were not directly supported by the evidence. This would be an enduring theme whenever anyone analyzed Laughlin's work. Hassencahl quotes the June 26th, 1923 memo written by Davenport directed at Laughlin:

> He feels especially that you ought not to go further in detail in regard to helping the committee on a definition of who may be acceptable as immigrant to the United States from Spanish America. The Spanish Americans are very sensitive on this matter as I, indeed, learned in Cuba and while it is the function of the Unites States Congress to lay such restrictions as it finds necessary, yet it will not do for the Carnegie Institution of Washington, or its officers, to take sides in this political question. I know you regard it properly as more than a political question and as a eugenical question but it is in politics now and that means that the institution has to preserve a neutrality. (Pg. 329, "Harry H. Laughlin, Expert Eugenics Agent," Hassencahl, University Microfilms, 1970)

The final report was entitled "Analysis of the Metal and Dross in America's Modern Melting Pot", and Laughlin delivered the results of his study to the House of Representatives, Sixty-seventh Congress, Third Session, on November 21st, 1922. The resulting work was published as the 1923 "Analysis of America's Modern Melting Pot: Hearings Before the Committee on Immigration and Naturalization." It focused mostly on the large amount of immigrants from Europe coming in through Ellis Island. It is of note that the 1924 Immigration Restriction Act, which resulted mainly from Laughlin's reports like the "Melting Pot," did not address immigration from the Southern border. This is certainly curious since Mexican and Oriental immigration was largely the impetus behind one of Laughlin's financial and ideological supporters, C.M. Goethe. There is no mention in the documents contained in the various archives as to why the 1924 Act did not address immigration of these two groups. As will be discussed later, the correspondence from C.M. Goethe does voice complaints about this aspect of the 1924 Act.

1923 - ERECTING THE GATES ABROAD

> *Mother of Exiles. From her beacon-hand*
> *Glows world-wide welcome; her mild eyes command*
> *The air-bridged harbor that twin cities frame.*
> *"Keep ancient lands, your storied pomp!" cries she*
> *With silent lips. "Give me your tired, your poor,*
> *Your huddled masses yearning to breathe free,*
> *The wretched refuse of your teeming shore.*
> *Send these, the homeless, tempest-tost to me,*
> *I lift my lamp beside the golden door!"*
> – Emma Lazarus – The New Colossus

Much of the opposition to immigration of those deemed eugenically undesirable was that they were not just unassimilable but that the gift of liberty was wasted on them. They were deemed incapable of adopting or adding to American style democracy. Frances Janet Hassencahl writes that in the 1920's the United States population had all but abandoned the ethos exemplified by the Emma Lazarus poem that is inscribed at the base of the Statue of Liberty. Lazarus wrote the sonnet entitled "The New Colossus" in 1883. The most recognized line from the poem asks the world for its "poor huddled masses," precisely the type of people the eugenicists wanted to keep out. In 1903, the poem was engraved on a bronze plaque and mounted inside the lower level of the pedestal of the Statue of Liberty, at the time when immigration numbers grew exponentially. Hassencahl cites the work of Thomas Bailey Aldrich, the editor of Atlantic Monthly, who became a prominent and vocal opponent of the increasing number of immigrants. Aldrich published a poem entitled "Unguarded Gates" in page 57 of the July 1892 issue of the Atlantic Monthly #70, No. CCCXVII. Hassenchal quotes the last for lines (Pg. 4):

> *O Liberty, White Goddess, is it well*
> *To have the gates unguarded? ...*
> *Stay those who to thy sacred portals come*
> *To Waste the gifts of freedom.*

The notion that the United States welcomed the "tired," the "poor," the "huddled masses yearning to breathe free" was an anathema to the likes of the Immigration Restriction League. They had no desire to include in the American experiment the "wretched refuse" from Europe, but rather to close the gates at the port of departure. This was the other tangible outcome of Laughlin's "Melting Pot" report before the United States Congress; the conscription of the U.S. Consulates abroad. Hassencahl documents that Laughlin secured an appointment as "Special Immigration Agent to Europe" on July 2nd, 1923 from James Davis, the Secretary of the Department of Labor. Davis was sympathetic to the cause of restricting immigration, and Laughlin had proved useful as the House of Representative's "Expert Eugenics Agent." Laughlin would write to E.S. Gosney, the prominent eugenicist from California, to inform him of the intentions of the project:

> I sail for Europe on August 8 with a commission as Special Immigration Agent to Europe, given by the Department of Labor which has control of our immigration administration. I shall make an effort to find out whether it is possible to go into the matter of **individual reputations and family pedigrees in selecting immigrants,** and shall try to find out how much it would cost the Government, per would-be immigrant, to make such studies a part of its normal administrative work. (Letter from Laughlin to E.S. Gosney, Aug. 7th, 1923, Folder 7.3 – Box 7, E.S. Gosney Papers, Cal. Tech Univ. Archives, emphasis mine)

Laughlin and his wife sailed from New York on the S.S. Belgenland on August 8th, 1923. They visited eleven countries including Sweden, Denmark, Germany, Holland, Belgium, France, Switzerland, Italy, England, Algeria, and Spain over a span of six months. Hassencahl describes Laughlin as a "dollar a year man," a term often used for experts employed during the Progressive Era of legislation, namely the New Deal era:

> The European filed studies served three purposes. First, they allowed him to trace, according to both theory and practice of international law, the authority of the home government of the immigrant and the authorized rights and activities of American consuls in these countries. Second, Laughlin tried to find out whether it would be possible, both from a legal and practical standpoint, to secure information about a prospective immigrant's personal history and family stock before he was allowed to sail for the United States. Third, he wished to conduct scientific researches in several American Consular districts to determine the fundamental "facts of history, geography, ethnology, statistics, economics, and social conditions" which affected immigration from that district to the United States. (Pg. 191, "Harry H. Laughlin, Expert Eugenics Agent," Frances Janet Hassencahl, University Microfilms, 1970)

Laughlin's main goal was to devise a plan to conduct eugenic screens prior to the emigrants stepping on a ship. Laughlin was in luck as all of his studies in Europe, with the exception of Italy, were coordinated with the eugenical societies of those countries. (Pg. 195, Hassencahl) These were very likely eugenicists that were already in touch with the Eugenics Record Office or some auspices of the International Federation of Eugenic Organizations. If Davenport did not have direct contact with them, then Leonard Darwin or Karl Pearson almost certainly did. The four-part investigation included a brief biography of the emigrant including standard data such as age and occupation. However, the tests went much further than that. They inquired into the immigrant's reputation in his community, as well as a battery of physical and mental measurements. The Yerkes-Bridges mental tests were used as part of the section labeled "racial tests."

Representative Johnson did not think that the proposal was outside of the scope of the House Committee, despite the fact that immigration fell within the jurisdiction of the State Department. Hassencahl documents that John C. Box of the Committee on Immigration did question the obvious issue of jurisdiction. Box submitted a brief entitled "Selection of Immigrants at the Source" which questioned the idea because consuls were established by treaties amongst nations, and such a plan called for the involvement of a deliberation much broader than that of a single committee. (Pg. 272, Hassencahl) However, some did see merit in the idea, even if not for the same reasons that Laughlin did. The acting Commissioner of Immigration, Fredrick A. Wallis, rightly pointed out that it was unjust to have the immigrant come to the United States after having sold their homes and possessions, only to be turned back penniless. Making a determination of entry abroad would avoid this dilemma.

Nor was Box the only one to see that such a significant undertaking abroad necessitated more than just the approval of a single committee. While the Secretary of Labor's endorsement was certainly helpful, Laughlin was presented with a political hurdle when the State Department became aware of the extensive amount of work being done in their consuls. Hassencahl points to a December 22nd, 1923 letter from Laughlin to Charles B. Davenport, and describes the dilemma that ensued:

> The Doctor later attempted to find out from the consuls whether or not European countries would cooperate in the genetic investigation of prospective immigrants, but he was stymied by the State Department when they discovered the nature of the information he was collecting. The questionnaire regarding the investigation of prospective immigrants was sent out under the auspices of the Department of Labor; the consuls, however, were under the authority of the State Department. A consul staff member had objected to the questionnaire on the grounds of a memorandum concerning the Regulation of 1896 in reference to mixed authority. Despite Laughlin's efforts to persuade them to the contrary, the State Department cabled the consuls and ordered them to relay only facts and not opinions regarding investigations abroad. The State Department was not in favor of eugenical investigations in Europe and saw that such investigations would require a negotiation of treaties with each country. Many countries would resent the implications of the inferiority of their citizens and the loss of control over the selection of emigrants. Better to reject the immigrants at Ellis Island than to open up a Pandora's Box by insisting on eugenical examinations abroad. (Pg. 192-193, "Harry H. Laughlin, Expert Eugenics Agent," Frances Janet Hassencahl, University Microfilms, 1970)

Unfortunately, it was precisely the eugenical testing that the consulates were opposed to that Laughlin most desired. He would try to use his position in the Carnegie Institution to see that the cooperation from the consulates kept going. Laughlin presented the plan to the Carnegie Institution accompanied by a letter from the United States Secretary of Labor, James J. Davis. The Secretary's letter of June 19th, 1924 acknowledged his support and asks the consulates operating under the Department of State to provide him with their full cooperation. (Laughlin files,

Carnegie Inst.) The title of the "working agreement" that Laughlin presented Charles Davenport and the Carnegie leadership had the lengthy title of "Memorandum and Outline of Tentative Working Agreement Between the Carnegie Institution of Washington, D.C. and the State Department of the Federal Government in Reference to Collaboration in the Collection of First-Hand Data on Immigration at its Source". The opening paragraph of the "working agreement" describes how on June 17th, Laughlin and President Merriam met at the Cosmos Club in Washington with "Honorable Wilbur Carr, Assistant Secretary of State in charge of the Consular Service." The agreement describes the close working relationship:

> In the matter of working out a practicable plan of operation, the representative of the State Department approved the suggestion that, in future collaborative studies in immigration between the Carnegie Institution and the Departments of the Federal Government, all work outside of the United States be done under the auspices of the State Department, while the investigations to be carried on inside of the United States be continued in collaboration with the Department of Labor, a Congressional Committee, or other purely domestic unit. (Laughlin files, Carnegie Inst., July 11th, 1924, Laughlin to Davenport)

The internal correspondence has an August 11th, 1924 letter by John C. Merriam to Walter M. Gilbert of Carnegie voicing doubts whether such an agreement was appropriate. Merriam did not want to strain the relationship with the State Department; though a later September 11th, 1924 letter from Gilbert to Laughlin describes Carr as "very favorably inclined toward cooperation." Whatever the agreement finally turned out to be, we can state that it accomplished Laughlin's goals. Laughlin, in fact, did conduct the investigation he had proposed. The accompanying memorandum from Gilbert to Merriam explains that Carr was very interested in Laughlin's work, but otherwise wanted to make sure the agreement conformed with government standards:

> I explained the situation to Mr. Carr and he stated that he would prepare a memorandum in turn with regard to what he considers the most desirable course of procedure in order to permit Dr. Laughlin to continue his collection of immigration data. ---- He thinks it will be desirable to issue appropriate instructions so that Dr. Laughlin may obtain the information he desires from American Consuls abroad, and he also considers it essential to define rather carefully the character and scope of the investigation and to institute a plan whereby the State Department may have full information concerning use of the material after it is procured. He expressed his interest in these immigration studies and in the work of our Department of Genetics as a whole and added that his main desire in checking the matter through rather carefully was to see that all steps were taken in conformity with established organization in the Department of State. (Laughlin files, MEMORANDUM CONCERNING PROPOSED ARRANGEMENT FOR CONTINUATION OF COLLECTION OF IMMIGRATION DATA FOR USE BY DR. LAUGHLIN, September 11th, 1924, Carr to Merriam)

On December 5th, 1924 Laughlin proposed that his official title be "Special Consul, detailed to Immigration Research." He included sample questionnaires he would utilize with State Department officials. Laughlin's suggested "MEMORANDUM ON IMMIGRATION" was a government immigration questionnaire that Laughlin had apparently developed with the Department of Labor. He adapted it for the needs of the Department of State Consular offices abroad. The form sought eugenic qualifications of the emigrating population including "Principal races, Prevailing religions, Physical Traits, General Mentality." The section entitled "Social and Economical Qualities" sought to determine the "initiative, inventiveness, altruism, business and organizing qualities" not of an individual, but of a population in general terms.

The discourse between Davenport, Laughlin, Merriam and Carr continued for several years. A December 1st, 1925 letter from Merriam to Laughlin is indicative of the support the Carnegie Institution, and likely the U.S. Government was voicing towards Laughlin's eugenic endeavors:

> Your outline for further research touching the subject of human migration as presented in pages 1425-1429 of the Hearings before the Committee on Immigration and Naturalization of the House of Representatives, 68th Congress, is an extremely interesting statement. If possible I hope to go over this with Dr. Rowe and Dr. Davenport and to see you some time before the end of the year. Of course you know in advance my great interest in the whole question of immigration and my desire to see the Carnegie Institution make contribution toward solution of the problems involved through fundamental studies in eugenics. I think it extremely important for us to consider those questions in the near future in order to outline a somewhat more definite program for the eugenics work of the Department of Genetics. (Laughlin files, Carnegie Inst., December 1st, 1925, Merriam to Laughlin)

Laughlin published the findings that resulted from the collaboration with the consuls and foreign governments. The work is entitled "Europe as an Emigrant-Exporting Continent and the United States as an Immigrant-Receiving Nation." It was presented to the 68th Congress on its first session of March 8th, 1924. (Pg. 191, Hassencahl) In conjunction with the "Analysis of America's Melting Pot," these presentations to the House Committee became the "scientific" and "expert testimony" upon which the 1924 Immigration Restriction Act would be based upon.

MEMORANDUM ON THE ARRANGEMENT BETWEEN THE CARNEGIE INSTITUTION OF
WASHINGTON AND THE DEPARTMENT OF STATE FOR CONTINUING THE RESEARCHES
ON THE SOURCES OF AMERICAN IMMIGRATION, BY HARRY H. LAUGHLIN.

...ed out by President Merriam and
...of November 17th.
...in the development of the pro-
...general principle.
...ar a year basis, as "Special
...ration Research," or other
...status.

MEMORANDUM ON IMMIGRATION

UNITED STATES DEPARTMENT OF STATE

Carnegie Institution of Washington
DEPARTMENT OF GENETICS
EUGENICS RECORD OFFICE
FOUNDED BY MRS. E. H. HARRIMAN

CABLE ADDRESS: "EUGEN COLDSPRINGHARBOR"   COLD SPRING HARBOR, LONG ISLAND, N. Y.

December 5, 1924.

CARNEGIE
INSTITUTION
DEC 7 - 1924
OF
WASHINGTON

President John C. Merriam,
Carnegie Institution of Washington,
Sixteenth and P Streets,
Washington, D. C.

Mr. President:

    I am wondering whether you found time to have your
conference with Assistant Secretary Carr in reference to the
feasibility of an agreement concerning the completion of my
researches on the sources of American immigration. In case
the meeting took place and an agreement was reached on the
general principles which would permit the work to proceed, I
am anxious to proceed with the investigations.

    I take the liberty to enclose with this letter two
papers: first, a proposed revision of the "Memorandum on Immigration," which outlines the general nature of the data which
we need from the American consuls. This revised form will, I
believe, cover the objections originally made by the State Department to the form used under the auspices of the Department
of Labor. The second paper is a sheet which lists some of the
practical items of special concern to be worked out in case the
Carnegie Institution of Washington and the State Department are
in general agreement.

    I trust that the matter has proceeded far enough to
permit me to take up the work directly with the State Department.

    Awaiting your instructions, I am,

    Very sincerely,

    Harry H. Laughlin

    H. H. Laughlin.

Encl.
HHL/IB

| 82d Congress | COMMITTEE PRINT |
| 2d Session | |

HEARINGS

BEFORE THE

PRESIDENT'S COMMISSION

ON

IMMIGRATION AND NATURALIZATION

Eugenics Research Association

ORGANIZED 1913

THIRTEENTH ANNUAL MEETING, COLD SPRING HARBOR, SATURDAY, JUNE 27, 1925

EXECUTIVE COMMITTEE

PRESIDENT, 1924-25	UNTIL JUNE, 1925	UNTIL JUNE, 1926	UNTIL JUNE, 1927
CHARLES W. BURR	LEWELLYS F. BARKER	STEWART PATON	IRVING FISHER
SECRETARY-TREASURER UNTIL JUNE, 1925	CHARLES B. DAVENPORT	MRS. WORTHAM JAMES	CLARK WISSLER
HARRY H. LAUGHLIN	FRANK L. BABBOTT	CHARLES W. BURR	FREDERICK L. HOFFMAN

COLD SPRING HARBOR, LONG ISLAND, N.Y.

December 15, 1924.

Mr. E. S. Gosney,
1011 Erie Street,
Pasadena, California.

Dear Mr. Gosney:

The Immigration Committee of the Eugenics Research Association is interested in securing additional copies of the report, "Europe as an Emigrant-Exporting Continent and the United States as an Immigrant-Receiving Nation," which is being published by the House Committee on Immigration and Naturalization. The Government prints 1000 copies for the use of the Congress, and then the laws of the United States permit the Committee on Printing to order additional copies to the cost of $200.00. $200.00 will, the public printer says, print 1700 extra copies. That will make a printing of 2700 at the cost of the government. The Committee felt that a larger edition were needed, and Mr. John B. Trevor has placed $100.00 at the disposal of the Committee, which will print 850 additional copies and increase the number to 3550. If we can secure another hundred dollar subscription, it will increase the edition still another 850 copies, or a total of 4400. If you care to subscribe a hundred dollars to this fund, the Committee would make good use of it and would be very grateful. So much has been put on the preparation of the report that our Committee is anxious to see that the printing will be large enough to supply the legitimate demand, and to see that the book does the greatest amount of practical good in applying eugenical or family-stock principles to the immigration policy of the country. Mr. Babbott had placed $250.00 to the disposal of the Committee, but this was to be used for preparation of the study and laying the facts before the Congress, rather than for printing extra copies of the hearing.

Very sincerely,

H. H. Laughlin.

HHL/I3

1924 - IMMIGRATION RESTRICTION ACT

> *"I had always hoped that this land might become a safe and agreeable asylum to the virtuous and persecuted part of mankind, to whatever nation they might belong."*
> – George Washington, letter to Francis Van der Kamp, May 28, 1788

The international eugenics movement reaped a major victory as a result of Laughlin's various appearances as the "expert eugenicist" to the United States Congress: The Immigration Act of 1924, or Johnson–Reed Act. (Pub.L. 68–139, 43 Stat. 153, enacted May 26, 1924) According to the U.S. Department of State Office of the Historian, the purpose of the Act was "to preserve the ideal of American homogeneity." The Act limited the number of immigrants who could be admitted annually from any nation to 2% of the number of people from that country who were already living in the United States per the Census of 1890. The law was aimed at further restricting the Southern and Eastern Europeans, many among them Jews who after 1890 escaped persecution in Poland and Russia. The Act also prohibited the immigration of Middle Easterners, East Asians, and Indians. This dubious method of using the Census from nearly half a century earlier would result in a reduction of total immigration from 357,803 in 1923–24 to 164,667 in 1924–25. The impact of the law varied with certain ethnic minorities suffering disproportionately by intention. For example, immigration from Italy fell more than 90% while immigration from Great Britain fell only 19%. The Act governed American immigration until the passage of the Immigration and Nationality Act of 1952, which revised it entirely.

The quota based on percentages of the 1890 Census was intended to lapse on July 1st, 1927, per the original text of the Act. As of that date, total immigration was supposed to be limited to 150,000, with the proportion of the total admitted from any nation based on that country's representation per the 1920 Census. This change would later be postponed to July 1st, 1929. The Act did have loopholes for relatives of U.S. residents, including their unmarried children under 21, as well as for their parents and spouses aged 21 and over. Non-quota status was accorded to the wives of U.S. citizens and their unmarried children that were under 18 and which were natives of Western Hemisphere countries. It also preferred immigrants aged 21 and over who were skilled in agriculture, as well as their wives and dependent children under age 16.

The 1924 Act also established the "consular control system," very likely as a result of Laughlin's work done in Europe under the auspices of the Department of Labor and the State Department. This provision allowed the U.S. consulate offices abroad to delve into the background of the applicants in order to obtain the information the eugenicists desired to possess prior to granting passage aboard a U.S. bound vessel. This provision divided responsibility for immigration between the State Department and the Immigration and Naturalization Service. It mandated that no alien should be allowed to enter the United States without a valid immigration visa issued by an American consular officer abroad. It imposed fines on transportation companies who landed aliens in violation of U.S. immigration laws. It defined the term "immigrant" and designated all other alien entries into the United States as "non-immigrant", or, in other words, temporary visitors. The Act's consular component would become the impenetrable bureaucratic wall that would prevent Jewish refugees from reaching the safety of U.S. shores. President Franklin D. Roosevelt's administration never came close to allowing the 25,000 slots/year available to European Jews by the Act. On average, the State Department under F.D.R. only allowed between 1,000 and 2,000 European Jews per year. Advocates for the Jewish cause would complain about the endless, and arguably pointless amount of paperwork imposed on those wishing to escape Hitler's henchmen.

As mentioned earlier, the Act set no limits on immigration from the Latin American countries, which set-off C.M. Goethe on a personal crusade to alter the Act. However, the Act successfully targeted people from the Asia–Pacific Triangle, which included Japan, China, Siam (Thailand), French Indochina (Laos, Vietnam, and Cambodia), Singapore (then a British colony), Korea, Dutch East Indies (Indonesia), Burma, India, Ceylon (Sri Lanka), Malaya (mainland part of Malaysia), and the Philippines despite the fact that it was then under U.S. control.

The Act had first been proposed in 1909 by Senator Henry Cabot Lodge along with Congressman Albert Johnson and Senator David Reed. It is fair to say that support had already been mounting by the time Laughlin arrived. The Act passed with strong congressional support. There were nine dissenting votes in the Senate and only a handful of opponents in the House. The most vigorous opponent was freshman Brooklyn Representative Emanuel Celler. Celler made the repeal of the Act his personal crusade; a mission he embarked on for the following decades. However, the opposition did not always form along ethnic lines. As has always been the case, financial and political concerns played a significant role. For example, the Progressive Congressman, Samuel Gompers, a Jewish immigrant and founder of the A.F.L., supported the Act because he opposed the cheap labor that immigration represented.

The debates leading up to the passing the Act are of historic value as they demonstrate the changing definition of the term "white." The hearings of March 8th, 1924 would include the presentation of the report which resulted from Laughlin's visit to Europe entitled "Europe as an Emigrant-Exporting Continent and the United States as an Immigrant-Receiving Nation". Laughlin used this report to document in an official manner his definition of what he called the "American Race." Evidently, the eugenicists did not consider German-Jews, Italians, or Eastern Europeans as "white". As documented earlier, this was a running conversation between Madison Grant, C.M. Goethe, and Laughlin. Laughlin's exclusionary policy would not only affect Jews, but any ethnicity that did not fit into his definition of "white" or "Caucasian". For example, Laughlin and his cohorts referred to Italians as "Mediterranean" immigrants. It is of note that in the ten years following 1900, about 200,000 Italians immigrated annually. With the imposition of the 1924 quota, this number was drastically reduced to only 4,000 per year. By contrast, the annual quota for Germany after the passage of the Act was over 57,000. About 86% of those permitted to enter under the Act's quota of 155,000 were from Northern European countries, with Germany, Britain, and Ireland having the highest quotas. So restrictive were the new quotas for immigration from Southern and Eastern Europe that in 1924 there were more Italians, Czechs, Greeks, Lithuanians, Yugoslavs, Hungarians, Poles, Portuguese, Romanians, Spaniards, Chinese, and Japanese actually leaving the United States than those coming in.

There should be no mistake as to the racialist intentions behind the legislation. Laughlin's 1924 report to the committee made it amply clear. They sought to propose that the term "Caucasian" be officially adopted by departments in the government, specifically those handling the Census and immigration control:

> If the American people had the habit of using the term "the American race," their foreign and especially their immigration problems, would be greatly simplified. We would have a standard to go by, and we would recruit to this standard from different European nationals in accordance with the qualities and proportions needed." (Pg. 1293, Hearing before the House Committee on Immigration, March 8th, 1924, "Europe as an Emigrant-Exporting Continent")

Laughlin concluded in his report that the American people "achieved a distinct nationality and race very early in its history." He claimed that through natural selection a small minority could grow to be a majority, and cited Charles Darwin in the process. (Pg. 277, Hassencahl) He would revisit this theme again and again, namely a speech entitled "The Definition of an American" given in Brooklyn to the Daughters of the American Revolution on February 20th, 1935. (Pg. 273, Hassencahl) Laughlin would also present a similar report to the New York Chamber of Commerce in 1938 while campaigning to ensure that the 1924 Immigration Restriction Act remain in force at the height of Nazi aggression towards German Jews:

> Racially the American people if they are to remain American, are to purge their existing family-stocks of degeneracy, and are to encourage a high rate of reproduction by the best-endowed portions of their population, can successfully assimilate in the future many thousands of northwestern European immigrants, but only such of these as are carefully inspected and selected. ----- But we can assimilate only a small fraction of this number of other white races; and of colored races, practically none." (Pg. 22, "Conquest by Immigration", Laughlin Papers, Carnegie, Truman)

The message was clear, and in 1938, thoroughly unmistakable, as this was the zenith of Hitler's aggression towards Jews in the streets of Germany. The gates to freedom would remain shut throughout the duration of The Holocaust, at all times justified by an alleged "biological" imperative presented by Laughlin. This biological imperative to protect the American populace from "degenerate stocks" was explicit on what entailed being an American in a "biological" sense.

The quotas remained in place with minor alterations until the Immigration and Nationality Act. However, prior to having the Immigration and Nationality Act of 1952 significantly alter the 1924 Act, the House of Representatives held hearings to evaluate the Johnson-Reed Act and its fallacies. The resulting report titled, "Hearings before the President's Commission on Immigration and Naturalization," documented the hearings held between September 30 and October 29, 1952. The U.S. House of Representatives printed the report for the use of the Committee on the Judiciary. It is important historically as it recalls precisely how influential Laughlin and Madison Grant were in the passing of the Johnson-Reed Act. The section titled "II. ORIGINS OF THE NEW-OLD IMMIGRATION DISTINCTION" quoted directly from Madison Grant's 1916 book, "The Passing of the Great Race":

> The conception of a new immigration inferior to the old began to take form in the writings of some sociologists and social thinkers in the 1890's. At root, this conception rested on racist notions that the peoples of the Mediterranean region were biologically different from those of Northern and Western Europe. ---- These new immigrants were no longer exclusively members of the Nordic race as were the earlier ones-The new immigration - contained a large and increasing number of the weak, the drunken, and the mentally crippled of all races drawn from the lowest stratum of the Mediterranean basin and the Balkans, together with hordes of the wretched, submerged populations of the Polish ghettos. Our jails, insane asylums, and almshouses are filled with this human flotsam and the whole tone of American life, social, moral, and political has been lowered and vulgarized by them. (Pgs. 1840-1841, "Hearings Before the President's Commission")

Grant's influence on Laughlin's work, and by extension the U.S. Congress is palpable. According to John Higham, author of the 1955 book "Strangers in the Land: Patterns of American Nativism: 1865-1924," the idea of quotas based on the national origins was conceived by Sen. David Reed of Pennsylvania, chair of the Senate immigration committee, and John Trevor, a colleague of Madison Grant and member of the Immigration Restriction League. Allan Chase, author of the 1975 book, "The Legacy of Malthus," documents that Trevor had attended Columbia Law School and Harvard. His wife was "one of Eleanor Roosevelt's oldest and most cherished friends." (Pg. 290) As documented earlier, the membership of the Immigration Restriction League was limited to those with the required racial and educational pedigree. The Immigration Restriction League had by this time become an expression of academic elitism at its worst. By 1924, the Immigration Restriction League was to include the presidents of Harvard, Stanford, Western Reserve, Georgia Tech, and the University of Pennsylvania's Wharton School of Finance, as well as scores of other university presidents and professors. (Pg. 113)

Chase verifies that Trevor's and Reed's 2% National-Origin quota was intentionally based on the 1890 Census, as opposed to the 1920 Census, precisely to further restrict the quota. They did not want that demarcation point to include the millions that had come to the United States between the turn-of-the-century and during World War I. Furthermore, the Jewish population that existed in the United States prior to 1890 were the refuges of the European Revolutions of 1848, and had been around long enough that Trevor counted them not as immigrants for the quota percentages but as American born.

In order to achieve their goal, the Immigration Restriction League had recruited a congressman they knew was sympathetic to the cause of immigration restriction. They had found that in Albert Johnson, who had been supporting immigration restriction measures since 1909. Johnson had been the editor of the Daily Washingtonian previous to becoming one of the most influential congressional leaders in the United States. According to Allan Chase, Rep. Johnson was "a high-school dropout and semiliterate" who owed his job to the lobbying of "the Immigration Restriction League's paid full-time Washington lobbyist, James H. Patten." (Pg. 289) Johnson was elected to the House in 1912 mainly due to his staunch opposition to the International Workers of the World, the notorious socialist and communist organization, which had caused trouble in the lumber mills in Johnson's hometown of Hoquiam, Washington. Hassencahl Documents that Johnson succeeded to the committee chair upon the death of Chairman John L. Burnett in 1918. (Pg. 207, Hassencahl) As Chairman, Johnson immediately called for a two-year suspension of all immigration, but the Senate refused to enact a total moratorium on immigration. The House and Senate compromised on a temporary measure that reduced immigration to 355,000 a year, and which provided a quota system as its basis. Johnson was given three years in which to develop a permanent legislation. Much of these three years were spent holding hearings, which is where Johnson leveraged the "expertise" of Laughlin. Professor Garland Allen documents how Laughlin and Johnson came to join forces in a common cause:

> Laughlin, long interested in the immigration issue, had made the initial contact with Johnson and, along with Madison Grant, had established a close personal and professional relationship with him. One consequence was that in 1924 Johnson, who was not then even a member, was elected to the presidency of the Eugenics Research Association. As "eugenics expert," Laughlin received congressional franking privileges, and he used them to assemble vast amounts of data about the institutionalized alien and native stock. The Carnegie Institution of Washington in turn officially allowed Laughlin to use his secretarial staff at the ERO to help compile data and figures for the congressional testimony. (Pg. 247, OSIRIS 1986, "The ERO at Cold Spring Harbor")

Johnson was also a member of the Republican Party. Hassencahl describes Johnson's political platform as "anti-Progressive." (Pg. 206, Hassencahl) This is seemingly a curious political position considering Laughlin's life-long commitment to Progressive causes. That is until one realizes that immigration has always served as the political fly paper that catches the worst aspects of American politics. According to Hassencahl, despite the fact that Johnson and Laughlin saw eye to eye on immigration matters, their allegiance was purely professional. Johnson and Madison Grant had a more friendly relationship. Johnson had known Madison Grant and made it a point to visit Grant whenever he was in New York. Hassencahl is of the opinion that the relationship between Laughlin and Johnson was "formal" and "strained" while Grant and Johnson chatted "like old friends" in their correspondence. (Pg. 208) Inversely, historians often paint Grant as a "right-wing conservative" despite the fact that he was a devoted Darwinist, the epitome of a North Eastern elitist, and staunchly opposed to limited or a *laissez-faire* form of government. The correspondence between Laughlin and Grant demonstrates a shared disdain for business interests that put profits above a eugenic consciousness. Hassencahl makes a similar observation about Grant's desire to rekindle the more "aristocratic" aspects of a eugenically superior "Nordic race", a running theme for eugenicists around the world:

> These aristocrats, by as much as their blood is pure, are taller and blonder than native populations, whether these be Alpine, in central Europe, or Mediterranean in Spain or in the south of France and Italy. (Pg. 213, Hassencahl quoting Grant, pp. 35, 152-153, "Passing of the Great Race")

Hassencahl also makes note later on in her unpublished dissertation of Laughlin's own disdain for big business and its want of cheap immigrant labor. She describes Laughlin's attitude towards big business when addressing the House Committee:

> Dr. Laughlin revealed that he shared in the Progressive Movement's dislike and distrust of big business. He did not hesitate to attack the economic basis which had been a major factor in determining the tide of immigration as short sighted and selfish because it did not consider what the long range effect of admitting mere labor would be upon America's hereditary qualities. ---- Laughlin reinforced the fears of his audience by arguing that an unrestricted immigration policy would bring undesirable immigrants who were motivated by easy money rather than "energy, initiative, love of liberty, and fine spiritual quality." (Pg. 238, "Harry H. Laughlin, Expert Eugenics Agent", Frances Janet Hassencahl, University Microfilms, 1970)

Laughlin did his best to dispel any notion that his employment in institutions philosophically committed to a political cause would taint his work as an "expert." Various historians have noted that his 1924 report to the Congress entitled "Europe as an Emigrant-exporting Continent" states:

> I made this biological investigation and put the facts on record here for the benefit of the Committee, which must draw its own conclusion. **I am not here as an advocate for or against any race.** Indeed, my position with the Carnegie Institution of Washington would prevent me from standing as an advocate of

special pleader. (Pg. 1318, "Europe as an Emigrant-exporting Continent: Hearings before the House Committee on Immigration and Naturalization, 68th Congress, First Session," Washington D.C.: U.S. Government Printing Office, 1924, emphasis mine)

Laughlin drew clear battle lines, and "Big Business" reciprocated the gesture by publishing their refutation of Laughlin's work. Hassencahl documents that the National Industrial Conference Board, an organization of thirty-one businesses and manufacturing companies, published a forty-two page report contesting the claims Laughlin made in his "Melting Pot" report. Their analysis called to question Laughlin's statistics and exposed them as fundamentally flawed as many others would point out in similar refutations of his work. It reiterated the questionable practice of using a 30-year-old census to arrive at conclusions about the population existing in institutions in 1920. The report accurately pointed out that the racial divisions utilized by Laughlin such as "Nordic", "Mediterranean", and "Alpine" were not in any way well defined or agreed to by other scientists or even other eugenicists. (Pgs. 291-292, Hassencahl) The National Industrial Conference Board sent one of their managers, a Mr. R.R. Lutz, to appear before the House Committee in order to personally refute Laughlin's "expert" report. According to Hassencahl, Mr. Lutz tried in vain to present himself as an "expert" on the matter, citing his career as the person responsible for training personnel at the Division of Planning of the Shipping Board. Interestingly enough, the committee members dismissed Lutz's testimony as the testimony of self-interested capitalists who sought to keep the doors open to cheap labor, and spent more time interrogating Lutz as to his motives than on the valid points and criticisms his group exposed.

Recall that Johnson was elected president of the Eugenics Research Association in 1924, despite the fact that he had not been a member prior to that. Thus, Grant, Davenport, and Laughlin effectively controlled the congressman in charge of House Committee holding the hearings. The bully tactics Johnson employed as the head of the committee ensured that Laughlin's testimony outweighed all others. Oscar Handling's Congressional 1952 report evidence the formidable influence Laughlin had on the congressmen. Johnson used his position to limit the amount of time the opposition had to debate. The section titled "APPENDIX: SPECIAL STUDIES MEMORANDUM BY OSCAR HANDLIN, ASSOCIATE PROFESSOR OF HISTORY, HARVARD UNIVERSITY" documents in its subsection "I. BASIC ASSUMPTIONS OF NATIONAL-ORIGINS QUOTA" just how skewed the hearings were:

> That assumption, embodied in the national-origins quota, is that the national origins of immigrants is a reliable indication of their capacity for Americanization. Generally, this assumption takes the form of an assertion that some people by their racial or national constitution are more capable of becoming Americanized than others. This is usually coupled with the assertion that the immigrants who came to the United States before 1880, the old

immigrants, were drawn from the superior stocks of Northern and Western Europe, while those who came after that date were drawn from the inferior breeds of Southern and Eastern Europe. (Pg. 1839, Handling, "Hearings Before the President's Commission")

Professor Garland Allen documents the "race crossing" aspect of Laughlin's testimony, which, incidentally touched upon the commonly held assumption by eugenicists that crossing "races" of humans was as undesirable as any improper breeding horses:

> In discussing the immigration issue, Laughlin was particularly disturbed by the specter of "race-crossing." He reported that a committee from the Eugenics Research Association had studied the matter and had failed to find a single case in history of two races living side by side and maintaining racial purity. Race mixture, Laughlin said, are poor mixtures, referring for corroboration to a study on race-crossing in Jamaica in which Davenport was then engaged. Like W.E. Castle, Edward M. East, and other geneticists at the time who had agricultural interests, Laughlin compared human racial crossing with mongrelization in the animal world. **The progeny of a cross between a racehorse and a draft horse, Castle once wrote, "will be useless as race horses and they will not make good draft horses . . . For similar reasons, wide racial crosses among men seem on the whole undesirable."** Like Grant, Laughlin felt that immigrants from southern and eastern Europe, especially Jews, were racially so different from, and genetically so inferior to, the current American population that any racial mixture would be deleterious. (Pg. 248, OSIRIS 1986, "The ERO at Cold Spring Harbor," emphasis mine)

In fact, the use of quotas based on national-origins can be said to have been the second attempt by eugenic-minded legislators to restrict immigration. They had tried to do so by employing mental tests devised by eugenicists, but these tests had proved insufficient in restricting immigration to the levels they desired. Oscar Handlin's summary recalls that the infamous literacy tests initially adopted in previous Congressional acts alone proved insufficient, thus the push for tighter methods of restrictions in the 1920s. The 1952 report cites Laughlin's "Report of the Immigration Commission" of the Congressional Record and provides an estimation of the importance of Laughlin's input upon the final decision to pass the Johnson-Reed Act:

> These theories were bitterly and inconclusively debated through the early years of this century. The decisive turn in the argument came when they seemed to receive validation from the reports of two governmental investigations. The first was the detailed study of the Immigration Commission under the chairmanship of Senator Dillingham. The second was a report by Dr. Harry H. Laughlin of the Carnegie Institution, expert eugenics agent of the House Committee on Immigration and Naturalization. ---- These reports had a direct impact upon subsequent legislation, for they supplied what had formerly been theoretical opinions privately held with a validation that was official and presumably scientific.

In the same way, **the Laughlin report** presented in 1922 and printed in 1923, laid the groundwork for the legislation of 1924. The report was **widely quoted** in quasi-scientific articles and **entered prominently into the debate** as a result of which the act of 1924 was enacted." It therefore becomes a matter of prime importance to investigate the nature of those reports and the soundness of their conclusions. (Pgs. 1840-1841, LXI, 558 - 73d Cong., 3d Sess., Hearings before the Committee on Immigration and Naturalization. House of Representatives, November 21, 1922. Serial 7-C, emphasis mine)

The article by Steven A. Gelb, Garland E. Allen, Andrew Futterman, and Barry A. Mehler titled "Rewriting Mental Testing History: The View from the American Psychologist," is posted in the archives of Ferris University's Institute for the Study of Academic Racism website. The paper describes Laughlin's presentation:

> In the 1922 testimony, Laughlin plastered the Committee room with charts and graphs showing ethnic differences in rates of institutionalization for various degenerative conditions, and verbally presented a barrage of data about the mental and physical inferiority of recent immigrant groups. These data included a "rogue's gallery" of photographs of "defectives" taken at Ellis Island, which purported to show "Carriers of the Germ Plasm of the Future American Population." Laughlin was a good showman, and effectively combined statistics and visual aids to create a strong fear of the feeble-minded in his listeners. (Pgs. 18-31, May 1986, Sage Race Relations Abstracts 11 #2, "Rewriting Mental Testing History," online version, www.ferris.edu)

As mentioned earlier, the small amount of opposition to the Act mirrored the opposition to other forms of heavy-handed government intrusion, such as Prohibition. Hassencahl opines that Democrat Adolph Sabath of Chicago, Republicans Isaac Siegel and Samuel Dickenson of New York represented the opposition of the committee. All three were Jewish, foreign-born, and from Russia and Eastern Europe, precisely the population Johnson, Grant, and Laughlin wanted to curtail. Sabath, a Democrat, had been opposing immigration restrictions in Congress since 1917, when literacy tests were proposed as a requirement. Sabath directed his ire towards Laughlin's influence when answering a question from another congressman about the intentions behind the proposed legislation:

> Because they believe these people are inferior. They have been fed by misinformation; they have been fed by new dope, as I may term it, by unrelated statisticians, and by Professor Laughlin's eugenic and anthropological false test, until they themselves believe there is some foundation for the unjustifiable conclusions contained in the so-called Laughlin report. (Pg. 223, Hassencahl, Pg. 5662, U.S. Congress, House, Representative Sabath speaking against H.R. 7995, 68th Cong., 1st Sess., April 5th, 1924, Congressional Record, V. 65)

Representative Emmanuel Celler, a Democrat, was very explicit in his complaints before the House Committee. He dismissed Laughlin's "Melting Pot" report by stating:

It is redolent with downright and deliberate falsehoods. The gentleman from Washington (Mr. Johnson) admitted to me that it contained certain inaccuracies, yet the committee has made no attempt to check its circulation. Verbatim parts and extracts from this vicious report are found in periodicals and magazines and newspaper articles all over the country, and so the errors and falsehoods are permitted to spread. ---- Why do I lay such heavy strictures on Mr. Laughlin? He claims that he has made an impartial investigation of the social inadequacies contained in our custodial institutions, so as to make an appraisal of the foreign born and native born of the United States. In truth and in fact Laughlin is predisposed in favor of the so-called Nordic superiority. He started out with the determination to show that the Nordics are a superhuman race. He supports this argument by the most dishonest methods. He has hoodwinked the Immigration Committee into believing his conclusions. (Pgs. 301-302, "Harry H. Laughlin, Expert Eugenics Agent," Frances Janet Hassencahl, University Microfilms, 1970)

The authors of the "Rewriting Mental Testing History" article also report on Rep. Celler's stand against Laughlin, as his efforts resulted in the calling of a potentially devastating expert on Laughlin's science. Recall that H.S. Jennings was rebuffed by Johnson:

Celler forced Johnson to call in another geneticist to respond to Laughlin's allegations. Herbert Spencer Jennings of Johns Hopkins University was invited to Washington, DC on the last day of the hearing, but given only a few minutes to testify. As Celler complained, Johnson stacked the hearings to favor the hereditarian eugenic position. Johnson had even gone further; with Laughlin and Henry Fairfield Osborn he had had the large exhibit on the inheritance of mental, moral and physical traits from the Second International Congress of Eugenics (held in New York in September 1921), shipped to and displayed in the Capitol Building in Washington, DC. There it remained for three years, providing the representatives and senators with "daily exposure to...exhibits on the heredity of criminality, idiocy, musical talent, epilepsy and other physical and mental traits." So successful were his efforts that Johnson could boast that before the debate on the floor of Congress ever began, "the biological questions of immigration. . . [had] already been settled in the minds of the members of the House and Senate." [sic.] ("Rewriting Mental Testing History," www.ferris.edu)

Rebuffed on the floor of Congress, Herbert Spencer Jennings did what scientists do when they disagree. Jennings, who had once been a student of Davenport's at Harvard, published a full critique of the eugenic assumptions expounded by Laughlin entitled "Heredity and Environment." The paper was derived in part from the testimony he had initially prepared for Congress. Jennings criticized the assumption that a person's abilities are predetermined by heredity and in no way affected by the environment the individual develops into a person:

[N]ot only what the cell within the body shall become, but what the organism as a whole shall become, is determined not alone by the hereditary materials it contains, but also by the conditions under which those materials operate. Under diverse conditions the same set of genes will produce very diverse results. It is not true that a given set of genes must produce just one set of characters and no other ... It is not true that what an organism shall become is determined ... (Pg. 319, Prof. G. Allen, "Eugenics and Modern Biology: Critiques of Eugenics, 1910–1945," Vol. 75, Issue 3, Pgs. 314–325, May 2011, Annals of Human Genetics)

In other words, being born Irish Catholic, Italian, or Eastern European Jewish in no way predetermined the quality of the person or the ability to contribute to society as the eugenicists were claiming as the basis for exclusion. Jennings' estimation of Laughlin's eugenics was simple enough even for a U.S. Congressman to understand:

> The characteristics of the adult are no more present in the germ cells than are those of an automobile in the metallic ores out of which it is ultimately manufactured. (Pg. 319, "Eugenics and Modern Biology")

Hassencahl documents that Jennings' article in the journal Science was the only one that Laughlin personally gave any thought to. H.S. Jennings was a fellow eugenicist after all. Robert De Courcy Ward of the Immigration Restriction League took Jennings' criticism seriously as well and asked Laughlin to draft a response in a March 30th, 1924 letter. (Pg.296, Hassencahl) Chairman Johnson was not shaken so easily. Johnson noted that the committee had been impressed with Laughlin's "Statistical Directory of State Institutions" and that if they accepted the severity of the problem, then they were inclined to accept the general notions extrapolated in the legislative proposals. Here was the "Precautionary Principle" at work; the congressmen had bought into the severity of the manufactured crisis. Thus, they were ready to implement any solution that was placed before them. Common sense was jettisoned as the wisdom expected of a statesman had been subcontracted to the "experts" like Laughlin.

In fact, the Congressman knew that the allegedly scientific facts and figures presented by Laughlin were statistically unsound. Laughlin had manipulated them, and anyone who was paying attention knew it. Well known newspapers like the New York Times and the Chicago Tribune made the questionable statistical tactics known to all. The New York Times article from June 1st, 1924, made it amply clear that Laughlin had cooked the numbers in order to justify his prejudices. The subtitle of the article was "Findings of Dr. H. H. Laughlin on Which Congress Acted Chiefly, Assailed as Unscientific":

> All the available data were not used, the board finds, and in commenting on this method of procedure it says: "Only if the concepts, methods and results of this basic investigation are sound can the country be assured that it has dealt, and will deal, with this vital problem in a scientific spirit, and has not merely clothed its wishes and prejudices in a body of facts and scientific ideas improvised to justify its purposes. Honest bigotry is less to be condemned than scientific pretension. (NYT, June 1st, 1924, "Call Immigration Problem Unsolved")

Professor Allen documents that Joseph Gilman, a professor in the School of

Business Administration at the University of Pittsburg had also noticed the statistical inconsistencies in the supposedly scientific study Laughlin had presented:

> Gilman noted that Laughlin had not corrected his sample for age or sex, especially important for comparisons since incarcerated populations tend to be largely male, between the ages of 20 and 30, while the general population includes both males and females and all ages. It was also well known, Gilman pointed out, that immigrant populations tend to include more males, since men come first to find work and establish themselves before bringing over families. (Pg. 320, "Eugenics and Modern Biology," Annals of Human Heredity, 2011)

Gilman also pointed out that Laughlin's study of prison populations referenced data from 1921 but compared against general population figures from the United States in 1910. Laughlin had done this intentionally as he knew that immigration rates had significantly increased between 1910 and 1914, thus disproportionately increasing the numbers found in prisons against those same nationalities found in the general population. In addition, Gilman found that the responses to Laughlin's survey from the prison authorities overrepresented prisons in the Northeast, where the immigrant populations naturally concentrated in that era because of the seaports on the coast. This is where those Mediterranean, Balkan, and Russian males were arriving and mainly staying to establish themselves economically prior to bringing their families. Gilman's observations would be reiterated in the criticisms of the 1924 Act found in the newspapers, but obviously not where it counted; in the halls of the U.S. Congress.

However, according to Hassencahl, Laughlin did receive favorable press from the Journal of Heredity, Scientific Monthly, and what she describes as an "avidly restrictionist" Saturday Evening Post. [sic.] Hassencahl also makes the observation that Henry Ford's infamous publication, the Dearborn Independent, gave Laughlin favorable reviews. (Pg. 284, Hassencahl)

Recall that this overreliance on the so-called "experts" in drafting monumentally important pieces of legislation came into fashion with the Progressive movement. As explained earlier, it was a practice brought into fashion by the eugenically minded Theodore Roosevelt explicitly to bolster the desired outcome of so-called "investigative" committees. Professor Allen writes about this aspect of law-making in his aptly titled paper, "The Role of Experts in Scientific Controversy":

> Sociological studies by Ralph Huitt, David Farnsworth, and David Truman suggest that more often than not congressional committees hold hearings to justify decisions already made, rather than to gain information for the formulation of a new policy or piece of legislation. ---- If we substitute the ruling class for congressional committee, the scenario has much broader applicability and, I think, shows the same forces at work. That is, the ruling class had its mind made up prior to the appearance of eugenicists on the scene: working-class people, Jews, eastern and southern Europeans, and blacks were a

dissatisfied and dangerous lot, and were, of course, biologically inferior. Eugenicists simply provided the seeming legitimation of that notion, just as experts legitimate congressional decisions that have, in effect, been decided before any testimony is given. (Pg. 194, "The Role of Experts in Scientific Controversy," 1987, Cambridge University Press)

This had always been part of the Progressive template, and certainly one of the goals of the eugenic intelligentsia. This is the belief system that they held in common with the British Fabian Socialists. The Progressive-minded legislators were willing to take Laughlin's Princeton degree along with the support prominent scientists like Davenport and Osborn gave him as proof that his views were "scientific." They made decisions that would negatively affect countless lives by subcontracting the analysis and deliberation to a zealot for no other reason that his title couched his obvious prejudices in science. Note Oscar Handling's summation of the process:

> A view of the actual circumstances of the compilation and of the nature of the methods used will show however that the Commission's report was neither impartial nor scientific, and that confidence in it was not altogether justified. No public hearings were held, no witnesses cross-examined by the members of the Commission. Largely the study was conducted by experts who each compiled their voluminous reports which were not printed until after the Commission had reached its conclusions. It is doubtful whether the Senators and Congressmen on the Commission ever had the time to examine the voluminous reports in manuscript. It is most likely they were compelled to rest their judgment upon the two-volume summary prepared for it by its body of experts. The final report was "adopted within a half hour of the time when, under the law, it must be filed." The identity of the experts must therefore become of some significance. (Pg. 1841, Handling, "Hearings Before the President's Commission")

Hassencahl agrees with this assessment. Her unpublished dissertation opines that the members of the United States Congress used an "expert" like Laughlin, not to inform, but to reinforce and justify actions they had already decided upon. She points out that the House had also appointed Alonzo G. Grace, a professor of history at Aberdeen South Dakota, as an "expert" as well, but curiously enough, he was never called to testify. (Pg. 230, Hassencahl) Laughlin had presented what Albert Johnson wanted, or in truth, the information that the Immigration Restriction League desired. The congressmen used Laughlin and the Immigration Restriction League to advance their agenda, and Laughlin and the Immigration Restriction League used the congressmen. This is the essence of politics, after all:

> Dr. Laughlin, served to justify action previously decided upon by the committee decision-makers. Although Dr. Laughlin did not persuade his audience, rather, he reinforced their views, the rhetorical situation was not a loss to him for it propelled the obscure scientist into the national scene and made possible both publicity and research, which organized eugenics could not have managed

otherwise. (Pg. iv, "Harry H. Laughlin 'Expert Eugenics Agent' for the House Committee on Immigration and Naturalization: 1921 to 1931" Hassencahl, 1970, University Microfilms)

Laughlin would utilize the network of eugenic-minded activists around the world to publicize the achievement of the 1924 Immigration Restriction Act. Laughlin's loyal supporter, C.M. Goethe, would write to his fellow eugenicists in California to brag about how this American piece of legislation was being used by Norway to keep Italian immigrants out:

> We have gained much in making our laws racially selective. I know you, as well as myself, are looking forward to the day when such legislation shall have become crystallized into a national habit, and when we can go further and make it individually selective. ---- Such a policy will have a profound influence on all mankind. You know Norway contemplates a Quota Act against Italy just because of such legislation in the United States. (Laughlin Papers, Box C-4-1:2, Truman Univ., Goethe to Popenoe, 1, 11, 1929)

The London Morning Post of Friday, December 18th, 1925 has an article written by Reverend W.R. Inge entitled "The Racial Test: Stringent U.S. Immigration Laws and the Justification – No Room for Bolsheviks." It is interesting to note that this article was kept in the files of the Carnegie Institution. Thus, it is likely that Laughlin sent it to his superiors as an example of the praise received for the work he was doing under the Carnegie Institution. It is clear that Laughlin was the impetus behind the article, as its opening paragraph states that "Dr. Harry Laughlin, of the Carnegie Institution of Washington . . . has sent me the Statement, which he made to the Committee of the House of Representatives on Immigration and Naturalization." The article is important as it announced to all the world that the United States, the country that was born out of an egalitarian creed, had officially created a barrier to entry based on racial and ethnic standards. The article says as much:

> The Report reveals the fact that there is one great democracy which is determined to pursue a scientific and enlightened policy in racial questions, putting in the forefront no longer the sentimental idea that America is the natural asylum for all the unfortunates of the world. (Laughlin files, Carnegie Inst., "The Racial Test", London Morning Post, Dec. 18th, 1925)

History proved just how this message was to resonate throughout the world, and the list of admirers and supporters of the 1924 Immigration Restriction Act only serves to underscore that fact further. The greatest and most historically significant praise for the Johnson-Reed Immigration Restriction Act came from Adolf Hitler himself, in the chapter of "Mein Kampf" titled "Subjects and Citizens":

> There is today one state in which at least weak beginnings toward a better conception are noticeable. Of course, it is not our model German Republic, but the American Union, in which an effort is made to consult reason at least

partially. By refusing immigration on principle to elements in poor health, by simply excluding certain races from naturalization, it professes in slow beginnings a view which is peculiar to the *folkish* state concept. ---- The *folkish* state divides its inhabitants into three classes: citizens, subjects, and foreigners. ("Mein Kampf," Vol. 2, Chp. 3)

As will be documented later, Hitler's government bestowed an Honorary Degree from Heidelberg University upon Laughlin. Laughlin's work on immigration restriction was one of the specific accomplishments that Hitler's government listed as justification for the Honorary Degree. Considering how micro-managed and obsessive the regime's propaganda wing was with international relations, it is only logical to assume that more than one of the higher-ups in the Third Reich had taken notice of Laughlin's work.

Frances Janet Hassencahl makes a very interesting observation. She analyzed Laughlin's worksheets and noted that amongst his scraps of paper were notes acknowledging that Jews held 3.45% of the patents but represented only 3.41% of the United States population, while scoring higher than the English in some metrics. (Pg. 348, Hassencahl) This, of course, went directly against any of Laughlin's contentions and disproved the leaps he made when arriving at his conclusions. It also proves that the statistical anomalies and errors that were often the criticism of Laughlin's work were not simple errors or oversight. At least, that is a fair conclusion one can arrive at when one sees the demeaning fashion in which Laughlin spoke of the European Jewish population, despite having scientific evidence to the contrary.

- 117 -

1924 - RACIAL INTEGRITY ACT

> "The scientist finds his reward in what Henri Poincare call the joy of comprehension, and not in the possibilities of application to which any discovery may lead."
> – Albert Einstein

Harry H. Laughlin would also significantly influence "Jim Crow" legislation inside the United States. Jim Crow was the name of the system of racial laws in the United States that were put in place just after the Civil War, between 1877 and the 1960s. While this system of laws and statutes is typically regarded as anti-black, Jim Crow was more than a series of rigid anti-black laws. It was targeted against any racial mixing that was deemed as undermining the "white race" by intermarriage, sexual, or even cultural relations with other races. The progeny of interracial relations was considered as a "mongrelization" of the white race, and the legal term commonly used for it was "miscegenation."

The Jim Crow era should be understood as distinct from the bigotry leading up to the American Civil War, as much of Jim Crow legislation was the result of the entrenchment of scientific racism in the United States. As discussed in the first book of this series, "From a 'Race of Masters' to a 'Master Race': 1948 to 1848," there was a significant upswing in the amount of racialist literature written in the guise of science after the Reconstruction. Recall that there existed a significant portion of the abolition movement in the North that resented the institution of slavery, not for its cruelty, but for the fact that it had brought a black population into their midst. Harvard's Nathaniel Shaler comes to mind here. This is how the proposal for the creation of the nation of Liberia came to be; where the emancipated slaves were to be sent in order to remove them from the American continent. Those interested in keeping the races separate, both in the North and the South, seemed to come to the conclusion that the effort to maintain the institution of slavery and racial supremacy had failed. Thus, it seems that a new approach became popular.

Also, keep in mind that at this point in history the work of both Charles Darwin and Theodore Roosevelt had become widely popular in the United States. Roosevelt had sounded the alarmist warnings about "racial degeneration." Darwin's "Descent of Man" had convinced a significant portion of academia that whites were at the pinnacle of evolution and that the colored races, namely Africans and Aborigines, were much further down the evolutionary ladder, literally closer to apes than man. The proponents of Jim Crow legislation took Darwin's and Roosevelt's observation very seriously. They were hardly alone. The fear of "degeneration" was a widespread phobia in turn-of-the-century Europe and America in a fervor that was arguably as pertinent then as fears of "climate change" are in the 21st Century. While this particular argument has been largely the contentious back and forth between Creationists and evolutionary scientists, this book aspires to evidence that the argument can be waged completely outside of a theological framework. One doesn't even need to go to Creationist tracts in order to find support for the observation that Darwin's evolutionary theory gave a significant bolster to the interests of racism. Remember that even the lauded expert on Darwin, Stephen Jay Gould, admitted that "biological arguments for racism" had "increased in orders of magnitude following the acceptance of evolutionary theory." (Pg. 127, "Ontogeny and Phylogeny")

Nor can it be said that these inflammatory concepts were relegated to political pamphlets. Theodore Roosevelt was an accomplished author, and the academics postulating about the practical applications of Darwin's evolutionary theory were expressing their concepts in respected scientific journals. The fact that they were adopting ideas deemed to be part of mainstream Darwinian evolution meant that these eugenic notions were included in mainstream texts. Professors and teachers at every educational level buttressed the belief that blacks were innately inferior to whites. The most famous textbook to forward these racialist evolutionary concepts was the "Hunter's Civic Biology" textbook that became the epicenter of the infamous Scope's Monkey Trial. The textbook had been written by none other than Charles B. Davenport. While academics have voiced outrage over the alleged disservice of attempting to keep evolution out of the classrooms, they have also feigned ignorance over the one chapter in the book that everyone should remember:

> **The Races of Man.** -- At the present time there exist upon the earth five races or varieties of man, each very different from the other in instincts, social customs, and, to an extent, in structure. These are the Ethiopian or negro type, originating in Africa; the Malay or brown race, from the islands of the Pacific; The American Indian; the Mongolian or yellow race, including the natives of China, Japan, and the Eskimos; and finally, **the highest type of all, the Caucasians**, represented by the civilized white inhabitants of Europe and America. ...
> **Improvement of Man.** - If the stock of domesticated animals can be improved, it is not unfair to ask if the health and vigor of the future generations of men and women on the earth might not be improved by applying to them the laws of selection. This improvement of the future race has a number of factors in which we as individuals may play a part. These are personal hygiene, selection of healthy mates, and the betterment of the environment.
> **Eugenics.** - When people marry there are certain things that the individual as well as the race should demand. The most important of these is freedom from germ diseases which might be handed down to the offspring. Tuberculosis, syphilis, that dread disease which cripples and kills hundreds of thousands of innocent children, epilepsy, and feeble-mindedness are handicaps which it is not only unfair but criminal to hand down to posterity. The science of being well born is called eugenics. (emphasis mine)

There is one curious aspect of the Monkey Trial that is rarely mentioned. The trials sidestepped the issue of eugenics. Neither of the famous lawyers broached the subject of eugenics despite the fact that Charles B. Davenport had written eugenics as being indistinguishable from Darwin's evolution in the very section of the textbook that supposedly offended the law. One can only speculate why, since

William Jennings Bryan's wife was an activist for the eugenics movement. Darrow had made it a point to voice his opinion about eugenics publicly before and after the famous trial. (See "Race of Masters") Then again, he was allegedly trying to defend the legitimacy of the scientific concepts portrayed in the textbook.

A March 1st, 1997, article in "Science News" provides a *mea culpa* about the role of science, namely its publications, had in the era of eugenics. "From News Wire to Newsweekly: 75 years of Science Service" by Anna Maria Gillis admits fault in the fact that the biased coverage of the Scopes Trial paved the way for its uncritical coverage of eugenics later:

> In its early days, Science Service did not always display the objectivity so prized in journalism today. The service clearly breached the objectivity barrier in 1925 during the trial of John Scopes, who challenged a Tennessee law that forbade the teaching of evolution. Science Service staffers Davis and Frank Thone went to Tennessee to cover the trial that summer, filing dispatches that went into daily newspapers and SCIENCE NEWS LETTER. At the same time, Science Service was helping Clarence Darrow's defense team gather expert witnesses to testify on Scopes' behalf. ----Throughout the 1920s, SCIENCE NEWS LETTER included extensive and uncritical coverage of eugenics, a favorite topic of many scientists and journalists at the time, including Davis, who was a member of the board of the American Eugenics Society. The Jan. 19, 1924, issue described a report of the Eugenics Committee of the United States that favored the immigration of northwestern over southeastern Europeans. "Will Blending of Races Produce Super-men?" dominated the Nov. 26, 1927, issue. Based on the comments of a geneticist at the Carnegie Institution of Washington, the article discussed, most often in negative terms, offspring of various mixed ancestries. Slosson wrote that the public needed to understood that "the fate of the nation depends . . . on how they combine their chromosomes. (p. S10)

Laughlin certainly contributed to Davenport's push to include eugenics as a topic of the scientific education of America's youth. As will be discussed later, Laughlin's greatest contribution to this effort was the distribution of the eugenic propaganda films produced by Hitler's Third Reich to classrooms across the United States. However, Laughlin's most direct influence in Jim Crow segregation was the veil of scientific legitimacy his work provided Virginia's Racial Integrity Laws.

One of the very influential Virginians to utilize Laughlin's expertise in passing legislation in the State was Dr. Walter Ashby Plecker, of the State's registrar of statistics. Plecker allied himself with the Anglo-Saxon Club of America in persuading the Virginia General Assembly to pass the Racial Integrity Law of 1924. The organization was founded in Virginia by John Powell of Richmond in 1922; within a year the club for white males had more than 400 members and 31 subsidiaries in the state. The leadership of the Anglo-Saxon Clubs was in touch with Laughlin, and both of the laws were Virginia's variations of his "Model Eugenical Sterilization Law," published two years earlier. This eugenic-minded lobby was successful in the passage of legislation to classify all persons as belonging either to the "white" or "negro" races. One of the major goals was to end "amalgamation" or "miscegenation" by racial intermarriage, whose progeny the racialists thought to contribute to "racial degeneration". On March 20th, 1924 the Virginia General Assembly passed two laws that had arisen out of these concerns. Both were motivated by an acceptance of the premises of eugenics by the activists in the Anglo-Saxon Clubs. The two pieces of legislation were SB 219, "The Racial Integrity Act" and SB 281, "The Sterilization Act." The former is described as "[a]n ACT to provide for the sexual sterilization of inmates of State institutions in certain cases." The Racial Integrity Act required that a racial description of every person be recorded at birth and divided society into only two classifications, white and colored, with Native Americans excluded from the classification. Thus, many mixed-ethnicity and African-Americans classified themselves as Native Americans in order to avoid segregation or sterilization. It defined race by the now infamous "one-drop rule," defining persons with any African ancestry as "colored." It also expanded the scope of Virginia's ban on interracial marriage by criminalizing all marriages between white persons and non-white persons.

Virginia's newly created Bureau of Vital Statistics under Plecker's direction aggressively policed the racial distinctions. Plecker and Laughlin were kindred spirits, both energetic, organized, and committed to their cause. The letters held at Truman University's Laughlin Papers proves that Plecker heavily relied on Laughlin for the science upon which Virginia's law was based. A January 10th, 1928 letter indicates that it was Madison Grant that introduced Plecker to Laughlin. Grant tells Laughlin that Plecker is "very much in earnest about race mixture and is the author of a good deal of important legislation in Virginia." (BOX D-4-3:12, Truman)

Plecker, like Laughlin, was very adept at leveraging the resources of the United States Census and the various genealogical databases. The Laughlin Papers at the Truman archives have a letter from Plecker to Mr. W.M. Steuart of the Bureau of the Census in Washington, D. C. The letter makes a request for data on the Pamunkey and Mattapony groups of Virginia native Americans. Recall that Native Americans were exempt from the 1924 Act. However, they were an obstacle for Plecker as many Virginians would claim Native American ancestry in order to escape the law:

> Under our new Racial Integrity law a white person cannot intermarry with one containing the slightest trace of negro blood, and for that reason I am interested in that subject as births and marriages are reported to us according to color, and I am called upon to establish that fact for the State. (Plecker to U.S. Census, Jan. 14th, 1925, Laughlin Papers, Truman Univ.)

One interesting aspect of the ongoing discussion between Laughlin and Plecker is a difficulty that plagued eugenic initiatives in both the United States and Hitler's Germany. Everyone seems to understand the general concept of 'race,' but scientifically describing them is something altogether more difficult, if not impossible. Eugenicists were never able to reach an agreed definition of race, and most disagreed on the racial boundaries or even the total number of races allegedly on the planet. Madison Grant, C.M. Goethe and Laughlin expended substantial effort in defining what a "white" person was in order to arrive at a legal definition in order to more effectively exclude anyone that fell outside of that description. The conversation between Laughlin and Plecker evidences this ongoing attempt to pin down a legal definition of the target and protected classes of people. The above-mentioned 25th of February 1928 letter continues along these lines:

> Our State Senate recently defeated an amendment to our Racial Integrity Act which would have defined a colored person as one with any ascertainable trace of colored blood. At present our law defines only a white person, and we find difficulty in prosecution. This bill was fought by the remnants of our so-called "Indians" who have in reality lost their identity by mixture with negroes and whites but who are still recognized as Indians. (BOX: D-4-3:12, Plecker to Laughlin, February 25th, 1928, Truman Univ. – Special Coll.)

Laughlin would write back to Plecker later on that year in order to gather legal or legislative research on racial definitions:

> Let me inquire whether you have any data concerning the definition of a white person listed in the laws of the several states. I have made a number of references to the Virginia racial integrity law which you have so well sponsored and just now I am anxious to find the definition by states. (BOX: D-4-3:12, Laughlin to Plecker, Nov. 22nd, 1928, Truman Univ. – Special Coll.)

This would be an integral part of the conversation that ensued between Plecker and the judges, attorneys, and legislators of the various States that were interested in copying Virginia's Racial Integrity Act. Plecker would copy Laughlin in a letter written to John C. Box, the Representative of Texas:

> Another defect in our law is that we define a white person but not a colored one. This has given us some trouble in court. Our law also defines that a person with a slight admixture of negro blood may not marry a white person nor register as a white in our office, but it does not specify that he shall not attend white schools nor ride in white coaches on trains. I would suggest that you make the law so as to be applicable for all purposes. (BOX: D-4-3:12, Plecker to Box, Aug. 16th, 1929, Truman Univ. – Special Coll.)

Keeping these efforts in mind, it is of note is that even a concerted effort to identify racial mixing in Hitler's Third Reich still struggled with the definitions of what it meant to be an "Aryan"; or more precisely, identifying who was and who was not Jewish. By the time Germany invaded Poland in 1939, a full six years after Hitler implemented his eugenic legislation, over 100,000 soldiers in Hitler's armed forces had some amount of Jewish ancestry. In some well-documented cases, some of the Third Reich's top military commanders had Jewish ancestry. The numbers were eventually whittled down. However, even as late as the push for Stalingrad, nearly 25,000 soldiers with one Jewish grandparent were still fighting for the

Nazis, mostly hoping and praying that their history would not come to light.

The issue spurned a back and forth between Laughlin and Plecker that took inventory of the various states that had begun to copy Virginia's 1924 Racial Integrity Law. For example, Plecker's November 24th, 1928 response states that Alabama and Georgia had "adopted laws based upon our Virginia Racial Integrity Law defining a white person as one with no trace of negro blood." Here was the "one-drop rule" at work. It is also known as the "one black ancestor rule," which is precisely the basis that Plecker used to terrorize the Virginia populace. It is popularly identified as a measure of the Ku Klux Klan influence on local governments. While that perception certainly holds some truth, the documents authored by Plecker and Laughlin indicate that it was the product of the political prowess of the American eugenics movement. Incidentally, some courts have called it the "traceable amount rule," with the concept of the traceability being directly derived from Laughlin's pedigree charts.

Other States used the 1924 Act as a model as well. A December 12th, 1928 letter from Plecker to Laughlin documents that "Hon. John R. Blake, Towson, Maryland, a member of the Maryland Legislature" requested a copy of the Racial Integrity Law. (Truman – Spec. Coll.) A May 24th, 1929 letter from Plecker to Laughlin claims that "at least eight other States seem to have laws forbidding the marriage of a white person to a negro or African, or person of negro or African descent." The majority of States were reluctant to follow Plecker's and Laughlin's lead, despite their efforts to effect change otherwise beyond what is regarded as the Jim Crow South. Plecker's letter continues along these lines:

> There is a disgracefully long list of states permitting the free intermarriage between whites and blacks. That is in reality the big problem as there is less tendency to intermarriage where there is any law at all forbidding intermarriage between the races, even though it be imperfect. A considerable number of our Virginia mixed breeds have migrated to Pennsylvania, New York and other northern states, I believe primarily to evade our marriage law. (BOX: D-4-3:12, Plecker to Laughlin, Nov. 24th, 1928, Truman Univ.)

It is also apparent that Laughlin utilized Walter A. Plecker's work to further his efforts abroad. A July 24th, 1929 letter from Plecker to Laughlin documents that Plecker sent "Professor Lundborg" of the "*Statens Institut for Rasbiologi*" in Uppsala, Sweden "samples of various publications issued from our office relating to racial integrity." [sic.] In other words, Plecker had sent one of pre-war Europe's leading eugenicists samples of Laughlin's work.

Information never dies. This is especially so when government uses it to extend its power over the population. It is a lesson that has yet to be learned, and the computer age only makes this fact increasingly more dangerous. Plecker continues his May 1929 letter by explaining how he was utilizing data from as far back as 1853 in order to round up racially-mixed individuals:

> Even since the passage of our 1924 Racial Integrity Act, near whites have been attempting, in some cases with success, especially when they leave home, to secure licenses to marry white persons. This law alone, with the determined insistence of our office that it be obeyed, and the education of the public as to the danger, has prevented many cased of miscegenation which would otherwise have occurred. A considerable number are leaving the State and being married elsewhere, especially in Washington. ---- Our office is gradually accumulating evidence as to the origin of mixed families and groups. We are greatly aided in this by being in possession of the old birth and death records secured during the period of 1853-1896 by the officers who visited the homes annually for the assessment of taxes. These officers were acquainted with the racial status of the people, and correctly listed the mulattoes, and before the war between the States, the free negroes and the slaves. Many descendants of these free negroes are now making determined efforts to secure white classification and to send their children to white schools. (BOX: D-4-3:12, Plecker to Laughlin, May 24th, 1929, Truman Univ.)

This is something to keep in mind as the 21st Century unfolds the capacity to collect population data on unprecedented scales. A 1928 letter from Plecker to Madison Grant explains that Plecker had also been relying on demographic data collected by the Virginia government in 1870. Plecker explains to Grant:

> It is impossible to estimate the value of these 1870 reports alone in establishing the racial status of those who were then classed as mulattoes, but who are now posing as white. ---- I am much interested in your statement of January 10th, 1928 that the ultimate aim of your group is to secure a card index representing each individual in the United States and that Prof. Irving Fisher, of Yale, thinks this is possible. If this would include the racial status of the individuals, it would be of extreme value. (BOX: D-4-3:12, Plecker to Grant, Jan. 13th, 1928, Truman Univ.)

Likewise, a letter from Plecker to Laughlin, written on the letterhead of the "Commonwealth of Virginia Bureau of Vital Statistics" in Richmond explains that Plecker sourced "marriage bonds" going back to about 1630. The same letter speaks of a "Montague Bill" which would instruct the Director of the Census to print the census records from 1800 to 1840. Plecker mentions that the "Genealogical Society" was backing the bill. The letter goes on to state:

> Our usual sources of information is our old birth and death records covering the period 1853 through 1896 and our marriage records going back to 1853. I do not think it is wise to emphasize this point as it might react against us, but I am counting much upon the census records in aiding us in establishing the racial status of our citizens. (BOX: D-4-3:12, Plecker to Laughlin, February 25th, 1928, Truman Univ.)

The use of census information for eugenic causes would of course have a much more pronounced impact in National Socialist Germany. Hitler's Third Reich used IBM tabulating machines, the predecessors to modern day computers, in order to identify any trace of Jewish ancestry in its population by cross-referencing census data. Edwin Black's famous book, "IBM and the Holocaust," documents how the Third Reich leased IBM machinery in order to scour genealogical data. IBM technical personnel were permanently stationed in all of the major concentration camps as part of this effort.

Plecker certainly persued his victims with the zeal of a Gestapo officer. The archives at Truman have a collection of letters documenting how Plecker viciously hounded the citizens of Virginia, mercilessly ignoring their pleas and pursuing them with the zeal of a Gestapo agent. Apparently, Plecker was proud enough of these efforts that Plecker would send copies of the letters to Laughlin for his inspection or amusement. Laughlin obviously valued them as they survived the closing of the Eugenics Record Office as part of his personal papers, which meant Laughlin intentionally kept them when he and his wife returned to their hometown.

Another piece of correspondence on the letterhead of the Commonwealth of Virginia documents Plecker's excitement. It also serves as evidence that the "science" which was used to pass the 1924 Immigration Restriction Act would be effectively turned against American families that had lived in the United States for generations:

> I have just received a report of your hearing before the Committee on Immigration and Naturalization, March 7, 1928, which I have read with much interest. I am delighted to see that your views which are in exact accord with those held by the State of Virginia were so forcefully presented to this Committee and that reprints have gone abroad. Since we have a Racial Integrity Law defining a white person as one with no trace whatsoever of non white blood and as our Legislature is not unanimous on the wisdom of such law, I would be glad to know if you can have copies of this report mailed to all of our legislators. As it is the duty of the Clerks to issue marriage licenses and to determine when it may be done, it would be well if they could receive copies also, as well as our Judges, Commonwealth's Attorneys, and county Superintendents of Schools. The question is constantly coming up as to the admission of mixed breeds into the white schools. Some are very careful as to that point and others less so. (BOX D-4-3:12, Plecker to Laughlin, June 28th, 1928, Truman Univ.)

In turn, Laughlin utilized Plecker's enthusiasm to further his efforts abroad. A July 24th, 1929 letter from Plecker to Laughlin documents that Plecker sent "Professor Lundborg" of the *Statens Institut for Rasbiologi*" in Uppsala, Sweden "samples of various publications issued from our office relating to racial integrity." [*sic*.] As will be discussed later, it was the Scandinavian countries, and not fascist Spain or Italy, which would join Germany in implementing ethnic cleansing and eugenic programs.

Aside from Plecker, Earnest Sevier Cox was yet another connection between Laughlin and the antagonists of the Civil Rights Era. Earnest Sevier Cox was a committed white supremacist who advocated on behalf of anti-miscegenation laws.

In 1922, Cox collaborated with the composer John Powell to create the Anglo-Saxon Clubs of America. Of note is that the elite white Virginians of the Anglo-Saxon Clubs worried that their efforts on behalf of the segregation might be confused with the more violent work of the Ku Klux Klan. Thus, they redoubled their efforts to present the laws as "scientifically" sound. They marketed the Racial Integrity Laws as progressive social policy based on science as opposed to the bigotry of the once Confederate South.

One only needs to peruse Cox's infamous book, "White America," to see that he clothes his argument with scientific claims. The book opens with the claim that "the problem of race is never a legal, economic, religious or even a social problem so much as it is a biological and political problem." Cox would reiterate this theme throughout "White America":

> It may readily be seen that the Negro problem is a part of the greater problem of heredity. When eugenics seeks to eliminate the unfit and establish the fit it has for its purpose not the betterment of physical types merely, but the establishment of those types of greatest value to progressive civilization. A race which has not shown creative genius may be assumed to be an unfit type so far as progress in civilization is concerned and is a matter of concern for the eugenist. Those who seek to maintain the White race in is purity within the United States are working in harmony with the ideals of eugenics. Asiatic exclusion and Negro repatriation are expressions of the eugenic ideal. (General Introduction, "White America," 1937 Edition)

Cox also quotes Professor William Bateson. Bateson is the British scientist best known for pioneering the science of genetics and coining the word "genetics." Cox cites Batson's "Heredity" speech, which was delivered before the Australian meeting of the British Association for the Advancement of Science in 1914:

> The factors which the individual receives from his parents and no others are those he can transmit to his offspring; and if a factor was received from one parent only, not more than one-half of the offspring, on an average, will inherit it. . . . I tis only quite recently that prominent horse breeders have come to see that the dam matters as much as the sire . . . The popular notion that any parents can have any kind of children within the racial limits is contrary to all experience, yet we have gravely entertained such ideas . . . At various times it has been declared that men are born equal and that the inequality is brought about by unequal opportunities. Acquaintance with the pedigrees of disease soon show the fatuity of such fancies. (Chapter 7, "White America," 1937 Edition)

These are the notions that Francis Galton popularized as part of his eugenic creed. The fact that Charles Darwin had incorporated Francis Galton's eugenics into "The Descent of Man," the book that followed "Origin of the Species," only served to help insulate eugenics it from criticism. Cox cites Darwin's "Descent of Man" as it was applied by Galton in "White America":

> When two races come into contact, one will expel the other from the commonly occupied or desired territory, or the races will adjust their differences through a

process of inter-race breeding, creating a mongrel race differing from the parent races but with a tendency to eliminate the specialized characters of the parent race. This result follows from the expression of biological laws and cannot be altered by educational program, legislative decree, or any amount of philanthropic interest. The characters of the higher race will tend to be obliterated in the mongrels, for the facilities of the higher race, the intellectual qualities which give it pre-eminence, are more specialized. The generalized characters of the lower race will eventually become established in the mongrel. (Chapter 3, "White America," 1937 Edition)

Cox used his fame and notoriety to muster publicity for the bill and, like Laughlin himself, appeared as an expert witness before the Senate Foreign Relations Committee. Cox used the influence that "White America" acquired for him to be chosen as an expert witness before Virginia's General Assembly in order to pass the 1924 Racial Integrity Act. Thus, it is of importance to understand that the racialist argument was not couched in the vitriol expected of the KKK types, but in the claims of Ivy League eugenicists. Of note is Cox's praise for Harvard's Lothrop Stoddard, the author of "The Rising Tide of Color" and Yale's Madison Grant's book "The Passing of the Great Race". Cox acknowledges in the General Introduction to "White America" that Grant read and critiqued the book prior to release, and thus generously cites him throughout. It is also interesting to see how Cox picked up where Laughlin, Madison Grant, and C.M. Goethe left of, in their untiring efforts to change the legalize which the argument was framed upon:

> It is well to state at this point that the writer is fully aware that the term "White Race" is not a satisfactory ethnological term. The term is used in its popular sense and is practically synonymous with the term "Caucasian Race". We know that the "White Race" in reality includes three or more "races". (Chapter 1, "White America," 1937 Edition)

According to Paul Lombardo's 2002 paper, "The American Breed," Cox had sought Madison Grant's help in getting "White America" published. When Charles Scribner's Sons, the publisher of Grant's various books declined, Cox printed the book under the auspices of the White America Society of Richmond, Virginia. Professor Lombardo recounts how Madison Grant used his contacts in Germany to give "White America" an audience with key members of the Third Reich's eugenic circle:

> White America also traveled to Europe. In 1930, Madison Grant asked that a copy be sent to Professor Hans Günther, "one of the most distinguished anthropologists of Germany," recently appointed to a new professorate at Jena. Günther was recognized as being the father of the German Nordic movement and was famous for developing a visual typology for classifying "racial types." Günther won his post at the University at Jena with the assistance of Nazi Party leader Wilhelm Frick; Hitler attended Günther's inaugural lecture. (Pg. 782, Lombardo, "The American Breed," Albany Law Review, Vol. 65, No. 3, 2002)

Günther had submitted a manuscript to J.F. Lehmann about Nordic knights at the time when Lehmann was trying to convince other German eugenicists to take up the cause of popularizing the Nordic lore. To put this into perspective, Lehmann was not just the publisher of Madison Grant's books in Germany but, if the reader recalls, also Hitler's publisher for "Mein Kampf." Paul Weindling's 1993 book, "Health, Race and German Politics Between National Unification and Nazism, 1870-1945," documents how Hitler's publisher, J.F. Lehmann, recruited Günther. :

> Lehmann persuaded Günther to write a piece on racial biological identity. He arranged for Günther to visit Lenz and Ploetz. Günther made revisions armed with an article by Lenz on 'The Nordic Race and the Blood-Mixture of our Eastern Neighbours'. Lenz, Ploetz and Lehmann all approved of the resulting work, and Lehmann invited Günther to write a racial study of the Germans. Lehmann supported Günther's research with money and such scientific materials as photographs of racial types, and encouraged him to acquire the skill of a practicing anthropologist. (Pg. 312, "Health, Race and German Politics")

Günther's 1922 "Racial Lore of the German Volk" became an instant success. Lehmann sold over 30,000 copies by 1932. Lehmann then leveraged the books contents to justify his political endeavors. He used the contents to justify the idea that people of "Nordic" ethnicity had a superior right to lead the nation and had the right to protect German "blood." Lehmann would perpetuate this by publishing a steady stream of Günther's books. Günther would remain indebted to the Americans. Stefan Kühl quotes Günther praising Madison Grant:

> In February 1934, Hans F. K. Günther, race anthropologist and a special protégé of the Nazis, explained to his audience in a crowded hall at the University of Munich that it was remarkable that "American immigration laws were accepted by the overwhelming majority, although the United States appeared the most liberal country of the world." He referred to Grant and Stoddard as the **"spiritual fathers"** of immigration legislation and proposed that the laws serve as a model for Germany. (Pgs. 37-38, "Nazi Connection," emphasis mine)

A January 7th, 1936, letter from Madison Grant to Laughlin, which is still held at the Laughlin Papers at Truman University's Special Collections, documents that Grant was able to obtain a copy of Hans Günther's book at a time when it was very hard to get. Grant leant Laughlin the copy of "The Racial Elements in European History." This copy was likely sent courtesy of J.F. Lehmann, as Lehmann was also be the publisher of Rudolf Polland's 1925 translation of "The Passing of the Great Race" into *"Der Untergang der grossen Rasse, die Rassen als Grundlage der Geschichte Europas."* Polland would contribute to "race hygiene" theories on his own in *"Die Rassenhygiene im medizinischen Unterricht,"* which appeared in the journal *"Wiener medizinische Wochenschrift"* in 1939 (Pgs. 875-878).

This is how WWII Nazi eugenics bridges over to significantly and negatively impact the post-war civil rights struggle in the United States. As specified by Günther, the Americans were the "spiritual fathers" of Nazi eugenics. He would

not be the first or the last one of Hitler's cohorts to make such a claim. More importantly, one of the men that was the impetus behind the Civil Rights opposition would recognize this sybiosis and leverage it further. Cox and Powell's Anglo-Saxon Clubs were not only instrumental in passing the 1924 Racial Integrity Laws in Virginia. Much of this work was done with the help of the very wealthy and influential, Wickliffe Draper, the person which Laughlin would found the infamous Pioneer Fund that ensured that eugenics would have financial backing even after The Holocaust. Cox first met Draper at the twenty-fourth meeting of the Eugenics Research Association in 1936. Earnest Sevier Cox and John Powell were both an instrumental part of the Pioneer Fund's eugenic campaign during the Civil Rights struggle in the United States. Cox's "White America" book would be released first in 1923, but would have editions in 1925, 1937, and as late as 1966. Amongst Cox's other racialist publications are:
- "Let My People Go" in 1925.
- "Lincoln's Negro Policy" in 1938.
- "Teutonic Unity" in 1938.
- "Unending Hate" in 1955.
- "Black Belt Around the World" in 1963.
- "Jim Crow's Defense" in 1965.

It is interesting to note that Cox not only distanced himself from the KKK's activities, but took a position of antipathy against the American South, namely in his 1926 book, "The South's Part in Mongrelizing the Nation" and his 1940 "Three Million Negroes Thank the State of Virginia." Professor Lombardo documents that Wickliffe Draper had purchased one thousand copies of "White America," of which 800 copies were to be distributed to whomever Cox suggested. Cox would send copies to every member of the United States Congress. The Racial Integrity Laws that Cox's infamous book helped pass stood until the U.S. Supreme Court's 1967 ruling in Loving v. Virginia, which declared Virginia's ban on interracial marriage to be unconstitutional. The Court unanimously held that prohibiting and punishing marriage based on racial qualifications violated the Equal Protection Clause of the Fourteenth Amendment. The Court held, "There can be no doubt that restricting the freedom to marry solely because of racial classifications violates the central meaning of the Equal Protection Clause." The Court also found that the Virginia law deprived the Loving family of liberty without due process:
> The freedom to marry has long been recognized as one of the vital personal rights essential to the orderly pursuit of happiness by free men.... To deny this fundamental freedom on so unsupportable a basis as the racial classifications ...is surely to deprive all the State's citizens of liberty without due process of law.

While Buck v. Bell has not been overturned by the Court, Loving v. Virginia certainly comes close with its invocation of the Equal Protection Clause. The Equal Protection Clause has since been interpreted to pertain to persons with "disabilities," which as we have seen, were the primary target of eugenic sterilization. Of course, the "equal protection clause" of the Fourteenth Amendment had preceded all of these so-called Progressive pieces of legislation. Therefore rendering the ever-changing conclusions of the Supreme Court only that much more frivolous, and disturbingly unpredictable.

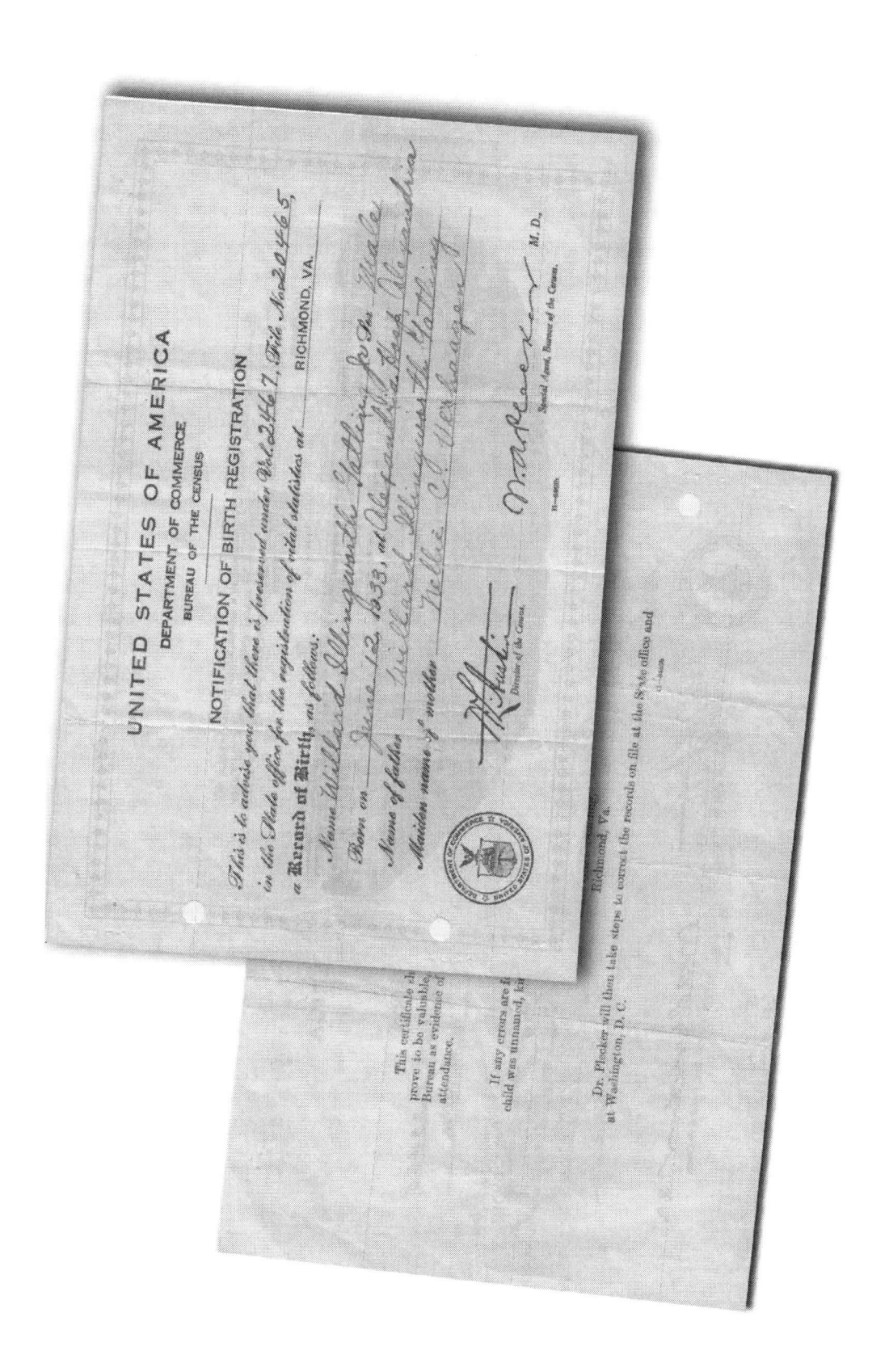

UNITED STATES OF AMERICA
DEPARTMENT OF COMMERCE
BUREAU OF THE CENSUS

NOTIFICATION OF BIRTH REGISTRATION

This is to advise you that there is preserved under Vol. 2467, File No. 20465, in the State office for the registration of vital statistics at RICHMOND, VA., a **Record of Birth**, as follows:

Name *Willard Ellingworth Gethins, for the Hale*

Born on *June 12, 1933*, at *Alexandria, Washington*

Name of father *Willard Ellingworth Gethins*

Maiden name of mother *Nellie C. Vershagen*

W.M. Austin, Director of the Census

N.A. Pleneary, M.D.
Special Agent, Bureau of the Census

This certificate sh[...]
prove to be valuable
Bureau as evidence o[...]
attendance.

If any errors are f[...]
child was unnamed, kin[...]

Dr. Plecker, Richmond, Va.,
at Washington, D. C. will then take steps to correct the records on file at the State office and

1925 - INT. FEDERATION OF EUGENIC ORGANIZATIONS

> *"For the several employments and offices of our fellows,*
> *we have twelve that sail into foreign countries*
> *under the names of other nations (for our own we conceal),*
> *who bring us the books and abstracts,*
> *and patterns of experiments of all other parts.*
> *These we call merchants of light."*
> *- Francis Bacon, in his 1626 Utopian vision "The New Atlantis."*

History is clear on the recurring circus of catastrophes that happen whenever some idealist has the brilliant inspiration of erecting a utopian society. Utopias, by their very nature, survive on the sustenance of ideas. Francis Bacon illustrated this in describing the role intellectuals played in the creation of his utopian vision, "The New Atlantis." These "merchants of light" provided that most ephemeral, but crucial ingredient, indispensable to the creation of utopias; these "merchants" traded in ideas. The "merchants of light" of 20th Century utopianism, perfectionism, or collectivism also peddled in the currency of ideas. Ideas, ephemeral as they may be, still have consequences.

The 20th century "merchants of light" injected the masses with precise dosages of utopian dogma through propaganda. In 20/20 hindsight, the differences between the Fascist, Bolshevik, or National Socialist versions of "total states" may be academic to us. However, to the "merchants of light," as it is with any good merchant, the miniscule differences between them and their bitter competitors were magnified beyond reason.

We must remember that Germany was trying to lift itself out of the devastation caused by World War I and the subsequent Great Depression. It can be said that the market was ripe for utopian schemes. Historians have adequately documented the street level violence that broke out among the different factions in the absence of direction or order. Historians have explained that this vacancy, this destitution in a decimated economy, led some to desire the heavy hand of the totalitarian state to provide what individuals were incapable of providing on their own in those circumstances. Through propaganda, they would sell the false virtues of surrendering to a statist utopia, to a "total state" that would lead them away from "degeneracy" and into world domination.

This becomes important to our dialog. These eugenicists, these "merchants" of elusive utopian ideas, were there ready to share all of the advances the United States and Britain had made in eugenic science and law. Eugenics had been a British creation by their proudest and most celebrated scientists. The international eugenic organizations run by Leonard Darwin, Laughlin, and Davenport became a beacon guiding anyone in the market for eugenic-utopian solutions. This is how Germany became the proving ground, the blank slate, for the most extreme of the eugenics movement's goals that could or would not be adopted by constitutional democracies committed to individual liberty. This is what drove the American eugenicists, Joseph DeJarnette, to utter that now infamous comment to the Richmond Times-Dispatch: **"The Germans are beating us at our own game."** According to Stefan Kühl, these professional jealousies were sentiments that were shared across the ocean:

> Professor Otto Reche, chairman of the Vienna Society for Racial Hygiene (Gesellschaft für Rassenpflege), expressed his concern over the fact that the Americans had become the world leaders in racial hygiene and urged Germans to catch up. (Pg. 117, "The Nazi Connection")

The eugenic organizations in the United States and Britain had long since been in correspondence and collaboration, and they had made it a point to recruit the Germans into their fold. Leonard Darwin had been instrumental in forwarding the Germans the work done by Laughlin on a "Model Eugenic Law." Truman University's Special Collections Department still hold a February 5th, 1925 handwritten letter from Leonard Darwin to Laughlin discussing the careful steps taken to recruit the Germans:

> Dear Mr. Laughlin, --- I am anxious that the Germans should join the commission but I am quite sure it would be unwise to put on any official pressure to make them do so. From my little experience they may not be very easy to deal with and they would become more difficult if any such pressure was applied. (Feb. 5th, 1925, Darwin to Laughlin, E-1-2:9, Truman Univ.)

Innocuous as the above letter may seem, it must be remembered that many historians paint the Germans as the impetus behind the eugenics that ultimately led to The Holocaust. This is not a view that can be supported by the evidence in the archives. Davenport founded the International Federation of Eugenics Organizations (IFEO) in 1925. It was headed up by Leonard Darwin. It was through Davenport's and Darwin's insistence and persistence that the Germans were brought into the organization. Darwin and Davenport insisted on including the Germans at a point where all others still nurtured animosities towards them in the wake of World War I.

A somewhat forceful letter from the Scandinavian eugenicists, Jon Alfred Mjöen illustrates the importance Europeans and Scandinavians gave to American eugenics as the driving force behind the movement:

> It seems to me that there must be a misunderstanding somewhere in regard to the scopes and aims of our <u>International</u> Eugenic work. And I do feel that it is my duty to express <u>my</u> opinion frankly. I was indeed very much disappointed with our last meeting. ---- What we need now is more science on one side and carefully worked out practical proposals on the other side, and less academic discussions. ---- The Americans (Davenport, Laughlin and others) have shown that even much more can be done. Indeed, they are making progress in a most promising way. But the Americans did not come to our Paris meeting. I am not astonished at it. It would hardly be worth while to travel from New York to Paris, to hear discussions of merely academic interests. ----- I read between the

lines of the American proposal, (Race crossing shall be discussed at Amsterdam 1927) that they want to be sure to have some result if they shall undertake a voyage to Europa to meet members of our International Commission. ----- It takes a good deal of patience to listen to so many banalities, so many words, words and again words without any ideas or views, or lines as were uttered by the French orators at our last meetings. ---- In short: The idea of "moving to Paris" must be dropped – and London continue as headquarters. The meetings must be so arranged that we are sure that the Americans will come and they will come if we are able to show <u>that our organization can take the lead in eugenic science and eugenic reform work.</u> [sic.] (Am. Phil. Soc., E.R.O. Records, TN 26977, Darwin, Leonard 1850-1943, Folder 1-4)

Thus, the American and Britons lead the way for key figures that would later assemble eugenic programs. Eugen Fischer, one of the leading eugenicists in Hitler's Germany was named the chairman of the IFEO's Commission on Bastardization and Miscegenation in 1927. Davenport aspired to create a "World Institute for Miscegenations," and "was working on a 'world map' of the 'mixed-race areas," which he introduced at a meeting of the IFEO in Munich, Germany in 1928. Some of the Third Reich's top eugenicists would ultimately fill positions of leadership at the IFEO. Ernst Rüdin would become the second president of the International Federation of Eugenic Organizations. A letter from Cora Hodson, the administrative secretary of the IFEO to Laughlin is still held at Truman University's Special Collection's Department:

> I have the honour to remind you that the Meeting of THE INTERNATIONAL FEDERATION OF EUGENIC ORGANIZATIONS is fixed this year for Thursday, Friday and Saturday, September 13th, 14th, and 15th. By kind invitation of Dr. Ploetz it will be held at:- MUNICH AND HERRSCHING, Nr MUNICH. (BOX: C-2-5:6, Hodson to Laughlin, May 30th, 1928, Truman Univ.)

The Laughlin Papers at Truman University hold the program distributed in Munich on September 13th through 15th of 1928. The document was titled "PROGRAMME FOR THE MUNICH MEETING OF THE INTERNATIONAL FEDERATION OF EUGENIC ORGANIZATIONS." On the 14th the conference planned "Lantern Lectures on race crossing" where Charles B. Davenport would talk about race crossing in Jamaica. Laughlin would address the conference on sterilization on the United States. The brief outline of the 1928 conference demonstrates Laughlin considering different titles around the general notion of "The Progress of Eugenical Sterilization in the United States." One of the bullet points is titled "Effectiveness as a means for race improvement." It is also interesting to see that Laughlin communicate his view of how eugenics paralleled horse breeding at this Munich conference:

> Most of the qualities which eugenics is concerned with in human heredity are, of course, different from racing capacity in the Thoroughbred horse, but they are similar and many of them if not all, are results of all the resources of the

individual.[sic] (Laughlin Papers, C-2-5:6 & D-2-2:7, "The Progress of Eugenical Sterilization in the United States," Truman Univ., undated)

It is of note that Laughlin made this presentation in Munich as early as 1928, as this evidences the fact that those prominent German scientists were interested in enacting eugenic-minded legislation much prior to Hitler's Third Reich. In 1928 most Germans had not heard of, and simply did not care about Adolf Hitler or his National Socialist party. Hitler was at that point regarded as the crank whose Beer-Hall Putsch had resulted in abysmal failure, and few, if any, foresaw the day that Hitler would be Chancellor. However, Laughlin's presentation takes on historical importance when one notes that amongst the other speakers were scientists like Alfred Ploetz, one of the other men responsible for the Third Reich's eugenic program. Davenport's presentation takes on historical importance when one notes that the Jamaican "race-crossing" study was conducted in collaboration with Eugen Fischer. Their study would later serve as the scientific basis for the sterilization of those with African ancestry in Hitler's Germany.

The PROGRAMME also addresses the issue of cooperating with the "International Birth Control Investigation Committee". Matthew James Connelly's 2008 book "Fatal Misconception: The Struggle to Control World Population" provides a quote from C.P. Blacker that illustrates the focus of this prominent British Birth Control association to the British Eugenics Society. Incidentally, the organization was started with support from the Rockefeller fund, as did the British, American, and German eugenics movements:

> Even the most sanguine supporter of sterilization must expect a considerable amount of time to elapse before dysgenic persons are sterilized in sufficient numbers to produce racial effects. And even after the lapse of years, it is possible that not more than a few hundred persons will be sterilized annually. Such results, excellent in themselves, would not have effects in any way comparable to those which would follow the discovery of a simple, reliable, and fool-proof contraceptive. **As an achievement of negative eugenics, such a discovery would have racial consequences thousands of times more important.** (Pg. 96, Connelly, 2008, "Fatal Misconception," emphasis mine)

Another key example is a September 17th, 1930 letter from Laughlin to Fredric Osborn written after attending the ninth meeting of the IFEO with Dr. Clarence Campbell. It explains, at least in part, why the Germans persisted in employing the otherwise outdated methods of phrenology. Leonard Darwin had been the host and Laughlin makes a point to state that "Human Measurement consumed a considerable portion of the attention of the Congress." "Human Measurement" was hardly more sophisticated than the infamous 19th Century science of phrenology, with eugenics adding slightly more robust behavioral statistics to the generalizations phrenology tried to make about the various ethnicities. This was the direct legacy of the founder of the eugenics movement, Francis Galton, who was known for his penchant for record keeping and statistical analysis. Extrapolations about human worth were made departing from this vast amount of information gathered. It is through the international eugenics movement that the 19th-Century phrenology would bridge over to the infamous measuring of humans that Hitler's National Socialists are now known for.

This multi-national group was reaching critical mass and ramping up its political influence just before the outbreak of a second world war. A "Fourth International Eugenics Congress" was planned to be held in Vienna in 1940. A letter from Laughlin to Ernst Rüdin documents how Laughlin passed onto Rüdin the latest information on immigration he had prepared for the U.S. Congress. This crucial package was sent just one month prior to the invasion of Poland:

> Dear Professor Rudin --- We have just received announcement of the Fourth International Congress of Eugenics. Workers in this field in all of the countries of Pan America congratulate the International Committee on its selection of Rudin as President, of Vienna for the site, and 1940 for the date. The whole setting presages a successful meeting. --- In order to hold the advances thus far made in building the science of Eugenics and to plan the next steps in research and trial, it is necessary that a new congress assembles soon; that its business be to take stock fo the world's knowledge of human heredity; to evaluate the technique of practical population-control; and to exchange experiences and plans among leaders in the biological betterment of mankind. --- I am taking the pleasure in sending by today's parcel post to your laboratory, addressed to the President of the Fourth International Congress of Eugenics, a package of books and papers. These comprise some records of the past congresses and current studies on the subject of eugenics as a science and as a practical art. [sic.] (BOX: C-2-5:3, August 12th, 1939, Laughlin to Rüdin, Truman Univ.)

Clearly, at this moment in history, the Americans were the recognized leaders of the international eugenics lobby. With so much evidence pointing to American leadership held in the various archives, it begs to question if this position of prominence was known to the general public of the era. American scientists are certainly no longer understood to be the impetus behind the movement that ultimately led to The Holocaust. Therefore, this author conducted a quick study of prominent newspapers of the era in order to reconstruct a profile of the American *zeitgeist* during the eugenics era between WWI and WWII. Two newspapers were selected: The New York Times and the Chicago Tribune, and key magazines such as TIME and LIFE were surveyed. Their online archives were mined for terms such as "eugenics," "race hygiene," "Nuremberg," "sterilization," "miscegenation", and other terms hand-picked to find long-forgotten newspaper articles. The date range utilized started with the year 1900 in order to capture what the international eugenics movement was publicized for leading up to WWII, and canvassed up to 1960 in order to capture any introspection or retrospection in the aftermath of the Nuremberg Trials. Several trends resulted:

1.) The American newspapers provided a pretty accurate description of what

eugenics in the U.S. and Britain was between 1900 and 1940.
2.) There was an in-depth and accurate understanding of the role of eugenics in Hitler's Germany, especially as the now infamous Nuremberg Laws were closely scrutinized between 1933 and 1935.
3.) Eugenics was understood as central to Hitler's National Socialism, and routinely depicted as such until up to 1942, upon which coverage serendipitously began to exclude any comparison between American and German eugenics.
4.) Eugenics was described and understood as an international movement, with Leonard Darwin, Karl Pearson, Charles Davenport, Eugen Fischer, Harry H. Laughlin, and others clearly documented as the champions of the cause.
5.) Any of the civil servants, lawyers, judges, or doctors in the 30 States in the Union that implemented Laughlin's "Model Eugenic Law" would have (or should have) easily recognized Hitler's three-panel eugenic courts as substantially similar, if not identical, to those in the United States.
6.) The term "eugenics" stops being mentioned as reports of the extermination began appearing. Newspapers that once reported the measures as part of National Socialism's eugenic policy started reporting them as something quite different.

More to the point, Hitler's policies were recognized as eugenic even prior to him assuming power and dominating the headlines. As early as 1931, the New York Times was characterizing Hitler's "racial purification" policy as based on a "criteria of race hygiene and eugenics." (NYT, Dec. 18th, 1931, "'Nazis' Would Assure Nordic Dominance, Sterilize Some Races, Ban Miscegenation") Another prime example of the eugenic aspect of National Socialism is the June 12th, 1938 New York Times article entitled "Bonus Marriages Boon To Germany." The article clearly explains Hitler's scheme of income redistribution to "eugenically desirable" couples. Anyone familiar with Leonard Darwin's work would have recognized the origins of the idea of income redistribution upon a eugenic criterion. The New York Times had covered the issue previously in an article entitled "Nazi Eugenics Policy Devised to Offset Increase of Slavs." The article is important as it documents the strong link between National Socialist eugenic sterilization and its racial policies:

> There are too many mental and physical defectives, whose support constitutes a serious burden on the State, declare the Nazis. Even if the decline in the birth rate should be arrested the proportion of elderly dependents will increase steadily, adding new burdens. At the same time the proportion of Slavs in Europe is increasing. This outlook does not please the National Socialists. Hence the many eugenic measures – the sterilization law, long-term loans to newly wedded couples and the measures designed eventually to eliminate all "non-Aryan" elements from Germany. (NYT, March 11th, 1934)

The same article documents the ban on "mixed marriages", and makes it amply clear that their eugenic policies deemed "non-Aryans" as "biologically inferior" and thus detrimental to the gene pool. Anyone in the United States, having to contend with anti-miscegenation laws such as Virginia's Racial Integrity law would have seen the similarities. These articles also cement National Socialist sterilization, segregation, and extermination policies as a form of "scientific racism" as opposed to the guttural type of racism typically attributed to it. It was clear that the fate of millions was firmly in the hands of doctors, as opposed to the infamous Brown Shirt street thugs.

An August 5th, 1933 New York Times article entitled "Purifying the German Race" makes the relationship between American and German scientists crystal clear. The article makes the observation that Hitler's eugenic program was substantially similar to those of other "civilized" nations. Most poignantly, it lays down the pretext that would be used by the eugenicists who supported Hitler's measures in the United States and Britain:

> When Goebbels, Nazi Minister of Propaganda, announced that the Germanic stock was to be improved by the application of eugenic principles a shudder must have run down many spines. If Hitler dared to revive belief in a discredited and wholly mythical Aryan as a racial ideal, what might be expected of a fanatical interpretation of Galton's teachings? But publication of the main provisions of the sterilization law to become effective on Jan. 1, 1934, dispels such fears. Indeed, the measure drafted to weed out physical degenerates who are beyond surgical aid, deaf-mutes and the feeble-minded differ in no important respect from those long advocated in every civilized country. Germany is by no means the first to enact laws to permit or compel sterilization of hereditary mental defectives. Some 15,000 unfortunates have thus far been harmlessly and humanely operated upon in the United States to prevent them from propagating their own kind. (NYT, Aug. 8th, 1933)

Another New York Times article appropriately entitled "The Week in Science: German Eugenics" also documented the link between American eugenic legislation being enacted by the Third Reich:

> Twenty-seven States have passed laws in this country to permit the sterilization of the hereditary feeble-minded and insane. By Jan. 1, 1930, more than 10,000 operations had been performed in twenty-five States. In California, the home of the **somewhat fanatical** Human Betterment Foundation, simple and painless operations have been performed on about 7,000 unfortunates, apparently with no harmful results. (NYT, July 23rd, 1933, emphasis mine)

This survey of the American *zeitgeist* at the eve of The Holocaust illustrates the amount of information the general public was privy to. This generation clearly understood that it was the professional ranks, involving scientists, doctors, nurses, lawyers, and judges that would carry out Hitler's eugenic program. More to the point, this generation understood that this program was not a product of the guttural racism as that practiced by the ranks of the Brown Shirts:

> Professor Alfred Schittenhelm of Kiel University --- He went on to say, however that a new era had begun in Germany in which the medical society would "actively and practically employ its energies in promoting national

reconstruction." This, apparently, is to be accomplished in part by having medical men and congresses pay more attention to the "race problem." Eugenics and heredity must be gone into when the society meets again next year, the professor announced. (NYT, Apr. 20th, 1933, "To Study 'Race Problem")

This is the critical importance of the IFEO, an institution that has gone largely overlooked by Holocaust historians. All the time that was saved by the IFEO in transferring ready-made laws literally translates to lives lost in the hundreds of thousands. Keep in mind that it took the likes of Laughlin and Davenport decades of work in the United States to mature these laws. Thus, having the benefit of their experience was a significant boon to the eugenicists in the Third Reich. Stefan Kühl, author of the 2002 book, "The Nazi Connection", documents how the IFEO was subsequently used by German eugenicists to justify the Third Reich's eugenic policies:

> In the summer of 1934, one and a half years after the Nazis came to power in Germany, the International Federation of Eugenic Organizations, meeting in Zurich, passed a resolution to which Nazi propaganda frequently referred in order to illustrate the international acceptance of their race policies. In this unanimously passed resolution, sent to the prime ministers of all the major Western powers, the IFEO stated that, despite all differences in political and social outlooks, the organization was "united by the deep conviction that eugenic research and practice is of the highest and most urgent importance for the existence of all civilized countries." It recommended that all governments "make themselves acquainted with the problems of heredity, population studies, and eugenics." It stated that eugenic principles should be adopted as state policies "for the good of their nations . . . with suitable regional modifications. German racial hygienists and Nazi race politicians viewed this resolution as confirmation of German and American dominance in the eugenics movement and as international approval of the 1933 German sterilization law. (Pgs. 26-27, "The Nazi Connection", Kühl)

To understand how much time was saved by German eugenicists, and thus how many lives were lost, one only need remember that the laws that Hitler's government implemented were verbatim translations from Laughlin's "Model Law." Recall that Laughlin had distilled his "Model Law" after almost a decade of surveying the laws of more than 30 states. Laughlin had spent decades gathering statistics and sourcing the expert opinion of the most prominent lawyers, judges, and legislators in the United States. Through the IFEO, Adolf Hitler was given access to tried and true law that had taken the best minds of the legislatures and courts of the United States various decades to mature. The perfecting of a model eugenic law had consumed a lot of Rockefeller, Carnegie, and Merriman money along with the sizeable staffs these institutions employed in Cold Spring Harbor to arrive at this work product. Through Ploetz, Fischer, and Rüdin, Hitler was given fully matured and proven legal mechanisms, and allowed to avoid having to start from scratch. The United States and Britain had enjoyed the luxury of developing these eugenic measures at the time when Germans could simply not aspire to do so because of the devastation following World War I and the Great Depression. This allowed the Hitler government to skip the decades that they had fallen behind in eugenics. One only need to gauge the numbers murdered per month by Hitler's henchmen to put a price on the true value of the time the American and British scientists saved for the Germans.

Juxtaposed against a timeline of history, this transfer of knowledge came at a fortuitous moment just after the Reichstag fire. It coincided with Hitler's consolidation of power by the passing of the Enabling Act of 1933. Most importantly, Hitler got what he wanted most: international legitimacy and the ability to claim that his racial laws were no different than those already adopted by the United States and Britain. The Laughlin Papers held at Truman University evidence that the relationship with Hitler's top scientists endured far into Hitler's reign and would have persisted if not for the outbreak of war.

INTERNATIONAL FEDERATION OF EUGENIC ORGANIZATIONS.

Vice-Presidents:
H. F. OSBORN, NEW YORK.
DR. PLOETZ, HERSCHING b. MUNICH.
DR. SCHLAGINHAUFEN, ZURICH.

Honorary President: MAJOR L. DARWIN, LONDON.
President: DR. CHARLES B. DAVONPORT.

Please reply to:
Administr. Secretary: MRS. HODSON,

THE INTERNATIONAL FEDERATION OF EUGENIC ORGANISATIONS.

President:
PROFESSOR RÜDIN,
Deutsche Forschungsanstalt
für Psychiatrie, Kaiser
Wilhelm Institut.
Kraepelinstrasse 2,
München N.23.

Honorary President: LEONARD DARWIN.
Hon. Vice President: H. F. OSBORN, New York.
Vice President: PROF. HERMAN LUNDBORG,
Statens Institut för Rasbiologi, Luna, Sweden.

Communications to—
Honorary Secretary:
Mrs. C. B. S. HODSON,
443 FULHAM ROAD,
LONDON, S.W.10.

Cables and Telephone—
LONDON: FLAXMAN 4817.

30th July, 1934.

Dr. H.H. Laughlin,
Eugenics Record Office,
Cold Spring Harbour,
Long Island,
New York.

Dear Dr. Laughlin,

    This letter is to introduce to you my very good friend, Dr. Gebhardt of Berlin, who sails for New York from Southampton on August 17th, and will be proceeding the first week in September to California where he is to show a Eugenics Exhibition taken in part from the two fine educational exhibitions which he has already created some years ago in Dresden and recently in Berlin.

    Dr. Gebhardt hopes later to visit Chicago and Baltimore, and is very anxious to meet not only people concerned with eugenic and genetical work, but also those who can show him of the health social services in the United States. He is anxious to meet you, and I know you will kindly give him introductions to other people who may either help him or in whose work he will be interested.

    Dr. Gebhardt and his wife stayed with me for a month a few years ago, when he spent a vacation in England for the purpose of studying our health services. He has been very kind and helpful to me ever since, and I am anxious to serve him in some way. Dr. Gebhardt's great knowledge and high character give him an exceptional position in Germany, where he stands quite outside all party concerns as an honoured personality and an acknowledged authority in his own particular field. Let me add my very hearty thanks for anything you are able to do for Dr. Gebhardt.

                  Yours very sincerely,

                    Cora Hodson

Address: Dr. Bruno Gebhardt,
c/o American Public Health Association,
50 West Fiftieth Street,
New York City.

1927 - BUCK v. BELL

> "We hold these truths to be self-evident, that all men are created equal, that they are endowed by their Creator with certain unalienable Rights, that among these are Life, Liberty and the pursuit of Happiness."
> – The Declaration of Independence

As soon as Virginia's Eugenical Sterilization Act was passed in 1924, the American eugenics lobby set out to find a test subject in order to test the constitutionality of the new law. In other words, they went in search of a guinea pig, a human they could legally deem "unfit" to reproduce, in order to test the new law. Albert Priddy had drafted Virginia's law with Aubrey E. Strode. It was based upon the "Model Eugenic Law" provided by Laughlin. They knew that in order to move the cause forward, the constitutionality of these newly passed eugenic sterilization laws would have to be "tested" at the Federal level. They selected 17-year-old Carrie Buck of Charlottesville. Carrie was at the time an inmate at Priddy's Virginia Colony.

Priddy was the superintendent of the Virginia Colony, also known as the Lynchburg Colony, or simply as the Colony. The Colony had become a collecting place for poor, uneducated, white Virginians who were regarded as "unfit" by the state. The fact that Carrie was a "ward of the State" also gave them the power to handpick the attorney that would defend her in court. They chose attorney Irving P. Whitehead, who not only had served on the Board of Directors of the Virginia Colony but was also a true believer in the eugenics movement. All three men knew one another politically, professionally, and personally for many years prior to the Buck litigation and Whitehead was chosen because he was ideologically reliable.

Laughlin did not personally attend the proceedings, but Dr. Arthur Estabrook, a member of the Eugenics Record Office appeared as an expert witness. Estabrook was not just a member of Laughlin's team at Cold Spring Harbor, but a seasoned eugenicists that had published "The Jukes in 1915" and "The Tribe of Ishmael." The Laughlin Papers held at Truman University have letters between Laughlin and Estabrook dated March 30th, 1928 and April 2nd, 1928 documenting that Estabrook worked for Laughlin. Estabrook was being used by Laughlin to travel around the country to collect information on the sterilization legislation of various states. Thus, the "experts" called by the courts in order to provide a supposedly impartial "medical opinion" of Carrie Buck were part of the organization responsible for drafting the law in question. They clearly had a conflict of interest. Professor Paul Lombardo's book, "Three Generations No Imbeciles" has become the authoritative account of this crucial episode in history. Lombardo reiterates the rancid political entanglements behind the eugenicist's <u>Buck v. Bell</u> initiative:

> Whitehead practiced law more than twenty-eight years before the *Buck* case, and he was no novice in the courtroom. Given this level of experience and the

compensation he received, it is only fair to evaluate his performance at Carrie Buck's trial as grossly negligent, but that description does not adequately portray the fraud he inflicted on his client and the court. Whitehead was not merely incompetent; his failure to represent Carrie Buck's interests was nothing less than betrayal. His poor showing in court was damning enough, but if the letter Aubrey Strode wrote recommending Whitehead for advancement to the position of general counsel to the Federal Land Bank at Baltimore the week before the *Buck* trial had become publicly known at the time, it might have raised serious suspicions about Whitehead's loyalties. Whitehead's duty to Carrie Buck was clear. Despite his friendship with Priddy, his connection to the Colony, and his personal support for sterilization, he had a duty to oppose Priddy's plan to sterilize her. Virginia cases long established every lawyer's obligation of loyalty to a client. Reporting regularly to your opponent's client and declaring your pleasure upon losing a case, as Whitehead did, violated every norm of legal ethics. Whitehead acted as if his real client was not Carrie Buck but his now-deceased friend Albert Priddy, whose sterilization program he had supported for over a decade. (Pgs. 154-155, "Three Generations No Imbeciles," Lombardo)

Aubrey E. Strode presented more than a dozen witnesses including four "expert" witnesses in the field of eugenics to prove Carrie's "feeblemindedness." One of them was Laughlin. Laughlin submitted sworn "expert" testimony analyzing Carrie and her family despite the fact he had never met any members of the Buck family. He confidently reasserted Priddy's statements that Carrie Buck and her family were members of "the shiftless, ignorant, and worthless class of anti-social whites of the South." Of significance to the legal proceedings was that Whitehead never challenged or contested Laughlin's allegedly "scientific" opinions.

One of the most flagrant injustices of the case was the contention that Carrie Buck was promiscuous and that promiscuity was a hereditary trait running in her family. Carrie Buck's foster parents had committed her to the Virginia Colony shortly after Carrie gave birth to an illegitimate child. The fact of the matter is that Carrie's pregnancy was the result of being raped by a relative of her foster parents, a point that Irving Whitehead also failed to raise during the court proceedings. They also claimed that Carrie's alleged promiscuity was hereditary by falsely claiming that Carrie herself had been an illegitimate child. This is a mischaracterization that could easily have been challenged since a marriage certificate existed proving that Emma, Carrie's mother, was married to Carrie' father. (See image at end of chapter.) They also called one of Carrie's school teachers to the stand. The teacher was brought in to testify that Carrie had passed flirtatious notes to schoolboys as evidence in support of the claim that she had inherited sexual precociousness from her mother.

Hereditary "feeblemindedness" was the technical charge used to degrade Carrie's biological worth, and by extension justify their claim that her genes were a danger to the society. Carrie's mother, Emma Buck, had been committed to the colony, so the foster family found an easy out of their troubles by accusing Carrie of being feebleminded. The logic was that since Emma and Carrie were already institutionalized then Carrie's allegedly illegitimate daughter, Vivian, was likely to grow up to be an "imbecile." A nurse testified "there is a look about it that is not quite normal," basing this claim on a single photograph of Vivian, and not an actual physical examination. Estabrook gave the expert opinion that at the age of six months, Vivian was "below the average," and likely to be feebleminded as well.

At no point during this onslaught of baseless accusations did Whitehead call witnesses in Carrie's defense. He made no challenges to the charges about Carrie's mental health. Nor did he call any experts question the science behind the eugenical theory espoused by the so-called expert witnesses. This failure to defend against the accusations had the legal effect of admitting to them. It also barred Carrie's defense to raise them at any appeal, as American jurisprudence disallows the entering of new evidence during the appeals process. Appeals courts in the United States cannot re-litigate a case. Therefore, the "expert" testimony by Laughlin's fellow eugenicists stood as the only medical opinion entered into evidence from the lower court all the way up to the United States Supreme Court.

The failure to defend can hardly be seen as an oversight when one remembers that the attorneys on both sides of the trial were avid supporters of the eugenics movement. Professor Lombardo's book, "Three Generations, No Imbeciles: Eugenics" convincingly documents how the outcome of the trial was the product of fraud and collusion:

> I found Carrie's grade school report cards and her daughter's honor roll record, proving the Holmes opinion false. Years later, I found the photos of the infamous "three generations" buried in the archives of a former eugenics expert; that collection showed how he head manufactured evidence to fit the state's case against Carrie Buck. Other research revealed handwritten minutes of an official meeting between Carrie's appointed lawyer and her adversaries. Those records confirmed that the case was not just a tragedy. It was a legal sham. (Pg. xi, "Three Generations No Imbeciles," Lombardo)

Professor Lombardo returns to the extreme negligence, or rather, overt collusion by Carrie Buck's lawyer:

> The evidence presented at Carrie Buck's trial was transparently weak; with even a modest amount of effort, a competent lawyer could have challenged both the scientific premises of the Virginia sterilization law and the description of Carrie Buck's family offered by the state. But that defense never materialized, in large part because Carrie's lawyer had o intention of defending her. He offered no rebuttal to the state's arguments for surgery; he called no witnesses to counter the experts who had condemned the Buck family; he never explained that Carrie had not become a mother by choice, but that she had been raped. (Pg. xi, "Three Generations No Imbeciles")

Professor Lombardo opines that the entire case, from lower court on up to the

United States Supreme Court, was nothing more than a planned and calculated scheme to significantly alter the laws of the nation in order to favor the legislative premises behind the eugenics movement:

> That lawyer, Irving Whitehead, was a founding member of the Virginia Colony's board of directors and a major supporter of the sterilization campaign of Dr. Albert Priddy, the Colony's superintendent. Following his failure at trial, Whitehead secretly met with Priddy and the Board and voiced satisfaction that the case was proceeding as planned. He had betrayed his client, defrauded the court, and set in motion a series of events that history has uniformly condemned.
> ---- Yet the Supreme Court was unaware of these details and, in a nearly unanimous vote, approved the state sterilization law. In retrospect, it would be reasonable to conclude that the result in Buck was inevitable. In fact, the very opposite is true. **Carrie Buck was the victim of an elaborate campaign to win judicial approval for eugenic sterilization laws.** (Pg. xi, "Three Generations No Imbeciles," emphasis mine)

Predictably, the Amherst County Circuit Court affirmed the validity of the sterilization law. Then in November of 1925, the Virginia Supreme Court of Appeals affirmed the ruling of the county court. A petition for certiorari was filed, briefs were submitted and on May 2nd, 1927, the United States Supreme Court upheld Virginia's eugenical sterilization law by a vote of 8 to 1. Justice Oliver Wendell Holmes, Jr. authored the opinion. Of note is the fact that Oliver Wendell Holmes, Jr also was Weld Professor of Law at the Harvard Law School, just like the long roster of Ivy League educated eugenicists. Note that according to Justice Holmes the case hinged on the determination of "due process":

> The case comes here upon the contention that the statute authorizing the judgment is void under the Fourteenth Amendment as denying to the plaintiff in error **due process of law** and the equal protection of the laws. (BUCK v. BELL, SUPERINTENDENT. No. 292. Supreme Court of United States. -- Argued April 22nd, 1927. Decided May 2, 1927, emphasis mine)

What exactly was the "process" being contested? The "process" in question was Laughlin's "Model Eugenic Law," which sought to satisfy "due process" by creating a three-panel eugenic court in order to determine a citizen's "fitness." Eight of the nine justices of the United States Supreme Court believed that Laughlin's "Model Law" satisfied the Constitution's requirement of "due process." The highest court in the land ruled that the forcible deprivation of reproductive capacity was lawful as long as the court procedure was orderly, with the opportunity for appeal, and consistent with the legal procedures typical of American jurisprudence. Not surprisingly, the Court's opinion ends with a justification of the State's prerogative over an individual's right to bodily integrity. The opinion is quoted here at length so its logic can be clearly understood:

> The attack is not upon the procedure but upon the substantive law. It seems to be contended that in no circumstances could such an order be justified. It certainly is contended that the order cannot be justified upon the existing

grounds. The judgment finds the facts that have been recited and that Carrie Buck "is the probable potential parent of socially inadequate offspring, likewise afflicted, that she may be sexually sterilized without detriment to her general health and that her welfare and that of society will be promoted by her sterilization," and thereupon makes the order. In view of the general declarations of the legislature and the specific findings of the Court, obviously we cannot say as matter of law that the grounds do not exist, and if they exist they justify the result. We have seen more than once that the public welfare may call upon the best citizens for their lives. It would be strange if it could not call upon those who already sap the strength of the State for these lesser sacrifices, often not felt to be such by those concerned, in order to prevent our being swamped with incompetence. It is better for all the world, if instead of waiting to execute degenerate offspring for crime, or to let them starve for their imbecility, society can prevent those who are manifestly unfit from continuing their kind. The principle that sustains compulsory vaccination is broad enough to cover cutting the Fallopian tubes. Jacobson v. Massachusetts, 197 U.S. 11. **Three generations of imbeciles are enough.** (BUCK v. BELL, SUPERINTENDENT. No. 292. Supreme Court of United States. -- Argued April 22nd, 1927. Decided May 2nd, 1927, emphasis mine)

Depending on where a particular historian falls in the highly polarized political dichotomy in the United States, Justice Oliver Wendell Holmes, Jr. is either remembered as a champion of the people or as a symbol of a government abusing its powers. If the recollection comes from the later, the portion of the Buck v. Bell opinion that states "**three generations of imbeciles are enough**" has come to exemplify the extreme arrogance of Justice Holmes. More to the point, it is an opinion that resonated around the world with eugenic-minded legislators. Lombardo rightfully describes the Buck v. Bell case an "egregious example of governmental malfeasance under color of law." He documents that the German defense team at Nuremberg submitted the Buck v. Bell opinion as evidence under the exhibit titled "Race Protection Laws of Other Countries." (Pg. 239, "Three Generations")

How could it be possible that the Supreme Court of the United States, the one body of government that should have been the shining beacon of individual rights, came to be aligned with the minds behind the eugenic laws of the Third Reich? The U.S. Supreme Court has justified its decision in the Buck case by clinging to the premise that the welfare of all citizens should take precedence over the rights of individuals to procreate. This "precautionary" posture was justified by citing a 1905 case that upheld as constitutional the forcible vaccination of citizens. It relied on the Jacobson v. Massachusetts, 197 U.S. 11 (1904) case which upheld a Massachusetts law requiring schoolchildren to be vaccinated against smallpox. The reader will recall that this case was specifically cited by Laughlin in his "Eugenical Sterilization" book that Judge Olson had printed and distributed to key members of the American legal community. Note the concept's prominence in the Supreme Court's opinion:

> It is better for all the world, if instead of waiting to execute degenerate offspring for crime, or to let them starve for their imbecility, society can prevent those who are manifestly unfit from continuing their kind. The principle that sustains compulsory vaccination is broad enough to cover cutting the Fallopian tubes. (Jacobson v. Massachusetts, 197 U.S. 11, 25 S.Ct. 358, 49 L.Ed. 643, 3 Ann.Cas. 765.)

It is of note that even institutions not necessarily known for a libertine ethos became outraged at the amount of intrusiveness these intellectual elites were intent upon. The Catholic Church put up the most consistent and formidable challenge to the eugenicists, and in turn, the leadership of the international eugenics movement identified it as their greatest opposition. The Catholic Church stepped in to try to rescue Carrie Buck from her fate, albeit too late and likely oblivious to the fact that Carrie's own legal defense team was in on the fraud. Professor Lombardo documents that Charles F. Dolle, the executive secretary of the National Council of Catholic Men, paid Whitehead to file a petition for rehearing. Unfortunately, this was too little and too late. Recall that American jurisprudence operates on the legal concept that no new evidence can be introduced at a rehearing or appeal. As discussed earlier, Carrie's defense had intentionally failed to present any evidence, call any witnesses, or challenge the allegedly scientific concepts presented. Thus, the petition Charles F. Dolle requested would have to be limited. Professor Lombardo documents that Whitehead, the man that had violated just about every ethical principle, argued against Dolle's insistence for a vigorous challenge as he was liable to be criticized for attempting to re-litigate in a superior court.

The petition would ultimately be written by a lawyer for the Roman Catholic's men's group. Even the "watered down" (Lombardo's term) petition challenged <u>Jacobson v. Massachusetts</u> precedent as inappropriate. That legal precedent permitted an intrusion of individual autonomy only when the general public health was seriously endangered. The legal standard applied to satisfy this "endangerment" would have to amount to an epidemic. Furthermore, the <u>Jacobson</u> decision merely imposed a relatively small fine on Reverend Jacobson for violating the vaccination law, as opposed to Carrie Buck's permanent bodily alteration by surgical procedure.

Carrie Buck was operated upon, receiving a compulsory salpingectomy, a form of tubal ligation. She was later paroled from the institution as a domestic worker to a family in Bland, Virginia. It is interesting to note that Carrie was an avid reader until her death in 1983. Vivian did very well in school despite Justice Holmes' "three generations" condemnation. It is worth noting that Vivian was listed on her school's honor roll of April 1931. Unfortunately, Vivian died of complications from measles in 1932.

Laughlin wrote that year to Judge Harry Olson, who had printed Laughlin's "Model Eugenical Law." Laughlin proudly reported to Olson that the case had been "a complete victory for the authority of a state to use eugenical sterilization for preventing the reproduction of degenerates." (Pg. 159, Hassencahl) This had after all been the goal of the international eugenics movement; the passing of legislation and its implementation.

Historically speaking, it is through the passing of legislation that governments give a veil of legitimacy to the deprivation of rights, and this process has historically been done under the guise of benefiting or protection of society. Court precedents open paths to scenarios unimaginable at the moment of their passing. More often than not, court opinions are what historians point to as the proverbial "slippery slope" upon which civilization descends. Even unrelated issues come into play. American jurists interpret the logic behind precedent in ways sometimes only tangentially related to the core issue of the cited reference. It is in this way that Justice Holmes used the 1905 Jacobson decision on compulsory vaccination, which was but a mild attack on an individual's bodily integrity, to justify compulsory sterilization that permanently removed an individual's reproductive capabilities. In 1973, courts even stretched the Buck v. Bell precedent to apply to the right to public education of minorities in the case of In San Antonio Independent School Dist. v. Rodriguez, 411 US 1 - Supreme Court 1973.

The State courts also revisited the Buck v. Bell opinion decades later in the Federal Court case of Poe v. Lynchburg Training School and Hospital, 518 F. Supp. 789 - Dist. Court, WD Virginia 1981. The issue before the court in 1981 was the following "due process" before depriving a citizen of "life, liberty, or the pursuit of happiness":

> In 1924, the Commonwealth enacted legislation providing for the sexual sterilization of "mental defectives" in certain cases. 1924 Acts of Assembly, Chap. 394. As set forth in defendants' memorandum in support of the motion to dismiss, the statute specifically prescribed certain preliminary procedural steps including notification to the individual, or his or her parent, guardian, or committee as might be appropriate.

As time passed, more and more individuals became aware that they had been victims and that they had been sterilized without even have been told. The victims brought their case before the Supreme Court of the State of Virginia:

> Several of the individual plaintiffs in this case underwent involuntary sterilization pursuant to the statute. These plaintiffs also purport to sue on behalf of all persons who have been involuntarily sterilized at governmental institutions in Virginia under color of state law. Two individual physicians have also joined as plaintiffs. These doctors also seek to represent a class of physicians who have provided or are willing to provide medical services to the involuntarily sterilized persons and who are unable to provide adequate services due to the defendants' alleged refusal to appropriately notify the sterilized persons as to their medical status and alternatives.

The State court threw out and dismissed part of the claim based mainly on the view that the doctors had acted according to a law that had been valid by contemporary standards. Most poignantly, the "highest court in the land," the United States Supreme Court, had upheld this decision in 1927:

> Regardless of whatever philosophical and sociological valuation may be made regarding involuntary sterilizations in terms of current mores and social thought, the fact remains that the general practice and procedure under the old Virginia statute were upheld by the highest court in the land in Buck v. Bell, supra. It is no answer for the plaintiff to allude to changing patterns of social and constitutional thought as a ground for reopening the inquiry.

According to the logic of Virginia's Supreme Court, the doctors were to be protected because at the time, the "highest court in the land" deemed these forcible and compulsory acts as legal. This is where the uncomfortable juxtaposition to the Nuremberg Trials of the German doctors is exposed. Clearly, the various German doctors could and did claim they were acting within the laws passed by their legally elected legislature.

The <u>Buck v. Bell</u> decision brings Thomas Jefferson's pleadings for limited government front and center. The fact that the government can be deemed to act lawfully in wantonly mutilating the bodies of its citizens is a warning to any citizenry that would trust too much in government. Pathetically enough, the court's review turned on the technical aspect of "notice," and not the grander principles at issue:

> The court now directs its attention to those portions of plaintiffs' complaint and prayer dealing with defendants' alleged failure to notify plaintiffs of the fact of their sterilization and to otherwise provide information and assistance as might be appropriate. As suggested above, the old Virginia statute contained provisions which insured, at least in theory, that persons considered for involuntary sterilization, and their representatives, **would be well advised prior to the surgery as to its purpose.** Plaintiffs have alleged facts which indicate that in at least some instances, such notification was not provided and that potential candidates were affirmatively misled as to the purpose of the surgery. Plaintiffs contend that many such persons who were inadequately or inaccurately informed have suffered and continue to suffer medical, emotional, and mental problems, arising in large part from unsuccessful and uninformed attempts to deal with their infertility. Plaintiffs contend that defendants continue to refuse to notify and inform all those affected persons despite the fact that defendants now have reason to believe that some involuntarily sterilized persons were not properly notified at the time of their hospitalization. In short, plaintiffs contend that, in actual practice, the notification provisions of the statute were often not honored and that state officials have continued to perpetrate the deprivation through their subsequent refusal to notify all involuntarily sterilized persons as to their status.

Judges and Justices have repeatedly stated that the definition of "due process" can only be said to be grounded in the premise of "basic fairness" and "decency," but that "due process" is otherwise a difficult concept to pin down. In essence, what the court was explaining was that Carrie Buck and her family had been given notification and an opportunity to appeal the decision of the panel, as prescribed by the law, and therefore they were acting in compliance with "due process." People outside of the legal profession probably have a hard time reconciling this reasoning. In the convoluted lawyer logic, it is ok to mutilate someone's genitals against their will, but apparently it is not ok to do so without notifying the victim of your intentions beforehand.

From a pedestrian standpoint, it is hard to understand the notion that an option for appeal ameliorates the injustice of coerced bodily mutilation. The cruel implications that any appeal to a governing elite, drunk with power and believing in their infallibility, is a reasonable recourse for the weakest amongst us is preposterous. Carrie Buck was certainly a person that can be said to be one of the weaker members of society, and in dire need of protection from the overwhelming power of the state:

> The court recognizes that in making these arguments, and in attempting to distinguish Buck v. Bell, supra, plaintiffs have relied primarily on what they perceive as a constitutional deficiency in the procedural aspects of the old Virginia statute. The court also recognizes that Buck dealt with an attack to the statute's substance rather than its procedure. Nevertheless, in delivering the court's opinion in Buck, Justice Holmes specifically noted that ". . . there is no doubt that . . . plaintiff in error has had due process of law." 274 U.S. at 207, 47 S.Ct. at 584.

While the crassness of Justice Oliver Wendell Holmes, Jr's pronouncement that "three generations of imbeciles are enough" has rightfully earned him scorn, we must remember that only one Justice voted against him. In hindsight, the fact that Hitler's henchmen used the Buck v. Bell case to defend themselves is embarrassing enough. However, the comparison goes beyond a superficial one. Historians must engage in serious introspection as to what exactly was the United Supreme Court truly deliberating. The United States Supreme Court proclaimed these eugenic concepts to be constitutional based on the finding that procedure was followed, and that the opportunity for appealing to a higher court satisfied "due process."

However, the true value of these legal formalities can be called into question when the defendants are prejudged as a consequence of their heredity. In other words, if the two preceding "generations" were "enough" to convince Justice Oliver Wendell Holmes, Jr. that Carrie should be forcibly sterilized, then of what use was the pretense of observing procedure? Carrie had been condemned before she ever entered the court, or for that matter, before she was ever even born, as a consequence of her mother's and grandmother's alleged eugenical worth.

This practice of predetermining worth, and by extension the results within the courtroom is too similar to the predetermined legal outcomes of Hitler's sham court system to ignore. These are the murky waters the American courts and State legislatures stepped into when they began to entertain eugenic legislation. Laws that predetermine rights by virtue of heredity are by their very nature the playthings of dictators and totalitarian states.

Every U.S. citizen has the right to question the Supreme Court's Buck v. Bell decision and judge if it is the product of a government drunk with power. One would have to be enamored with centrally-planned utopias and totalitarian state solutions to not see the abuse of power displayed. Apparently, the U.S. Supreme Court did not believe those "certain inalianable rights" to be so, well, inalianable from the individual citizen. The American court system had taught the world how to deprive citizens of their rights under the "color of law." Professor Lombardo documents the pleasure Oliver Wendell Holmes took in writing the Buck v. Bell opinion:

> One decision that I wrote gave me pleasure, establishing the constitutionality of a law permitting the sterilization of imbeciles. (Pg. 173, "Three Generations," Lombardo)

There are other fundamental legal concepts at play here that must also be discussed. The United States Constitution was authored to protect a citizen's fundamental rights by enumerating the powers allowed to the government. It is therefore understood that the Constitution is a "negative charter," as it limits the government's powers whenever it encroaches on a citizen's rights. This argument of "positive" and "negative" rights goes back all the way to the founding of the nation. The U.S. Constitution was meant to take away the "positive" powers of a monarch to do as he pleased with his or her "royal subjects."

The Progressive movement has been a one-hundred year-long effort to reverse this "limited government" aspect of our nation's founding. Progressives understood that "command and control" legislation, namely eugenics, could not survive a constitutional challenge if the fundamental concepts of the nation's founding were observed. Eugenics cannot be anything other than the legislation of a "command and control" economy. Another term used by Progressives is a "centrally-planned economy", which in reality is not at all dissimilar to that which is centrally located in the powers of a king or queen. Incidentally, some of the media coverage of the Buck v. Bell reveals its appeal to those that believed in government as the "caretaker" of the populace:

> The New York Times covered the Buck decision, quoting liberally from the Holmes opinion, which had given states the **"right to protect society"**. ----- A wire service reporter quoted the U.S. surgeon general, who called the decision a "step toward a super-race." (Pgs. 174-175, "Three Generations No Imbeciles," Lombardo, emphasis mine)

Interestingly enough, the petition that was submitted by the Catholic Church addressed the importance of an individual's right to bodily integrity. It questioned a government intent on violating an individual's bodily autonomy citing the founding notion of government "limited" in its ability to impose its will upon the populace. It did so by quoting an opinion drafted by ex-President and now Chief Justice William Howard Taft:

> Quoting an opinion of Chief Justice Taft from the 1921 Supreme Court case Truax v. Corrigan, the brief attacked the attempt to deprive a person of "fundamental rights." As Taft had written: "The Constitution was intended, its very purpose was, to prevent experimentation with the fundamental rights of the individual." (Pg. 180, "Three Generations No Imbeciles")

The citation of an opinion by Taft was appropriate in order to remind the Justices sitting in that session of the United States Supreme Court the fundamental concepts the history of the very court was based upon. The petition could have gone much further, as there are countless historical and legal documents pointing to the fact that the Constitution is based on "enumerated powers." Eugenics, as the Taft citation appropriately indicated, is best described as "experimentation with the fundamental rights of an individual":

> Eugenics had always had a set of progressive followers who thought it appropriate that the rights of individuals should be subordinated to the collective whole; and, for some, the New Deal seemed to prove the wisdom of placing the public's rights above those of individuals. Harry Laughlin, sterilization's great crusader, would proclaim that eugenics was the "inherent right" of the community, invoking the notion of the community's right of self-defense against the harms imposed by the "unfit". (Pg. 125, "In Reckless Hands," 2008, Victoria F. Nourse)

Laws that elevate the government's or society's "rights" over that of the individual are the tools of despots lusting for power over the populace. One must take Hitler's carefully calculated actions as evidence towards this question. Hitler was an impulsive and impatient man, to say the least. The fact that he carefully, patiently, and deliberately made it a point to follow practices and procedures in his ascension to the position of Chancellor indicates that Hitler himself placed a high value on legally legitimizing his reign of power. Furthermore, the concerted effort to make the eugenic aspirations of the Third Rich observe internationally respected legal measures is indicative of the importance Hitler placed upon the image of legality. Stephen Trombley, author of the 1988 book "The Right to Reproduce: A History of Coercive Sterilization," quotes Hitler as stating:

> I have studied with great interest the laws of several American states concerning the prevention of reproduction by people whose progeny would, in all probability, be of no value or be injurious to the racial stock. (Pg. 116, "The Right to Reproduce")

The fact that Hitler makes reference to "several American states" is an indication that Hitler was citing Laughlin's publication of the eugenic laws passed by the individual States. Recall that this publication of eugenic laws and practices was eagerly passed on to the German members of the IFEO, namely Alfred Ploetz,

Ernst Rüdin, and Erwin Baur. Recall that Hitler's publisher, J.F. Lehmann, was also the publisher of German translations of American eugenic texts. Historians must also take note of the fact that the eugenic notions Adolf Hitler wrote into much of "Mein Kampf" became the foundations of the Nazi T4 Euthanasia program:

> If for a period of only 600 years those individuals would be sterilized who are physically degenerate or mentally diseased, humanity would not only be delivered from an immense misfortune but also restored to a state of general health such as we at present can hardly imagine. If the fecundity of the healthy portion of the nation should be made a practical matter in a conscientious and methodical way, we should have at least the beginnings of a race from which all those germs would be eliminated which are to-day the cause of our moral and physical decadence. (Pg. 346, "Mein Kampf," Bottom of the Hill, June 2010)

Now compare the above sentiment from Adolph Hitler's to those voiced by Dr. Joseph S. DeJarnette, one of the "expert witnesses" for the Buck v. Bell case:

> Reproduction among the "unfit," said DeJarnette, was "a crime against their offspring and a burden to their state," and he demanded their sterilization. He decried those who constantly invoked "The so-called inalienable rights of man" to oppose surgery and compared accepted rules of stock breeding with the deference paid to "the syphilitic, epileptic, imbecile, drunkard and unfit." In contrast to the political sentimentalists, DeJarnette believed in a Darwinian scheme where "only the fit survive." A good farmer, he said, "breeding his hogs, horses, cows, sheep, . . . selects a thoroughbred"; even crops are grown from the "best seed." Yet "when it comes to our own race any sort of seed seems good enough." (Pgs. 121-122, "Three Generations No Imbeciles," Lombardo)

Did the Third Reich comply with "due process" and "rule of law" when it faithfully copied the three-panel eugenic courts per Laughlin's recommendation? The Supreme Court of the United States seems to provide an uncomfortable answer to that question. Significant portions of Laughlin's "Model Law" were adopted verbatim by the Germans in 1933 precisely because a prominent American eugenicist was its author. More importantly, by 1933, the most respected of all courts of law had deemed these compulsory eugenic measures "constitutional."

The Buck v. Bell case would directly result in the forcible sterilization of 70,000 to 80,000 Americans, depending on whose count you choose to trust. Who was liable to fall under the law for compulsory sterilization in Germany? Who was to sacrifice their "fallopian tubes" when "called upon" to do so by the Führer? Anyone considered a threat to the social body due to their allegedly inferior hereditary traits. The first 250,000 victims of The Holocaust were otherwise "Aryans" with birth defects and mental ailments deemed a danger to Hitler's precious gene pool. The first "test case" under German jurisprudence was that of an infant born with birth defects. The case is known as the case of "Baby Knauer." Hitler instructed his underlings to use the opportunity to cement the legal precedent for the Third Reich's eugenic legislation.

MARRIAGE LICENSE.

Virginia, Charlottesville, To-wit:

TO ANY PERSON LICENSED TO CELEBRATE MARRIAGES:

You are hereby authorized to join together in the HOLY STATE OF MATRIMONY, according to the Rites and Ceremonies of your Church or Religious Denomination and the Laws of the Commonwealth of Virginia, *F. W. Buck* and *Miss Emma Harlow*

Given under my hand as Deputy Clerk of the Corporation Court of the City of Charlottesville, this 23rd day of Sept., 1896.

E. T. Fitts, Deputy Clerk

CERTIFICATE TO OBTAIN A MARRIAGE LICENSE.

To be annexed to the License

Time of Marriage	Sept 23rd 1896
Place of Marriage	Charlottesville Va
Full Name of Husband	Frank W. Buck
Full Name of Wife	Emma Adeline Harlow
Color	White
Age of Husband	42
Age of Wife	20
Condition of Husband (widowed or single)	Single
Condition of Wife (widowed or single)	Single
Place of Husband's Birth	Albemarle Co.
Place of Wife's Birth	Charlottesville Va
Place of Husband's Residence	
Place of Wife's Residence	
Names of Husband's Parents	Fleming & Richetia Buck
Names of Wife's Parents	Richard & Adeline Harlow

Most Immediate Blood-Kin of Carrie Buck.
Showing illegitimacy and hereditary feeblemindedness.

Legend:
- F = Feebleminded.
- ? = Name unknown.
- Dotted Line = Illegitimate mating.
- ➤ = Central figure.

Generation I: ?¹, F² (Addie Emmitt), ?³, ?⁴, F⁵ (Frank Buck)

Generation II: F¹ (Carrie Buck), ²(Clarence Garland), F³ (Roy Smith), F⁴ (Doris Buck)

Generation III: F¹ (Vivian Alice Elaine Buck, b. 1924. Test at 7 mo. showed backwardness.)

1928 - STERILIZING THE "GREATEST GENERATION."

> "It is difficult to get a man to understand something when his salary depends upon his not understanding it."
> - Upton Sinclair

Historians typically state that the Buck v. Bell decision was reversed by the Skinner v. Oklahoma decision. Professor Lombardo dismisses this notion in his 2008 book, "Three Generations, No Imbeciles." Skinner and Bell are parallel decisions that do not cancel each other out. The reader should recall that Laughlin intentionally removed any aspect of criminal law from his "Model Law" in order to sidestep the Constitution's prohibition on "cruel and unusual punishment." The Skinner decision pertained to the rights of a criminal only, and that is how it has been cited by the courts. The Buck decision, on the other hand, has influenced Supreme Court outcomes all the way up until the passing of the Americans Disabilities Act of 1990. The States conducted involuntary sterilizations up until 1973. Sterilization rates under eugenic laws in the United States climbed after 1927. Virginia's state sterilization law was repealed in 1974, but by this time over 80,000 sterilizations had been conducted in the United States. Professor Lombardo provides a warning:

> There is a common misconception that the Supreme Court decision in Skinner all but overruled Buck and that the post-war revelation of Nazi practices led to a general rejection of eugenics. But eugenically based assumptions about heredity as a basis for law survived well beyond Skinner, just as they outlived the Third Reich. Years after the case, Justice Douglas himself reiterated that there was no desire by the Skinner court to overrule Buck. Douglas was "very clear" on the case's constitutional validity. The eugenic foundations of Buck were safe because of the procedural protections that Virginia law included. (Pg. 232, "Three Generations")

It is more than disturbing that the Buck v. Bell opinion continued to be used despite the fact that its past was severely tainted by Nazism. As late as 1968, the Nebraska Supreme Court Case made reference to it in the case In the Matter of the Sterilization of Gloria Cavitt. Keep in mind that this is two decades after the Nuremberg Trials supposedly exposed the evils of the Nazi government's tyrannical control over the people's reproductive lives:

> It can hardly be disputed that the right of a woman to bear and the right of a man to beget children is a natural and constitutional right, nor can it be successfully disputed that no citizen has any rights that are superior to the common welfare. Acting for the public good, the state, in the exercise of its police power, may impose reasonable restrictions upon the natural and constitutional rights of its citizens. **Measured by its injurious effect upon society, the state may limit a class of citizens in its right to bear or beget children with an inherited tendency to mental deficiency, including**

feeblemindedness, idiocy, or imbecility. It is the function of the Legislature, and its duty as well, to enact appropriate legislation to protect the public and preserve the race from the known effects of the procreation of mentally deficient children by the mentally deficient... In re Cavitt, 182 Neb. 712, 157 N.W.2d 171 (1968). (emphasis mine)

Most notably, it was cited by the landmark abortion decision of Roe v. Wade that resulted from Margaret Sanger's efforts with International Planned Parenthood. Note the defense of the state's interests and prerogative:

> As noted above, a State may properly assert important interests in safeguarding health, in maintaining medical standards, and in protecting potential life. At some point in pregnancy, these respective interests become sufficiently compelling to sustain regulation of the factors that govern the abortion decision. The privacy right involved, therefore, cannot be said to be absolute. In fact, it is not clear to us that the claim asserted by some amici that one has an unlimited right to do with one's body as one pleases bears a close relationship to the right of privacy previously articulated in the Court's decisions. The Court has refused to recognize an unlimited right of this kind in the past. Jacobson v. Massachusetts, 197 U. S. 11 (1905) (vaccination); Buck v. Bell, 274 U.S. 200 (1927) (sterilization). We, therefore, conclude that the right of personal privacy includes the abortion decision, **but that this right is not unqualified and must be considered against important state interests in regulation.** (ROE v. WADE, 407 U.S. 113 U.S. Supreme Court 1973, emphasis mine)

Ironically, it is the generation we now refer to as "The Greatest Generation" that was the target of the sterilization campaigns that followed the 1927 Buck v. Bell decision. The story of the WWII veteran, Raymond Hudlow, serves as an example of just how asinine the goals of the eugenics movement, and by extension the decision of the United States Supreme Court, truly were. Raymond Hudlow was one of those brave soldiers to land on the Normandy shores on D-Day. He served in General Patton's army which rumbled in to liberate Bastogne in the historic Battle of the Bulge in Ardennes forest in Belgium. Hudlow also served in Holland during Operation Market Garden, where shrapnel wrecked his left knee. German soldiers captured him, beat him and nearly starved him while captured. Yet, according to Raymond Hudlow, none of these instances inflicted the amount of pain as the sterilization that the State of Virginia performed on him at the age of 16, just two years prior to landing on "Bloody Omaha." Stephen Buckley of the St. Petersburg Times interviewed Hudlow for a November 11th, 2001 article.

Raymond Hudlow had been one of over 8,000 individuals we know that were forcibly sterilized by the State of Virginia. The truth is that it is highly improbable that Raymond Hudlow was the only American veteran who had suffered such a fate, considering the great number of youths like Raymond serving in the U.S. Armed Forces, and the tens of thousands of sterilizations forced on youths prior to D-Day and WWII. The total numbers of sterilized is unknown, namely because sterilizations of African-Americans and Native-Americans were not officially recorded. To make matters worse, many doctors performed them without notice or record prior to the U.S. Supreme Court decision. Beyond that, a sizeable amount of the sterilizations were done without the knowledge of the victim. Many did not find out about their condition until visiting doctors decades later after futile attempts to have children. The true numbers are reported as low as 60,000 sterilizations in the United States, with the last state-sanctioned operation officially being conducted in 1979. The number is very likely closer to 80,000 based on known records. In fact, many of those sterilized in the 20th century did not find out until the 21st century. The official apology to Raymond Hudlow reads in part:

> Commending Raymond W. Hudlow. -- Agreed to by the Senate, January 17, 2002 -- Agreed to by the House of Delegates, January 25, 2002
> WHEREAS, the now-discredited pseudo-science of eugenics was based on theories first propounded in England by Francis Galton, the cousin and disciple of famed biologist Charles Darwin; and
> WHEREAS, in 1924, Virginia passed two eugenics-related laws, the second of which permitted involuntary sterilization, the most egregious outcome of the lamentable eugenics movement in the Commonwealth; and
> WHEREAS, under this act, those labeled "feebleminded," including the "insane, idiotic, imbecile, feebleminded or epileptic" could be involuntarily sterilized, so that they would not produce similarly disabled offspring; and
> WHEREAS, in 1941, Raymond Hudlow, a 16-year-old boy who repeatedly ran away from home to escape an abusive father, was committed to the Virginia Colony for Epileptics and Feebleminded near Lynchburg; and
> WHEREAS, on June 17, 1942, an Amherst County Circuit Court judge granted the Virginia Colony's request that Raymond Hudlow be sterilized; and
> WHEREAS, in October of 1943, Raymond Hudlow was released from the Virginia Colony, was drafted into the United States Army two months later, and in August 1944, was at Omaha Beach in France two months after D-Day; and
> (2002 SESSION - SENATE JOINT RESOLUTION NO. 79)

The ACLU helped Raymond Hudlow to sue the State of Virginia in 1985. Surprisingly enough, all Raymond received was the above apology and much resistance from those nervous about further litigation. Other stories began to surface thereafter. A news bulletin titled "Eugenics: U.S. Marine Vet of Two Wars was Sterilized by State at 13" by Ray Reed documents the story of Lewis Reynolds. Reynolds was institutionalized at the Lynchburg Training School at age 13:

> The institution's doctors initially evaluated Reynolds, then 12, as a "fairly normal, intelligent boy", according to records that Reynolds obtained recently from the Central Virginia Training Center. The documents show he was admitted to the "Colony" on Aug. 21, 1941, and had two epileptic seizures within the first few months. "He should make a rather well-behaved patient once he becomes adjusted to institutional life. Sterilization, of course, is indicated," a doctor wrote in the records on Aug. 25, 1941, four days after Reynolds was admitted. (The News & Advance, Sept. 15th, 2012, "Eugenics: U.S. Marine Vet of Two Wars Sterilized")

It is unclear if Reynolds' seizures were the product of a hereditary trait, as he remembers them starting when his older cousin hit him on the head with a rock at around the age of three. Thus, Reynolds was socially adept and functional as the doctor's records and his military service evidence. More importantly, it was logical to believe that sterilization was a worthless measure as the reason for his seizures was not hereditary.

Reynolds would go on to serve under General MacArthur and reached the rank of sergeant while fighting in both the Korean and Vietnam Wars. Reynolds went on to be an electrician in civilian life, and conducts the occasional electrical job even after retirement. Reynolds would marry twice. His first marriage came to an end after his wife wrote him a "Dear John" letter that stated the reasons for leaving him was the inability to have children. He is quoted in the article:

> Sometimes I cry when I see a lady pregnant or something like that. I always wanted children and never could have them. Sometimes I get off by myself and cry. (The News & Advance, Sept. 15th, 2012, "Eugenics: U.S. Marine Vet of Two Wars Sterilized")

Michael D'Antonio wrote the 2004 book titled "The State Boys Rebellion" about the Fernald State School in Boston, Massachusetts, where boys like Hudlow and Reynolds were taken:

> At home, eugenics' targets became, arguably, the most violated and least acknowledged victims of government abuse in American history. As mere children, they were railroaded into institutions by officials who misused IQ tests. Once locked away, they endured isolation, overcrowding, forced labor, and physical abuse including lobotomy, electroshock, and surgical sterilization. Some of these practices continued as late as 1974 when hundreds of seemingly normal children and adults were discovered at state training centers for the retarded in Florida. Many had been held for more than twenty years. (Pg. 5, "State Boys Rebellion")

Boys like Hudlow and Reynolds were part of eugenic round-ups intended to identify and restrain youths deemed to be "unfit." Journalist Welling Savo wrote a bombshell of an article for Boston Magazine titled "The Master Race" in December of 2002. In it he tells the story of Shutesbury, a town just 90 miles West of Boston. It was one of the small rural towns targeted by eugenicists in their nation-wide sterilization project. Savo documents how boys as young as 14 were sterilized for their "poor moral condition." Savo tells a story where the metropolitan elites took a gaze at the rural population just outside of their city, and embarked on a campaign to cut them out of history:

> The Shutesbury study, which was carried out in 1928, was part of a campaign to promote sterilization, segregation, selective breeding, and immigration restrictions a campaign with leadership and widespread support among academics from Harvard and other top New England colleges and universities. (W. Savo, "The Master Race")

Of course, the eugenic masterminds in the United States were the impetus behind these efforts. Leon Whitney, a leading member of the American eugenics movement and the International Federation of Eugenic Organizations was the leader behind the Shutesbury sterilization campaign:

> In fact, the Northampton man behind the Shutesbury study was corresponding with German scientists, whose sterilization policies he called "courageous" and "admirable." And that man, **Leon Whitney a thin, bespectacled dog breeder whose book, The Case for Sterilization, won him an admiring personal letter from Adolf Hitler was no crackpot loner.** There was a whole movement behind him, legitimized by scientists, academics, and influential policymakers. And Massachusetts was one of its epicenters, beginning at a time when Hitler was an aimless Austrian barely in his teens. (W. Savo, "The Master Race", emphasis mine)

Michael D'Antonio documents the voraciousness of these campaigns, making it clear that they were not in any way confined to the unlucky few:

> To make sure every last moron was captured, many states, including Massachusetts, would establish traveling "clinics" to administer IQ tests at public schools. Often these clinics identified as feebleminded, children who had been deemed by teachers and parents to be normal. Many of these boys and girls would be separated from their families by officials who pressured parents to accept that an institution offered their child the best possible future. Parents who did not volunteer their children for admission often lost custody of a son or daughter in court. (Pg. 12, "State Boys Rebellion")

These sterilization campaigns mostly targeted "white" rural populations. More precisely, the "shiftless" and "poor" whites that were directly referenced in the Buck v. Bell trial by "expert eugenicists" like Estabrook:

> With so many supposedly subnormal people being sterilized, the eugenicists should have reduced the number of low-IQ children being born, and the population of institutions should have stabilized. Instead, the number of children who were locked away continued to grow, and buildings on state school campuses became overcrowded. This happened because the criteria for the diagnosis "moron" had become looser with time. (Pg. 18, "State Boys Rebellion")

The above quote is bound to enrage considering the suffering at the hands of these eugenicists. Why would these doctors and scientists keep institutionalizing and sterilizing so many children after realizing that their measures did not produce the results they claimed they would? The reason was explored in earlier chapters. These scientists were building their careers by building the movement along with the corresponding institutions that flourished from in its wake. It is in the nature of institutions to act in the interests of its own survival, and as a result to take steps to ensure survival. Anyone that understands how budgets are managed by government departments knows that budgets never get smaller. Budgets are not allowed to shrink as this is treated as an admission that the need for the institution is diminishing. It is no secret that jailhouses and other similar institutions become the kingdoms of the warden, where its inmates are his source of power, labor, and treated as his subjects:

> Superintendent Ransom Greene offered many reasons to explain why so few people left Fernald for the outside world. Among them was the institution's need for the unpaid labor of brighter inmates, who worked as custodians, caretakers, gardeners, cooks, etc. --- "The upper level of mental defect helps in the care of those less able to care for themselves, or we would have a very much larger employee roster," noted Greene. To keep the place running smoothly, the trustees decreed that Greene adjust admissions to make sure that at least 38 percent of the Fernald population was composed of higher-functioning children and adults. (People who today would be regarded as normal). (Pg. 19, "State Boys Rebellion")

The above describes an institution engaging in a practice worse than indentured servitude as indentured servitude would imply a debt owed. This was outright slavery by government corruption and coercion, especially in the "borderline" cases that were by most accounts fully healthy people from vulnerable families without the means to defend themselves from powerful government bureaucrats. Keep the above 38% number in mind:

> The population at Fernald School was nearly 1,900. Across the nation, eighty-four institutions housed a total of 150,000 children, and twenty-six more state schools were under construction. Fernald was about to be expanded, even though officials in Massachusetts acknowledged at the time that about 8 percent of the children in its state schools were either almost normal, or not at all retarded. This figure suggests that nationwide, at any given time, more than 12,000 American boys and girls of relatively normal intelligence were locked away. (Pgs. 18-19, "State Boys Rebellion")

Consider the gravity of these facts. If the State publically claimed that 8% of the institution's population was likely "normal" but adjusted their admissions so 38% were at or near "normal," then the actual number of healthy boys was obviously much higher than 8%. These are the consequences of imbuing the state with the power of a caretaker. The governed quickly become the "subjects" of institutions amassing influence, territory, and funding.

All of this is an aspect of eugenics and WWII history that has escaped the generally accepted history of The Holocaust. While anti-Semitism was a driving force behind Hitler's murderous policies, the more comprehensive history of eugenics demonstrates a much broader and deeper impact to society in general. The eugenicist in the different nations or geographical locations focused their angst towards whatever ethnic minority happened to cross their paths. Eugenics did not begin or end with the anti-Semitism of the Third Reich. In fact, the eugenics of the

Third Reich with its expansion into the infamous T4 Euthanasia Program began with the eugenic sterilization of mixed-ethnicity European-African children, not the German-Jewish community. In the American Southwest, C.M. Goethe was interested in leveraging eugenics to rid himself of the Mexicans and Oriental immigrants. Laughlin and Davenport were focused on the Irish and Italian Catholics as well as the Eastern European immigrants coming into the American Northeast. Hitler's ire was focused on the German Jews, but his first target group were the children of Europeans and Africans (French-Algerian). The evidence indicates that Hitler's regime would still have systematically sterilized or exterminated any mixed-ethnicity population even if there would never have been a German-Jewish population. Hitler would still have embarked on a perpetual campaign of euthanizing infants with birth defects and sterilization of those deemed a danger to the "Aryan" gene pool. This was the conception of Hitler's version of a hyper "nationalized" and "socialized" state. A November 19th, 1933 Chicago Tribune article aptly entitled "In a Planned Society" makes it sufficiently clear that the eugenic measures were integral to a highly collectivized venture. Those deemed to be drains on society were the primary target:

> IN A PLANNED SOCIETY. German gynecologists, discussing the Nazi sterilization law at a meeting of their society in Berlin, approved the measure, which goes into effect Jan. 1. ---- Dr. Eugene Fischer, anthropologist of the Kaiser Wilhelm institute, observed that the eugenics law would make a fundamental change for the surgeon. Heretofore he had considered the personal interests of his patient. Hereafter he would consider the public weal. (Nov. 19th, 1933, Chicago Tribune)

This was Hitler's "eugenic utopia." This was the purpose of the T4 Euthanasia Program, which murdered half a million Germans of otherwise "Aryan" ethnicity that the eugenic laws labeled as "useless eaters" or "lives unworthy of living."

> As Hermann Hebestreit of the German Labor Front put the matter, the aim was to reduce the difference between the age of retirement and the age of death – ideally zero. Werner Bockhacker, chief of the DAF's health office, put forward pretty much the same idea – as did Hellmut Haubold, who characterized the elderly as people "no longer useful to the community." In the idealized Nazi scheme of things, workers would work long and hard and then die – saving for the *Volksgemeinschaft* the financial burdens of the elderly and "unproductive" infirm. (Pg. 119, "Nazi War on Cancer")

Clearly, the practice of eugenic sterilization has not been connected back to the eugenics practiced by the Hitler regime; at least not in the mind of the general public. The proof is that eugenic sterilization, despite its obvious connections to the Third Reich was somehow able to remain not just legal, but also commonly practiced in the United States until the late 1970s. The pattern of practice had always been the same. It is what in earlier generations was called an "Appalachian Appendectomy." Those targeted were those individuals deemed to be consuming the resources of the state as welfare recipients or inmates; what Hitler's henchmen referred to as "useless eaters" or "lives unworthy of living". This is the flip-side of a zero-sum conception of a "nationalized" and "socialized" welfare state. The economic "pie" is understood as having finite resources to be divided and distributed amongst an ever-growing populace. The available resources become precious and the growing population competing for those resources, a potential liability. It is precisely under this logic that a child from the socially unadjusted is perceived as a threat to the social body.

Historians tell us that men like Raymond Hudlow were part of the "Greatest Generation" for risking life and limb in order to dislodge the great evil of National Socialism from Europe. National Socialism is rightfully regarded as one of the greatest evils in history. We consider Hitler's government to be abhorrent precisely because its actions went beyond what is merely despotic and embarked on the most notorious campaign of "racial cleansing" in history. It is precisely because of individuals like Raymond Hudlow, this "greatest generation," that the Allies were able to bring Hitler's henchmen to justice. It was those simple-living farm boys, the Native Americans, African Americans, and first and second-generation immigrants from Europe, which made up this "greatest generation." Ironically, it was precisely these Americans that were the target of the eugenic laws in the United States. The 1947 Nuremberg Doctor's Trial displayed for the entire world the barbarity of Hitler's doctors and scientists. Ironically, people like Raymond Hudlow fought and died in order to force the defeated Germans to repeal and repent for such laws. The same law that the German doctors held up in their defense at Nuremberg is still valid case law in the United States.

Grand Jury Association of New York County

"To Increase the Efficiency of the Grand Jury System"

105 WEST 40TH STREET, NEW YORK

January 4th, 1937.

Mr. John C. Merriman, President
Carnegie Institution of Washington
16th and P Streets,
Washington, D.C.

Dear Mr. Merriman:-

We feel sure that you will be pleased to be advised of the very informative, intelligent and interesting address made before our Association by Dr. Harry H. Laughlin on the "Legal and Biological Aspects of Sterilization" at our recent annual meeting. Copy of invitation is enclosed.

Our members have heard much of sterilization in the last few years without taking a position, therefore, we were especially interested in ... Laughlin's arguments were ...

Other Volumes published in
THE FORUM SERIES.

The Forum Series.—No. 19.

HUMAN STERILIZATION TO-DAY

DEJARNETTE STATE SANATORIUM
J. S. DEJARNETTE, M.D.
SUPERINTENDENT

Box 270

STAUNTON, VA.
November 24, 1943

Mr. E. S. Gosney
Human Betterment Foundation
Pasadena, California

Dear Mr. Gosney:

We are attempting to renew the interest of eugenic sterilization in Virginia, though we are proud to say Virginia is next to your State who is leading in the number of sterilizations done in the United States, and your State has done almost half of the sterilizations in the United States.

If you have some extra copies of the last report on the number of sterilizations done in the various states in the Union I shall be very glad if you will forward me about 150 copies as I want to use them at the meeting of our next legislature. If there is any charge please forward me the bill.

I want to take this opportunity to thank you for your cooperation with me in the past years. You have been very cooperative in sending me your literature.

You have a wonderful State and you have made great progress in cutting down the reproduction of the unfit and raising the intelligence of your people. I wish to congratulate you on the great work done in your State. The people of California should rise up and call you blessed, in fact, all of the States who are following your example - some feebly and others fairly well, and they should thank you for the great impetus you have given to sterilization.

Sincerely yours,
J. S. DeJarnette, M.D.
Superintendent
DeJarnette State Sanatorium

JSD/

The pamphlets were used

1928 - EUGENICAL ASPECTS OF DEPORTATION

> "I hate the impudence of a claim that in fifty minutes you can judge
> and classify a human being's predestined fitness in life.
> I hate the pretentiousness of that claim.
> I hate the abuse of scientific method which it involves.
> I hate the sense of superiority which it creates,
> and the sense of inferiority it imposes."
> - Walter Lippmann, The New Republic

It seems like the worse life became in Europe between WWI and WWII, and the more that sought refuge in the U.S., the more vigilantly that the American eugenicists sought to enforce the 1924 Immigration Restriction Act. The correspondence held at Truman University's Special Collections Department helps illustrate how Laughlin and C.M. Goethe, the wealthy California landowner and founder of the Save the Redwoods organization persistently pursued the cause of eugenic-minded immigration policy. Laughlin was sent to survey and develop immigration policies with the United States Consulates in Europe. At around the same time, C.M. Goethe took it upon himself to conduct his own field recognizance. A March 15th, 1926 letter from Goethe to Laughlin documents that Goethe, using his Immigration Study Commission, acted upon the conviction that immigration needed to be controlled at the source:

> My dear Dr. Laughlin: - Answering your inquiry:- The immigration Study Commission has been quietly making overseas field studies of immigration for a long while. I have subscribed its budget since its organization. Its inception came in my studies of my customers. (BOX: C-4-1:2, March 15th, 1925 – Goethe to Laughlin, Truman Univ.)

The correspondence held at Truman University also holds letters from Goethe to third parties, which Goethe copied Laughlin on. A letter to Mr. S.W. Ward of the very powerful Commonwealth Club of San Francisco illustrates the "studies" of the customers Goethe referred to in the March 15th, 1925 letter to Laughlin:

> Dear Mr. Ward: - In connection with your proposed work on the Mexican Immigration, you asked me to describe in a letter the racial complexion of our installment business. --- We are making practically no installment sales of either farm lands or city lands to Sicilians, Greeks, Darmatians, Croats, etc. --- We are of course, no longer making sales to Japanese, who were once quite a factor. We have however, a considerable new element in the Mexican. I am trying in my own business to avoid them. This is not because I do not want to make sales. It is because we never make cash sales to them. As installment customers they are most troublesome. They cannot grasp the theory of contracts, as do even the negroes who are coming in to California from the South in considerable numbers. [sic.] (BOX: C-4-1:2, Feb. 26th, 1926, Goethe to Ward, Truman Univ.)

C.M. Goethe had established the "Goethe Fund" at Cold Spring Harbor for the explicit purpose of having Davenport's and Laughlin's team study and develop restrictions on U.S. immigration based on race, nationality, and culture. In turn, Goethe's fieldworkers reported back from Haifa, Palestine, Smyrna, and Florence, Italy. On March 15th, 1926, the fieldworker reported from Haifa to Goethe and Laughlin:

> These men are usually illiterates. – The Johnson Immigration Act is a powerful strainer, at the very spot where such a strainer is needed. (BOX: C-4-1:2, Laughlin Papers, Truman Univ.)

From Smyrna on April 1926 the fieldworker reported his findings at length for Goethe and Laughlin; here in part:

> Their accompanying children constitute an interesting example of race hybridization. Some showed inherited characteristics so mixes as to be tragic. One felt that here, in human shape, were examples of the trite proverb. "One cannot unscramble eggs. American sociologists declare that in just such hybridization were the seeds of the decay of Egypt, Greece, Rome. They say, hopefully, however that, while the causes of such decay are in operation today, that we now have the knowledge and can organize the will to prevent similar destruction of our civilization. (BOX: C-4-1:2, Laughlin Papers, Truman Univ.)

The fieldworker's letter of June of 1926 from Florence, Italy is interesting. The vast correspondence between Goethe and Laughlin documents their desire to pin down a legal definition of the "American Race," which explicitly stipulated "Caucasian" as opposed to "White" because Italians could claim to be "White." The report from the "famous old Baptistery in Florence" states in part:

> This high excess of Italian births not only constitutes Italy's chief problem, but is also a world problem, causing concern even in all European countries with high standards of living. England and Germany, both weighted down with unemployment problems, are discussing barring aliens from nearby low-wage areas. Switzerland is worried over Fascist threats from Italian immigrants in her Italian-speaking canton. France complains that not only Tunis, but certain parts of southern France, are becoming Italianized. – Against such population pressure, America's only dyke is the Johnson Immigration Restriction Act. Should this weaken, the Chinafication of our country will have begun. (BOX: C-4-1:2, Laughlin Papers, Truman Univ.)

Of course, all of Goethe's and Laughlin's work would eventually end up presented as "evidence" before the U.S. Congress. Back on April 26th of 1926, the Committee had decided to "set aside" the matter of deportation for a later date appearance before Congressman Albert Johnson's Committee on Immigration. Laughlin returned to address the House Committee on February 21st, 1928 to complete the deportation section before the Seventieth Congress, First Session. (Hearing No. 70.1.4) The resulting publication was "The Eugenical Aspects of Deportation: Hearings before the Committee on Immigration and Naturalization House of Representatives." The report was presented as a continuation of

Laughlin's "Analysis of America's Modern Melting Pot" report. Congressman Johnson introduced the topic by quoting a memorandum prepared by Laughlin detailing the scope of the work:

> The European sources of American immigration. – The first material for this particular research was gathered in Europe under the joint auspices of the Committee on Immigration and Naturalization and the Department of Labor. Satisfactory data were secured from 67 of the 123 consular districts in Europe and the Near East. The completion of this investigation and the analysis of its findings for the use of the committee will depend upon a common agreement among this committee, the president of the Carnegie Institution of Washington, and the Department of State of the United States. (Pg. 2, "Eugenical Aspects of Deportation," U.S. House of Rep., 70th Cong., 1st Sess., Hearing No. 70.1.4)

As such, much of the data had been gathered in the various projects, not only from Laughlin's visits abroad, but from the extensive surveys done by the Eugenics Record Office of the State and Federal jails, hospitals, and other institutions that housed the "unfit." Laughlin describes his survey of 684 institutions as such:

> We studied the relation between the total number of foreign-born inmates in State custodial institutions and the number of such inmates who are deportable, by specific types and classes. --- In our immigration law and practice, deportation is the last line of defense against contamination of the American family stocks by alien hereditary degeneracy. (Pg. 3, "Eugenical Aspects of Deportation," U.S. House of Rep., 70th Cong., 1st Sess., Hearing No. 70.1.4)

It is clear from the papers that Laughlin was frustrated by the fact that of the 74,170 foreign-born inmates he singled out as those he desired to deport, only 5.12% or 3,798, were actually deportable according to the law. He cites three reasons why 98.22% of those he wanted to get rid of could not be deported and thus justified the radical changes he delineated in his presentation:

> First, the foreign-born person may be a naturalized citizen; second, he may have been in the United States more than five years; and third, he may have become inadequate from causes arising since his admission. (Pg. 5, "Eugenical Aspects of Deportation," U.S. House of Rep., 70th Cong., 1st Sess., Hearing No. 70.1.4)

Laughlin thus reiterated his desire that eugenic examinations be conducted at the consuls abroad prior to allowing any immigrant to board a ship towards the United States. Again, he qualified this measure as "one of the greatest humanitarian advances" and in the interests of "justice, peace, and eugenical soundness." Note the insistence on gathering the type of information that could at best be described hearsay at best, and libel at worst:

> The principal remedy would seem to provide for more thorough examination into the individuals and family histories of the would-be immigrant. A great advance in this direction has been made by beginning the examination of immigrants in their home towns. The feasibility of such examinations was first demonstrated by my studies made as a representative of the United States

Department of Labor and of this committee. We made successfully such actual experimental examinations in Europe in 1923 and 1924, in perfect consonance with international law. (Pg. 6, "Eugenical Aspects of Deportation," U.S. House of Rep., 70th Cong., 1st Sess., Hearing No. 70.1.4)

As documented earlier, the definition of "white", or more precisely what nationalities were white enough, played a significant part in the conversations between C.M. Goethe, Madison Grant, and Laughlin. The Congressional hearings delved in similar prejudices. An exchange between Congressman Hays B. White, a Republican from Kansas and Bird J. Vincent, a Republican from Michigan made it clear as to what races were deemed desirable as they debating completely shutting down immigration from any other country outside of the "northern" European countries such as England, France, and Holland. (Pg. 26) One can only conclude that by "northern" they meant to exclude problem immigration from countries like Italy and Eastern Europe.

It is telling that Congressman Johnson admitted that the foreign-born criminals identified by Laughlin were not any more likely to land in jail than the American-born criminals and differed only in their propensity for crimes violating the Volstead Act, otherwise known as the National Prohibition Act or "liquor laws," which had been the prerogatives of Protestantism and Progressivism of the era. (Pg. 31) As explained earlier, the political lines defined by Prohibition played a part in the debate. Gangster culture and its links to recently arrived immigrants loomed large in the discussion.

Laughlin railed against a practice he termed as "dumping" and asked those responsible to push for the adoption of the following rule at the international level. Note that Laughlin's "immigration" principles also restricted movement at the county and State level:

> It is clear that when once the biological principle of human migration is firmly established in our policy of government, the following rule will be put into effect: "Any county, State, or nation which is responsible for the production of a degenerate or defective must be made to take care of that individual and not impose his custody, expense, and care upon another community." (Pg. 17, "Eugenical Aspects of Deportation," U.S. House of Rep., 70th Cong., 1st Sess., Hearing No. 70.1.4)

At the core of Laughlin's anti-dumping policy was a "biological" consideration. Laughlin returns to the various eugenic studies of "degenerate" families like the Hill Folk, the Jukes, the Ishmaels, and the Nams in order to redirect the conversation towards the topic of breeding better citizens. These are what Laughlin called the "white degenerates" living in the "outskirts" of great cities. One can only surmise that Laughlin was referring to towns like Shutesbury, the town his colleague Leon Whitney raided. Laughlin reminded the committee that 23 States had adopted "eugenical sterilization" laws largely as a result of the <u>Buck v. Bell</u> case. It is important to understand just what the scope of what Laughlin's proposal truly was, as it focused the might of the Federal Government inwards in order to vigilantly control the population within the States. Recall that "outdoor relief" was a term for any help provided by a charity for an individual that did not live in a hospital or institution. Note that even these people would be counted as a "public charge" unworthy of the liberty of mobility or reproductive rights, and if Laughlin got his way, subject to segregation, institutionalization, and eventual sterilization:

> For the purpose of this act, a public charge is a person maintained in whole or in part by public funds in a Federal, State, city, county or township custodial or charitable institution, or who receives outdoor relief at public expense. (Pg. 41, "Eugenical Aspects of Deportation," U.S. House of Rep., 70th Cong., 1st Sess., Hearing No. 70.1.4)

This is also where the report goes far beyond that of legislation pertaining to immigration and emigration, and where Laughlin frames his view in the language of a horse breeder primarily concerned with "mate selection" and family stock crossing, two concepts that have no place in a conversation about the legalities of what is otherwise the liberty of movement in a free society. Laughlin provides his "expert" opinion in order to justify the assertions made by Congressman Johnson, that the Federal Government be reorganized to operate as a central-planning body, responsible for the "mate selection" and "family stock crossing" of the nation. Take note of Laughlin framing his observations in the language of a horse breeder:

> The "pure sire" principle in race mixture has had the biological effect of breeding up the lower races, and the only thing that has prevented the complete mixture of races where the two come in contact is the high virtue and the high mate selection standard of the women of the dominant classes. (Pg. 19, "Eugenical Aspects of Deportation," U.S. House of Rep., 70th Cong., 1st Sess., Hearing No. 70.1.4)

Congressman John C. Box, the Democrat from Texas, brought up the question of "differential fecundity," fearing that the "upper classes" supposedly reproduced at a slower rate. Laughlin answered Congressman Box's worries. Consider the potential consequences of the radicalism in Laughlin's response:

> Yes, sir; and that is a matter of differential fecundity that call for still another study. The time will come when the several States, rather than the Federal Government, in making marriage laws, and the people in building up their customs, will have to demand fit mating and high fertility from the classes who are better endowed physically, mentally, and morally by heredity, and to prevent, either by segregation or sterilization or otherwise, the reproduction by the more degenerate classes. That is the job of the biological control of population, and immigration, of course, is one of the three great factors and the only one the Federal Government can now use effectively. (Pg. 19, "Eugenical Aspects of Deportation," U.S. House of Rep., 70th Cong., 1st Sess., Hearing No. 70.1.4)

One has to wonder how these congressmen, those counted on by the electorate to uphold the various concepts enshrined in the Declaration of Independence, which championed the sovereignty of the individual, could not see the traitorous notions expounded by Laughlin. Laughlin can hardly be said to have disguised his contempt for the legal traditions of the United States. In fact, he explained his departure from them in no uncertain terms:

> The immigration laws of the United States and our immigration policy formerly were based upon the asylum idea; let everyone come to the United States who cares to come. The next step in advance was to base the immigration policy on economic grounds. Then the third basis is the one we are just entering on now, the biological. ---- The time will come when this country will have to face, more courageously than it has at the present time, the mater not only for race and of individual quality, but also of pedigree or family stock, and we will also have to face boldly and courageously the matter of race. (Pgs. 20-21, "Eugenical Aspects of Deportation", U.S. House of Rep., 70th Cong., 1st Sess., Hearing No. 70.1.4)

Here was the "biological aristocracy," which Laughlin and his cohorts so yearned, expounded and championed in the halls of the United States Congress; the halls of the institution created by men who mounted a rebellion against kings, queens, and the notion that an individual's worth is tied to his "family pedigree". The guarantee of "individual rights" written into the Declaration of Independence was never meant to be qualified by the biological "quality" of an individual. The promise of "equality before the law" is not contingent upon "heredity."

One very telling portion of Laughlin's report is the section titled "PARALLEL BETWEEN RECRUITING THOROUGHBRED STOCK BLOD BY PURCHASE AND NATIONAL FAMILY STOCK BLOOD BY IMMIGRATION." This section of the report, as the title indicates, was a literal comparison between allowing a human being into the country and the purchase of a horse. Laughlin studies of horses were part of his work at Cold Spring Harbor. This work, like all others, had an outside sponsor with the Carnegie Institution managing and contributing to the expenses. Work in the study of race horses at Cold Spring Harbor started in 1923 when Walter J. Salmon, the owner of Mereworth Stud, the horse breeding farm in Lexington, Kentucky, offered to finance a study. The idea was to arrive at a formula for breeding a winner on the race track. According to Frances Janet Hassencahl, the notoriety of arriving at a scientific formula for breeding a winning race horse actually aroused more interest and publicity than Laughlin's work on humans. (Pg. 83, Hassencahl) The project would produce seven papers that were published by the National Academy of Sciences, Scientific Monthly, and several privately printed compendiums that Laughlin pushed Carnegie into publishing into a series of books. Laughlin makes direct reference to these projects in his juxtaposition between immigrants and race horses:

> I have made some studies with regard to a closely parallel thing for Mr. Walter J. Salmon of New York, one of the most distinguished and successful

breeders of thoroughbred horses in the United States. When this gentleman recruits his stud farm, he never even considers acquiring a mare or a stallion not of the top level, judged by excellence of near-kin, and he has been very successful in racing for that reason. He weeds out from the lower levels and recruits by purchase, analogous to immigration in man, to the top levels. Man is an animal, and so far as heredity and future generations are concerned, there is considerable real basis for the comparison made. (Pgs. 44-45, "Eugenical Aspects of Deportation," U.S. House of Rep., 70th Cong., 1st Sess., Hearing No. 70.1.4)

For the purposes of this book, it is interesting to note that Laughlin's methodology in studying animal breeds and that which he applied to humans hardly differed. Laughlin's thoroughbred study is also important to analyze as it is a prime example of how Laughlin manipulated data in order to arrive at the desired outcome as well as his willful ignorance of the facts of life. To make a long story short, Laughlin's study of the race horses demonstrates obliviousness to the fact that the competitors often cheated any way they could in sporting events that involve gambling. Laughlin was equally naïve about the influence of money in sporting events as he was about the influence of power on government officials.

1932 - ONE-WORLD EUGENIC UTOPIA

> *"Some of the biggest cases of mistaken identity are among intellectuals who have trouble remembering that they are not God."*
> *- Thomas Sowell*

What is truly astonishing is how little "science" was discussed in the vast amount of correspondence among the international eugenic think-tanks. The vast majority of the correspondence among these "scientists" covered legalistic and legislative topics. Most of their effort was focused on drafting, reporting and maturing the laws, statutes and codes by which a eugenic mindset would be applied to government, as opposed to proving or developing the "science of eugenics." An inordinate amount of time was expended at creating a eugenic utopia by using the various parliaments, legislatures and court systems to establish laws about sterilization, euthanasia, segregation and immigration policies. While this surely proves some measure of disingenuous intent from these eugenicists, more importantly it proves just how dependent eugenics was upon utopian or collectivist governmental structures. Eugenics is politics, as no eugenic measures can be put into effect without extensive governmental intervention into the lives of otherwise autonomous individuals.

Utopian ventures, in turn, are fueled by the lofty ideals of those lustful of the power a farmer has over animals. This is the reason all of the top eugenicists spent so much of time either dreaming up fictional worlds or why so many fictional authors, namely H.G. Wells, wrote fictional accounts of eugenic utopias. H.G. Wells studied under prominent Darwinists like T.H. Huxley and was an avid supporter of the eugenics movement. Francis Galton, would write "Kantsaywhere" in order to provide a vision of the eugenic world he envisioned, and before him T.H. Huxley would write "Prolegomena" to postulate the implications of manipulating evolution. Both Wilhelm Schallmayer and Alfred Ploetz, two German eugenicists indispensable to the Third Reich's "racial hygiene" policies, were devout followers of Edward Bellamy. Bellamy had written one of the most politically influential utopian visions after which countless Progressive proposals were modeled. Ploetz himself traveled to the United States explicitly to study Bellamy and the utopian colonies that had sprung up during the era.

Clearly, the most recognizable of these authors was H.G. Wells. H.G. Wells debated eugenics with Francis Galton himself, and would be one of those "Merchants of Light" that would throughout his life sell the gospel of eugenics. It is also no coincidence that the height of H.G. Well's fame came at the turn-of-the-century. His work was consumed by a public poised upon embarking on a new century. Published in 1901, his first non-fiction bestseller was "Anticipations of the Reaction of Mechanical and Scientific Progress Upon Human Life and Thought." The book predicted what the world would be like in the year 2000. His other works persist along the line of eugenic utopian thought: "Mankind in the Making" (1903), "A Modern Utopia" (1905), "Men Like Gods" (1923), "The Science of Life" (1930), and "The Work, Wealth and Happiness of Mankind" (1931)

The 1905 "A Modern Utopia" and the 1901 "Anticipations" were the most revealing of all of H.G. Wells' utopian visions. His Malthusian population theory combined with the critical view of free-market capitalism in order to create what Wells called a "modern" vision of an ideal society, and most interestingly, a "New Republic." Wells acknowledges at the beginning of "Modern Utopia" that the book is neither a novel nor an essay. "A Modern Utopia" is the result of what Wells called "a peculiar method," one which he believed to be "the best way to a sort of lucid vagueness that has always been my intention in this matter." This "lucid vagueness" is the ambiguity necessary to keep the reader believing in the viability of the utopian scheme. Wells knew that too much reality was detrimental to utopian schemes. Wells oscillated between specificity and ambiguity, never allowing the reader to approach close enough to their creation to reveal its true nature. Wells peddled in platitudes to maintain this "suspension of disbelief," this "lucid vagueness," for the reader to be enamored of the proposed future:

> And the ethical system of these men of the New Republic, the ethical system which will dominate the world state, will be shaped primarily to favour the procreation of what is fine and efficient and beautiful in humanity beautiful and strong bodies, clear and powerful minds, and a growing body of knowledge and to check the procreation of base and servile types -- To do the latter is to do the former ; the two things are inseparable. ---- In the new vision death is no inexplicable horror, no pointless terminal terror to the miseries of life, it is the end of all the pain of life, the end of the bitterness of failure, the merciful obliteration of weak and silly and pointless things. . . (H.G. Wells, "Anticipations," The Faith of the New Republic)

Another common thread in the utopian description of Fabian futurisms are their intolerance to adversity or change. Statist proposals are by their very nature static, vulnerable to the consequences of change. Utopias by definition cannot withstand change, as they pretend to have arrived at perfection. However, their prescribed equilibrium is easily disturbed by the injection of a new technology, a different culture, a different art, a disproportion between male and female, a rise or fall in productivity, a rise or fall in population, or an element of the population which refuses to adhere to their predetermined lives. Utopias are fragile playthings of a single individual. They cannot withstand participatory collaboration.

> Humanity has set out in the direction of a more complex and exacting organization, and until, by a foresight to me at least inconceivable, it can prevent the birth of just all the inadaptable, useless, or merely unnecessary creatures in each generation, there must needs continue to be, in greater or less amount, this individually futile struggle beneath the feet of race; somewhere and in some form there must still persist those essentials that now take shape as the slum, the prison, and the asylum. (H.G. Wells, "Anticipations")

"A Modern Utopia" is a one-world state, using modern transportation and communication technologies to provide for a unified citizenry.

> If the surmise of a developing New Republic a Republic that must ultimately become a World State of capable rational men, developing amidst the fading contours and colours of our existing nations and institutions be indeed no idle dream, but an attainable possibility in the future. (H.G. Wells, "Anticipations," The Faith, Morals and Public Policy of The New Republic)

H.G. Wells recognized the primary reason why the preceding utopian schemes are static by nature. Wells was aware that in order to maintain the guarantee of providing everyone a minimum economic life, resources must not be depleted or strained by an ever-growing population. In other words, to redistribute wealth equally and comfortably, this overall wealth cannot be overtaxed by a population that increases beyond the availability of commodities. As such, the one major restriction in Wells' "Modern Utopia" is a eugenic restriction:

> For a multitude of contemptible and silly creatures, fear-driven and helpless and useless, unhappy or hatefully happy in the midst of squalid dishonor, feeble, ugly, inefficient, born of unrestrained lusts, and increasing and multiplying through sheer incontinence and stupidity, the men of the New Republic will have little pity and less benevolence. To make life convenient for the breeding of such people will seem to them not the most virtuous and amiable thing in the world, as it is held to be now, but an exceedingly abominable proceeding. (H.G. Wells, "Anticipations")

Professor Garland Allen and Randall D. Bird document the fact that Laughlin was an "internationalist," a political belief that went hand in hand with very specific political affiliations in the early Twentieth Century. Laughlin had been a member of the permanent Immigration Commission of the International Labor Office of the League of Nations in 1925. Progressives like Laughlin were considered "Internationalists" especially because of their support for one-world organizations. However, Laughlin's version of "Internationalism" must be qualified. To be more precise, Laughlin was an "internationalist" because was a eugenicist:

> Laughlin's involvement with eugenics spread well beyond the borders of the United States. In his eugenical outlook he was clearly an internationalist, maintaining that decisions about issues such as immigration could not be left up to individual countries, but required worldwide discussion. The instrument for achieving international agreement, Laughlin thought, was a common world government. ("The Papers of Harry Hamilton Laughlin," Annals of the History of Biology, Vol. 14, No. 2)

One must go back to the correspondence between him and C.M. Goethe about the Johnson-Reed Act as the "strainer" stopping immigration at the source in order to understand Laughlin's intentions. A June 13th, 1932, letter from Laughlin to Grant provides an explanation for "The Fundamental Instrument for the Common

Government of the World," the title of Laughlin's own utopian vision:

> The reason most of us have for condemning the so-called internationalist is primarily because he strives to break down national barriers instead of coordinating sovereign nations. In this book I have gone over the unusual formula for world government and have changed it to call for organization, not by breaking down national and racial boundaries but by providing for the development of each race and culture independently. Instead of breaking down immigration bars my draft gives international sanction to control absolutely its own immigration policy. It also enjoins upon each nation the moral obligation to control its own population numbers and to direct its own racial evolution in accordance with its own ideals. Migration control is, of course, the one thing which makes such a long time international program possible. Consequently migration control on the basis which we have many times discussed, should constitute a cornerstone of future international polity. Incidentally my proposed draft calls for complete control over deportation of aliens by the host country, and for the abolition of dual citizenship. (BOX: B-5-2B:6, June 13th, 1932, Truman Univ. - Spec. Coll.)

Laughlin understood that a high degree of cooperation and coordination amongst the nations of the world would be necessary if immigration and emigration were to be controlled to the degree he desired. It would not be enough to simply close the doors of the United States. Laughlin also voiced his desire for legislation to serve his eugenic demands at a world-wide level in a 1925 article entitled "Eugenics in America":

> The United States and the Colonies of Great Britain, Canada, Australia, New Zealand, and South Africa have a great problem in common. ---- The races of Southern Europe and Eastern Europe and the Oriental races are crowding on the borders of these so-called Colonies. But the word "Colony" should, of course, be restricted to a group of people who go from a country to plant themselves in new regions and there build a new and better civilization of the parental type. Unless the United States and the self-governing Colonies or Dominions of the British Empire can get together in some sort of concerted action to admit only emigrants who are of assimilable [sic.] races and of good family-stocks – immigrants who will raise the physical, mental and moral standards and help to carry on the European and especially the British type of civilization, I am afraid that in the long run not only the United States, but, even earlier than the United States, the self-governing Dominions of the British Empire will suffer greatly. (Pg. 85, "Eugenics in America," Eugenics Review, April 1925)

Laughlin's eugenic zealotry was not a patriotic one, despite his allusions in public statements. Laughlin was equally interested in preserving the "white" race in Europe. The fact that he was willing to subsume the sovereignty of the United States under a one-world government clearly evidences that Laughlin's eugenic zealotry trumped any patriotic feelings he claimed to have for his country. Thus, Laughlin, like many of his cohorts, spent an inordinate amount of time dreaming up his eugenic utopia. Laughlin would spend a formidable amount of time while at

Cold Spring Harbor drafting a constitution for a one-world government. This proposal currently archived at the Special Collections at Truman University has been largely ignored by historians. However, the document is essential in evidencing the megalomania inherent in Laughlin's eugenics. According to Frances Janet Hassencahl, Laughlin started working on his "dream – half prophetic, half wistful" constitution for a one-world government during his college years. The first draft was 15 pages long and is dated January 1st, 1901. (Pg. 47, Hassencahl) She describes later revisions:

> Drafts written in the post-war period showed that he saw only one advantage to the world war. It made a preliminary experiment in world government, The League of Nations, possible. Laughlin, who had served as a captain in the National Guard during the war, was anti-war and predicted a second conflict if some sort of democratic world federation did not progress rapidly enough. (Pg. 47, "Harry H. Laughlin, Expert Eugenics Agent," Hassencahl, University Microfilms, 1970)

Hassencahl opines that Laughlin's proposal was "extremely idealistic and displays a political naiveté which he fails to rid himself of in later revisions." Laughlin's proposal would be one of the 22,165 entries for the Bok Peace Prize of 1924. (Pg. 47, Hassencahl) Laughlin's mail evidences that in 1932 Laughlin also presented his one-world utopian plans to Scribner's Publishers with the help of Madison Grant. Laughlin's June 13th, 1932 letter begins by informing Madison Grant that he had forwarded a copy to Mr. Maxwell E. Perkins, the editor at Scribner's. The Special Collections Department at Truman University holds a June 15th, 1932 response from Grant stating that he had personally spoken to the staff at Scribner's about Laughlin's manuscript. Laughlin's June 13th, 1932 letter to Grant continues:

> Perhaps the second most striking difference between our views and those of internationalists concern the basis of representation in the World Council. The internationalist puts forth two theories of such basis, one on the equality of all sovereign countries big or little and second, the allotment of voice on the basis of population. Both of these are, of course, impossible. I feel that in rejecting these two bases a better basis should be offered. In accordance with this feeling I have computed, for each country, the allotment of voice... (BOX: B-5-2B:6, June 13th, 1932, Truman Univ.)

The other "command and control" mechanisms in Laughlin's vision are worth dissecting. Laughlin proposes in this utopian one-world constitution that the world government be broken down to six continents with a "federated" structure mimicking that of the U.S. federal government and its independent state governments. While Laughlin employs the politically correct catch words like "freedom," "peace," and "democracy," the actual application of the government policies betray the real purpose of the effort. In fact, one just needs to refer to the related correspondence to get an explanation of what the purpose of the utopian effort was. While the document text itself provides extensive lip-service to the politically correct notions of a one-world government, the actual numbers of a "federation" of nations betrays precisely where the power lies. Laughlin's June 13th, 1932, letter to Madison Grant explains:

> ...the allotment of voices in World Council, based on the following formula: Area counts 5 percent, wealth 10 percent, total population 15 percent, literate population 35 percent, and world commerce 35 percent. This works out, for example, by making the representation **value of one man in the United States equal to more than 25 times the representation value of one man in India**. This seems sound and fair. (emphasis mine)

The June 13th, 1932 letter goes on to explain precisely how Laughlin's version of "internationalism" is intended as a target to the traditional Communist or Socialist version of "internationalism." Adolf Hitler would concur on this point as this was precisely Hitler's opposition to Bolshevik style Communism. What Adolf Hitler referred to as "International Communism", or "International Bolshevism", or "International Socialism" would break down racial and ethnic barriers in a borderless one-world Bolshevik style government. That was the stated intent of the so-called Communist International, "*Comintern*", or "*Kommunisticheskiĭ Internatsional*" in Russian. Hitler's "National" form of "Socialism" or his "*Nationalsozialistische Deutsche Arbeiterpartei*", of course, was an intentional contrast and juxtaposition to the "internationalism" of the Bolsheviks. Hitler's "National Socialism" did not bicker with the Bolshevik's collectivism. Hitler was offended by the notion of a world order without borders and without racial hierarchies, with the seat of power administered by those he considered racially inferior, the Slavs. Laughlin's June 13th letter expounds on this belief:

> This book is an invasion of the territory of the internationalists and hits what I believe to constitute their weakest part – their tendency to abolish migration barriers on the theory that the whole earth belongs to all of its inhabitants in common and that all men are created equal. (BOX: B-5-2B:6, June 13th, 1932, Laughlin to Grant, Truman Univ.)

Laughlin's entire scheme is about institutionalized inequity. As stated above, neither Laughlin nor Grant believed "all men" to be "created equal." Eugenicists had from the onset been at odds with the egalitarian values of the new democracies popping up around the world. Francis Galton explicitly says so in his article "Hereditary Improvement," which appeared in a January 1873 edition of "Fraser's Magazine":

> As regards the democratic feelings, its assertion of equality is deserving of the highest admiration so far as it demands equal consideration for the feelings of all, just as in the same way as their rights are equally maintained by the law. But it goes farther than this, for it asserts that men are of equal value as social units, equally capable of voting, and the rest. This feeling is undeniably wrong, and cannot last. (Pg. 85, As quoted by A. Chase, "Legacy of Malthus")

One of Laughlin's one-world drafts entitled "America and The Common Government of the World: A draft of a World Constitution in Accordance with Unhampered American Ideals" also peddles in the typical catch words of American values. However the essence of the document betrays any faux respect for the founding principles of the American Revolution. While Laughlin may mimic the "federal" model of the U.S. Constitution in his proposal, he certainly held it with bitter disdain. Laughlin describes his proposal as a "federal form of government" for "a group of free states" under a "democratic world government" only to qualify these initiatives with the paternalistic views of an all powerful government:

> A strong world government would not issue territorial mandates but would administer at first hand the government of its backwards and its immature nations, and would educate them in sanitation, self-government and modern learning. (BOX: B-5-3B:1, Laughlin Papers, Truman Univ.)

True to its Progressive notions, Laughlin's proposal postulates that his was necessary as a bulwark against "international injustice, which we call oppression" and as a method to prevent "national murder which we now call war." Here, Laughlin employs the typical one-world government argument:

> **The principle of arming the state and disarming the constituent individual** is perhaps the only plan which will make for the destruction of militarism and competitive armament. – The fact that a world government would have no coordinate competitor would relive it of the necessity of arming competitively, the people of Wars cannot yet get at us to do military violence. (BOX: B-5-3B:1, Laughlin Papers, Truman Univ., emphasis mine)

Laughlin's proposal is a direct attack on the "right to bear arms" otherwise guaranteed by the 2nd Amendment of the United States Constitution. Laughlin's proposal was intent on "disarming" all "individuals," a topic continuously revisited in his proposal and yet another credential for Laughlin's Progressivism. Instead, Laughlin proposes to mimic the court system of the U.S. governments to resolve all disputes among individuals and nations. However, he proposes an "armed police force" to enforce the mandates of these courts as a replacement for the right to bear arms. Comically enough, Laughlin frames his proposal as "dedicated to individual liberty, to national patriotism."

The section labeled "Empire vs. Federal Democracy" provides insight. Laughlin aptly points out that "all empires have been and are motivated primarily by desire for mastery and gain." His analysis of earlier versions of one-world structures, such as that of the Romans or the Spaniards, certainly underscores his pseudo-Marxist opinion that all world history was dictated by the desire for "mastery and gain." Laughlin's one-world proposal may not have been about "gain," but it certainly was about "mastery"; control over the outcome of immigration and emigration in a broader scope, and control over human reproduction at the individual level.

An example of how Laughlin made sure to weave the goals of his one-world eugenic controls into the agenda of the I.F.E.O. can be found in a memo Laughlin wrote for Cora Hodson. The memo was written in preparation for that first meeting of the I.F.E.O. that was held in Munich on September of 1928. The memo addressed what Laughlin wanted to cover in the "migration conference" as to what to do with "surplus population":

> If international law ever becomes **codified**, it must include the present **unwritten rule** which, in substance, states: "Every sovereign nation and self-governing colony has the sovereign right to control its own migration policy – that is, **to determine whether one of its own nationals may emigrate from its own territories** and whether a particular alien may immigrate into its territories. (BOX: D-2-2:7, Laughlin Papers, undated, Truman Univ., emphasis mine)

There are several curious aspects to Laughlin's "migration" memo. First, it is curious to see Laughlin propose the existence of "unwritten rules" in the even international law ever was "codified." How one "codifies" and "unwritten rule" Laughlin does not explain, but it betrays the fact that even he did not feel entirely comfortable about having his most zealous ideals out in the open. Second, it is yet another demonstration of the feudal conception Laughlin had of the role of government when he voiced the right of a government to restrict the right of free movement of a law abiding individual, all with the employment of "unwritten rules." One can easily argue that Laughlin intended to use the force of government to keep those of desirable racial qualities from leaving the nation the eugenicists slotted them into, as if they were breeds of horses to be corralled.

It is by no surprise that Laughlin understood his one-world government had to disarm the individual in order to maintain such a coercive control, lest these individuals rebel against the controls imposed. At the individual level, Laughlin envisioned his one-world proposal would "forbid human slavery" and "abolish the death penalty for crime," and even prohibit "cruel and unusual punishment" for its "duly qualified" citizens. "Section 6" of the "Common Government of the World," defines precisely the requirements for a citizen to have the right to vote. Clearly, the compassion Laughlin voiced was only as genuine as the compassion the farmer has for the animals he slaughters::

> The right to vote shall not be denied or abridged by the World, or by any of its political subdivisions of any degree, on account of race, sex, belief, or station; but throughout the World the right to vote shall be vouchsafed and limited in each political unit to citizens thereof who have attained the age of personal responsibility, who are intelligent, literate, sane, patriotic, and obedient to law, who have visible means of support, and who have duly qualified as voters, according to the just and equal standards and tests legalized for the particular unit. (BOX: B-5-3B:1, Truman Univ.)

In other words, to be a "duly qualified citizen" in Laughlin's utopian government, one had to pass the tests that eugenicists used to determine "fitness."

One could not be a "useless eater" as the German "racial hygienists" would later define, and still have rights in Laughlin's utopia.

Nowhere in Laughlin's decades long attempt at a one-world utopia is the healthy fear of an overwhelmingly powerful government or the concept of "limited government" present. The Founding Fathers of the American Revolution had a justified fear of all-powerful governments, namely the British Empire under King George, and thus enshrined the "right to bear arms" into the Second Amendment to the U.S. Constitution. The Founding Fathers were not trying to prevent future wars between Britain and France but further incursions on their individual liberties by their government. The founding concepts of "balance" and "separation" of powers were explicitly written into the founding documents to create a "limited government" precisely to prevent the centralized power that Progressives and Fabian Socialists desired; in this instant case, the power to enact their "race betterment," "racial hygiene," "population control" and other "eugenic" policies.

The Founding Fathers created a template for "self-government," precisely to prevent bureaucrats like Leonard Darwin, H.G. Wells, C.M. Goethe, Madison Grant, Alfred Ploetz, and Ernst Rüdin impose their will on the individual citizen. The Second Amendment can be said to be the most important aspect of the founding documents that creates a "balance" and "separation" of powers, as the Founding Fathers intended. It distributes and balances power between the government and its constituents by respecting the right of the individual to defend themselves against an over-zealous government. This is a concept that would certainly come front and center as eugenicists like Laughlin and Leon Whitney scoured the countryside to sterilize children that they deemed "inferior" or "unfit."

Planned societies are precarious ventures, whom by their very nature teeter on the tightrope walk that is staying on the plan charted by the expert and central planner. The one factor most likely to shake the foundations of a planned economy and culture is either an unplanned for growth or decline in population. Population ebbs and swells are the Achilles' heel of centrally planned communities. Population ebbs and swells conspire to spoil socialized insurance and pension schemes. Population ebbs and swells destroy any plans for the planned distribution of all major and minor resources such as housing, health care, food, and education. It is by no surprise that the icons of American Progressivism and British Fabian Socialism shared a leadership with their corresponding eugenic institutions. Thus, Laughlin was hardly the only Progressive with calculations for one-world government schemes. This template can be seen repeated whenever Progressives drafted similar proposals for one-world governments. A Chicago Daily Tribune article entitled "World State's Super-Secret Constitution" documents how the eminent New Dealer under President Franklin D. Roosevelt, Rex Tugwell, was amongst a group of American Progressives found to be drafting plans for a one-world government:

> A highly restricted secret document, setting up the constitution and plan of a new world government which would supplant the United Nations, abolish the United States and all other countries as nations, and govern, tax, and regulate the world's people with power to seize and manage private property has been obtained exclusively by THE TRIBUNE. (Nov. 17th, 1947, Chicago Daily Tribune, "World State's Super-Secret Constitution")

Curiously enough, one of the most important aspects of the New Dealer's one-world government was the abolishment of the right to bear arms, much like Laughlin's one-world constitution emphasizes. The article goes on to document another aspect of this one-world government which was perfectly in line with the ethos subscribed to by Tugwell and fellow New Dealers:

> One interesting agency of the proposed world government is a planning group of 21 members, who under the draft constitution would prepare the global budget, and also be empowered to pass on the social usefulness of new inventions and the exploitation of natural resources, and suppress them if it saw fit. (Nov. 17th, 1947, Chicago Daily Tribune, "World State's Super-Secret Constitution")

Laughlin worked on his own utopian vision for decades. He was working on this one-world constitution while he was serving as the Congressional expert on immigration. A February 19th, 1921, letter to H.G. Wells documents the fact that Laughlin sent Wells an early copy of the utopian proposal. Laughlin would also leverage the various prestigious contacts that Chicago's Municipal Court Judge Olson would provide him in the distribution of "Eugenical Sterilization" in 1921. The reader will recall that one of the recipients of Laughlin's book was ex-President and Supreme Court Justice, William Howard Taft. According to Professor Lombardo, Laughlin would write to Taft at least a dozen times. Notably, Taft was also part of the faculty at Yale University Law School. Laughlin would seek out Taft again in order to forward his one-world government initiative. According to Professor Lombardo, Laughlin "somewhat grandiosely asked the former president for an introductory note that could be published with the text." (Pg. 89, "Three Generations") Taft would decline this request, but despite Taft's otherwise sober approach to American jurisprudence, the ex-president would be amongst the handful of Republicans that would flirt with eugenics, including Presidents Theodore Roosevelt and Calvin Coolidge.

Frances Janet Hassencahl notes an additional list of influential individuals that received Laughlin's proposal for a one-world government. According to Hassencahl, Laughlin sent copies to Ramsey McDonald, the Prime Minister of England, Heinrich Bruening, Chancellor of Germany, M. Ariside Briand, the Minister of Foreign Affairs in France, and to President Herbert Hoover, at all times "expecting that they would read it and comment on the merits of his plan." (Pg. 48, Hassencahl) Her dissertation continues on to comment on this aspect of Laughlin's propagandizing:

Such expectations appear to be typical for Laughlin; he tended to present his solutions for various social problems and to step back and wait for the accolade. Consequently, Laughlin received many disappointments for his failures to analyze his audience and to prepare them for his proposals. Fortunately for his self-esteem he never saw himself as being a lone unknown voice. (Pg. 48, "Harry H. Laughlin, Expert Eugenics Agent," Frances Janet Hassencahl, University Microfilms, 1970)

A September 19th, 1933 letter from the Under Secretary at the Secretary of State's office documents that Laughlin sent copies to President F.D. Roosevelt and Secretary of State Cordell Hull. Laughlin made sure that his proposal was not received blindly, as the September 9th, 1933, letter to Secretary of State Hull reminds the Secretary that Laughlin had been an expert advisor to the Committee on Immigration and Naturalization. Laughlin can hardly be said to have been aiming too high by passing this proposal to the President and the Secretary of State, as the influence he wielded over key pieces of legislation proved he certainly had more than just a foot in the door.

WORLD'S FAIR
CHIC
1833 · A CENTURY
ADULTS 50¢ MAY 27TH
A CENTURY OF PROGRESS
I WILL
1833
1933
SOUVENIR
IGOROT
VILLAGE
PHILIPPINE PHOTOGRAPH CO.
WORLD'S FAIR
ST. LOUIS. · · · 1904.
COPYRIGHTED 1904, PHILIPPINE PHOTOGRAPH CO.

1933 - A CENTURY OF PROGRESS

> *"The advance of science and the evolution of humanity and charity made it known to us that whatever is the result of human agency is capable of correction by human intelligence."*
> – Postmaster General, James A. Farley, Dedication of the 1933 World's Fair

The name of the 1933 World's Fair held in Chicago was "A Century of Progress International Exposition." Originally, the fair was scheduled to run until November 12th, 1933, but it was so successful that it remained opened to run from May 26th to October 31st, 1934. The fair helped the nation's morale as it began to emerge out of the Great Depression. Technological innovation was the theme of the fair along with the slogan "Science Finds, Industry Applies, Man Conforms." Eugenic ideology fit right into the theme and a eugenics section was planned for the fair. Laughlin and the Eugenics Record Office would create the presentation, as well as make themselves available at the exhibit in order to answer questions from the visitors. Robert W. Rydell, author of the 1993 book, "World of Fairs: The Century-of-Progress Expositions," recalls the success of the eugenics exhibit:

> After the congress closed, eugenics exhibits remained open to the public for a month. No accurate attendance figures were kept, but museum officials estimated that between five thousand and ten thousand visitors saw the displays, with over eight hundred signing a register intended to record names of individuals interested in becoming involved in promoting eugenics. Throughout the duration of the exhibition, staff members from the Eugenics Record Office remained at the museum to explain exhibits. Davenport and Laughlin personally escorted biology teachers around the museum. A far more momentous event occurred when the exhibits were dismantled. Many displays were returned to exhibitors, but those that "pertained directly to immigration were installed on the walls of the [U.S. Congress's Committee on Immigration] in Washington for the use of the Committee in analyzing certain historical and new data in reference to immigration." In less than three months, Laughlin's exhibits, originally intended for popular education, became sources for shaping national policy as well. It may be overstating the case, but not by much, to claim that Laughlin converted a U.S. congressional committee into an plenary session of the eugenics congress. (Pg. 48, "World of Fairs")

Laughlin would publicize the effort. Laughlin completed a write-up describing the project entitled "The Eugenics Exhibit at Chicago." It is held at the Laughlin Collection at Truman University and was a short description of the wall-panel entitled "Survey of Eugenics" as exhibited in the Hall of Science in the Century of Progress Exposition. Laughlin describes the installation as:

> As finally installed the four-chart eugenics exhibit was favorably placed along a well-lighted wall in one of the main wide corridors of the Hall of Science, near other biological and particularly anthropological and genetic subjects. (BOX: E-1-2:16, Pg. 3, "The Eugenics Exhibit at Chicago," Laughlin Papers, Truman Univ.)

There is a corresponding article that reads like the final version of Laughlin's write-up. The write-up was published by the Journal of Heredity as "The Eugenics Exhibit at Chicago: A Description of the Wall-Panel Survey of Eugenics Exhibited in the Hall of Science, Century of Progress Exposition, Chicago, 1933-34." Note how Laughlin places eugenics in the upper echelon of the sciences:

> The Century of Progress Exposition was the first world's fair to include eugenics as a matter of course in the classification of the basic sciences. For this reason the exhibit has an historic interest, rather greater than its size, and an account of it is consequently of value as a reference record. (Pg. 155, Journal of Heredity, Vol. XXVI, No. 4, of April 1935)

Laughlin's article continues to describe the panels:

Panel 1a. The Eugenics Tree. This symbolic treatment defines eugenics as "The self-direction of human evolution," and it extends the metaphor by stating the "like a tree eugenics draws its material from many sources and gives them organic unity and purpose." It is half diagnostic and half descriptive. It is "the picture of the introductory chapter of the principles of eugenics." ---- Panel 1b – "What is Eugenics All About" ---- Panel 2 is a chart entitled: "How Families, Communities, Races and Nations May Change Greatly in Capacity Within a Few Generations." (BOX: E-1-2:16, Pg. 4, "The Eugenics Exhibit at Chicago," Laughlin Papers, Truman Univ.)

Chart number two delved into "The Outcome of Differential Fertility," expounding the well-worn argument that the "unfit" reproduced at a much higher rate than those deemed biologically or racially worthwhile. Panel number 3 documented the infamous Ishmael Family as an example of the "unfit", and panel number 4 juxtaposed the Ishmaels with "The Roosevelts." Laughlin explains the juxtaposition in his write-up as "placed side by side for the purpose of contracting qualities in the hereditary equipment of different family-stocks." (Pg. 4) Laughlin describes the charts as delving further into this comparison by charting the presidential family pedigrees of the Adams and Harrison families. The presentation made the laughable claim that "Washington was known to be an aristocrat," despite the fact that this president risked life and limb in order to abolish the monarchy, as well as aristocratic titles and positions. (Pg. 5) Laughlin would continue by describing the reactions of the visitors viewing the charts and what he believed the visitors gleaned from them:

> Human family-stocks and strains of plants and animals in their hereditary behavior present basic analogies too close to dispute successfully. While this analogy was not brought out directly by the exhibit, the facts were presented in such a manner that the visitor with a little knowledge of plant and animal breeding readily supplied the analogy himself. In this the intelligent farmer who treasured hereditary quality in his plant and animal stocks had the necessary background for building up in his own mind the basic pedigree concept of eugenics. The parallel with his own efforts to improve a breed of poultry, hogs or

cattle on his own farm was too close to be denied mental reflection when human pedigrees were brought to his attention. ---- Thus the pedigree-idea spreads, -- that is, the general appreciation of hereditary quality. It came first in reference to domestic animals, cattle and horses, then spread to other farm animals, then to grains and other plants, and last of all to man. Within the human realm, as a principle of general appreciation, it applied first to racial traits, Chinese produced Chinese; Negroes, Negroes; white people, white people, if the blood, that is the pedigree, was clear. (BOX: E-1-2:16, Pg. 7, "The Eugenics Exhibit at Chicago," Laughlin Papers, Truman Univ. – Special Coll.)

Laughlin would make sure to send President Franklin D. Roosevelt a photograph of the curious eugenic pedigree. Correspondence held in the Laughlin Papers at Truman University documents the exchange between Laughlin and the White House. Laughlin sent the photo on September 18th, 1933 and on the 21st, Luis M. Howe, the Secretary to the President, responded thanking him on the President's behalf. Laughlin's letter is interesting as it makes no effort to disguise the racial prejudices behind the exhibition:

Mr. President: Permit me to enclose a photograph of one of the charts exhibited at the Century of Progress Exposition. This chart was one of a series of four, the first describing the relation between racial and family-stocks, national welfare and happiness generally; the second a statistical account of population turn-over with reference to quality; the third showing an inferior family which, despite opportunity, could never get on; and the fourth a superior family. For this latter we could find no better example than the Roosevelt family-stock. (BOX: C-2-2:4, Laughlin to Pres. F.D.R., Sept. 18th, 1933, Truman Univ.)

The management of the International Exposition must have considered the eugenics exhibition to be a success as they wrote Laughlin requesting permission to keep the exhibit past the originally planned closing of the Chicago fair. A November 4th, 1933 letter held at Truman by C.W. Fitch, the Director of Exhibitions to Laughlin makes the official request. Further correspondence held at Truman demonstrates that the interest extended beyond the International Exposition. There are letters from the Associated Merchandising Corporation and the Buffalo Museum of Science asking both the Eugenics Record Office and the Carnegie Institution for the right to purchase or display the boards, with Laughlin ultimately promising them to the Buffalo Museum.

A more disturbing aspect about the 1933 fair must also be recalled. The 1933 fair, like most world's fairs preceding, had exhibits of other cultures that historians now refer to as "human zoos", which were all too common and accepted at the time. "Human Zoos," sometimes called "negro villages," were 19th and 20th-century exhibits of humans, typically in their alleged natural or primitive state. The displays typically emphasized the cultural differences between those of European descent and non-European peoples. These ethnographic zoos were intended as educational shows, often the part of actual zoos, museums, and most prominently, World Fairs.

Human zoos could be found in Paris, Hamburg, Antwerp, Barcelona, London, Milan, New York, and Warsaw with crowds of 200,000 to 300,000 visitors attending each exhibition. The fact that these zoos gained significant popularity in the 1870s clarifies the "educational" message they intended to communicate. There is an important aspect to "Human Zoos" that must be extrapolated in a book about eugenics. "Human Zoos" were not isolated phenomena, but integral and parallel in the Darwinian roots of eugenics. "Human Zoos" thrived in the golden age of Darwinism, and they purported to display the lesser evolved "savages" in contrast to allegedly higher evolved descendants of European civilizations. For enhanced effect, the displays would often be exhibited physically next to the laudatory displays of Western technology and culture.

The Century of Progress Exposition of 1933 sought to emphasize this hierarchy by juxtaposing displays of "primitive" peoples alongside ones that demonstrated the purported superiority of the white Anglo-Saxons. Thus, for example, the fair organizers erected a quaint "Indian Village" in the looming shadow of the General Motors Tower, a modernist temple dedicated to the ascendant American auto industry. The real Native Americans who inhabited the ersatz tepees of the Indian Village served as reminders of an earlier way of life; a way of life that had been rendered obsolete by the steam engine, the automobile, and other advances produced by "white" American civilization. Now vanquished and domesticated on reservations, Native Americans were seen largely as harmless or even ennobled, more deserving of pity than of fear.

Laughlin and company erected their eugenic display in the prominently located Hall of Science Pavilion, The "tribe" the eugenicists displayed with photographs and family pedigrees was the Tribe of Ishmael. According to the Hall of Science exhibition, these modern day "savages" were:

> A Degenerate Family ... which, despite opportunities, never developed a normal life. Shiftless, begging, wanderers, sound enough in body, their hereditary equipment lacked the basic qualities of intelligence and character on which opportunity could work.

Just as the Indian Village stood next to the General Motors Tower, juxtaposing the gulf between them, the eugenicists display exhibited "A Superior Family: The Roosevelt Family-Stock" on panels adjoining those dedicated to the Ishmaels, a family line of alleged rural "degenerates." At the head of the Roosevelt family tree stood Jonathan Edwards, the famous Puritan theologian. Portraits of Theodore Roosevelt and Franklin Delano Roosevelt framed the genealogical tree with the legend reading: "Pedigree showing the distribution of inborn qualities in a family which produced two presidents of the United States."

It must also be clarified that the 1933 fair was not the first time a prominent eugenicist from the United States toyed with the idea using humans for anthropological exhibits. In 1906, Madison Grant, acting as head of the New York

Zoological Society, had Congolese pygmy Ota Benga put on display at the Bronx Zoo alongside apes. At the behest of Grant, the zoo director William Hornaday placed Ota Benga in a cage with the chimpanzees, then with an orangutan named Dohong. Curiously enough, they labeled Benga as "The Missing Link."

Historically speaking, the most notorious example of humans exhibited in this fashion was that of Saartjie Baartman of the Namaqua, often referred to as the 'Hottentot Venus.' Author Sadiah Qureshi of Christ's College in Cambridge tells the story of Saartjie ("little Sara" in Dutch) in her article "Displaying Sara Baartman, the 'Hottentot Venus'." No record of Baartman's real name exists. Baartman was brought to Liverpool, England in 1810 by Alexander Dunlop, an exporter of museum specimens from the African Cape. Baartman went on display in the Piccadilly neighborhood in London. Later, Baartman was exhibited in Paris by the animal trainer S. Réaux in 1814.

Not all of Little Sara's life was spent as entertainment for the masses. In the spring of 1815 Baartman spent three days at the Jardin des Plantes under the observation of the professors of the *Muséum d'Histoire Naturelle*. She posed in the nude for images that appeared in the first volume of Étienne Geoffroy Saint-Hilaire's and Frédéric Cuvier's now iconic *Histoire Naturelle des Mammifères*. It is important to note that this was the effort of a scientific elite, and not necessarily the exploits of circus exhibitors such as those of P.T. Barnum. According to Stephen Jay Gould, author of the Mismeasure of Man, Cuvier was "widely hailed in France as the Aristotle of his age, and a founder of geology." The images of Baartman are prominently displayed in the opening pages of the book and are the only portraits of a human in this extensively illustrated tome. The remainder of the book depicts a vast variety of mammals, including numerous species of apes and monkeys. Quereshi notes that Baartman's poses are disturbingly similarly to the other mammalian specimens in the volume.

In December 1815, Baartman died from an illness Georges Cuvier diagnosed as *"une maladie inflammatoire et eruptive."* Cuvier's autopsy report reveals his belief that she represented an inferior human form. Cuvier's extended discussion of Baartman's face confirms his political and scientific convictions. Cuvier included his observations of a living Baartman in his report. He opines on her supposedly rapid and unexpected movements as being similar to those of a monkey. Cuvier justifies his categorization by pointing to the features of her head. According to Cuvier, her ears were small and weakly formed, and like an orangutan, she frequently jutted her lip outwards. Cuvier claimed that Baartman's skull resembled a monkey's more than any other he had examined. Cuvier's decision to categorize her as a *Boschimanne*, rather than *Hottentote*, further suggests that for Cuvier Baartman was as close as possible to an ape. Qureshi summarizes the phenomenon:

> Throughout the history of colonial occupation at the Cape, many representations of indigenous peoples have been used to facilitate their

subjugation. Wildness and savagery characterized depictions of the Khoikhoi during the seventeenth century, quickly establishing them as the 'link' between ape and human in nature's great hierarchy. -- Flora, fauna and people were all commodities to be collected. The agricultural relevance of botanical knowledge fuelled nationalist interest in plants, whilst animals caged in menageries provided the public with entertainment and evidence of imperial success.

Georges Cuvier's work influenced several generations of 'scientists' that were all too eager to categorize humanity into an evolutionary hierarchy, from ape to man. Cuvier held other beliefs common to the eugenicists that would follow him. He believed environmental influences on evolution were minimal, that anatomical and cranial measurement differentiated the human races, and that physical and mental differences between the races were an indication of their place in this evolutionary hierarchy.

According to Clifton C. Crais and Pamela Scully, authors of the book "Sara Baartman and the Hottentot Venus: a Ghost Story and a Biography," Cuvier's writings, were "particularly influential to Charles Darwin as he began elaborating his theory of evolution." Darwin's understanding of the Hottentot shaped his ideas on human diversity and sexuality." (Page 144-145) By extension, it is instrumental to understand that Galton's hierarchy of the so-called "races of man" was central and an integral part of what he defined as part of his eugenic "science":

> In short, classes E and F of the negro may roughly be considered as the equivalent of our C and D—a result which again points to the conclusion, that the average intellectual standard of the negro race is some two grades below our own. (Pg. 338, "Hereditary Genius")

The European public of Cuvier's time also had a strange obsession with the physical aspects of African females. Francis Galton shared this fetish. He undertook expeditions to see and measure the bodies of these females under the guise of 'scientific' curiosity. Observing a Khoikhoi woman in the distance, he writes:

> I profess to be a scientific man, and was exceedingly anxious to obtain accurate measurements of her shape; but there was a difficulty... I did not know a word of Hottentot... I therefore felt in a dilemma as I gazed at her form, that gift of bounteous nature to this favoured race which no mantua-maker, with all her crinoline and stuffing, can do otherwise than humbly imitate. The object of my admiration stood under a tree, and was turning herself about to all of the compass, as ladies who wish to be admired usually do.

Of course, the foreboding presence of Nazism was palpable at the World's Fair. Clifton C. Crais and Pamela Scully point out that the undesirable and underdeveloped image of the African Hottentot directly contributed to the National Socialist's 1935 laws prohibiting mixed marriages. Incidentally, one of the highlights of the 1933 World's Fair was the arrival of the German airship Graf Zeppelin on October 26th, 1933. The airship was a prominent reminder of the ascendancy of Adolf Hitler to power earlier that same year. This triggered dissension in the days following its visit, particularly within the city's large German-American population.

Likewise, Hitler too would use art and popular culture to sell his eugenic vision to the German public. The Third Reich would sponsor fairs and art exhibitions that also practiced a comparative approach between the "fit" and the "unfit." The expositions put on by the National Socialists also juxtaposed the races deemed to be of a higher evolutionary value and those "degenerating" back towards a state of savagery. The infamous Degenerate Art exhibition mounted by the Nazis in Munich in 1937 displayed the intentionally contorted human figures of modern art as evidence of a "degenerate" Jewish or Bolshevik mind. The *"entartete Kunst"* exhibition was intentionally placed next door to traditional, or classical, German art that intentionally celebrated the anatomically correct depictions of Aryan or Nordic figures. The exhibits traveled in conjunction to several other cities in Germany and Austria, always displayed next to each other for the intended juxtaposition. Clearly, hyper-politicized minds think alike.

AMERICAN EUGENICS SOCIETY, INC.
1790 BROADWAY, NEW YORK 19, N. Y.

EUGENICAL
NEWS

AMERICAN EUGENICS SOCIETY, INC.

Vol. XXXII   JUNE, 1947   No. 2

EUGENICAL
NEWS

A REVIEW OF EUGENICS, AND RELATED PROBLEMS
OF HUMAN HEREDITY, POPULATION
AND THE FAMILY

WITH SPECIAL REFERENCE TO EDUCATION
AND SOCIAL ACTION

Published Quarterly
AMERICAN EUGENICS SOCIETY, INC.
NEW YORK, N. Y.

1933 - EUGENICAL NEWS

> *"National Socialism is nothing but applied biology."*
> – Rudolph Hess quoting Fritz Lenz

Harry H. Laughlin used his clout and professional reputation to paint National Socialism's eugenic policies in a positive light at a time when the rest of the world was still unsure of what to think about Adolf Hitler. He did so mainly by using the journal published by the Eugenics Record Office. Eugenical News was the central publication of the American eugenics movement from 1916 until 1953. It was the most influential eugenics periodical throughout the world from the time of its founding until the start of World War II. Although Eugenical News primarily served as a newsletter for eugenical activity in the United States, it increasingly included news and editorials from European eugenicists and organizations. This was especially true at the time the Third Reich's eugenic policy was being implemented.

The first several volumes were published by Davenport's and Laughlin's Eugenics Record Office. All of this is documented by a September 11th, 1934 memo still held by the Carnegie Institution entitled "MEMORANDA ON ORIGIN OF THE EUGENICAL NEWS AND THE RELATION OF THE EUGENICS RECORD OFFICE AND THE EUGENICS RESEARCH ASSOCIATION IN ITS PUBLICATION." Laughlin prepared the memo for Dr. Albert F. Blakeslee, the Acting Director of the Carnegie Institution's Department of Genetics. The memo details that the editorial committee of Eugenical News consisted of Charles B. Davenport as the chairman, along with Laughlin and Morris Steggerda. Publication was then taken over by the Carnegie Institution of Washington from 1918 to 1920. It also serves to clarify that the Eugenical News eventually became the official organ of the International Federation of Eugenics Organizations. Publication was later taken over by the American Eugenics Association and other successor organizations, which was first called the "Conference of Field Workers of the Eugenics Record Office." The first of these "conferences" was held at the Eugenics Record Office in 1913. The American Eugenics Association and the Eugenics Record Office at times tried to act as two distinct groups, although their rosters betray their unison.

Recall that the International Federation of Eugenic Organizations was not only the group that mounted all of the international eugenic congresses and symposiums, but the organization where German, American, and British eugenicists actively collaborated. Interestingly enough, the above memoranda describes how central Laughlin's and Davenport's Eugenics Record Office was to the international eugenics movement:

The cost of printing the Eugenical News is borne wholly by the Eugenics Research Association. This Association has about 390 paid up members, scattered quite largely over the United States with a few foreign members. The Eugenical News is also the official organ of the International Federation of Eugenic Organizations, which organization sponsors the International Congress and Exhibit of Eugenics. In this formative period of making eugenics into a science the ideals of the Eugenics Record Office, of the Eugenics Research Association, of the International Congress and Exhibits of Eugenics and of the Eugenical News are identical. (Laughlin files, Carnegie Inst., MEMORANDA ON ORIGIN OF THE EUGENICAL NEWS, Sept. 11th, 1934)

Thus, the importance of the Eugenical News goes far beyond that of a racially charged medical journal, as it has been described by historians. It helped legitimize the Third Reich's eugenic policies at a crucial point in history by providing a prime example that scientists from the United States and Britain endorsed and cooperated with the regime.

Historically speaking, the most important article Laughlin wrote for the Eugenical News was his "Eugenical Sterilization in Germany" in V. XXVIII, No. 5, of the September-October issue of 1933. The article was a translation by Laughlin of the June 28th, 1933 address by *Reichsminister* for the Interior, Dr. Wilhelm Frick. "German Population-and-Race Politics" had been read by Frick at the first meeting of the Expert Council for Population-and-Race Politics held in Berlin. It was translated from the German for the Eugenical News by "A. Hellmer" according to the Truman files. Of note is that Frick served in Hitler's cabinet from 1933 to 1943 and was one of the criminals tried and executed for war crimes at the Nuremberg Trials.

Paul Lombardo wrote in "The American Breed" that William Gregory, the curator of the American Museum of Natural History in New York, asked Laughlin to read the paper at a meeting of the Galton Society. Lombardo quotes a letter held at Truman University's Laughlin Collection where Laughlin applauded Frick's speech and predicted other nations would be "compelled to look primarily to eugenics" for the solution to national problems:

> We sent to Germany for Dr. Frick's paper . . . . We propose devoting an early number of the Eugenical News entirely to Germany, and to make Dr. Frick's paper the leading article. Dr. Frick's address sounds exactly as though spoken by a perfectly good American eugenicist in reference to what "ought to be done," with this difference, that Dr. Frick, instead of being a mere scientist, is a powerful Reichsminister in a dictatorial government which is getting things done in a nation of sixty million people. (Pg. 762, P. Lombardo, "The American Breed," Albany Law Review, Vol. 65, No. 3, 2002, quoting Laughlin to Grant letter, Jan., 13th, 1934)

Professor Lombardo clarifies that as Hitler's *Reichsminister* of the Interior, Frick had jurisdiction over the Third Reich's domestic policy. This meant that Frick was

the bureaucrat responsible, not just for the sterilization program, but for the infamous "purity of blood" Nuremberg decrees enacted against the so-called "Jewish degeneracy." It s through this program that the German-Jewish population was defined as detrimental to Hitler's precious "Aryan" gene pool. In other words, Wilhelm Frick was the person where eugenics and anti-Semitism bridged and became indistinguishable from one another. Professor Lombardo lists some of Frick's academic papers, which serve to illustrate this point:
1.) Population Turn-over Within Nordic Civilization
2.) Neighbors of the Nordic Civilization.
3.) Race-hygiene as a Common Duty of all Civilized People.
4.) Contributions to Racial Anthropology.
5.) Race-culture of the Nordic Civilization.

One important point must be made. Frick should not be confused with the likes of Alfred Rosenberg or Adolf Hitler. Neither Rosenberg nor Hitler possessed the scientific education or even the original thinking necessary to have authored the eugenic concepts that are so prominent and frequent in their speeches. Hitler and Rosenberg were largely parroting what scientists like Frick and Laughlin pioneered. Note the tone and phraseology utilized by Frick, one of the men we now regard as one of the architects of The Holocaust:

> However, not only the figures are alarming, but, in the same degree, the quality and composition of our German nation. Since we have not yet taken any heredo-biological census, we are confined to estimates. While we may assume that the cases of serious physical and mental hereditary diseases number about 500,000, the number of minor cases is considerably higher. According to some authors 20% of the German population are considered to be hereditary defectives, whose progeny is therefore undesirable. (BOX: D-2-2:24, "GERMAN POPULATION-AND-RACE POLITICS," Truman Univ.)

The reader will note that Frick's address reads no different than the work of British and American eugenicists cited herein. The speech provides a glimpse of how relatively innocuous legislative intent may seem when delivered by scientists. Frick's intentions are expressed in the same exact scientific terminology and are devoid of the overt racism of speeches given by Hitler, Alfred Rosenberg, or Joseph Goebbels. Yet, Frick was as guilty, if not guiltier of the crimes, as he was one of the men actively involved in the day to day execution of the Third Reich's murderous policies:

> In Berlin alone approximately 4000 immigrants from the East were naturalized in 1930, these were mostly of foreign stock and to a great extent eastern Jews. - - - Besides being threatened with increasing hereditary and biological inferiority, we must carefully watch the progressing race-mixture and race-deterioration of our people, since the German man and the German woman no longer are conscious of their blood and their race. (BOX: D-2-2:24, "GERMAN POPULATION-AND-RACE POLITICS," Truman Univ.)

Consider the importance of the above statement. The above statement clarifies that not only the Germans, but also the readership of the Eugenical News, understood that the Third Reich's eugenic sterilization and immigration program was indistinguishable from their policy towards the German-Jewish population. Their alleged "biological" inferiority was deemed as a threat to the German nation, and eugenics was touted as the solution:

> In order to avert the threatening disaster, it is urgent to reform the entire public health system, as well as the attitude of physicians; it is necessary to change our duties from the point of view of race-hygiene, population-and-race politics. When it will have become the main object of the State and public health service to provide for the unborn generation, only then shall we be able to speak of a new era and of a constructive population-and-race policy. (BOX: D-2-2:24, "GERMAN POPULATION-AND-RACE POLITICS," Truman Univ.)

It is important to note that the Germans sought to revamp their entire healthcare system in order to make the eugenic goals possible. It is curious to see that Frick's address also included the type of income redistribution schemes typical of Progressive politics, with the focus being on redirecting income to families deemed to be eugenically desirable. Frick calls for an "adjustment of the tax reductions" and what we would call a "living wage" in order to accomplish this:

> The salary of an official should not only be a compensation, but afford sufficient income for the family. An income necessary to support a family of 3 or 4 children should be adopted as the standard form which salaries may be graded upwards and downwards. ---- In order to carry out such measures during the difficult financial situation of the country, we certainly need relief from other burdens: e.g. unification and adequate economy in the social insurance system. (BOX: D-2-2:24, "GERMAN POPULATION-AND-RACE POLITICS," Truman Univ.)

In hindsight, it is also important to see how the Nazis understood that eugenic policy had to be by necessity an integral part of Hitler's "Total State", or what we now refer to as "Totalitarianism." This was not just a system of systematic inclusion and exclusion, but also an endeavor to put the full might of government to guard the purity of the "hereditary stocks" of the nation. This was an all-out war, not just on unwanted ethnicities, but also on unwanted "racial poisons." As author Robert Proctor documents in his book "The Nazi War on Cancer," Hitler's government was the most pervasive anti-tobacco, anti-alcohol, and anti-food colorant government in history. Not surprisingly, the regime was also committed to a campaign for animal rights and natural eating. Alas, the grounds of the Dachau concentration camp were the single largest organic produce farm of the era, and a significant portion of the SS funds came from the sale of organic herbs. Frick's speech continues along these lines:

> The Reich, the States, and the communities must test and revise our entire administration from the point of view of population politics. Besides the financial and economic reorganization, our public health system should be

unified and placed in the service of race-hygiene by constructive measures. Together with the present sanitary regulations it will be necessary to banish the dangers of hereditary defects in accordance with our knowledge of heredity and race-hygiene. This would insure the propagation of hereditarily sound and fit human stock. (BOX: D-2-2:24, "GERMAN POPULATION-AND-RACE POLITICS," Truman Univ.)

Frick closes with the type of statement that Adolf Hitler and Joseph Goebbels were known for; calling on the youth to awaken their "national" and "social" sentiments towards the building of a "master race." However, instead of it being saturated with aggressive anti-Semitism, Frick's words fit perfectly in line with eugenical dissertations:

> Here again it is up to the educated youth to recognize the value of the German hereditary constitution, to preserve race-purity and to strive toward improvement of their own family-stocks by suitable matings. Miscegenation must be labelled what it is: namely the foundation for mental and spiritual degeneration and alienation from the native stock. Family pedigree study and anthropology should be cultivated in a manner to stress the value of the blood above wealth and comfort. We must have the courage to rate our population according to its hereditary value, in order to supply the State with leaders. [sic.] (BOX: D-2-2:24, "GERMAN POPULATION-AND-RACE POLITICS," Truman Univ.)

The Law for the Prevention of Genetically Diseased Offspring in National Socialist Germany was enacted on July 14th, 1933. The law allowed for the compulsory sterilization of any citizen who in the opinion of a "Genetic Health Court," or *Gr. Erbgesundheitsgericht*, suffered from a list of disorders thought to be hereditary. The law was mainly the work of Ernst Rüdin, Arthur Gütt and the lawyer Dr. Falk Ruttke of the Reich's Committee for Public Health Service. Frick's translated address is held together with a letter from Dr. Falk Ruttke at Truman University's Laughlin Collection. It serves as evidence of the relationship between Hitler's propaganda department and Harry H. Laughlin. The cover letter is headlined as a "Publication Series", and the English language it is written in evidences that Frick's speech was distributed for the consumption of the public outside of Germany:

> The Reich's Committee for Public Health Service begins with this number a series of pamphlets which will essentially differ from the publications issued by the Committee for Popular Hygienic Education. The national-socialist government is the first government to make an example of putting Eugenics and Race-culture (Race-hygiene) in the service of the State. This fact will be particularly stressed by the present series. **Everyone is requested to help circulating these publications.** (BOX: D-2-2:24, "Publication Series of Reich's Committee for Public Health Service," June 28, 1933, Berlin, Truman Univ., emphasis mine)

The above document can justly be characterized as an example of Laughlin willingly acting as a propaganda mouthpiece for Hitler's government and using the circulation of Eugenical News towards that end. In turn, Laughlin likely understood that most of his countrymen would find his collaboration unpalatable. Thus, many of the articles that provided praise for the movement's accomplishments were unsigned editorials written by Laughlin. The September 11th, 1934 memorandum admits as much:

> For me personally the Eugenical News requires a great deal of hard work; in it I have published many unsigned papers for which I have received no authorship or bibliographic credit. Still I feel that it is quite worthwhile as a constructive contribution to the development of eugenics. (Laughlin files, Carnegie Inst., MEMORANDA ON ORIGIN OF THE EUGENICAL NEWS, Sept. 11th, 1934)

Of course, this is a coy evasion by Laughlin, as his leadership position allowed him the power to give himself credit for authorship whenever credit was due. A January 16th, 1934 letter from Madison Grant to Laughlin discussing Hitler's eugenical sterilization program is telling. Grant warns Laughlin that "most people of our type" would be in sympathy but that they would "have to proceed cautiously in endorsing them." (Laughlin Papers, Truman Univ.)

However cautiously they chose to proceed, disguising racism with scientific terminology, there was the ever present newspaper coverage defining the German legislation as "eugenic." The Chicago Tribune and New York Times made sure to cover every development inside of Germany and accurately describe them as "eugenic." Anyone familiar with the aspirations of American eugenicists would have recognized the programs enacted by Hitler's government as substantially similar, if not identical. Frick's address in the Eugenical News certainly demonstrated that the German scientists responsible for The Holocaust considered their eugenics to be cut from the same cloth as that of the American and British eugenics. The printing of Frick's address, along with the remaining stream of favorable coverage the Eugenical News disseminated evidences not only approbation but a camaraderie as would be expected from individuals working towards a unified cause. Paul Lombardo points out in "The American Breed" that the close ties amongst the eugenicists became crystal clear when Ruttke, Rüdin, and Eugen Fischer were named part of the Advisory Board of the Eugenical News. (Pg. 772) Here was the International Federation of Eugenic Organizations admitting to the monolithic nature of their movement.

The letter from Dr. Falk Ruttke to Laughlin asking for the publication and dissemination of Frick's speech raises matters to a more serious level. All of this resulted in the murder of millions. Evidence of this kind would build towards what prosecutors call a "criminal conspiracy" if one were in a court of law. The military tribunal at Nuremberg, in fact, determined that the acts and events directly overseen by Frick were "criminal" in nature and as part of a "conspiracy." As mentioned earlier, Frick was sentenced to death by the Nuremberg tribunal. One wonders if this all-too-cozy relationship between Laughlin and his Nazi cohorts raises to the level of "aiding and abetting the enemy"? It certainly should have raised the curiosity of the otherwise highly aggressive investigations into any individual suspected of collaboration with the Nazis.

Acclaims Hitler

Leon F. Whitney
Hailing Chancellor Adolf Hitler as "one of the greatest statesmen and social planners in the world," Leon F. Whitney, of New Haven, Conn., former executive secretary of the American Eugenics Society, endorses Hitler's sterilization program, which is to be applied to 400,000 Germans considered defectives.
(Central Press)

A publication of the
THE STERILIZATION LEAGUE OF NEW JERSEY
Princeton, New Jersey

MAJOR PROVISIONS for POPULATION CONTROL ABROAD

With Special Reference
To Medical Leadership

By Mrs. Marion S. Norton

...months of European travel in 1936 gave ...ity to accumulate information on for-...ation control policies and to confer ...leaders in eugenic sterilization pro-... outstanding difference from the move-... the United States lies in the fact that ...ilization legislation abroad the initia-... been taken by physicians, the whole ...as been developed by and is administered ...sional people, while for the most part ...al public remains unaware of what is ...d entirely a medical question.

...LAND: Canton of Vaud. The sterilization ... 1901 and 1921 covered persons afflicted ...ntal disease, but the law which went into ... in 1929 extended the scope to the feeble-... if according to all foresight, he can ...ly defective offspring," and to those ad-... to drugs, and to alcoholics, when "their ...ion necessitates care or offers dangers to ... or to themselves." The Board of Health ... the authorization, after investigation and ... prognosis of two physicians appointed by it.

"What is done is done by the doctors quietly. ...ublic have never had their attention drawn ...he subject."

Canton of Bern. Voluntary sterilization ...rations are performed on persons who have al-...y a family that they cannot properly support. ... does not mean dependents only but also those ... can just make ends meet with the family they ...e. It is done mostly upon women. There is no ...urt procedure, but a private doctor must get the ...sent of the municipal doctor. Every town sup-...orts public birth control clinics with free con-...ltation; clients pay only for their supplies.

"The Catholic Church has never tried to in-...terfere. How could they influence things as long ...as they are only 20-25% in this canton?" (the ...same proportion as in the state of New Jersey)

Charles Fauconnet, M.D., Vice-Director of the
National Public Health Service.

Sweden	Norway	Germany	Finland	Estonia	Denmark	
x	x	x	x	x	x	Mental Deficiency
x	x	x	x	x	x	Mental Disease
		x		x		Epilepsy
		x	x			Nervous Disease
		x		x		Gross Physical Defect
					x	
x					x	
					x	
x	x	x	x	x		
x		x				
					x	
x	x	x	x	x		
x	x	x	x	x		
			x	x		
x				x		
		x	x			
x						
		x	x			
x						
					x	

1933 - TOURING HITLER'S EUGENIC UTOPIA

"The Germans are beating us at our own game."
- Joseph DeJarnette

The version of Holocaust history we are often presented with claims that few people in the United States knew what was happening inside Hitler's eugenic utopia. Professor Victoria F. Nourse, author of the 2008 book, "In Reckless Hands: Skinner v. Oklahoma and the Near Triumph of American Eugenics" documents a December 22nd, 1933 article in the New York Daily Times. Professor Nourse recalls that American academia and the popular press has adopted an intentional policy of amnesia for this early adoration of Adolf Hitler:

> When the German sterilization law was first proposed, the press emphasized the analogy to American laws. In 1933, the New York Times's editorial page explained that the Nazi program, upon examination, turned out to be little different from those advocated in "every civilized country." (Pg. 32, "In Reckless Hands")

Professor Nourse opines that it was Hitler's antagonism and militarism that first opened the door to criticism from these previously supportive political circles. She cites the New York Times' science editor, Waldermar Kaempffert:

> Given "Germany's present reign of political terror, geneticists wonder whether a law which has much to commend will be enforced with strict scientific impartiality." Presciently, Kaempffert asked, "What is to stop the governor of a concentration camp from recommending sterilization for a malformed Communist or member of the Catholic Center?" (Pg. 34, "In Reckless Hands")

The answer to Kaempffert's question should have been obvious. A "centrally-planned" society leverages a single voice in government and has "total control." These are the consequences of governmental solutions that lack a "balance" or "separation" of powers. It is what Americans call "same hands powers." Any American that understood and the basic notion of "limited government" should have been keen to the abuses that come when there is a "diss-balance of power" or when the power of the state is held in the "same hands." To the contrary, the abuses become part of the institution of government, as those in power demand the collaboration of their subordinates. Professor Nourse continues by documenting how doubts emerged as scientifically questionable applications of the law were reported. Nourse is insightful as it gives one an idea of the speed by which the situation in Germany deteriorated:

> In January 1934, it was reported that Germany's sterilization law would apply to children as young as ten. Two weeks later, the Germans ordered a census of incurables and demanded that the German criminal courts be scoured for "hereditary defectives" (despite the fact that the original Nazi

statute did not cover habitual criminals). Doctors who failed to report a defective individual were to be fined heavily. In February, it was reported that eugenics authorities were insisting on the immediate sterilization of the "Negroid children in the Rhineland and the Ruhr," the legacy of "invading French colonial troops" during World War I. (Pgs. 34-35, "In Reckless Hands")

More to the point, the coercive aspects of the legislation should have been obvious to anyone that took notice of the egregious amount of gloating coming from eugenic circles when the Germans adopted their recommendations. The "German criminal courts" that Nourse refers to were in fact the "Genetic Health Courts" which consisted of a judge, a medical officer, and medical practitioner, much in the same way in which Harry H. Laughlin's "Model Eugenic Law" recommended, and precisely in the same way which the U.S. Supreme Court found to be sufficiently observant of "due process" in the 1927 case of <u>Buck v. Bell</u>. One only need to refer to Section 21 of Laughlin's "Model Eugenic Law" to see the same coercive provisions that would later seem objectionable when practiced by Hitler's dictatorship:

> **Section 21. Punishment of Responsible Head of Institution for Dereliction.** The responsible head of any public or private custodial institution in the State who shall discharge, release or parole from his or her custody or care any inmate who has been duly ordered by a court of this State to be eugenically sterilized, before due consummation of such order as herein contemplated, unless, as herein provided, such particular inmate be discharged, released or paroled into the custody of the State Eugenicist, shall be guilty of a misdemeanor, and shall be punished by not less than — months imprisonment or — dollars fine, or both; or by not more than — months imprisonment or — dollars fine, or both.

These were the banal mechanisms through which evil was perpetrated, albeit in the guise of legality, scientific legitimacy, and governmental authority. The <u>Buck v. Bell</u> decision by the United States Supreme Court was highly publicized along with the measures individual States began to implement in earnest as a result. At this juncture, approximately thirty States in the American Union had implemented eugenic sterilization laws and were actively enforcing it. Furthermore, prominent scientists and doctors from the most prestigious schools and institutions were propagandizing their movement in the most public of forums, including the World's Fair and the New York Museum of Natural History. Towns across America were holding the now infamous "Fitter Families" contests to reward families that were deemed eugenically fit and superior. In California, young couples considering marriage were being counseled to seek out an evaluation by expert eugenicists prior to marriage to determine if the coupling was eugenically desirable. Grade school students across the United States were learning eugenics directly from the

"Hunter's Civic Biology," whose section on humanity had been written by Charles B. Davenport and was overtly white-supremacist and strictly eugenic. At least two Presidents, Theodore Roosevelt and Woodrow Wilson, had vociferously supported eugenic legislation for decades. Jim Crow legislation was in full force, and anti-miscegenation laws and segregation based on race were part of daily reality. This was the American *zeitgeist* at the time when the Third Reich first enacted eugenic legislation.

The members of the American and British eugenics movement certainly understood just how interwoven eugenics was in the hierarchy of the Third Reich. Several influential American eugenicists would travel to Hitler's Germany to survey the scope of the program. These visits would prove to be crucial, historically speaking, as they provided Hitler's government precisely what they needed in order to answer the accusations of the international public. They provided National Socialism's "applied eugenics" a veil of scientific legitimacy. The vocal approbation by British and American scientists was utilized by Hitler's propaganda machine to answer the criticisms that his domestic policy was the creation of thugs and bigots. For example, Paul Popenoe, whom sat on the board of the American Eugenics Society, and was the founder of the Human Betterment Foundation, wrote in the Journal of Heredity about the permeation of eugenics in the Third Reich:

> Hitler is surrounded by men who at least sympathize with the eugenics program . . . . The policy of the present German government is therefore to gather about it the recognized leaders of the eugenics movement, and to depend largely on their counsel in framing a policy which will direct the destinies of the German people, as Hitler remarks in Mein Kampf, "for the next thousand years." (Pg. 56, "California's Nazi Eugenics," EIR Investigation, Vol. 22, No. 11, March 10th, 1995)

Stefan Kühl quotes Paul Popenoe voicing an opinion that the eugenics practiced by the Third Reich was the product of the eugenics that had been developed over decades by the international eugenics movement:

> The law that has been adopted is not a half-baked and hasty improvisation of the Hitler regime, but is the product of many years of consideration by the best specialists in Germany . . . I must say that my impression is, from a close following of the situation in the German scientific press, rather favorable. (Pg. 45, "The Nazi Connection")

Of course, none of this would have been news to the eugenic insiders. Charles Davenport, Harry H. Laughlin, and Leonard Darwin had been collaborating with the German eugenicists for decades prior. The letterhead of the International Federation of Eugenics Organizations (IFEO) prominently displays Davenport, Laughlin, and Darwin alongside Ernst Rüdin, Eugen Fischer, and Alfred Ploetz as the leadership of the IFEO. Thus, the relationships were undeniable. The IFEO network facilitated key pieces of information. Laughlin's "Model Eugenical Law" was put in the hands of the German eugenicists primarily responsible for authoring and implementing the Third Reich's eugenic program. They corresponded and met in IFEO sponsored congresses and symposiums on a regular basis. Take note of the opening statements of the address Davenport delivered at the 1932 congress. This curious statement seemingly echoes Hitler's desire to have a "Total State" breed a race of "supermen":

> Can we by eugenical studies point the way to produce the superman and the superstate? (Pg. 56, "California's Nazi Eugenics", EIR Investigation, Vol. 22, No. 11, March 10th, 1995)

Clearly, the international eugenics movement did not see their close relationship with Hitler's government as a negative. To the contrary, they both publicized the advances made by Hitler's government in the field of eugenics and took credit whenever it was apparent that Hitler's scientists had utilized the work of their American counterparts. An important example of this was the "24th Annual Report of the Colony for Epileptics and Feeble-Minded" that Dr. John Bell, the named party in the Buck v. Bell case, wrote in 1933:

> In his last report for the Virginia Colony, Bell praised the "principle of genetic control" enshrined in Virginia law and heralded the new German law for sterilization. He predicted that the German law, which applied not merely to institutions but also to the country's entire population, would provide "a vast advantage in the elimination of the unfit." He called for a federal sterilization law in the United States, urging the nation to "apply the pruning knife with vigor." (Pg. 208, "Three Generations No Imbeciles")

The Third Reich's implementation of Laughlin's "Model Eugenic Law" was celebrated by other key members of the Buck v. Bell initiative. Recall that Joseph DeJarnette, the man who bemoaned the fact that the "Germans were beating us at our own game," kept track of the numbers sterilized to justify his jealousy for Hitler's accomplishments. According to Professor Paul Lombardo, DeJarnette tallied the numbers sterilized in Germany and in the U.S. from 1935 to 1939, "chiding his countrymen for falling behind" the pace of the Germans. DeJarnette reported that Germany had already sterilized 56,224 people by the end of the first year. (Pg. 209, "Three Generations No Imbeciles")

Other prominent members of American medicine and science would follow. Stefan Kühl, documents that William W. Peter, the secretary of the American Public Health Association, also spent six months in Germany. Peter traveled between 1933 and 1934 "visiting every major section of Germany and met with officials who were responsible for the new health measures." (Pg. 54) Again, William W. Peter's endorsement was no small accomplishment for the Third Reich. The American Public Health Association is the oldest and most diverse organization of public health professionals in the world. It still exists as a Washington, D.C.-based professional organization for public health professionals in the United States. Founded in 1872 by Dr. Stephen Smith, APHA has more than

30,000 members worldwide. Kühl explains the importance of William W. Peter's endorsement:

> Peter's experiences convinced him that the Nazi government was applying eugenics measures in a "legally and scientifically fair way." He judged Germany as the "first modern nation to have reached a goal toward with other nations are just looking, or approaching at snail's pace." --- Back in the United States, Peter --- published an article in the American Journal of Publish Health and The Nation's Health. In this article he reassured the American scientific community that several safeguards would prevent potential abuse of the Law on Preventing Hereditarily Ill Progeny. The Hereditary Health Courts and Hereditary Health Supreme Courts, he argued, would guarantee the correct application of the law. (Pg. 54, "The Nazi Connection")

C.M. Goethe, Laughlin's supporter and founder of California State, Sacramento University, would also travel to Germany and report back to his various eugenic-minded cohorts the extent to which the Third Reich's eugenic policies were based upon American eugenics. The one person he made a point to contact was his fellow Californian, E.S. Gosney, whom apparently took great joy in the Goethe's praise. The correspondence is still held at the E.S. Gosney collection at the Cal. Tech archives:

> It is well known, however, that their leaders in the sterilization movement depended largely upon the material accumulated by the Human Betterment Foundation, using this as a California data foundation upon which to rear their present remarkable structure. (Folder 5.15 – Box 5, E.S. Gosney Papers, Cal. Tech University)

Marion Stephenson Norton, wife of Princeton professor Paul R. Coleman-Norton was another prominent Ivy League educated eugenicist to survey Hitler's eugenic program. She was a product of Princeton University and had founded the Sterilization League of New Jersey in 1937. Olden conducted her professional activities under the name Marion S. Norton until about 1941 when, after marrying her fourth husband, she styled herself as Marian (sometimes Mariann) S. Olden. She would become one of the most vocal proponents of New Jersey's eugenic legislation under then Governor Woodrow Wilson. She chaired the Social Hygiene Committee of the Princeton chapter of the League of Women Voters beginning in 1933 or 1934 in which capacity she began her activism on behalf of eugenic sterilization. Her activism extended past the end of WWII and The Holocaust, as she also helped to found Birthright, Inc., a national organization advocating compulsory sterilization in 1943 and served as its executive secretary until 1948. She was one of a handful of prominent Americans to tour Hitler's Germany with the specific goal of reporting back how the Third Reich's eugenic legislation was being implemented. She published a pamphlet titled "MAJOR PROVISIONS FOR POPULATION CONTROL ABROAD – With Special Reference To Medical Leadership." It was widely distributed and advertised as a publication of "THE

STERILIZATION LEAGUE OF NEW JERSEY, Princeton, New Jersey", with her name Marion S. Norton as the principal author. The opening paragraph of the pamphlet states:

> Seven months of European travel in 1938 gave an opportunity to accumulate information on foreign population control policies and to confer with the leaders in eugenic sterilization programs. The outstanding difference from the movement in the United States lies in the fact that with sterilization legislation abroad the initiative has been taken by physicians, the whole project has been developed by and is administered by professional people, while for the most part the general public remains unaware of what is considered entirely a medical question. (Folder 9.3 – Box 9, E.S. Gosney Papers, Cal. Tech Archives)

According to Stefan Kühl, Norton had come under the German government's radar due to the pamphlet that her New Jersey organization used to influence New Jersey law. The 1937 pamphlet titled "Selective Sterilization in Primer Form" as well as the 1935 pamphlet "Sterilization and the Organized Opposition" fell right in line with National Socialism's political convictions. Most importantly, the assessments she returned helped keep The Holocaust as a "rumor" until the U.S. Armed Forces liberated the extermination camps:

> She countered claims that sterilization in Germany was used to eliminate Jews, and complained that such rumors stemmed from the "cunning effort on the part of Catholics to emotionally stampede people, who otherwise would support a measure for social health." She criticized the "strangulating power' of Pope Pius XI's opposition to all forms of population control that he reiterated in his Encyclical *Casti Connubii* on December 31, 1930. Nazi race politicians used Norton's pamphlet when confronting Catholic opposition to the Law on preventing Hereditarily Ill Progeny. On September 18, 1937, Gottfried Frey, member of the health department of the Reich minister of the interior, wrote a report for the Reich Chancellery about the "fight of the Catholic Church against the Law on Preventing Hereditarily Ill Progeny.'" In the report he quoted Norton to prove that the opposition of the Catholic Church was coordinated "from abroad (Rome)" rather than from Germany. (Pg. 59, "The Nazi Connection")

Of note is that Norton's pamphlet covers all of the countries she recognized as pioneers of eugenic legislation aside from Germany. This included countries who were considered to be at the forefront of progressive legislation including Denmark, Norway, Sweden, Finland, Latvia, and the British Empire including Australia and Canada. Of note is that none of these aside from Germany would have been considered Fascist, militaristic, highly nationalistic, or "right-wing" by any stretch of the imagination. The portion on Germany is the most extensive and it states:

> The law effective Jan. 1, 1934 has proved to be the best sterilization law on any statute book. It is eugenically effective and is safeguarded from political interference by having its own system of Courts for the Prevention of Hereditary Diseases. These are especially fitted to handle eugenic questions and such cases are never committed to the ordinary courts. ---- Competent American

investigators, **C.M. Goethe**, ex-president of the Eugenics Research Association, and **Dr. Marie E. Kopp**, have reported that "the law is administered wisely and without racial cruelty," that "all possible safeguards are taken to forestall miscarriage of justice in whatever form it may occur," and that discrimination of class, race, creed, political or religious belief does not enter into the matter." The problem of safeguarding the administration of a sterilization law from political influence seems to have been solved, and to **consist in placing the whole program in the hands of legal and medical experts under a system of special Health Courts, divorced from all criminal and civil proceedings**. (Folder 9.3 – Box 9, E.S. Gosney Papers, Cal. Tech Archives, emphasis mine)

Norton makes reference to a Dr. Marie E. Kopp, another eugenicist that also toured and published a paper upon from returning from Hitler's Germany in the American Sociological Review:

I interviewed many leaders, including laymen as well as superintendents of hospitals and institutions, judges of the Hereditary Health Courts, and a large number of physicians, surgeons, psychiatrists, and social workers, who are called upon to give testimony in court and to carry out the provisions of the new laws. (Pg. 761, American Sociological Review, Volume I, No. 5, October 1936, "Legal and Medical Aspects of Eugenic Sterilization in Germany," Box 5.15 – Folder 4, E.S. Gosney Papers, Cal. Tech Archives, emphasis mine)

It is interesting to note that Kopp's translation of the German sterilization law is a verbatim copy of Laughlin's "Model Eugenic Law":

Five mental and three physical groups are specifically named as hereditary in origin, and hence come under the provisions of the law. The mental groups are (1) hereditary feeble-mindedness, (2) schizophrenia, (3) manic-depressive insanity, (4) hereditary epilepsy, and (5) hereditary Huntington's chorea. The physical groups are (6) blindness, (7) deafness, and (8) severe physical deformity, so far as any of these are hereditary. The law also covers (9) severe habitual drunkenness. (Pg. 763, American Sociological Review, Volume I, No. 5, October 1936, "Legal and Medical Aspects of Eugenic Sterilization in Germany", Box 5.15 – Folder 4, E.S. Gosney Papers, Cal. Tech Archives)

Dr. Kopp very likely understood that the so-called "Hereditary Health Courts" were an adaptation of Laughlin's legislative recommendations, as she points out that the Germans had followed the scientific "experts" in the implementation of three panel courts.

Like Laughlin, Davenport, and Darwin, Kopp had established relationships with the leadership of the Kaiser Wilhelm Research Institute by the time she returned to Germany in 1935. Kopp had initially traveled in 1932 under an Oberlaender Fellowship, an organization that itself was already under criticism for some conspicuous connections to the Third Reich. The Oberlaender Trust discusses this openly in the biographical profile of Gustav Oberlaender, the German-born textile magnate and philanthropist in an article posted on its web page entitled "The Problem of Nazism and Oberlaender's Legacy". The Oberlaender

Trust partnered with the Carl Schurz Memorial Foundation, the *Vereinigung Carl Schurz* (Carl Schurz Association, VCS). By 1933, the VCS had become sympathetic to the Nazi cause. The American foundation and the Oberlaender Trust publicly distanced themselves from the Nazified VCS, while they continued to work with it in sponsoring cultural exchanges. The relationship became public when Propaganda Minister Josef Goebbels praised the Oberlaender Trust in an October 1933 speech calling for more German-American support of Nazism.

Kopp clearly understood the depth of the Third Reich's commitment to eugenics. She begins her ten page praise of Hitler's eugenic venture by explaining that the regime was dedicated to using its position of power towards the "biological improvement" of its populace:

> The National Socialist Government of Germany has as one of its avowed aims the improvement of the biological and racial qualities of the German people. For this purpose it has undertaken a variety of measures, carried on as part of the public health and social welfare services of the state. The measures are not arbitrary experiments. Every one of them is **part of a large, permanent public health program**. (Pg. 761, American Sociological Review, Volume I, No. 5, October 1936, "Legal and Medical Aspects of Eugenic Sterilization in Germany," Box 5.15 – Folder 4, E.S. Gosney Papers, Cal. Tech Archives, emphasis mine)

The reader should revisit the above quote, as its casual tone betrays the true nature of Hitler's "nationalized" form of "socialism." The mass media has ingrained in our general public the notion that the "crimes against humanity" were the result of impulsive and unadulterated hatred. It is a dangerous notion that underestimates the human capacity for calculated and systematized criminal acts, or to be more precise, the capacity for governments to disguise the most heinous of crimes under the veil of legality. Even more important is the fact that the so-called "willing executioners," as some famous Holocaust historians have referred to them, were not necessarily motivated by a simmering hatred but were true believers in the "science." It is the approach that Kopp refers to as a "permanent public health program," administered with the cold calculation of professionals. The most intriguing aspect of Kopp's paper is the description of how the Third Reich's eugenic program permeated into every method in which the government interacted with the German populace. She lists the methods she found intriguing:

1.) Marriage loans are offered to encourage early marriages among healthy and intelligent persons by financing new homes for them.
2.) Municipalities have become the sponsors of the third and fourth children in more competent families.
3.) Subsidies are granted for the children of healthy parents on farms, thus attempting to make up for the deficiency in births among the urban population.
(Pg. 762, American Sociological Review, Volume I, No. 5, October 1936, Box 5.15 – Folder 4, E.S. Gosney Papers, Cal. Tech Archives)

At this juncture, the reader will recognize that these measures were hardly new concepts to the international eugenics movement. To the contrary, they were pretty much the consensus amongst all of its leadership beginning with Francis Galton and proceeding on through Leonard Darwin and Charles Davenport. A New York Times article from 1929, printed years prior to Adolf Hitler consolidating power, quotes Clarence Campbell calling for precisely the types of measures that Kopp would later praise the Third Reich for:

> To make it possible for those best fitted to have a minimum of four children, Dr. Campbell urged the remission of taxes for such persons. A contributory tax by those who make no contribution to racial reproduction and replacement, similar in that proposed by Mussolini. (NYT, June 2nd, 1929, "Urges Endowment to Improve Race")

The article's subtitle was "Eugenist Says Funds Should Be Given to Aid Best Families to Rear More Children." The article continues along the lines that so many eugenicists, namely Leonard Darwin, proposed as income redistribution schemes towards eugenic ends:

> "Eventually the State must come to recognize the social and economic value of endowing offspring from its efficient stock, a policy for which the social body should receive a hundredfold in return," Dr. Campbell maintained. "It would seem to be incontestable that the social body should not only have the right to exercise discreet supervision over such social replacement, but be under the obligation to supply, or adequately supplement, the means to this. The application of the principles of taxation in the primary socio-economic need of population replacement is both warrantable and just." (NYT, June 2nd, 1929, "Urges Endowment to Improve Race")

Later chapters will discuss how the eugenic-minded institutions that survived the negative taint of The Holocaust, namely Wickliffe Draper's and Laughlin's Pioneer Fund, would embark on projects precisely as described in Kopp's points 1 to 3:

> The German sterilization law is not a hasty enactment, as some people believe. Educational work along eugenic lines goes back four decades. The first sterilization legislation was discussed before the Reichstag in 1907, about the time an American sterilization measure first became law in Indiana. ---- The leaders in the German sterilization movement state repeatedly that their legislation was formulated only after careful study of the California experiment as reported by Mr. Gosney and Dr. Popenoe. It would have been impossible, they say, to undertake such a venture involving some one million people without drawing heavily upon previous experience elsewhere. (Pg. 763, American Sociological Review, Volume I, No. 5, October 1936, Box 5.15 – Folder 4, E.S. Gosney Papers, Cal. Tech, emphasis mine)

Furthermore, the reader should take note that these are the measures of progressive-minded governments, as they employ the "income redistribution" scheme common to their politics. The adage about the road to hell being paved with good intentions applies here, especially when discussing an apparently sober-minded scientist like Marie Kopp. Kopp's paper serves to dispel any doubt that her admiration of Hitler's measure is their collectivist nature:

> The present prevailing philosophy, therefore, is that if the social and cultural standards of the nation are to be maintained, **the interests of the community must take precedence over individual interests even in very personal matters.** (Pg. 763, American Sociological Review, Volume I, No. 5, October 1936, Box 5.15 – Folder 4, E.S. Gosney Papers, Cal. Tech, emphasis mine)

Kopp makes it a point to emphasize several key aspects of the legal requirements, which incidentally, are in perfect observation of the provisions which the United States Supreme Court singled out as necessary in order to make the sterilization law "constitutional" in the 1927 Buck v. Bell case. The most important one was fact that the German law made no provisions for sterilization as a punitive measure for criminal acts. (Pg. 768, Kopp) Recall that this was a requirement recommended by the eminent civil rights attorney, Louis Marshall in Laughlin's 1914 "Legal, Legislative, and Administrative Aspects of Sterilization."

The list of American eugenicists that toured Hitler's eugenic utopia continues. The other famous American eugenicist to offer favorable publicity and support for Hitler's adoption of eugenic legislation was Leon F. Whitney. Whitney was the direct descendant of the famous inventor of the cotton gin, Eli Whitney, and had a familial relationship with Wickliffe Draper. Whitney was also the man that was primarily in charge of the round-up of "defective" children at Shutesbury. Leon F. Whitney's 1934 book, "The Case for Sterilization," gave open praise for Hitler's sterilization policies. Stefan Kühl cites Whitney openly praising the Third Reich in his book:

> Many far-sighted men and women in both England and America have long been working earnestly toward something very like what Hitler has now made compulsory. (Pg. 36, "Nazi Connection")

Whitney's statement about "far-sighted men and women" from England and America would not have been controversial in the pre-Holocaust era. In fact, Leon Whitney's eugenic goals were as ambitious as those of the German eugenicists, and most leading American eugenicists agreed with the scope and scale of Whitney's eugenic aspirations. Leon Whitney proposed sterilizing 10 percent of the entire population of the United States. At the time 10 percent of the American population would have been around 10 million "hereditary defectives." Furthermore, Whitney was openly jealous of the power the Third Reich wielded towards this effect. (Pg. 59, "The Case for Sterilization") Allan Chase, author of the 1975 book titled, "The Legacy of Malthus: The Social Costs of the New Scientific Racism," provides some figures to put this all into perspective. At the end of the war the Allies came to learn about the German Central Association of Sterilized Persons. This was the organization that ran the eugenic courts and that had ruled that at least two million human beings were eugenically unfit. These individuals would be systematically sterilized during the twelve years of the Third Reich. In other words, the Nazis sterilized against their will an average of 165,000 people every year. This was done at a pace of 450 forced sterilizations per day. (Pg. 135, "Legacy of Malthus") Whitney apparently knew something about these institutions as his book's first paragraph makes a direct reference to the National Socialist's sterilization project:

> CHAPTER I – Sterilization, A Burning Issue To-Day. ---- Since the year 1934 opened there has been a startling increase in the attention given to the subject of sterilization, an increase which among American newspaper-readers is probably due largely to the news from Germany that Hitler has undertaken to have some four hundred thousand Germans sterilized – nearly a hundredth part of the population. Whether this order is or is not directed exclusively at the Jews, it is so grave a decision as to justify fully the recent discussion of it among thousands of persons in our own country who may never before have taken any real interest in the subject. ---- Many far-sighted men and women in both England and America, however, have long been working earnestly toward something very like what Hitler has now made compulsory. Ridiculed, even vilified, they have fought courageously and steadily for the legalization of what they consider a constructive agency in the betterment of the race.

The condescending tone of Whitney's book will ring familiar to 21st Century readers. Whitney's book asks for an "enlightened understanding" of sterilization, free from the typical "uneducated" objections from the "religious," as well as free from the "abuse the supporters of sterilization" receive from these sectors of the concerned public. Whitney is clear on the point that eugenics as practiced in the Third Reich and as intended by the leadership of the international eugenics movement, was synonymous with "social planning." This was another way of stating that eugenics was part of a "centrally-planned" society, the likes of which were being proposed by the economist John Maynard Keynes. Keynes, incidentally, was a lifelong member and part of the leadership of the British Eugenics Society. Whitney continues along these lines:

> No one can deny that our present trend is toward a planned society – planned biologically as well as economically; and no planned social order is attainable without careful consideration of the kind of people we want to have forming the race of the future. ---- I believe that sterilization is but a part of the general discipline that we call social planning, and it is from this point of view that I shall discuss it.

Herein lays the honest truth, brazen and arrogant. Whitney states the obvious: Society is to be planned, and the members of this planned society are to be selected by the upper echelon of society, among which he undoubtedly includes himself. Whitney is equally honest about the drastic change for scientists; no longer as the impartial truth-seeker, but as part of the central-planning and political leadership:

> My position is not that of the scientist of earlier days, who was supposed only to

collect facts and was not expected to publish the views he had derived from them except through learned scientific monographs that could hardly reach the people.

Rather, Whitney applauds the practical application of eugenics by openly stating: "Many thousands of men and women have been sterilized under the laws of the United States, and thousands others have been sterilized privately." Whitney asserts that he "interviewed in person a considerable number of the people." Whitney was referring to the work of Paul Popenoe and E.S. Gosney of Pasadena, California, "Sterilization for Human Betterment: A Summary of 6000 Operations in California, 1909 – 1929." Note how Whitney portrays eugenic sterilization as "therapeutic" and as an aspect of "social control":

> We live in an age of social control, and here – in eugenics – lies our most glorious opportunity of controlling the quality of our children and our children's children. ---- **The doctors, too, may sometimes exceed their duties.** I know of one young woman who was told by the surgeon after she came out from an appendectomy, "Now, my dear, there is one burden that you have off your mind forever. **While I was taking out your appendix I tied off your tubes, and you'll never have to worry for fear you'll have babies. Isn't that nice?**" (emphasis mine)

Whitney proudly claims that "more than 16,000 persons have been sterilized in our public institutions since the practice first became authorized by law," and is clear as to who were his supporters and detractors:

> The Superintendent of the Eugenics Record Office, Dr. Harry H. Laughlin, has been of the greatest assistance to the legislators of many States. To him they have turned for information in their endeavors to get sterilization laws enacted. – Dr. Laughlin's correspondence with interested legislators and laymen has been voluminous.

Most importantly, historically speaking is that Whitney was clear as to the scale and scope of the Third Reich's eugenic efforts:

> The 400,000 known defectives in Germany who become subject of the new law are about equally divided into men and women ---- **And this represents but a small beginning, we are told!** Though not all of us, probably, will approve of the compulsory character of this law – as it applies, for instance, to the sterilizing of drunkards – we cannot but admire the foresight revealed by the plan in general. [sic.] (emphasis mine)

Whitney engages in the slight-of-hand that was utilized by other prominent American eugenicists that surveyed the Third Reich's eugenic policies. Whitney accurately portrays the law as being devoid of a "religious bias," as he knew this was important to Americans who valued as "separation of church and state" and freedom from religious prosecution:

> American Jewry is naturally suspecting that the German chancellor had the law

enacted for the specific purpose of sterilizing the German Jews, but I believe nothing to be further from the truth. The German law provides for the sterilization of hereditary defectives only. It safeguards the rights of every individual, and where it sterilizes it will not maim. The measure is solely eugenic in its purpose, and were it not for its compulsory character it would probably meet with the approval of all who are free from religious bias.

This is not to say that the eugenics of the Third Reich did not emerge out of prejudice and racism, but that the Nazis could have cared less about the religious beliefs of the German Jews. The German Jewish population was considered "biologically" inferior per the dictates of their eugenic beliefs. Conversion or acceptance of Christian beliefs was not the goal of the Nazis as it had been, by contrast, the goal of the Spanish Inquisition. More precisely, you could not escape being sent to an extermination camp by converting from Judaism to Christianity as you could during the Spanish Inquisition. To the contrary, Hitler has been quoted praising the marriage traditions of Judaism for its preference for marrying within the religion and culture.

Another prominent American to note that the Third Reich's eugenic policy was not necessarily driven by "religious" bias was T.U.H. Ellinger. Ellinger, like Laughlin, came from a plant and animal breeding background. According to the 1920 "Annual Report of the Indiana Corn Grower's Association," Ellinger had previously been employed by the Union Stock Yards of Chicago to travel to Europe and study their plant and animal breeding practices. (Pg. 51) According to Stefan Kühl, Ellinger would return to Germany between 1939 and 1940 to survey Hitler's human breeding program despite the onset of war in 1939. He met with Eugen Fischer and Wolfgang Abel at the Kaiser Wilhelm Institute. According to Kühl, Abel was a member of Hitler's SS and an anthropologist known for his research on Gypsies. Abel was also active in the sterilization campaign against mixed ethnicity blacks, which had been in turn identified by Fischer's *Rheinlandbastarde* study that Fischer had conducted with Charles B. Davenport:

> After his return to the United States, Ellinger explained to readers of the Journal of Heredity that the treatment of Jews in Germany had nothing to do with religious persecution. Rather, it was entirely "a large-scale breeding project, with the purpose of eliminating from the nation the hereditary attributes of the Semitic race." ---- Ellinger speculated that the idea behind the cruel treatment of the Jews "might be to discourage them from giving birth to children doomed to a life of horrors." In 1942, the year that witnessed the installation of the gas chambers in Auschwitz, Ellinger argued that if the cruelties "were accomplished, the Jewish problem would solve itself in a generation, but it would have been a great deal more merciful to kill the unfortunate outright." (Pg. 60, "The Nazi Connection," emphasis mine)

Dr. Clarence Campbell was the other prominent member of the Eugenics Research Association to chime in and provide glaring support for the Third Reich's eugenical sterilization. Most importantly, Dr. Campbell attempted to dissuade the notion that the Third Reich's eugenic laws were racially motivated. Clearly, Dr. Campbell knew this was not the case. He was a eugenics insider and knew very well how racial prejudices were woven behind the scientific rhetoric. On the other hand, he was also revealing an important concept about eugenics; that it could, in fact, operate without racial bias. Some of the very first victims of the Third Reich's sterilization laws were otherwise "Aryans" or "Nordics" with birth defects. It is also important to understand that in the event that the Third Reich survived WWII, its eugenic sterilization program would have been carried out in perpetuity, weeding out the "lower tenth" of the German population in an ever persistent strive towards breeding a "master race." In a speech given to the Social Services Club of Delaware in 1934, Dr. Campbell stated:

> One thing it is desirable for us to known is that this German programme is not in its primary intent an anti-racial measure. Contrary to the somewhat hysterical accusations that have been made, before ever the programme went into effect, there is nothing to indicate that these laws will be administered any more unfairly than our own, or other than in the best interest of racial improvement. This programme embodies and follows closely the principles of race improvement that have been carefully worked out by German anthropologists and eugenists in the last twenty years. Eugenists can only endorse these principles, and it would be intellectual dishonesty to deny their soundness. Professor de la Pouge, the great French anthropologist, whom we would hardly suspect of being pro-German, has said that to Hitler goes the credit of being the first statesman to realize the importance to a country of a eugenics national policy. While some might form adverse opinions from reports which are obviously biased, no eugenists can doubt that the German Nation stands to derive great and lasting benefit from the improvement in racial quality which this programme gives every promise of producing. Whatever may be thought of the Germans, there is probably no people in the world that is more whole-heartedly devoted to its country than the German Nation. And it evidently regards the eugenic endeavor to improve its racial quality as the most effective way in which it can show its patriotism, and serve its fatherland. How long shall we need to wait until the American Nation shows an equal devotion to its national future? (BOX: D-2-3:5, "Race Betterment and Sterilization," Feb. 13th, 1934, Campbell, Truman Univ. – Special Coll.)

Campbell's and Ellinger's summation of Hitler's eugenic policies coincided with that of Leon Whitney's, and were in truth a somewhat accurate depiction of National Socialism's murderous policies. In truth, neither Hitler nor any of his henchmen deliberated much about the religion of the Jewish-German population. Theirs was a "scientific racism" through and through. They fully believed in the long-held notions of the anthropologists, biologists, and eugenicists that ranked the "races of man" in a hierarchical fashion with the "Nordic," "Teutonic", and "Aryan" races at the top, and Africans and Aborigines at the bottom. If there had been a greater population of African descent in Germany at the time that Hitler took power, then, The Holocaust would certainly have been a catastrophe that included many more victims of African descent. Thus, it is not surprising that so many of the top eugenicists came from animal and plant breeding backgrounds like Laughlin. The opinions that they gave after surveying Hitler's domestic health policies were perfectly in line with the surveys of the type that Ellinger had once delivered from an agricultural point of view. They were fully devoid of any recognition in the sanctity of human life. They treated humans as biological assets no different than livestock.

By this token, it is interesting to see the eminent Julian Huxley both support and condemn the type of measures employed by the Hitler regime. To qualify Huxley's position we first go to the New York Times article entitled "Huxley Envisages the Eugenic Race: Predicts Application to Human Propagation of New Artificial Livestock Breeding Methods":

> The next step in the goal of scientific eugenics toward the production of a better race of men will be the application to human propagation of the very same artificial methods now employed in breeding thoroughbred horses and cattle. It was stated in an interview today by Dr. Julian Huxley, noted British biologist, who is attending the annual meeting here of the British Association for the Advancement of Science. ---- **"if you are going to take eugenics seriously and if you want to get a quick rise in the standards of the human population, you have to take into consideration these remarkable new methods of artificial sterilization now so successfully employed in breeding better animal stock,"** Dr. Huxley said. (The New York Times, Sept. 6th, 1937, "Huxley Envisages the Eugenic Race," emphasis mine)

Huxley was a lifelong and vocal supporter of eugenics. He was well versed in the long history of racialism inherent in the eugenics proposed by his British counterparts as well as those in the United States, Canada, Sweden, Denmark, Finland, and other supposedly benign countries. Yet, Huxley would criticize the very methods he was vigorously lobbying for when applied by the German government he found distasteful. Huxley split hairs between his eugenics and Germany's eugenics, despite knowing full well that they had developed in full cooperation between British and German scientists:

> We find in Germany today an example of the absurdities claimed in the name of eugenics. It is a shocking story the way the scientific method is being prostituted to perpetuate the Aryan myth. Of course, every one knows there is no such thing as an Aryan race, but even if such a race existed more than three-quarters of the German people would be **non-Aryan, including Hitler himself.** [*sic.*] (NYT, Sept. 6th, 1937, "Huxley Envisages the Eugenic Race", emphasis mine)

Huxley's argument was revisionist at best and flat out disinformation at worst. This is the myth that the eugenicists clung to, and which would endure after WWII, namely Huxley, would propagate in order to both save face and preserve the eugenic calculations they had for humanity. Interestingly enough, after decades upon decades of being the face of eugenics by appearing in articles, and writing books and papers on the subject, Julian Huxley would completely sanitize his deep involvement with the movement when writing his memoirs. Nowhere in his 1970 autobiography, "Memories," is there even the slightest mention of the mountains of work he did for the eugenic cause.

The most interesting of these tours taken by American elites was Lothrop Stoddard. As an American journalist and author, Stoddard enjoyed unimpeded access into Adolf Hitler's "racial state." In fact, Stoddard enjoyed more access than would have been given to a European journalist and more freedom than a writer/journalist under Goebbels' Propaganda Ministry. Lothrop Stoddard is an indispensable figure in the effort to understand the nature of National Socialism and eugenics. Stoddard was born in Brookline, Massachusetts, and attended Harvard College. Stoddard received a Ph.D. in History from Harvard University in 1914. Stoddard is remembered for his book, "The Rising Tide of Color against White World-Supremacy" in 1920. Margaret Sanger partnered with him the following year to create the American Birth Control League, the forerunner to International Planned Parenthood. The infamous Madison Grant wrote the introduction to Stoddard's book, and together with Grant and Laughlin, Stoddard was integral in the effort to pass the 1924 Johnson-Reed Immigration Restriction Act.

Stoddard had earned his "white supremacist" and eugenic credentials with the publication of his "racialist" books, and Hitler deeply appreciated the propaganda value of having a famous American reporter write a piece about National Socialism's eugenic policies from the American eugenic viewpoint. Hitler personally made sure Stoddard's visit into the institutions of National Socialism would be unimpeded and that the most important figures in the National Socialist state would be his hosts. Stoddard's thorough inspection resulted in his 1940 publication of the book "Into the Darkness." In the book "The Men Behind Hitler: A German Warning to the World," Bernhard Schreiber documents Lothrop Stoddard's investigative survey of National Socialism. As documented by the book review, Stoddard had largely unimpeded access into the infamous eugenic courts. In a conversation with an earnest young man who was officially in charge of the tuberculosis section of the public health service headquarters he was told that:

> The treatment given a tuberculosis patient is partly determined by his social worth. If he is a valuable citizen and his case is curable no expense is spared. If he is adjudged incurable he is kept comfortable of course but no special effort is made to prolong slightly an existence which will benefit neither the community nor himself. Germany can nourish only a certain amount of human life at a given time. We National Socialists are in duty bound to foster individuals of social and biological value.

Stoddard was apparently impressed by the health measures taken by Hitler's National Socialist government and later in his book recounts his participation in the sessions of the Upper Court for Hereditary Health in Berlin-Charlottenburg. This is of true importance. Stoddard, the American eugenicist, was given access to the eugenic courts that sealed the fate of so many Europeans. As this book documents, these infamous eugenic courts were copied from the proposals that Laughlin made years prior to them being adopted by the Third Reich. Stefan Kühl documents Stoddard's visit to these courts and their historical importance:

> At the Hereditary Health Supreme Court in Charlottenburg, Berlin, he joined two regular Nazi judges, a psychopathologist, and a criminal psychologist. Stoddard reported on four cases that he reviewed in order to illustrate the urgency of sterilizations:
> » An "apelike" man with a receding forehead and flaring nostrils who had a history of homosexuality and was married to a "Jewess" by whom he had three "ne'er-do-well children.
> » An obvious manic-depressive, of whom Stoddard wrote that "there was no doubt that he should be sterilized."
> » An eighteen-year-old deaf-mute girl with several "unfortunate" hereditary factors in her family.
> » A seventeen-year-old mentally retarded girl employed as a helper in an inexpensive restaurant. (Generally from Pgs. 62-63, "Nazi Connection")

Stoddard's lack of sympathy for the defenseless and weak comes through just as clear as the ease with which he depicts his socializing with Hitler's henchmen. Of note is the matter-of-fact way in which Stoddard treated the "Jewish Question":

> He viewed racialism, on the other hand, as a "passing phenomenon." Stoddard claimed in 1940 that the "Jews problem" is already settled in principle and soon to be settled in fact by the physical elimination of the Jews themselves from the Third Reich. (Pg. 62, "Nazi Connection")

Stoddard's collaboration with the administration of Hitler's racial policies perfectly parallels the running theme of this book. One has to seriously question why American historians have missed this jaw-dropping event in world history. "Into the Darkness" is remembered for its journalistic account of Nazi Germany. However, Stoddard's political affiliations to Margaret Sanger, Harvard University, or the significance of his stint as one of the judges in Hitler's eugenic courts is conveniently forgotten. Here was one of the founders of the most prominent American political organizations dedicated to reproductive rights directly collaborating in the administration of Hitler's racial and eugenic policies. Here was Laughlin's "Model Eugenic Law" in practice, with an American eugenic expert sitting in judgment of the defenseless in precisely the three-panel courts that the U.S. Supreme Court had found to be constitutional in the 1927 case of <u>Buck v. Bell</u>.

On a broader perspective, these eugenicists catalogued for posterity the progress made by the international movement in the countries that chose to implement the pieces of legislation they proposed. A grander lesson can be gleaned from the different degrees in which these different types of government adopted eugenics. Eugenicists like Laughlin, Leon Whitney, and Leonard Darwin were quite blunt about the fact that they wanted to remove significant swaths of the population from the gene pool. Yet, they encountered much more resistance and had to accommodate their goals to the political realities of the types of governments they operated in. Adolf Hitler encountered no such resistance. Once the Reichstag bent to his will, it became nothing but a tool for the hyper-centralization of power.

This is where the concept of "separation of powers" enshrined in the founding documents of the American Revolution can be deemed as prophetic. The concentration of powers in the "same hands," to both "make" and "enforce" the law is the very definition of "dictatorial" prerogative. Yet, German eugenicists were following the path American and British eugenicists had prescribed for decades. The German eugenic "solutions" included deportation, segregation, sterilization, and finally when all else failed, euthanasia; exactly as eugenicists throughout the movement had prescribed for decades prior.

By this time there existed no viable avenue to contest the actions of the Nazi controlled government. There existed no "checks and balances" on the Fuhrer's powers. Holocaust historians point to the Wannsee Conference as the point where the "final solution to the Jewish problem" was decided upon by the Nazi leadership. We have the transcripts of the conference, and the conversation evolves precisely along these lines. Eichmann and company discussed the failures of deportation to Madagascar and Palestine as well as the lack of desire to continue feeding a segregated population even if measures were taken to sterilize them. It is by no coincidence that the Nazis literally transplanted the doctors, nurses, and instrumentation of the T4 Euthanasia Program that was used to eradicate the "hereditary defectives," to the death camps where the Final Solution would be carried out. Any doubts held by those questioning the extreme nature of the "final solution to the Jewish problem" were stamped out by top down dictates and directives, or by force if necessary. It is at that point that Hitler's wish became the command that they acted upon without hesitation or further deliberation. The political machine behind the Third Reich was unified by a single purpose, ready to act, without need for the 'obstruction' of a parliamentary body or the voice of the governed.

Reprinted from
AMERICAN SOCIOLOGICAL REVIEW
Volume I, No. 5, October, 1936

LEGAL AND MEDICAL ASPECTS OF EUGENIC STERILIZATION IN GERMANY

MARIE E. KOPP
New York City

THE National Socialist Government of Germany has as one of its avowed aims the improvement of the biological and racial qualities of the German people. For this purpose it has undertaken a variety of measures, carried on as part of the public health and social welfare services of the state. These measures are not arbitrary experiments. Every one of them is part of a large, permanent public health program which includes full records as to health and family history and an evaluation of the intelligence and competence of the people. With this goes a eugenic program designed to diminish the transmission of qualities making for lower standards of health, and for lower degrees of competence and well-being among the German people.

In the summer of 1935 the renewal of an Oberlaender Fellowship gave me an opportunity to study this new system, and to compare it with what I had previously seen in 1932. Through the kindness of a friend at the Kaiser Wilhelm Research Institute, I received official permission to interview officials and visit any public service within the scope of my study. This permitted me to observe people's reactions in the farming, industrial, and shipping sections of the country, as well as among various racial groups. I interviewed many leaders, including laymen as well as superintendents of hospitals and institutions, judges of the Hereditary Health Courts, and a large number of physicians, surgeons, psychiatrists, and social workers, who are called upon to give testimony in court and to carry out the provisions of the new laws. Aside from religious scruples, I found relatively few objections to the "compulsory" sterilization law. It is accepted as beneficial legislation designed to minimize the difficulties of those afflicted.

Three out of every hundred Germans are afflicted with physical and mental diseases which are believed to be hereditary, and which seriously interfere with their ability to earn a livelihood. In some sections of the country hereditary feeblemindedness afflicts about six

1934 - A REORIENTATION OF THE PROBLEM

> *"Eugenics is the self-direction of human evolution."*
> - Second International Eugenics Congress, NY, 1921

The American Neurological Association, working with funding from the Carnegie Institution, set off to review and document the work of the international eugenics movement, and all of the major publications it had produced. The committee was made up of Abraham Myerson, M.D., James B. Ayer, M.D. Tracy J. Putnam, M.D., Clyde E. Keeler, ScD, and Leo Alexander, M.D. on May of 1934. Alexander would later be appointed as the scientific expert for the American prosecution team at Nuremberg. The choice of Meyerson, by itself, likely reveals the intentions of the American Neurological Association. They were looking for a strong voice effectively to create a gulf between the Association and the science of eugenics. Ulf Schmidt wrote the 2004 book "Justice at Nuremberg: Leo Alexander and the Nazi Doctors' Trial." According to Schmidt, Abraham Meyerson openly attacked the leading proponents of eugenics, namely Davenport and his minion Laughlin, as being "anti-democratic":

> Meyerson enjoyed attacking 'harebrained' eugenic ideas that called for the sterilization of all 'potential parents of socially inadequate offspring'. Future eugenicists, he argued, would need to be clairvoyants with supernatural powers to detect whether someone fulfilled the criteria. He felt that the proposal to sterilize people on the assumption that their future offspring might be socially inadequate was 'naïve beyond [the] ... powers of expression'. 'Imagine the graft, the blackmail and the generally muddled and corrupt social reactions involved in this proposal!', he told his audience. (Pg. 56, "Justice at Nuremberg")

Schmidt reports that the introduction of Hitler's compulsory sterilization law of 1934 gave enough people at the American Neurological Association reason to begin distancing themselves from previous eugenic beliefs. Ulf Schmidt documents how Alexander, feeling pronounced regrets for the work on eugenics he did in his native Germany, contacted Meyerson to offer his assistance with the inquiry in July of 1934. (Pg. 55, "Justice at Nuremberg") "Eugenical Sterilization, a Reorientation of the Problem," would be the book resulting from this committee, and it stands as one of the most comprehensive rebuttals of eugenics as a science:

> The report showed that sterilizations often originated as eugenic measures, but ended up as social ones. In the eyes of the authors, the concept of eugenics was riddled with methodological errors and it was lacking scientific support from modern genetic studies. Evidence from countries like Germany, where sterilizations were carried out with 'characteristic thoroughness', also showed that in many cases eugenics was linked with Aryan racism and Nordic mysticism. (Pg. 57, "Justice at Nuremberg")

The committee published a preliminary report, and Carnegie later funded the publication of the book-length version in 1936. The introductory statement sets the tone:

> The most primitive form of sterilization is undoubtedly castration. The impulse to inflict injury upon an enemy's genitalia as a measure of punishment and insult is a deeply rooted one in the human race, which finds expression at times among the most civilized modern nations, as well as among savages. ---- The suspicion of a sadistic motive must always arise when genitalectomy is advocated for any group of physically healthy people. . (Intro, "Eugenical Sterilization")

Most importantly, the Carnegie book continues its introduction by pointing to the fact that eugenics has lagged behind the science of genetics, which begun with Gregor Mendel's work:

> Many an eloquent voice has been raised against the pollution of the race which might be feared as a result. The term "eugenics" originated with Galton, who based his social doctrines upon what was then known of heredity, a field of study in which he was a pioneer. Enormous strides have since been made in the field of genetics. It may, however, be seriously questioned whether many of the eugenic proposals now current take into account the newer genetic data; and further, whether the data upon which some are based – derived from experiments upon plants and lower animals – are applicable also to man. (Pg. 2, "Eugenical Sterilization")

The book continues by documenting the gulf between Mendelian genetics and eugenics, likening it to the difference between "hard" and "soft" science:

> On the whole, eugenics receives scant support on any scientific basis from genetics. Genetics has largely concerned itself in the past twenty-five years with those experimental procedures by which, in lower animals especially, the genes have been discovered and their laws of appearance and combination have been formulated. (Pg. 69, "Eugenical Sterilization")

The committee makes it clear that the inability to precisely define the characteristics of the allegedly hereditary phenomena made them impossible to study with the rigor that Mendelian science otherwise provided:

> It is true that many men have set up the hypothesis of Mendelian recessiveness of one type or another in the case of the conditions we are studying. But nothing like proof has been adduced. The leading geneticists, at least of America and England, have been very cautious in their pronunciamentos concerning eugenics, and it is apparent from their writings that they look with disfavor upon the sweeping statements made popularly and, to some extent, in the scientific literature concerning eugenic measures. (Pg. 70, "Eugenic Sterilization")

Recall that the methodology of cataloguing human pedigrees could only mimic the practice of charting the pedigrees of fruit flies and peas:

> ...we discuss the heredity of schizophrenia, manic-depressive psychosis, feeblemindedness, epilepsy, and crime, more or less as if these were definable entities, and thus that it is possible to study them statistically and scientifically.

No psychiatrist of first rank believes this to be the case; for him the term dementia praecox, for example, represents the best we can do in the way of classifying what is obviously a group of conditions which is very likely of heterogeneous composition. (Pg. 81, "Eugenic Sterilization")

In fact, the committee which authored "Eugenical Sterilization" calls the eugenicists to task for their unscientific use of the term "Mendelian":

> The term *Mendelian* has merely been substituted for *deviation from normality* in the widest possible sense, and all of its value as a precise method of studying heredity has been thrown overboard. (Pg. 101, "Eugenic Sterilization")

Most importantly, the committee treated the claims of the eugenicists as one monolithic international movement. After all, this is how the movement presented itself to the world:

> Such men as Rüdin, and Whitney, stress the fact that insanity is increasing at a terrific rate and imply quite definitely that the biological unfitness is thus threatening two swamp the race. Joseph Mayer quotes this change in the statistics of the cultural countries as alarming. The writings of Laughlin, Baur, Fischer, Lenz, Mjöen and, practically speaking, all the important books echo these statements and stress eugenic measures as the only possible protection society has against further deterioration. (Pg. 25, "Eugenical Sterilization")

Historically speaking, it is interesting to see the committee recognize that the eugenic measures being implemented by Hitler's government predated Hitler by various decades. Furthermore, that these laws followed the legislative recommendations of the prominent international eugenicists of the time:

> It is fair to state that it is not a product of the Hitler regime, in that its main tenets were proposed and considered several years before the Nazi regime took possession of Germany. – It will be seen that this law is very precise and, as appears later, conforms closely with the present knowledge of medical eugenics. (Pg. 22, "Eugenical Sterilization")

The book continues to analyze the claims of the international eugenics movement on a case by case basis, focusing on the more important publications by the eugenics movement. The committee offers its scientific dissection of the various works, illuminating just how deficient the studies are from the perspective of a rigorous and empirical science. One of the most important observations was to debunk the studies of the various "cacogenic" families, such as the Jukes, the Nams, and the dozens of other allegedly scientific studies by several generations of eugenicists. The committee clarified that in order to arrive at scientifically sound data, the studies would have to include samples upwards of 15 to 25 million individuals, as opposed to the paltry thousands of these infamous studies. The committee goes into detail, and further explains the deficiency of the staff utilized to conduct these studies. They criticize the amount of data arrived at by assumption as opposed to empirical observation.

Interestingly enough, this committee of scientists, also documents where the opposition to the eugenics movement came from and singles out the Catholic Church as one of the "leading forces" offering resistance to the movement. It quotes the Pope's encyclical at length, cited here in part:

> Finally, that pernicious practice must be condemned which closely touches upon the natural right of man to enter matrimony but affects also in a real way the welfare of the offspring. For there are some who over-solicitous for the cause of eugenics, not only give salutary counsel for more certainly procuring the strength and health of the future child – which, indeed, is not contrary to right reason – but put eugenics before aims of a higher order, and by public authority wish to prevent from marrying all those whom, even though naturally fit for marriage, they consider, according to the norms and conjectures of their investigations, would, through hereditary transmission, bring forth defective offspring. And more, they wish to legislate to deprive these of that natural faculty by medical action despite their unwillingness; and this they do not propose as an infliction of grave punishment under the authority of the state for a crime committed, nor to prevent future crimes by guilty persons, but against every right and good they wish the civil authority to arrogate to itself a power over a faculty which it never had and can never legitimately possess. (Pgs. 60-61, "Eugenical Sterilization")

Curiously enough, this extract from the Roman Catholic Pope cited by the committee hardly reads like liturgy, but rather reads like the declarations of "inalienable rights" proclaimed by the Founding Fathers of the American Revolution. The citation continues along this secular tone:

> Public magistrates have no direct power over the bodies of their subjects; therefore, where no crime has taken place and there is no cause present for grave punishment, they can never directly harm, or tamper with the integrity of the body, either for the reasons of eugenics or for any other reason. (Pg. 61, "Eugenical Sterilization")

For the purposes of this book, it is important to point out that the committee also made reference to the dangers of establishing a tyrannical utopia. The committee quotes the warnings of Charles A. Ellwood:

> It is a counsel of perfection, which modern science has given us in the doctrines of eugenics; but like all such counsels it is socially valuable and is obviously closely allied with idealistic social religion. If eugenics were ever made the basis of a code of minute legislative prescriptions regarding marriage and reproduction, doubtless it would become an intolerable tyranny. (Pg. 64, "Eugenical Sterilization")

The criticism was spot on. Eugenics was applied at a "minute legislative" level by Hitler's Third Reich, and as history evidences, the effect was an "intolerable tyranny." The committee concludes its study by recommending a retreat from sterilization justified by eugenics. The committee is clear in its discomfort with the impending doom of any governmental policy that implements the recommendations of the international eugenics movement. The book anticipated the problem posed by the uncomfortable commonalities between American eugenics and those implemented by Hitler's government. Ultimately, it served as a precursor to the various steps the Carnegie Institution took to separate itself from Laughlin, Davenport, and the Eugenics Record Office. Eugenics could no longer be talked about as a theoretical proposal as the positive and negative press of Hitler's eugenic Third Reich emerged.

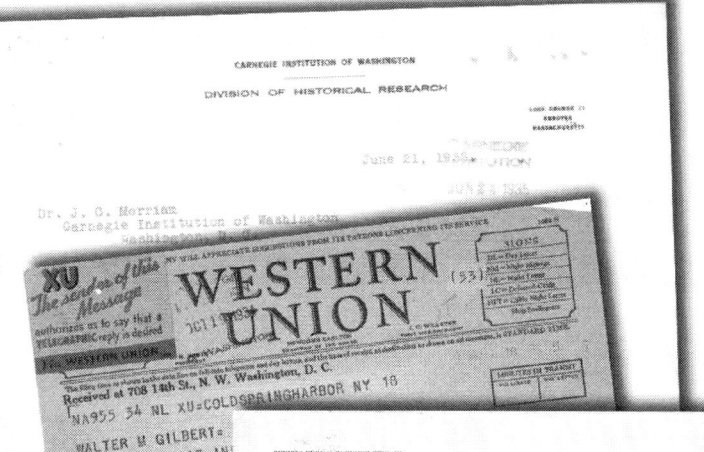

CARNEGIE INSTITUTION OF WASHINGTON
DIVISION OF HISTORICAL RESEARCH

June 21, 1935

Dr. J. C. Merriam,
 Carnegie Institution of Washington
  Washington, D. C.

WESTERN UNION

Received at 706 14th St., N. W. Washington, D. C.

NA955 34 NL XU=COLDSPRINGHARBOR NY 16

WALTER M GILBERT=
 CARNEGIE IN[STITUTION]

EUGENICS EXHIBIT
FORTY POUND PACKA[GE]
TWENTIETH RAIL T[O]
TRANSPORT WILL [BE]
DOLLARS ONE CENT[S]

H H LAUGHL[IN]

DEPARTMENT OF STATE
WASHINGTON

In reply refer to
PC 540.1 A 2/

August 22, 1934

Dr. Charles B. Davenport,
 C/o Carnegie Institution of Washington,
  Cold Spring Harbor, New York.

Sir:

An invitation has been received from the Government of Argentina, extended through its Embassy in Washington, for the United States to be represented by official delegates at the Second Pan-American Conference on Eugenics and Homiculture which will be held in Buenos Aires from November 23 to November 25, 1934. A copy of the Embassy's note is enclosed.

The Acting Secretary of the Smithsonian Institution, to whom the question of representation was referred, has suggested that the matter be brought to your attention as one who is directly interested in the subject of eugenics and allied lines. Your opinion as to the desirability of participation, as well as the names of any suggested delegates

Acknowledged 8/24/34.

1934 - PAN AMERICAN CONGRESS

> "The 20th century was a test bed for big ideas
> - fascism, communism, the atomic bomb."
> - P. J. O'Rourke

By 1935, the American eugenics movement had solidified its influence internationally. Most importantly, this leadership position began to be recognized by the highest offices in the United States government. Foreign governments began to request assistance in developing their immigration, sterilization and marriage laws. The U.S. Government apparently felt comfortable enough to have the leaders of the American eugenics movement represent the nation in international symposiums. The documentation provided to this author by the Carnegie Institution provides evidence to this point. The best example is the research Laughlin provided the Pan American Union. The Pan American Union was strategically located in Washington D.C., but met throughout Latin America regularly. The Carnegie correspondence still holds letters from high officers in the United States and the Pan American Union, and the letterhead of this organization describes its mission as follows:

> The Pan American Union is the international organization maintained by the twenty-one American republics for the development of good understanding, friendly intercourse, commerce, and peace among them; controlled by a governing board composed of the Secretary of State of the United States and the diplomatic representatives in Washington of the other republics. (Standard letterhead of Pan American Union, Laughlin files, Carnegie Inst.)

In other words, the Pan American Union was the way the President of the United States, through his Cabinet and the Department of State, exerted his formidable influence over the Americas. This was hardly an insignificant diplomatic effort, as prior to World War II, the United States was still pushing away the European imperialism that would not truly begin to dissipate from Latin America until after the war. The correspondence held at Carnegie includes letters from, to, and making direct reference to the Secretary of Labor, the Secretary of State, and President Franklin D. Roosevelt. These high officials were both the initiators and the decision makers in the relationship that ensued between Carnegie's Eugenic Record Office and the Pan American Union's foreign diplomats. The initial invitation came from the government of Argentina. An August 22nd, 1934 letter written in Department of State letterhead and addressed to Dr. Charles B. Davenport of the Carnegie Institution reads as follows:

> An invitation has been received from the Government of Argentina, extended through its Embassy in Washington, for the United States to be represented by official delegates at the Second Pan-American Conference on Eugenics and Homiculture which will be held in Buenos Aires from November 23 to November 25, 1934. A copy of the Embassy's note is enclosed. The Acting Secretary of the Smithsonian Institution to whom the question of representation

was referred, has suggested that the matter be brought to your attention as one who is directly interested in the subject of eugenic and allied lines. (Laughlin files, Carnegie Inst., Assistant Sec. of State to C.B. Davenport, August 22nd, 1934)

All of this is important as it helps illustrate exactly how close the international eugenics movement came to become a truly formidable entity of worldwide clout and influence. The Pan American Study is also of historical importance as it is one of the occurrences that clued the leadership of the Carnegie Institution exactly what Laughlin and Davenport had entangled them in. Laughlin described how the Pan American Conference originated in his September 7th, 1934 letter to Walter M. Gilbert, likely in an effort to bring the Carnegie management up to speed on the relationship with the Latin American wing of the international eugenics movement:

> The Pan American Conference (and Office of Eugenics and Homiculture) was set up in Havana, Cuba, as Cuba's outgrowth of the Second International Congress of Eugenics which was held in New York in 1921. The moving spirit of this Pan American organization was Dr. Delgado F. Ramos, Calle 11, Vedado, Havana, Cuba. Ramos was a frequent visitor to New York and Cold Spring Harbor, and professor of medicine in the University of Havana and was one of those men thrown out of Cuba by the student rebellion against President Machado's regime. The University of Havana was the headquarters of the Pan American Office of Eugenics and Homiculture, which in turn called the Conferences. For a number of months Ramos has been back on his job in the University of Havana and is seeking to re-establish with some Pan American support the Pan American Office of Eugenics and Homiculture. The word Homiculture is only a pet word of Dr. Ramos. Pan American office of Eugenics would sound better to Americans but the Latins need a little decoration. (Laughlin files, Carnegie Inst., Sept. 7th, 1934, Letter from Laughlin to Gilbert)

Laughlin also responded to the Secretary of State on September 5th, 1934 offering a broader list of individuals that could represent the United States at the Pan American Conference. Laughlin suggested Henry Fairfield Osborn, the president of the American Museum of Natural History and uncle to Fredrick Osborn of the Eugenics Research Association, as well as Clarence Campbell, also of the E.R.A.. Charles Davenport had retired from the directorship of the Eugenics Record Office by this time.

Laughlin very much intended to attend, instead of just preparing the scientific study as the Carnegie leadership wanted. The internal correspondence reveals that the Carnegie leadership was worried about Laughlin attending the conference even without approval or support from the Carnegie Institution. According to an October 22nd, 1934 letter from Laughlin to Gilbert held at the Carnegie Institution, Dr. Ramos spent two weeks at Cold Spring Harbor with Laughlin before sailing to Buenos Aires. An October 23rd, 1934 memorandum prepared by Gilbert for Dr. Merriam demonstrates Laughlin's persistence:

> The inference is that Laughlin is determined to go ahead with his plans even if they are not supported by the Institution. Even if he is willing to pay the

necessary expenses from his own pocket, it may be inadvisable from the Institution's point of view for Laughlin to proceed with some of his plans. (Laughlin files, Carnegie Inst., MEMORANDUM FOR DR. MERRIAM, Oct. 23rd, 1934, Gilbert to Merriam)

This was an uncomfortable situation that would repeat itself. By 1924, Laughlin was recognized as one of, or the most prominent leader of the international eugenics movement with Charles Davenport and Leonard Darwin reaching old age. Laughlin would not only be invited to Argentina, but also to Cuba and Germany. According to a June 11th, 1935 letter from Laughlin to Dr. Merriam, Laughlin had attended the "Migration Congress" held in Havana, Cuba in 1928. Thus, he was already familiar with those interested in eugenics in Latin America. All of this fervor coincided with a time when the Carnegie leadership was quickly becoming aware of the practical reality of eugenics as Hitler's government zealously applied it to every aspect of German life:

> Dr. Domingo F. Ramos, who is now in charge of health and welfare in Cuba as a member of the cabinet of President Mendieta has invited me to come to Havana for the purpose of drafting an immigration law for Cuba – a Latin American country which has set its own racial ideals and desires that future immigration work toward these standards. Cuba, which is now about two-thirds white and one-third colored, is still an immigrant-receiving country, and immigration will play a very substantial part in the character of its future population. Cuba was the first of the Latin American countries to enact a modern national sanitary code, and Ramos, who is well acquainted with the Pan American feeling and needs in the matter of immigration control, is anxious that Cuba be the first Pan American country to enact an immigration-control law which will work definitely toward the racial standards which the particular nation may set up for itself. (Laughlin files, Carnegie Inst., June 11th, 1935, Laughlin to Merriam)

To put this letter into historical context, by 1935 Laughlin had already influenced the legislative efforts of Hitler's Germany, as well as several Scandinavian countries wishing to mimic his "Model Law." As demonstrated earlier, Laughlin had made sure to disseminate copies of this work to key members of the international eugenic lobby, and in turn, these members provided public praise for the legislative efforts within the United States. Dr. Merriam repeatedly voiced enthusiasm for these achievements. However, the internal correspondence at Carnegie shows that his mid-level staff was beginning to worry. Evidently, Dr. Merriam took note of the complaints. He began to regularly send copies of Laughlin's work to other scientists within the Carnegie Institution to get second opinions. A June 12th, 1935 follow-up letter from Dr. Merriam to Dr. George L Streeter, the Director of the Department of Embryology at Carnegie, demonstrates the growing unease:

> Inclosed is a copy of a letter from Dr. Laughlin concerning which I would be glad to have any opinion which you might wish to express. I know that the work in Cuba is important and probably Laughlin is one of the persons best qualified to

aid. My principal hesitation relates to question of policy as to the influence of the Institution in development of what might be the national program of another country. [sic.] (Laughlin files, Carnegie Inst., June 12th, 1935, Merriam to Streeter)

Dr. Streeter reviewed the work and responded back voicing some serious concerns and reservations about the consequences of allowing Laughlin to have too much input in a foreign government's legislation:

> Your letter from Dr. Laughlin raises the fundamental question as to our interpretation of the Institution's function in the field of Eugenics. ---- Dr. Ramos in this undertaking may be performing a very fine service to Cuba and there could be no objection to our placing at his disposal any of the fundamental facts that we have that bear on his problems. But to cooperate with him in any official way in his application of these facts in the drafting of a law might be **a very dangerous thing for us to do. It is very easy to slip into propaganda and patriotic endeavors**, as you brought out two days ago. (Laughlin files, Carnegie Inst., June 13th, 1935, Streeter to Merriam, emphasis mine)

The issue of Laughlin attending these conferences, even at his own expense, was raised again by Dr. Streeter. The implications concerned Dr. Streeter as he made it a point to write a subsequent letter to Dr. Merriam in order to reiterate his worries:

> I was concerned in discussion yesterday with the committee set up by the National Resources Board with regard to closely related questions, namely, the social and political implications of various aspects of studies in eugenics. ---- Although the Institution can make it clear that it is free from responsibility if Dr. Laughlin takes leave, it become difficult to make this clear to the large number of people who might not be aware of the arrangements for leave and might assume that we are responsible. (Laughlin files, Carnegie Inst., June 14th, 1935, Streeter to Merriam)

Dr. Streeter's letter is an acknowledgement that at this point the Carnegie leadership felt tied at the hips to Laughlin. Merriam understood that Laughlin's actions would be traced back to the Institution even if Laughlin was working independently. Laughlin's international notoriety as a racially-minded eugenicist had turned into a potential liability. Even the Carnegie scientists that worked on eugenics had the presence of mind to understand the political implications of Laughlin's aspirations. The Carnegie leadership was evaluating the implications of Laughlin's immigration work abroad at the same time that it had directed a committee to evaluate the work of the Eugenics Record Office. The eugenicist A.V. Kidder headed up that effort and kept Merriam informed on Laughlin:

> Although I feel very strongly that universities and other institutions should make no attempt to control the personal utterances of members of their staff, I believe that to give Laughlin leave for the purpose of advising a foreign government would be tantamount to putting the seal of the Institution's

approval on his actions while abroad. And although Laughlin is continually stating that his attitude is that of a scientific investigator rather than a propagandist, his published writings (most of which I have read within the last few weeks) all indicate a very strong tendency toward certain definite pints of view. With most of his ideas I heartily agree, but I am equally certain that many of them are based on racial or nationalistic sentiments rather than on scientifically ascertained fact. Even so, I would hesitate to recommend that Laughlin should not be allowed to go were it not for the fact that the Advisory Committee, whose report you will receive in a few days, **expressly recommends that the Record Office be divorced from all forms of propaganda**. (Laughlin files, Carnegie Inst., June 21st, 1935, Kidder to Merriam, emphasis mine)

It seems that the mounting newspaper coverage of the events unfolding in Germany along with the coverage of race relations at home finally began to create doubts in the mind of one of Laughlin's most consistent supporters. Dr. Merriam's response to A.V. Kidder says so in no uncertain terms:

I appreciate very much your letter of June twenty-first regarding the matter of the request for Laughlin's services to Cuba. Your views and those of the advisory committee which has just met with you at Cold Spring Harbor run closely parallel with mine regarding the nature of Laughlin's work and the dangers involved. Although I have been much concerned regarding the situation for some years, I am perhaps particularly impressed with the importance of the matter at the moment due to the study being made by the National Resources or Planning Board with reference to the social implication of scientific studies. Incidentally, I notice that this matter is coming to the front in the newspapers now due to agitation for deportation of aliens. This is a case in which we should not avoid considering the social implication of scientific problems, but it is also a time in which the scientific basis from which the implications arise must be examined with the greatest care in order to be sure that we are not deceived as to the significance of data secured by research. Although I have not yet seen the report of the committee, I am in sympathy with the idea that the Eugenics Record Office should be so set up as to prevent distinctly racial or nationalistic propaganda. Of course it is difficult to distinguish between what we call propaganda and what may be called the adequate interpretation of scientific truth. (Laughlin files, Carnegie Inst., June 24th, 1935, Merriam to Kidder)

Dr. Merriam then quotes from the Carnegie Institution's Presidential Report of 1931 to touch on the fundamental principles, which in truth, should have kept such a reputable institution far away from politicized scientists like Laughlin in the first place. Unfortunately, Laughlin, like Leonard Darwin, Julian Huxley, Charles B. Davenport, and even the father of eugenics, Francis Galton, were able to sponge more than an air of respectability from their relationship with Charles Darwin as well as from their Ivy League educations. The quotes that Dr. Merriam recalls are worth repeating here as they are indicative of the scientist's conceit and aloofness to the consequences of their ideas and ideals:

"Harm can be done through unwarranted philosophical or religious application of incomplete scientific hypothesis, but the evils which develop are not necessarily to be charged against the new knowledge as such. Generally they are compounded from inadequacy of knowledge and failure to recognize the need of additional correlated information. Human frailty in taking the form of selfishness in the use of new materials is a menace coordinate with the dangers of ignorance and bad judgment." (Laughlin files, Carnegie Inst., June 24th, 1935, Merriam to Kidder)

The quote is indicative that Dr. Merriam had become tuned into the troubled waters the Institution had navigated itself into. At the same time, it is indicative that Dr. Merriam suffered from the same conceit that Julian Huxley and Leonard Darwin suffered from. He seemed to believe that it was only the misapplication of eugenics that was the cause of the danger, and not the concept itself:

"Science is only the truth about ourselves and the world around us, but truth in partial statement must be interpreted carefully and applied with every caution until the story is known in completeness." (Laughlin files, Carnegie Inst., June 24th, 1935, Merriam to Kidder)

Dr. Merriam's observations are certainly accurate for the most part. However, they are guilty of intellectual abstraction and a departure from reality. At some point, those that empowered scientists like Laughlin should have taken the words of the eugenicists at face value. They should have pondered what it truly meant to "eliminate" or "segregate" as much as 15% of the nation's total population. This is especially true in this very scenario, when Laughlin's superiors were contending with the implications of departing the world of theory and into actual implementation in real world scenarios. By 1935, Hitler's henchmen had made good on their promises, and the topic of eugenics could no longer be treated as theory alone:

"The safety of humanity does not require a moratorium on the increase of honest knowledge, while half-truths and unrelated and uncoordinated facts constitute a real source of danger. What we need is more truth and the acceptance of knowledge for precisely what it is." (Laughlin files, Carnegie Inst., June 24th, 1935, Merriam to Kidder)

Dr. Merriam seems to have understood the "dangers" that Dr. Streeter and Dr. Kidder voiced and tailored his response to Laughlin accordingly:

The idea of securing the best scientific data upon which to base an immigration law for Cuba is a project to which we must give the highest consideration, and I hope that in drafting such a law it will be possible for us to furnish all of the scientific data which we have available that could be used profitably in such a study. I am, however, of the opinion that it is wise for us as an institution to refrain from participating in the drafting of laws for another country which have to do specifically with relations between countries. Among other questions it is necessary for us to bear in mind the fact that in the consideration of international relations our own country is included, and it is doubtful whether we should influence the judgment of another agency with reference to formulation of its views toward the country in which we live. I know that the data which have been brought together by researches and conferences in the past ought to be extremely valuable, and I sincerely hope that the careful scientific study of the immigration law for Cuba will result in something that will be a real pattern for study of other nations. It is my feeling, however, that the Carnegie Institution ought to limit its relations to have for utilization in such a study, without official representation or participation. (Laughlin files, Carnegie Inst., June 28th, 1935, Merriam to Laughlin)

The Carnegie Institute under Dr. Merriam would hardly be able to claim that they were unaware that Laughlin continued to zealously promote his work in Latin America and Nazi Germany as well. Laughlin published an article in the *Zeitschrift Für Rassenkunde*, a periodical whose name translates to "race-science." The Stuttgart-based periodical was headed up by the popularizer of "Aryan" mythology, Hans K. Günther. Recall that Günther and Hitler shared a politically engaged publisher in J.F. Lehmann. Lehmann would not only publish "Mein Kampf", but also bring Hitler the eugenic textbooks and publications from which the eugenic notions in "Mein Kampf" were gleaned from. Günther became the deputy editor of *Zeitschrift Für Rassenkunde* between 1935, two years after Hitler came to power, and 1944. At the same time *Zeitschrift Für Rassenkunde* regularly reviewed books of an explicitly pro-Nazi stance. Laughlin was one of the various members of the international eugenics movement that contributed to the periodical.

The Laughlin files still held at Carnegie have a copy of the article he provided along with the October 19th, 1935 note requesting that Dr. Merriam review the article. Laughlin's article is entitled "Researches in Pan American Population History." Laughlin describes the project as a study of the "differential fecundity" with a focus on "race and family-stock quality" as a result of the racial mixing of the influx of the "14 generations" of inhabitants from the "Old World" into the "New World." Most importantly, Laughlin identifies the project as being part of the Eugenics Record Office of the Carnegie Institution of Washington.

Laughlin sent the *Zeitschrift Für Rassenkunde* article to Dr. Merriam along with another article about the Pan American project published in the Eugenical News of November-December of 1935. Laughlin describes the project as an analysis of the "fundamental forces in the biological evolution of people", and claims that the League of Nations was one of the institutions backing the project. The most interesting aspect of Laughlin's description is the "Proposed Institute of Pan American Population Research." Laughlin called for the creation of an anthropological institute for collecting census information from all participating countries towards a eugenic end. Of course, Laughlin's proposal required that the census of all these nations conform to a uniform format tailored towards its eugenic goals. The section of the article in the Eugenical News entitled "Mate selection in each Pan American country" is indicative of its intent. The "Race-Crossing" portion asks the census taker to grade the "quality of offspring" produced by the marriage.

GERMANY

Meanest Mother

Sullen Frau Charlotte Juenemann, though with child, had her head struck off in Berlin last week. Notorious since her arrest early this year as the "World's Meanest Mother," Frau Juenemann let her three young children starve to death in a cellar while she spent her last few

CHARLOTTE JUENEMANN
Her unborn babe went with her.

marks making the rounds of Berlin's cheaper night clubs. Since Herr Juenemann is in an insane asylum, Germany's New Justice assumed that her unborn babe would be a debit to the race.

Praise for Nazis

Sore from the slings and arrows of foreign criticism, Germans heard gratefully last week a warm, approving speech from Dr. Clarence Gordon Campbell, president of the American Eugenics Research Asso-

---

teasers was slated for sterilization

Though many U. S. eugenists felt last week that the Hitler program is too bold, Atlantic City Psychiatrist Dr. Cole Davis called not merely for the sterilization but for the "merciful destruction" of the incurably insane.

In his Christmas address to his College of Cardinals, His Holiness Pope Pius XI hurled from Vatican City a potent re-

1935 - POPULATION CONGRESS IN BERLIN

"To that great leader, Adolf Hitler!"
– C. Campbell, E.R.A.

The relationship between the American and German eugenicists would become excruciatingly clear in 1935. TIME Magazine would cover the event. The International Congress for the Scientific Investigation of Population Problems that was held in Berlin, Germany. Paul Lombardo, the author of "Three Generations No Imbeciles," documents the importance Hitler's government gave to this 1935 conference. Top members of Hitler's cabinet sponsored and spoke at the congress. Wilhelm Frick, the Reich Minister of the Interior in the Hitler Cabinet whose speech Laughlin printed in Eugenical News, was the honorary chairman of the conference. After the end of World War II, Frick was tried for war crimes at the Nuremberg Trials and executed. Professor Lombardo documents the event:

> His cabinet post as Reichminister of the Interior gave him jurisdiction over German domestic law, and promulgating the compulsory sterilization legislation had been among his first official acts in 1933. Frick's keynote address reviewed laws the Nazis had designed to reinvigorate Germany; laws to reduce unemployment would focus on "economic security for the hereditarily sound family," and "hereditary degenerates" would be eugenically sterilized. (Pg. 207, "Three Generations No Imbeciles")

Dr. Ruttke had made it a point to send Laughlin an English language review copy of this speech several months prior on March 4th, 1935. (BOX: C-4-4:7, Truman) The presentation was entitled "The German Law for the Prevention of Hereditary Defective Progeny and the Scandinavian Legislation for Sterilization." (BOX: D-5-5:9) Laughlin would print it in Eugenical News just like all the previous documents provided to him by Hitler's deputies. This particular speech is important as it documents how Hitler's leading eugenicists presented their policies to a worldwide audience invited to survey Nazi eugenic legislation. The very title displays an intention to parallel Nazi Germany's eugenic legislation with the progressive Scandinavian countries. Leading American eugenicists such as Lothrop Stoddard, Leon Whitney, Paul Popenoe, Marion S. Norton, and Marie Kopp would regurgitate the contents of this address in the fashion that political minions repeat the talking points of the party heads. The one point that would be repeated in all of their books and articles was the comparison Dr. Ruttke made between Hitler's eugenic policies and the eugenic legislation of progressive nations such as Denmark, Finland, Norway, and Sweden. Thus, providing for the sympathetic international audience the veil of scientific legitimacy that Hitler's top eugenicists so desired. Note the way Dr. Ruttke presents the German legislation in the section entitled "Must sterilization be carried out within a certain period of time?" He describes the German version of the law as complying with the legal "due process" requirements that Laughlin had prescribed in his "Model Eugenic Law":

> In <u>Norway</u>, the law prescribes nothing in this regard; in <u>Denmark</u>, sterilization must take place as soon as possible. In Germany, the commissioned physician must send the person to be sterilized a written summons, after the decision of the court for heredity cases has issued the decision for sterilization, demanding the person to be sterilized within two weeks. In <u>Finland</u>, the sterilization must not take place any later than a year after the conclusion of the board of health has become legal; likewise, in <u>Sweden</u>. Exceptional provisions are only provided for in <u>Germany</u>. (Box D-5-5:9, "German Law for the Prevention of Hereditary Defective Progeny," Truman Univ., emphasis theirs)

Of course, it is only prudent to believe that at least some, or many of the scientists operating under Hitler's National Socialism were true believers in the eugenic measures. These were the infamous "murderers in white coats." Scientists, judges, and doctors are perfectly capable of lending their credibility to the perogative of the political elite. Many times, they are enticed into cooperation precisely because they believe their scientific beliefs justify their actions. The testimony and interrogations of Dr. Karl Brandt at Nuremberg prove that he truly believed in the social benefits of eugenic euthanasia, sterilization, and segregation. Ruttke's presentation touches on this sentiment:

> The legislation in <u>Germany</u> and <u>Scandinavia</u> has begun to fight hereditary affected, particularly feeble-minded, mentally affected, other hereditarily affected, and sexual degenerates. All of these measures do nit indicate a return to the dark Middle Ages, as occasionally has been claimed, - no – they are bitter necessities for the government conscious of its responsibilities for the future of its nation. It as a greater humanity take care of the propagation of hereditarily sound, racially more valuable, orofolic families than to work against the check placed on defective inheritance. Is it not charactrising, that a short time ago, in a general inquiry made by several newspapers of Brasil concerning the German bill for the prevention of hereditarily affected progeny, such measures were hailed various experts, very prominent scholars? [sic.] (Box D-5-5:9, "German Law for the Prevention of Hereditary Defective Progeny," Truman Univ., emphasis theirs)

Dr. Ruttke's presentation goes a long way to evidence that these utopian social planners certainly thought they were addressing the needs of society in a legal and orderly way. These bureaucrats knowingly forfeited their responsibilities. As pointed out when analyzing Laughlin's "Model Eugenic Law," the mechanisms of a tyrannical centrally planned and all-powerful government were written into the compliance controls of the law. Ruttke's presentation explains why it was impossible for a doctor operating under the heavy hand of National Socialism to object on moral or ethical grounds, or to speak out against the measures:

> The laws of <u>Germany</u> and <u>Norway</u> provide penalties only for the violation of secrecy. Besides, the Reich's and Prussian Minister of the Interior, in Germany, in a decree, directed the competent boards to set themselves against agitation against the law, and to make arrests in cases which have become known for

violating § 110 of the "RStGB" (public challenge to disobedience of the law), or against the law against malicious attacks on the government and party. (Box D-5-5:9, "German Law for the Prevention of Hereditary Defective Progeny," Truman Univ., emphasis theirs)

Ruttke's presentation also makes reference to the necessary propaganda play that was necessary for such a type of legislation:

> If a people is to understand this legislation, it must be popular among the people. Thus requires a general, intelligible language of the legislator, which avoids the use of foreign words as for as possible. Such laws which regulate the sterilization should, therefore, bear the title "Law for the Prevention of Hereditarily Diseased Progeny", and not "Sterilization Law". If a people is to have confidence in this sort of legislation a very extensive secrecy for those involved in the process in any way whatsoever must be ordered, besides. The operation must take place only in institutions approved of by the government, and executed by physicians schooled accordingly. [sic.] (Pg. 18, Box D-5-5:9, "German Law for the Prevention of Hereditary Defective Progeny," Truman Univ.)

Ruttke's 1935 presentation is of significant historical importance. Ruttke makes direct reference to the International Federation of Eugenic Organizations as the reason the Germans felt there was widespread approbation for their eugenic program abroad. More poignantly, Ruttke points to the international eugenic movement as the source from which much of National Socialism's eugenic policy came from:

> The national legislation will, under all points of view, have to guarantee that the compulsory castration and sterilization will be executed only with the extremest care, and according to an orderly method which provides for a thorough investigation of the case by a board of lawyers and physicians. The second resolution of the International Federation of Eugenic Organizations, accepted on the 21st of July 1934 at Zurich, upon the suggestion of Dr. Mjöen, Norway, lay in the same direction. "The participants of the assembly who are present upon the occasion of the 2th Conference of **International Federation of Eugenic Organizations** in Zurich, and who represent the various countries of the world, ascertain that in the four day discussions, they have, **in spite of all of the differences of their political or general point of view, agreed that racial hygiene research and practice is most essential and unavoidable for all civilized countries. The Congress advises the governments of the world to study the problems of hereditary biology, the policy of population and race hygiene, in a similar and objective manner, as has already been done in some of the countries of Europe and America, and to apply their results for the benefit of their nations.**" A new era is being created. In conceivable time, there will hardly be any country which will not have decreed such a legislation, through which the flow of hereditary defects will be checked. [sic.] (Pgs. 16-17, Box D-5-5:9, "German Law for the Prevention of Hereditary Defective Progeny," Truman Univ., emphasis mine)

Here was a high-ranking Nazi pointing to the organization created by Leonard Darwin and Charles B. Davenport as the source of their eugenic knowledge. Here was a prominent leader in Hitler's government using the work of respected international scientists as justification for their aggressive policies towards ethnic minorities. Here were Hitler's henchmen announcing to the world that they had adopted the policies suggested by that institution that Laughlin, Darwin, and Davenport championed.

Ruttke outright claimed that the members of the international eugenics movement, namely the Americans, approved of the legislative measures. This claim was verified by an American delegation. Laughlin was not able to attend the conference, but asked Dr. Clarence Gordon Campbell, the president of the American Eugenics Research Association, to read the speech Laughlin would have given himself during the 1935 congress. This is confirmed by a July 31st, 1935 letter from Laughlin to "Professor Dr. Eugen Fischer." Dr. Eugen Fischer was serving as president of the congress as he was recognized as a prominent German eugenicist since the infamous "Baur-Fischer-Lenz" book that Hitler read in preparation for "Mein Kampf." Laughlin wrote to Fischer:

> I am enclosing with this letter a paper entitled "Further Studies on the Historical and Legal Development of Eugenical Sterilization in the United States." The paper is illustrated by 12 charts, pictures of which accompany the manuscript. In accordance with your suggestion, my distinguished colleague Dr. Clarence G. Campbell, who will attend the Population Congress in person, has kindly consented to read my paper. (BOX: C-4-4:7, Laughlin to Fischer, July 31st, 1935, Truman Univ.)

Consider the implications. Here was Laughlin again providing Hitler's top deputies with a highly detailed survey of the eugenical legislation implemented in the United States as a way of confirming that the United States government was equally supportive of the racial and eugenic laws implemented by Hitler's Third Reich. This letter also documents that Laughlin provided Hitler's government with insider information of the proceedings held by the United States Congress in its adoption of eugenic and racially minded exclusionary and isolationist 1924 immigration legislation:

> For this exhibit I have sent also a number of books and pamphlets. Among these pamphlets are a set of hearings held before the Committee on Immigration and Naturalization of the House of Representatives of the United States Congress. Some of these hearings were held ten years ago, but they show the nature of the testimony taken during the development by the United States of its biologically based policy for the control of immigration. By the use of scientific studies the American people are gradually working out a sound biological basis for their national and state policies on such matters as the control of immigration, of deportation, of marriage, and of eugenical sterilization. (BOX: C-4-4:7, Laughlin to Fischer, July 31st, 1935, Truman Univ.)

Clarence Campbell would present Laughlin's "German and Scandinavian Laws Regarding Sterilization," which also contained "MS Further Studies on Eugenical Sterilization in the United States." (BOX: D-5-5:9, Truman) The speech prepared by Laughlin was accompanied by a plethora of charts and figures documenting compulsory sterilization by the States. The presentation claimed to document American sterilization policies up to January 1st, of 1935. To put this into historical context, at this point in history the Nazi government was looking for international support in its efforts to deport its Jewish population, namely to Palestine or Madagascar. A presentation from the "scientific expert" for the United States Congress stating that the land of egalitarianism and individual rights had engaged in such legislation was precisely what Hitler's deputies needed. It was precisely the kind of information the Germans wanted for the entire world to hear in this international population congress. More poignantly, Laughlin identified himself as part of the "Carnegie Institution of Washington." Hitler's propaganda ministers could not have asked for more. They had an American scientist, working for one of the most renowned American institutions, declaring that the eugenics practiced in the United States was substantially similar to that being practiced in Nazi Germany. Laughlin's presentation included recommendations for eugenically-minded sterilization, segregation, and immigration policies encompassing forcible deportation of undesirables. Laughlin outright sanctioned the practice of having the dominant ethnicity both breed better examples of themselves as well as to "eliminate" those deemed "unfit":

> Once the standard is set, it is necessary for the particular reproductive group to act in both the positive or constructive, and the negative or eliminative phases of the problem. (BOX: D-5-5:9, "Further Studies," Truman Univ.)

Keep in mind that Laughlin was also recognized as the "Expert Eugenics Agent" for the United States Congress, the Labor Department, and the Department of State. Here was the renowned "expert" bragging to Hitler's eugenicists of the tens of thousands of sterilizations conducted in the United States thus far, and telling them that such numbers were purely part of the beginning of a much larger program:

> The latest first-hand survey of the enforcement of the eugenical sterilization statutes for the several States shows that 21,539 operations have been performed under these statutes up to January 1, 1935. (See chart.) ---- From the negative side of eugenics it must be stated that the sterilization of only a few more than 20,000 persons in thirty years in a country of vast population like the United States, while of considerable importance itself, is relatively quite insignificant as a national remedy for hereditary degeneracy. These first years and few operations, however, are looked upon by the different States largely as experimental. (BOX: D-5-5:9, "Further Studies," Truman Univ.)

Nor can it be said that Campbell and Laughlin were simply posturing for an international audience made up of his colleagues. As documented earlier, Laughlin had voiced a goal of sterilizing as many as 15,000,000 Americans when speaking in Battle Creek, Michigan decades earlier. Leon one, his cohort in the American Eugenics Society, wrote in his book that he wanted to sterilize as many as 10,000,000. These were not rough figures either. They were the amount of people eugenicists claimed they had to sterilize in order to make a dent in the evolution of a society due to the way recessive genes and other factors of biological inheritance operate. Under the section entitled "The Compulsory Aspect," Laughlin and Campbell communicate to the Nazi scientists an endorsement of the use of strong-arm policies in the enforcement of eugenically-motivated legislation:

> The motive for eugenical sterilization is basically biological; it is the prevention of the birth of children with degenerate or inadequate hereditary endowment. Vaccination has also a biological purpose; it is designed to protect both the individual and his fellows from smallpox. A generation ago the courts fought out the matter of compulsory or voluntary vaccination, and the legal result is that now any State may quite legally seize an individual and, if necessary, quite contrary to his wish and against his vigorous protest, vaccinate him. In general the compulsory element in eugenical sterilization has allowed a parallel development. The courts have held quite uniformly that the State may seize the individual and perform an operation of sexual sterilization for eugenical purposes, in cases so decided by due legal procedure, regardless of the consent or objection of the individual or of his or her kin or advisors. (BOX: D-5-5:9, "Further Studies," 1935, Truman Univ.)

Laughlin and Campbell were describing for the Germans the salient portions of the Unites States Supreme Court's 1927 <u>Buck v. Bell</u> opinion. Much of Laughlin's presentation reads like a summary of the 1927 <u>Buck v. Bell</u> opinion, legitimizing eugenical sterilization as a biological necessity, as opposed to a barbaric castration:

> One reason why, in the United States, great pains were taken for the individual whom the State proposed to sterilize, was because many of these early statutes had elements of punishment in them, and any kind of punishment by the State without due court hearing is held to be illegal and contrary to the Bill of Rights. There is a growing tendency for the States to set up quasi-judicial bodies to hear the cases when the State proposes to sterilize certain residents as falling within the natural class defined by the law as subject to eugenical sterilization. (BOX: D-5-5:9, "Further Studies," 1935, Truman Univ.)

Laughlin's presentation continues later with the theme of the biological basis for eugenical sterilization as sanctioned by the United States Supreme Court, and singling out "Justice Oliver Wendell Holmes" by name:

> Finally, experimental legislation and litigation clarified the matter, and, with later statutes, provided for the sexual sterilization of certain natural classes within the population on the basis of hereditary degeneracy; all penal motives and reference of all sorts were eliminated. Thus placing the statutes on a biological or pedigree-basis paved the way for the support of the Virginia statute by the Supreme Court of the United States. The Virginia statute was a purely eugenical one, with a biological basis but not penal feature. On May 2, 1927, in

the case of Carrie Buck vs. A.S. Priddy, Superintendent, Associate Justice Oliver Wendell Holmes who wrote the decision, said, in reference to the particular subject which the State of Virginia proposed to sterilize, that "three generations of imbeciles are enough." The eugenical sterilization laws which have been upheld by the courts make no reference whatever to race, religion or punishment. Thus legalized sexual sterilization, as developed by the several States in the United States, is purely biological or eugenical institution. (BOX: D-5-5:9, "Further Studies," 1935, Truman Univ.)

This was not the only time Campbell lectured about American eugenics. Dr. Campbell had previously voiced similar views in a lecture he delivered before the Social Service Club of Delaware at Wilmington in 1934:

> Perhaps the one fact that emerges more clearly than any other from all such study is that no one of all these sciences offers any evidence of human equality. But it is found that the changes which occur in the process of human evolution are due to the variation and inequality in individuals. The fact not only needs to be recognized that human equality is a gross fallacy, but that the variations and inequalities need carefully to be discriminated and correlated. ---- For a century and more, all social thought was based upon a social philosophy of egalitarianism and environmentalism, which its advocates are still by no means disposed to relinquish. ---- The egalitarians and environmentalists now feel compelled to admit that there are certain variations in individuals which are of hereditary origin. [sic.] (BOX: D-2-3:5, "Race Betterment and Sterilization," Feb. 13th, 1934, Truman Univ.)

Of course, this is a misreading of the founding principles of the country Campbell and Laughlin were born into. The founding documents of the American Revolution do not promise an equality of results, but only an equality of "opportunity" and treatment before the law. However, these founding principles stood as a formidable obstacle to the very core of their eugenic goals. Dr. Campbell went on to describe his belief that society was within its rights to practice "negative," or coerced, eugenics. Campbell understood that it would be difficult to convince the "fit" to choose the best mate, a practice often called "positive eugenics", but using the coercive power of the State to prevent those deemed "unfit" from reproducing was allegedly within the government's rights, legally speaking:

> Eugenists, as you no doubt well know, stress the desirability of perpetuating and increasing that eugenic population element that possesses that highest survival value, and of diminishing that other dysgenic element that is only a detriment to the racial prospect. As you also no doubt know, the efforts to increase this eugenic stock is called positive eugenics, and those to decrease the dysgenic stock is called negative eugenics. As we are here directing our attention more particularly to the decreasing of the dysgenic stock, we will need to pass over the highly important subject of positive eugenics. We may note however the radical difference between the nature of the efforts that are to be made in positive, and in negative, eugenics. By forcible control, or by other effective

means, we can prevent people from producing dysgenic offspring. But we cannot force people to produce eugenic offspring. We can only persuade them by appealing to their sense of racial duty, and by acquainting them with the personal rewards they should derive, (or by some form of subsidy or endowment) or by striving for more favorable external conditions for the production of such offspring. Hence no law can promote positive eugenics further than to offer inducements to individuals. Negative eugenics on the other hand is entirely amenable to the law, both in respect of sterilization laws, and of laws which will regulate or forbid the entrance into the population of stocks regarded as racially undesirable, or to enforce the deportation of such stocks. (BOX: D-2-3:5, "Race Betterment and Sterilization," Feb. 13th, 1934, Truman)

Dr. Campbell continues later on to address "individual rights" in the United States as the hurdle of the eugenics movement, and makes direct reference to the 1927 United States Supreme Court case of <u>Buck v. Bell</u>:

There is also the opposition to sterilization on the grounds of trespass on the individual's rights. The legal and constitutional aspects of this objection to sterilization have already been disposed of and settled by the United States Supreme Court. In experience, the adherence to the doctrine of individual rights is found to be anything but consistent. This doctrine is often invoked as the main support for claims that are otherwise weak and untenable. But it is found that what people are disposed to regard as inalienable individual rights are often revoked when the majority decide that they are against the common interest. Indeed when the common and the racial interests are at stake, how can it be maintained that individual rights, which go to injure this interest, should be allowed to stand? (BOX: D-2-3:5, "Race Betterment and Sterilization," Feb. 13th, 1934, Campbell, Truman Univ.)

Dr. Campbell would continue on in his "Race Betterment and Sterilization" lecture to make clear the extent of the "dysgenic", or "undesirable racial element" of the population:

An approximately accurate estimate of this whole element goes to show that even in normal times it constitutes no less than 10% of our population. It is perfectly obvious that the moral, intellectual, social, and economic conditions, and the future prospects, of any racial or national group would be greatly improved by the **extermination of these undesirable racial elements** that are both a constant burden upon the remainder, and a menace to the racial future. (BOX: D-2-3:5, "Race Betterment and Sterilization," Feb. 13th, 1934, Campbell, Truman Univ., emphasis mine)

Everything evidences that in 1935, Laughlin and Campbell were acting in concert with Hitler's scientists, and, in fact, giving aid and support to their eugenic venture. Laughlin's 1935 presentation revealed that eugenics, both in the United States and Hitler's Germany, was more than just petty bigotry run amok. Eugenics began and was intended to continue in Hitler's "Thousand-year Reich" long after the eradication of those unwanted ethnic elements. It was meant to be a perpetual program of biological purification. Case in point, Laughlin's 1914 presentation at

Battle Creek, Michigan clearly states the goal for eugenic sterilization in the United States to continue on through the 1980s and beyond. Hitler's scientists were equally aware that to perfect their "Master Race" they too would have to perpetuate eugenics after their plans for the Jews had been fulfilled. Laughlin continued along these lines:

> There is a fundamental parallel, in their biological aspects, between the **establishment and maintenance of human racial and family-stock standards**, on the one hand, with the development and maintenance of racial and breed characteristics of domestic plants and animals, on the other. (BOX: D-5-5:9, "Further Studies," 1935, Truman Univ.)

Laughlin referring to the individual targeted for sterilization as "subjects of the State" is curious, as it reveals the relationship between governed and government that Laughlin subscribed to. Apparently, Laughlin thought of the State as supreme and the individual living in subservience. Keep in mind that the group Campbell and Laughlin were addressing were the scientists in Hitler's Germany directly responsible for the implementation and execution of National Socialist eugenic policies, including the infamous Nuremberg Laws and the T4 Euthanasia program.

The 1935 Population Congress was also of significant historical importance because through it, Laughlin provided the bridge between National Socialism and some of the most formidable forces in opposition to the Civil Rights movement that followed in the United States. Laughlin asked Eugen Fischer in that July 31st, 1935 letter to welcome Wickliffe Draper, the man Laughlin would help with the creation of the infamous Pioneer Fund. The letter introduces Draper as "one of the staunchest supporters of eugenical research and policy in the United States", and as such, these prominent Germans welcomed Draper with enthusiasm. Truman's archives also hold an August 15th, 1935 letter from Laughlin to Draper. In it Laughlin confirms that Draper had been named "an official delegate" of the "Executive Committee of the Eugenics Research Association" for the congress upon Laughlin's request. Draper responded with a letter written on the letterhead of the Hotel Adlon in Berlin:

> Dear Doctor Laughlin, Please accept my belated thanks for the credentials as delegate from the Eugenics Research Association which you so kindly sent me. I have already got in touch with Doctor Campbell and met several Germans who may be able to give me the information I seek, and which I look forward to discussing with you on my return. With renewed thanks, believe me, Very sincerely yours, W.P. Draper (BOX: D-2-3-14, Draper to Laughlin, Aug. 28th, 1935, Truman Univ.)

The importance of this symposium cannot be overemphasized. Here was the future of American racial segregation put in touch with the eugenic leadership of National Socialist Germany. As mentioned, TIME covered the event and described the immediate impact this population congress had. The TIME article was titled

"Praise for Nazis" and it appeared in the September 9th, 1935 edition of this leading periodical. The article clearly depicts the inseparable link between population control, birth control, and the "Nazi eugenists' plans for breeding Germans like prize cattle":

> Sore from the slings and arrows of foreign criticism, Germans heard gratefully last week a warm, approving speech from Dr. Clarence Gordon Campbell, president of the American Eugenics Research Association, delivered before the World Population Congress in Berlin.

TIME Magazine quotes Campbell:

Dr. Campbell sat down last week, Chief Arthur Gutt of the German Public Health Department bluntly told the Congress: "Our penal code will shortly make compulsory a health examination for all marrying persons. The purpose of this is first to dissuade bodily or mental inferiors from marrying and especially from procreation. Second, to prevent marriages between hereditarily tainted persons, the same as a marriage between an Aryan and a non-Aryan. Third, to influence the choice of life partners from a health as well as a racial viewpoint."

The event certainly raised eyebrows. The Laughlin files at both Carnegie and Truman University hold several letters, some supportive, but many angry. An interesting one was directed at Laughlin by a J. H. Sandman written on the stationary of "The College of the City of New York", the old name for N.Y.U. Despite the fact that Mr. Sandman was a member of the Eugenics Research Association, he was somehow shocked that eugenics was part of Nazi ideology:

> However, as President of the Eugenics Research Association, in which capacity he served, he owes allegiance to its constitution and its members. I hate to believe that the Eugenics Research Association, dedicated to eugenics as a science, has been prostituted to further false propaganda. (BOX: D-2-3:5, Letter Sandman to Laughlin, Sept., 13th, 1935, Truman Univ.)

The reader will recall Waldemar Kaempffert, the Science Editor of the New York Times, who had been writing about the development of eugenic legislation in Nazi Germany. Kaempffert wrote to Laughlin to voice his displeasure over Laughlin's publication of Frick's speech. His letter found the publication of Campbell's address in Eugenical News objectionable due to its contents. His claims are certainly strange, as anyone that read the Eugenical News regularly would not have found the content outside of the norm:

> Dear Sir: Am I to infer that because you publish the presidential address of Dr. G. Campbell in your September-October 1935 number you endorse all its out-moded and questionable statements about Nordic "races" and mongrelization? Or do you have to give him space simply because you are the official organ of the Eugenics Research Association? [sic.] (BOX: D-2-3:5., Letter Kaempffert to Laughlin, October 15th, 1935, Truman Univ.)

Here was a well-publicized conference that linked Nazism to the racialists that would later be the impetus behind the obstructionist antagonism towards the American Civil Rights movement. Yet, the event has been overlooked in much the same way that Laughlin has by mainstream historians. TIME Magazine provides a quote from Campbell that should make every American shiver cold to their bones:

> Socialite Dr. Campbell's boldest dicta: "The difference between the Jew and the Aryan is as insurmountable as that between black and white. . . . Germany has set a pattern which other nations must follow."

In other words, Dr. Campbell was of the opinion that Hitler's policies towards the Jews should be applied to American blacks. Needless to say, the image of prominent American scientists participating in one of Hitler's propaganda ploys, and worse, saluting the dictator, was too much to stomach for Americans back home. TIME Magazine described Dr. Campbell closing Congress by raising his arm in the infamous stiff-arm salute and proclaiming: **"To that great leader, Adolf Hitler!"**

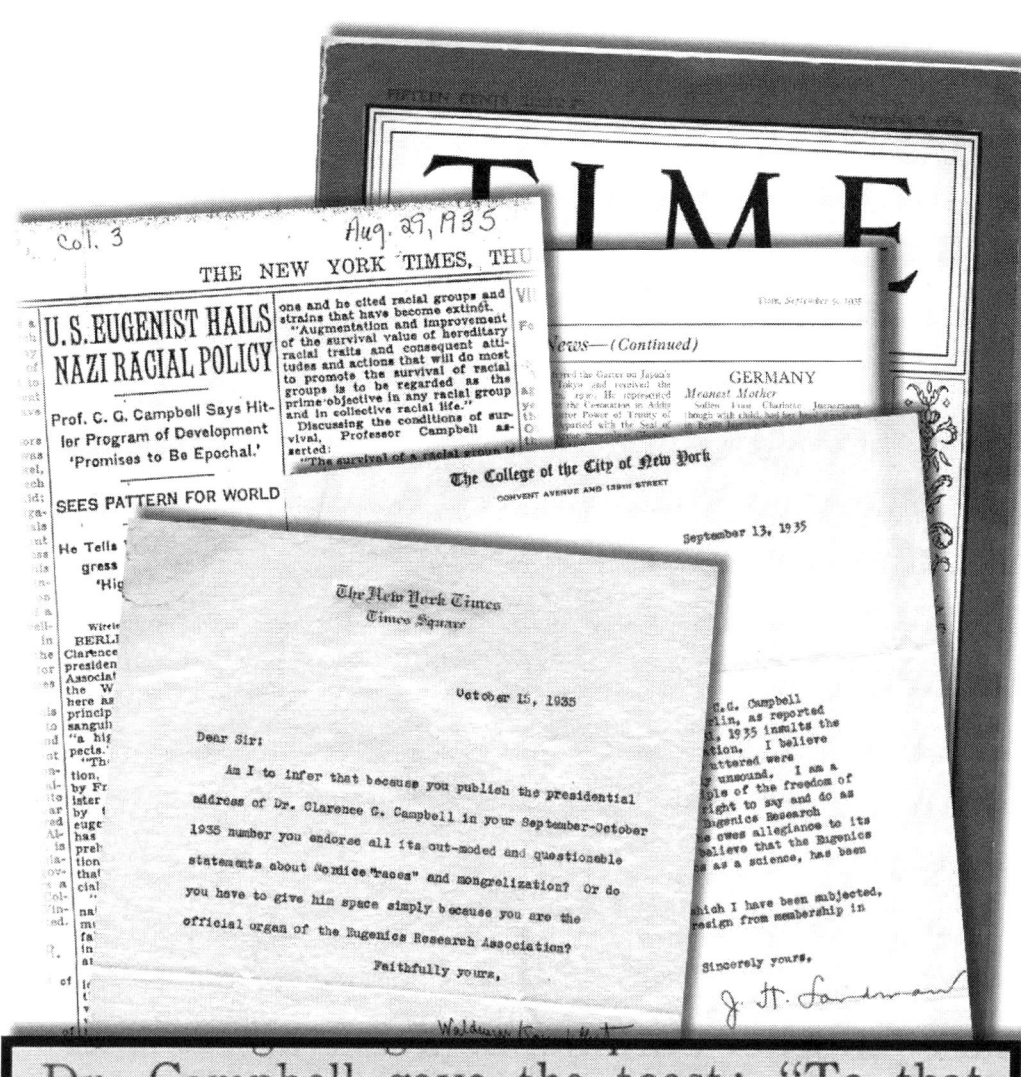

THE NEW YORK TIMES, THU[RSDAY, Aug. 29, 1935]

U.S. EUGENIST HAILS NAZI RACIAL POLICY

Prof. C. G. Campbell Says Hitler Program of Development 'Promises to Be Epochal.'

SEES PATTERN FOR WORLD

one and he cited racial groups and strains that have become extinct.

"Augmentation and improvement of the survival value of hereditary racial traits and consequent attitudes and actions that will do most to promote the survival of racial groups is to be regarded as the prime objective in any racial group and in collective racial life."

Discussing the conditions of survival, Professor Campbell asserted:

Time, September 9, 1935

News—(Continued)

GERMANY

Meanest Mother

The New York Times
Times Square

October 15, 1935

Dear Sir:

Am I to infer that because you publish the presidential address of Dr. Clarence G. Campbell in your September-October 1935 number you endorse all its out-moded and questionable statements about Nordic "races" and mongrelization? Or do you have to give him space simply because you are the official organ of the Eugenics Research Association?

Faithfully yours,

The College of the City of New York
CONVENT AVENUE AND 139TH STREET

September 13, 1935

...C. G. Campbell ...lin, as reported ...l, 1935 insults the ...tion, I believe ...ttered were ...y unsound. I am a ...ple of the freedom of ...right to say and do as ...ugenics Research ...e owes allegiance to its ...elieve that the Eugenics ...n as a science, has been

...ich I have been subjected, ...resign from membership in

Sincerely yours,

J. H. Landman

Dr. Campbell gave the toast: "To that great leader, Adolf Hitler!"

Cold Spring Harbor, L.I., N.Y.

1935 - CARNEGIE'S FIRST ADVISORY COMMITTEE

> *"Only a fool of a scientist would dismiss the evidence and reports in front of him and substitute his own beliefs in their place."*
> - Paul Kurtz

It seems that while under the presidency of John C. Merriam the Eugenics Record Office had enthusiastic support from the Carnegie leadership. As mentioned earlier, the internal correspondence still held at the Carnegie Institution reveals that the doubts emerged from the middle ranks and scientists in other departments. While Gilbert, Blakeslee, and others voiced such concerns, it seems that Dr. Merriam, at least when speaking to Laughlin and Davenport, was consistently supportive of the work being done at the Eugenics Record Office. A February 19th, 1935 letter from Dr. Merriam to Laughlin concerning the donations by a wealthy Miss R.H. Verne is an example of the enthusiasm Dr. Merriam often voiced:

> I am glad to hear through you of the interest of Miss R.H. Verne in the Institution and the Eugenics Record Offices. It is pleasant to know that others look upon what we are doing as valuable. Personally, I feel that there is an opportunity in eugenics to do a great work for mankind, and I hope others will take the same attitude toward the subject. I hope that you will give Miss Verne opportunity to see what we are doing and also to know fully regarding our ideals and purposes. (Laughlin files, Carnegie Inst., Feb. 19th, 1935, Merriam to Laughlin)

The correspondence between Laughlin and Merriam on the potential donation from Miss Verne reveals the level of ignorance on the part of both Merriam and Miss Verne. A January 17th, 1935 letter demonstrates that Laughlin was willing to benefit from this ignorance:

> The particular interests of the possible prospective testator seem to be an aversion to race-mixture, opposition to Hitler, favor of eugenical immigration control for all Pan America, the study of Aztec and Mayan history, and the sterilization of degenerate human stocks. (Both Miss Verne and testator have evidently traveled widely throughout the world, particularly in Latin America. Miss Verne herself is of French and Spanish descent and speaks several languages.) (Laughlin files, Carnegie Inst., Jan. 17th, 1935, Laughlin to Merriam)

It does not seem that Miss Verne ever contributed to the Eugenics Record Office financially, or if she became wise that her mixed-ethnicity was precisely what eugenic zealots like Laughlin found as inferior. She certainly did not seem to understand that her "opposition" to Hitler contradicted her personal aversion to "race-mixture."

Whatever the case, the constant barrage of negative press inspired Dr. Merriam to fund a second investigation into the work done at Cold Spring Harbor.

The Carnegie Institution conducted at least two major reviews of the work done by the Eugenics Record Office while Laughlin and Davenport headed it. The on-site review was headed up by A.V. Kidder, whom despite his belief in the general goals of eugenics, had serious doubts about the work done by Davenport and Laughlin. Paul Lombardo's paper, "Pioneer's Big Lie," documents that A.V. Kidder described Laughlin as having "a messiah attitude toward eugenics." Kidder corresponded with Dr. Streeter stating that Laughlin was more of a "propagandist" and was out of place in a scientific institution. The criticism was spot on, as Laughlin was much more interested in getting legislation passed than in the actual research necessary to back up his claims. John C. Merriam would eventually accept the committee's conclusions along with the premise that there needed to be a separation between "fundamental research and propaganda."

A specifically damaging letter of June 3rd, 1935, by the man subsequently appointed to review the work done at the Eugenics Record Office came from Professor L.C. Dunn of Columbia University. Dunn's opinion carried some weight in the matter. The letter from Dunn to the Institution directly questions whether the work that had been done at Cold Spring Harbor was political or fact based:

> In this connection I think it is open to question whether it is wise to continue such a record office under the patronage of a research institution as a "Eugenics Record Office." "Eugenics" has come to mean an effort to foster a program of social improvement rather than an effort to discover facts." (Item ID#1092 – 1096, www.eugenicsarchive.org)

Professor Lombardo quotes the L.C. Dunn on the growing distance between geneticists and eugenicists:

> Eugenical research was not always activated by purely disinterested scientific motives. – Eugenics has come to mean an effort to foster a program of social improvement rather than an effort to discover facts. (Lombardo, "Pioneer's Big Lie")

L.C. Dunn expanded his comments to clarify the consequences of the commonality between German and American eugenics. Paul Lombardo clarifies that "as early as 1935, Dunn was willing to draw parallels between the most virulent American eugenics propaganda and Nazi abuses in the name of science":

> I have just observed in Germany some of the consequences of reversing the order as between [social] program and discovery. The incomplete knowledge of today, much of it based on a theory of the state which has been influenced by the racial, class and religious prejudices of the group in power, has been embalmed in law . . . The genealogical [sic] record offices have become powerful agencies of the state, and medical judgments even when possible, appear to be subservient to political purposes. (Lombardo, "Pioneer's Big Lie")

Professor Garland Allen has also studied this episode and quotes L.C. Dunn's opinion of the quality and value of the work done at Cold Spring Harbor:

> The records, upon which so much effort and money have been expended, have to date been extremely little used, to judge by the number of publications based upon them. Thus the Office [Eugenics Record Office] appears to be accumulating large amounts of material, and devoting a disproportionately great amount of time and money to a futile system for indexing it, without certainty, or even good probability, that it will ever be of value. (Pg. 317, Annals of Human Genetics, 2011, "Eugenics and Modern Biology")

The truth is that the gargantuan amount of data being collected had in all of those decades been useful only to those with political motivations and intentions. In hindsight, it may have been counterproductive for eugenicists like Laughlin to actually engage in rigorous science. It did not serve his goals as genuinely scientific efforts in a field as complex as human genetics would have likely marginalized or been too complicated for the judges, lawyers, and legislators to use effectively. Simple terms and concepts lend themselves to political zealotry. Lombardo describes the scientific validity of the work being done by the ERO in his article "Pioneer's Big Lie":

> They described the records collected at the ERO as a "vast and inert accumulation," "unsatisfactory for the scientific study of human genetics" and judged the "system of recording . . . unsound." The auditors recommended a new direction for Laughlin's program to insure that it was "divorced from all forms of propaganda and the urging or sponsoring of programs for social reform or race betterment such as sterilization, birth-control, inculcation of race (sic) or national consciousness, restriction of immigration, etc." A change to the name of the Eugenical News was recommended to avoid the negative connotations of the word "eugenics," which the auditors suggested was "not a science." – (Lombardo, "Pioneer's Big Lie," Volume 66, Albany Law Review)

Unfortunately, both Davenport and Laughlin were allowed to be part of this committee, and it seems that the harsher judgments did not make it to the final report or determination. An example of this can be seen in the hand-written side notes that A.V. Kidder wrote on Laughlin's suggestions for the future of the office. The 1935 letter from L.C. Dunn was copied to Laughlin, and it suggested closing the Cold Spring Harbor facility and focusing any future efforts on a pure science-based research on "human heredity." It seems that Laughlin tried to insert himself into the changing directions of the Carnegie Institution. He submitted proposals that adopted Dunn's suggestion that the focus of "eugenics" be dropped and "human heredity" and "genetics" be adopted. Correspondence in 1938 from Laughlin to the Carnegie Institution heads titled "Proposed Clinic of Human Heredity" were part of his negotiations according to the archives (Item ID# 1795 – 1804, www.eugenicsarchive.org). Also, a memorandum entitled "FOUR POINTS DESIRED IN THE IMMEDIATE FUTURE POLICY" had been written by Laughlin and presented to John C. Merriam on December 7th, 1934 when the committee concluded its review. The memorandum had a grandiose closing paragraph which called for "An institution of the type herein described would contribute to the world's knowledge about mankind's numbers and quality, and it would aid in the conservation of the racial and family-stock values of the American people." A.V. Kidder's hand written reaction states:

> This implies a <u>knowledge</u> of the fundamental superiority of the American stock which, in fact, we ___ have ___ the specific objective of the E.R.O. the attempt to evaluate the abilities of various studies? But his strong predisposition in favor of the "Nordics" would probably render him unfit to direct such studies. A more purely biological problem would probably be better handled by any group which L. (Laughlin) might head? (Laughlin files, Carnegie Inst., "FOUR POINTS DESIRED," annotated by A.V. Kidder, <u>illegible portions omitted</u>)

The annotated memorandum is held together with the letter that Laughlin wrote president Merriam, so it is very likely that it was Merriam that handed it to Kidder to review. While Merriam would not adopt Laughlin's recommendations, the record shows that the leadership of the Carnegie Institution would support Laughlin and Davenport throughout Merriam's tenure. It seems that in 1935, the clear parallels to Nazi Germany were not enough to cause Merriam sufficient alarm to justify a drastic change in direction. The history of the regime was still developing, and, after all, the National Socialist leadership was adopting the recommendations of prominent minds in the United States and Britain. In Britain, you had Winston Churchill, Leonard Darwin, and John Maynard Keynes vociferously championing the eugenics cause. In the United States warnings against "race suicide" had been popularized by President Theodore Roosevelt along with the most respected intellects of Ivy League pedigree. Thus, the warnings of sober-minded scientists like L.C. Dunn, prophetic as they may have been, were yet to reveal their true wisdom. Kidder's observation that Laughlin had a predisposition to believe in Nordic superiority was accurate. Nevertheless, the fact is that Laughlin's beliefs were also the beliefs of the most famous and respected scientists of the time, beginning with Francis Galton on through to Charles B. Davenport.

1936 - CONNECTICUT STUDY

*"If a man is in too big a hurry to give up an error
he is liable to give up some truth with it."*
- Wilbur Wright, 1902

John C. Merriam may have entertained the observations and warnings of L.C. Dunn and A.V. Kidder. However, the internal documents evidence that he turned right around and continued to extend his campaign to showcase the Eugenic Records Office. The opportunity to further the research, as well as the practical implementation of Laughlin's eugenics presented itself when a prominent legislator from Connecticut voiced interest. In January of 1936, Laughlin would provide Merriam and the Carnegie leadership a proposal for a eugenic study. The title of this study is telling. Laughlin entitled "A Sample Human-Resources Inventory," with "inventory" apparently meaning what the term entails in a stockyard or farm:

> DEFINITION: A new and first-hand field inventory of all the inhabitants of a small geographical or political unit in the United States, but representative in respect to the nation's population and population problems. Such an inventory should determine and record the facts concerning the history, physical anthropology, blood-kinship, occupation, **economic value, social value**, health, intelligence, education, religion and personality of each individual. (Laughlin files, Carnegie Inst., "A Short Statement on the Definition, Purpose, Place and Cost of a Sample Human-Resources Inventory," emphasis mine)

True to Laughlin's penchant to build upon political connections, this initial proposal would conveniently find its way to the eyes and ears of several like-minded legislators. In turn, they would play their part and request Laughlin's work as if the idea had initiated with them. With the benefit of hindsight, one can pull together the internal correspondence and note how this simple proposal would later become a full-fledged project under the auspices of the State of Connecticut. The proposal would call for an expansion of and furtherance of previous projects and experiments. For example, the project calls for the employment of the "resources in the census" in order to provide the raw data for the "inventory." It requested that the Census capture "blood-kinships" in order to track the "economic" and "social" value of each individual as well as the "racial constitution" of each "family stock." This is, in essence, what IBM punch card readers were helping Hitler's government accomplish with the German census. Notably, Laughlin understood the problems that individual rights posed. Therefore, he addressed the need for a "legal definition" of what a "resident" was. More importantly, Laughlin was astute enough to be concerned with the legal aspect of the "privacy of public records."

Taking an inventory of humans and their "economic and social value" was a eugenic notion that dated back to Francis Galton's utopian novel, "Kantsaywhere." Galton proposed a committee made up of eugenic elites that would determine the rights and privileges of each individual "resident." Needless to say, those deemed of lesser value were allowed a diminishing number of rights in accordance with their perceived biological worth.

Much of the statistical documentation originated from work the Eugenics Record Office had already done for the State. Laughlin had studied the costs necessary for the upkeep of Connecticut's twelve institutions for the so-called "socially degenerate" in 1916. At that point, Laughlin had estimated that 20.5% of the Connecticut's total expenditures went to these institutions.

Senator F. Walcott of Connecticut showed interest and Laughlin's work. Walcott also held the position of Commissioner of Welfare for the State of Connecticut; a position that possessed the power to create policy for the various institutions in question. An October 5th, 1936 letter from Laughlin to Dr. Merriam discusses Walcott's interest. Of course, one of Laughlin's suggestions was to send the Senator a copy of his "Model Eugenic Law":

> I am sending also to your address in Washington a few reprints on eugenical sterilization which may be of use in case Senator Walcott is interested in a further development of this instrument by the State of Connecticut for the protection of the state's future population against reproduction by certain family-stocks of proven hereditary degeneracy. (Laughlin files, Carnegie Inst., Oct. 5th, 1936, Laughlin to Merriam)

It is especially interesting to see Dr. Merriam's continuing interest in effecting eugenic-minded legislation within the United States, despite the dire warnings given to him by A.V. Kidder and L.C. Dunn. Note that Dr. Merriam all but ignores the warnings to step over the line of scientific research into the realm of practical and political application of eugenics:

> I would appreciate it greatly if you could meet with Senator Walcott, or Dr. Davenport if you can not go, and **do everything feasible in making practical application of eugenical data in this connection.** This appears to me a very exceptional opportunity and one in which we should do our utmost to aid. [sic] (Laughlin files, Carnegie Inst., Oct. 14th, 1936, Merriam to Laughlin, emphasis mine)

There is no chance that Dr. Merriam was unaware of the implications of the implementation of eugenic-minded policies as Laughlin's response makes it amply clear what the Connecticut Study entailed:

> While this excellent custodial care of its inadequates is all very well, the Senator feels that it is time for the State of Connecticut to do something **to purge the population of its degenerate strains** which the present custodial system tends to conserve and to increase. In the policy in handling its known inadequates the State of Connecticut has reached a definite mile post, and the Senator is anxious that his commonwealth be one of the first to codify its laws in the field of population-conservation covering *such* matters as the commitment to custodial institutions, provisions for sterilization and parole, interstate deportation of inadequates, locating more definitely om the particular

community which produces an inadequate the responsibility to care for him, better coordination with the Federal Government in the deportation of aliens, and with local educational and social offices and organizations in the location of degenerate family-stocks, and the revision of the state's standard for marriage license.[sic.] (Laughlin files, Carnegie Inst., Oct. 24th, 1936, Laughlin to Merriam, emphasis mine)

By this time, newspapers with coverage of international events were documenting the extent of Hitler's aggression. The National Socialist regime had begun to reveal its fangs in the early months of that year. On February 10th, 1936 the SS and the Gestapo became unified into one powerful and intimidating agency capable of delivering the aggression promised in the speeches and rallies. Gestapo Law was enacted in Prussia, giving this police force exclusive right to make arrests, and entitled it to investigate all activities considered hostile to the state. On March 7th, 1936 Hitler sent German troops into the Rhineland Province, defying the Treaty of Versailles once again and making National Socialist militancy a palpable reality.

More to the point, Laughlin's statement to Merriam was also an accurate description of how the Third Reich had implemented its early eugenic policy. With the exclusion of euthanasia Laughlin proposed segregating and sterilizing undesirable "strains," while promoting families that met the racial standards. Laughlin wanted to deport those that did not meet his biological standard, as well as to limit their reproduction and marriages. Laughlin can hardly be said to have been ambiguous or unclear:

> The Senator is working to find a plan which would promise the elimination of definitely defective stocks and strains, and which would encourage fit matings and higher fertility among the better-endowed families. [sic.] (Laughlin files, Carnegie Inst., Oct. 24th, 1936, Laughlin to Merriam)

The impetus behind the study would survive Laughlin. It seems that Walcott never lost interest in the study, even as the "rumors" about the Third Reich revealed themselves to be the horrid reality we now recognize as Holocaust history. As late as 1943, with the stories of how Hitler's government employed eugenics to subjugate its population, Senator Walcott still had an interest in formalizing Laughlin's study. The Carnegie files have a document with the long heading of "Report on the information supplied by the 1937 Survey on the Human Resources of Connecticut, prepared by Dr. U. Fano, Carnegie Institution of Washington, at the request of Senator F. Walcott, and presented to the meeting of the Commission at Hartford, Connecticut, on January 4, 1943." The 1943 date is of interest, as the "rumors" of The Holocaust atrocities had begun to surface two years earlier in American newspapers. The report covered research up until October 1st, 1938 and interestingly enough, it states that it was "prepared at the Genetics Record Office," with "Genetics" already formally replacing "Eugenics" as the name of the Cold Spring Harbor facilities. Senator Walcott later visited Cold Spring Harbor in 1942 to request that the study be "reexamined and critically summarized." It is, therefore, of note that the report could not resist its eugenic impetus:

> Of course any action opposing natural selection tends in the long run to increase the over-all frequency of harmful hereditary factors, even though they are hidden because of being recessive. However, the beneficial effects of such an action are immediate, while it has been shown by Haldane that the harmful effects would be expected to become important only in the course of 1000 years. (Objections may be raised on principle as to the advisability of interfering with natural selection. However, the fact remains that whenever hereditary factors produce too disastrous results, the State finds it necessary to intervene in some way – from charitable if not from eugenical motives. The resultant financial burden is exactly what the State is now endeavoring to avoid.) (Laughlin files, Carnegie Inst., 1943 Report on the Connecticut Study)

While the above text backpedals the impulse to tinker with natural selection, it clearly falls prey to the temptation to have the state play God in order to rid itself of the burden of inconvenient individuals. Alternatively, in the words of Hitler's top deputy, Rudolf Hess, to enact a program of "applied biology":

> Finally, it is possible to reinforce selection, instead of opposing it, by preventing the reproduction of carriers of harmful heredity. This aim may be furthered through education, legislation, segregation, or sterilization, although it meets with obvious difficulties. (Laughlin files, Carnegie Inst., 1943 Report on the Connecticut Study)

There are two very interesting aspects to the report. First, it finds that the vast majority of its "problem" population was between the ages of "7 and 21". Thus, it corroborates the reports of the mass sterilization campaigns like the ones conducted at Shutesbury. Second, it admits that the "feeble-minded" were the least of the state's problems, contributing only to what is described as only a "minor share of the State burden." This, of course, contradicts that most fundamental and enduring claim of the international eugenics movement. It is interesting to see the study generate this conclusion once the prejudices of its original author were removed and replaced with that of another scientist. The conclusions and recommendations of the report were hardly benign:

> The specific measures that might be taken in this matter are not clear to me. It might, however, be well to comb the State population in order to control and segregate the totality of these cases. Then there is the problem raised by the less serious cases, which are uncontrolled and at large in the population. Most of these cases are only partially inadequate, but their number is very high and might well reach 50,000 (3% of the population). This class of persons probably constitutes a dangerous reservoir of low-grade heredity. (Laughlin files, Carnegie Inst., 1943 Report on the Connecticut Study)

Would not history be served if we could study exactly whom these 50,000 individuals were? More specifically, would history not be served if we could see what families and individuals would have been prevented from existing if this plan had been implemented? The above statement reveals the dangers of imbuing centrally-planned governmental institutions with the power to deprive individuals of all of the "inalienable" rights that are guaranteed by the United States Constitution and Declaration of Independence. The hubris inherent in the above statement boils to the surface when one realizes that this 3% of the population, these 50,000 individuals, were described to not be as serious, and in actuality, difficult to diagnose. How much of a menace to society could they have possibly been if their condition was difficult to discern? Yet, the author is fully prepared to deprive these individuals of their right to "life, liberty, and the pursuit of happiness" based on nothing more than a best guess as to their biological worth. The author clearly viewed himself as empowered to act as the farmer, the breeder, the caretaker of the "reservoirs" of breeding stocks, fully entitled by his position of power to rid the society of the "dangers" of the individuals that he deemed to be of "low-grade heredity."

Die Universität Heidelberg

die älteste Hochschule des Deutschen Reiches, begeht in den Tagen vom 27. bis 30. Juni 1936 die Feier ihres

550jährigen Bestehens.

Ich würde es mit zur Ehre anrechnen

Herrn Prof. Harry H. Laughlin

in diesen Tagen [...]
fen. Ihre Ant[...]
damit Ihnen [...]

UNIVERSITÄTS-BIBLIOTHEK HEIDELBERG

Nr. A 2032

HEIDELBERG, den 15. Juni 1936.

Wir bestätigen mit verbindlichstem Dank den Empfang von

A decade of progress in Eugenics. 1934
Laughlin, A Report of the Special Committee on Sterilization, 1934
- *The Legal Status of Eugenical Sterilization.*
- *Eugenical Sterilization in the United States, 1922.*
- *Europe as an Emigrant-exporting Kont, 1924.*
- *Analysis of (the) America's mod. melting pot, 1923.*
- *Biological Aspects of Immigration. 1931.*
- *Eugenical Aspects of Deportation. 1928.*
- *Am History in Terms of Human Migration. 1928.*
- *21 Reprints.*

Der Direktor,
UNIVERSITÄTSBIBLIOTHEK HEIDELBERG
AKZESSION

An
Eugenics Record Office

Cold Spring Harbor

1936 - HEIDELBERG DEGREE

> *"Man prefers to believe what he prefers to be true."*
> *- Francis Bacon*

Laughlin would be honored by Hitler's Third Reich for the work that was so instrumental in creating the "racial state" that was Hitler's Germany. In 1936, Laughlin received an invitation from Carl Schneider, a professor of racial hygiene. The invitation was for the 550-year Jubilee at Heidelberg University and for Laughlin to receive an honorary Doctor of Medicine degree. Paul Lombardo documents that the date had ideological connotations, as it was the anniversary of Hitler's 1934 purge of the Jewish faculty at Heidelberg University. The relevant correspondence is still held at Truman University's Laughlin Collection. A letter from a Dr. Carl Schneider, the Dean of the Faculty of Medicine at Heidelberg University, announced the honors:

> The Faculty of Medicine of the University of Heidelberg intends to confer upon you the degree of Doctor of Medicine h.c. on the occasion of the 550-year Jubilee (27th to 30th of June 1936) (BOX: E-1-3:8, Translated letter from Schneider to Laughlin, May 16th, 1936, Truman Univ.)

Laughlin was supposed to personally and ceremoniously receive the honorary degree. The German press speculated that the invitations would provide a "foreign endorsement" to the regime. (Pg. 212, "Three Generations") The implications could not be clearer, and the invitation letter ended with a list of Laughlin's work on eugenics as the justification for the honors:

1.) A decade of progress in Eugenics. 1934
2.) Laughlin, A Report of the Special Committee on Immigration, 1934.
3.) The Legal Status of Eugenical Sterilization, Eugenical Sterilization in the U.S., 1922.
4.) Europe as an Immigrant-Exporting Cont., 1924.
5.) Analysis of (the) America's Mod. Melting Pot, 1923.
6.) Biological Aspects of Immigration, 1927.
7.) Eugenical Aspects of Deportation, 1928.
8.) Am. History in Terms of Human Migration, 1928

Laughlin would respond to Dr. Schneider on May 28th, 1936, making sure to praise the racial qualities of the German people:

> I stand ready to accept this very high honor. Its bestowal will give me particular gratification, coming as it will from a university deep rooted in the life history of the German people, and a university which has been both a reservoir and a fountain of learning for more than half a millennium. To me this honor will be doubly valued because it will come from a nation which for many centuries nurtured the human seed-stock which later founded my own country and thus gave basic character to our present lives and institutions. (BOX: E-1-3:8, Translated letter from Schneider to Laughlin, May 16th, 1936, Truman Univ.)

Laughlin's honorary degree received minimal press coverage in the United States. The Laughlin Collection at Truman has a small one-paragraph clipping from the Huntington Times of July 9th, 1936 entitled "Dr. H.H. Loughlin of Carnegie Honored." [sic.] However, the event in general instigated the ire of the American and British press. Laughlin made a point to keep these press clippings in his files, which survive to this day at Truman University's archives. Many of the American and British scientists invited refused to attend out of principle. An article entitled "Science at Heidelberg" makes a point to highlight the very curious choice of words from Dr. Bernhard Rust, Hitler's Minister of Science, Education and People's Education:

> "The charge of enmity to science is true of the National Socialist regime if the complete absence of preconceptions and predispositions, unrestrained objectivity, are to be taken as characteristics of science . . . The old idea of science based on the sovereign right of abstract intellectual activity has gone forever. The new science is entirely different from the idea of knowledge that found its value in an unchecked effort to reach the truth. The true freedom of science is to be an organ of a nation's living strength and of its historic fate and to present this in obedience to the law of truth."

The author of the article responds to Dr. Rust:

What scientist worthy of the name will be willing to assent to a proposition so false and so shameless? What true scientist has there been from Empedocles to Einstein, from Pythagoras to Newton, from Thales of Miletia to Darwin, from Anaximander to Herbert Spencer, who could have been persuaded that not a search for absolute truth but a search for substantiation of preconceived opinion bearing upon current political philosophy has been or is the true goal of science? What earnest scholar poring over test tube or microscope is prepared to admit even now that instead of being self-disciplined search for knowledge science ought to be a governmentally disciplined inquiry into the historic sources of national vanity? (BOX: E-1-3:8, Heidelberg Degree press clippings, Truman Univ.)

The negative press on Nazi eugenics would only get worse from here on. In fact, there is one curious little episode that is worth recounting because of who wrote it and who it ultimately reached. The March-August 1936 edition of "Living Age" did a book review of Heinrich Krieger's work in an article titled "Heil Lincoln!" Littell's "Living Age," also known simply as "The Living Age," was an American magazine largely consisting of selections from various English and American publications. It was published weekly from 1844 to 1941 by Eliakim Littell and Robert S Littell. It documented that *"Die Tat,"* the monthly publication of National Socialism, used Krieger's work in juxtaposing American race laws to those of the Third Reich. In the process the process, it made some controversial claims that must have raised eyebrows across the United States:

Kreiger states that Lincoln was 'far removed from the sentimental idea of equality with which his name has time and again been falsely coupled', and 'often and vigorously supported the expulsion of the Negroes from the United States. (Pg. 257, "Heil Lincoln!")

The article goes on to blame the "crushing burden of ideology" as the culprit for a lack of effort towards America's "racial salvation":

> Visitors to the United States whose instincts have not been adultered are stirred and deeply revolted by the form which racial co-existence has taken, especially in the great cities of the East. (Pg. 257, "Heil Lincoln!")

The article goes on to make some poignant recommendations in order to achieve the "racial salvation" it desires for the "Nordic" Americans:

> First and most important: the ideology of racial equality must be relinquished. In particular there must never be, not even in theory, legal equality between Nordics and Negroes. ---- Second: The Fourteenth and Fifteenth Amendments to the Constitution must be repealed. This would lead to the disenfranchisement of the Negroes and do away with all enforcement legislation. – Third: Lincoln's plans for expulsion should be taken up again and gradually realized. The promising manner in which Germany is attempting broadly and finally to liquidate centuries of racial mixture undoubtedly will in due time attract notice in America. (Pg. 257, "Heil Lincoln!")

Interestingly enough, the article alludes to the fact that some in the United States agree with the stated goals of "racial salvation," and proposes to find the culprit for the alleged resistance:

> It is understandable that the underminers of the American Nation's Germanic character are fanatically at work inculculating into Americans the paralyzing ideology of racial equality. The Jews, with an exemplary instinct for their own welfare, here, too, are in the van. --– As racial comrades we Germans hope and wish that Germanic America will increasingly find its way back to the principles of its great statesmen, Washington, Jefferson and Lincoln, who were worlds removed from the liberalistic idea of racial equality. [sic.] (Pg. 258, "Heil Lincoln!")

Krieger's book caught the attention of key policy making bodies back in the United States. The Council of Foreign Relations reviewed Heinrich Krieger's 1936 book in "Foreign Affairs." The July 1937 review in "Foreign Affairs" stated:

> The Nazis point to American racial discrimination in support of their laws against ethnic minorities. The present work is a description of the legal disabilities enforced against Negroes and Indians in the United States.

This one piece of negative press coverage is singled out here because catching the attention of Foreign Affairs was no small matter. Foreign Affairs has been the leading forum for serious discussion of American foreign policy and global affairs since its founding in 1922. Foreign Affairs is published by the Council on Foreign

Relations, a non-profit organization dedicated to improving the understanding of U.S. foreign policy and international affairs. The earliest origin of the Council stemmed from a working fellowship of about 150 scholars, called "The Inquiry," tasked to brief President Wilson about options for the postwar world when Germany was defeated. It was precisely the publication that the State Department and institutions of international scope like Rockefeller and Carnegie consulted in order to get a beat on world events.

Heinrich Krieger's 1936 book and the honorary degree lavished upon Laughlin must have raised eyebrows at the most influential offices in the United States. The Rockefellers were at the same time funding the Kaiser-Wilhelm Institute in Berlin, the German counterpart to Cold Spring Harbor. The fact that the Council of Foreign Relations and its Foreign Affairs bi-monthly publication were also a Rockefeller creation serves to evidence the uncomfortable tangle had begun to be an issue for these powerful American institutions. These seemingly innocuous occurrences such as the Pan American Conference seem to be where the high and mighty in the United States pivoted from their cautious support to all-out damage control.

Curiously enough, it was none less than the Secretary of State, Cordell Hull, who acted to prevent Harry H. Laughlin to travel to Germany. Jan Anthony Witkowski, author of the 2008 book "Davenport's Dream: 21st Century Reflections on Heredity and Eugenics," documents that "Laughlin was told by the State Department not to go to Germany to pick it up and he instead received his honor at the German embassy in Rockefeller Center in New York" (Pg. 67).

Heidelberg, den 16.5.36

Sehr geehrter Herr Kollege!

Die medizinische Fakultät der Universität Heidelberg beabsichtigt, Ihnen anlässlich des 550 jährigen Jubiläums(27.-30.6.1936)die Würde eines Doktoren der Medizin h.c. zu verleihen. Ich wäre Ihnen dankbar für eine Mitteilung,ob Sie bereit sind,die Ehrendoktorwürde anzunehmen und,

---

May 28th 1936.

Dr. Carl Schneider,
Dean of the Faculty of Medicine,
University of Heidelberg,
Heidelberg, Germany.

My dear Dr. Schneider,

I acknowledge with deep gratitude the receipt of your letter of May 16th in which you state that the Faculty of Medicine of the University of Heidelberg intends to confer upon me the degree of Doctor of Medicine h.c. on the occasion of its 550th jubilee-year 27th - 30th of June, 1936.

I stand ready to accept this very high honor. Its bestowal will give me particular gratification, coming as it will from a university deep rooted in the life history of the German people, and a university which has been both a reservoir and a fountain of learning for more than half a millenium. To me this honor will be doubly valued because it will come from a nation which for many centuries nurtured the human seed-stock which later founded my own country and thus gave basic character to our present lives and institutions.

I regret more than I can say that the shortness of time before the jubilee-date makes it impossible for me to arrange to leave my duties at Cold Spring Harbor to visit Heidelberg, to participate in the ceremony and to receive this highly honored diploma in person.

With highest regards,

Very respectfully yours,

HARRY HAMILTON LAUGHLIN

In Charge of the Eugenics Record Office,
Carnegie Institution of Washington,
Cold Spring Harbor, Long Island, N.Y.

1937 - PIONEER FUND

> "A man may die, nations may rise and fall, but an idea lives on."
> - John F. Kennedy, February 8th, 1963

With events like the 1935 Population Congress in Berlin, Laughlin had proved that he had the international clout to replace Charles B. Davenport as the leading eugenicist in the United States. By this time, Davenport was slowly withdrawing from prominence as his old age and ill health began to take its toll. With the Carnegie Institution growing cold to the prospect of continued funding for eugenics, Laughlin needed to find another willing source of wealth to draw from. He found this in Wickliffe Draper.

Laughlin had been working on Draper for some time, but the turning point came with the 1935 population congress in Berlin where Laughlin appointed Draper as a delegate along with Dr. Clarence Campbell. Laughlin asked Dr. Eugen Fischer of the Kaiser Wilhelm Institute to receive Draper in the 1935 congress in Berlin with the appropriate fanfare. Lombardo comments on the historical importance:

> After his success linking German supporters of eugenics and his colleagues from the United States at the Berlin Population Congress, Laughlin was in a good position to take advantage of his relationship with Wickliffe Draper. When Draper returned to the United States still excited about having seen Nazi eugenics in action, Laughlin put the finishing touches on another project that would advance his ambitions toward a national eugenic policy. Together, Draper and Laughlin completed plans for establishing a U.S. foundation called the Pioneer Fund that would subsidize "research into the problems of heredity and eugenics." (Pg. 213, "Three Generations No Imbeciles")

Wickliffe Preston Draper was an American multimillionaire and lifelong advocate of strict racial segregation. Born in Hopedale, Massachusetts, he was the son of George A. Draper, the textile machinery manufacturer known as Draper looms. He served in the British army at the beginning of WWI, transferring to the US Army as the Americans entered the war. Draper was the fund's primary benefactor and, therefore, the de facto final authority. Draper served on Pioneer's Board of Directors from 1937 until 1972.

The archives at Truman hold the correspondence that lead up to the formation of the Pioneer Fund. A February 24th, 1937 letter from Laughlin to Draper has Laughlin responding to Draper's request that he write the "tentative program" for the new organization:

> I shall be very anxious in connection with my work on your Board to serve the purpose of race conservation and improvement to the fullest. I am sure that if the possibilities of practical eugenics, which your foundation makes possible, are realized that great and lasting good will be accomplished in the most patriotic development of racial ideals and in their maintenance by the American people. (Laughlin to Draper, Feb. 24th, 1937, Laughlin Papers, Truman Univ.)

Wickliffe Draper committed $50,000 (1937 money) as seed money, and four names were proposed for the new foundation including "The Eugenics Fund," "The Genetics Fund," "The Pioneer Fund," and "The Research Foundation." According to Professor Lombardo's 2002 Albany Law Review paper, "The American Breed," Draper's lawyer, Malcolm Donald, warned against using the term "eugenics." Interestingly enough, Fredric Osborn and Laughlin would agree that it was not politically convenient to use the term in the name of the organization. (Pg. 788)

The first five directors were the eugenic faithful including Wickliffe Preston Draper, Frederic Osborn, Malcolm Donald, John Marshall Harlan II, and Harry H. Laughlin. Malcolm Donald was also the Draper family lawyer and trustee of the Draper estate. Donald was a former editor of the Harvard Law Review. John Marshall Harlan II had been appointed to the Supreme Court of the United States by President Dwight D. Eisenhower. His firm had also provided legal work for the Pioneer Fund. Harlan was the only director whose name did not appear on the incorporation papers. The Pioneer Fund would also be financially supported by Harry H. Laughlin's friend and founder of California State University, Sacramento and land developer, C.M. Goethe.

The Pioneer Fund was officially incorporated on March 11th, 1937. Its founders left correspondence that indicates that they knew that their relationship with the Carnegie institution was quickly eroding probably as early as 1934 and definitely as early as 1935. A January 30th, 1939 letter from Goethe to Laughlin documents the end of the Eugenics Research Association and Cold Spring Harbor:

> My dear Dr. Laughlin:- I have marked off the offer of the Goethe Prize to the Eugenics Research Association, as I understand that organization has practically gone out of business. I am now trying to make my plans to complete my contribution to eugenics in 1939. It seems to me that in addition to Dr. Gosney's work in sterilization, with which I am in close contact, that there are two things which are moving toward real practical results politically. The first is your own work in Connecticut, which I trust is being supported by the powers that be. The second is the work in South Dakota which seems to be spilling over into Nebraska. I will write of the latter later, as soon as I dispose of accumulated "bread-and-butter" business. (Goethe to Laughlin, Laughlin Papers, Truman Univ.)

The 1937 incorporation papers of the Pioneer Fund list two purposes for the creation of the organization. The first was aimed at encouraging the propagation of those "descended predominantly from white persons who settled in the original thirteen states prior to the adoption of the Constitution of the United States." It is by no coincidence that the program bears a strong resemblance to the infamous Nazi *Kinderreich* (child-rich) breeding program, as it is an idea that had been discussed by the members of the IFEO for decades prior. In fact, this type of income redistribution to eugenically desirable couples is one of the major components in Francis Galton's eugenic utopia, "Kantsaywhere," and other similar ideas contemplated by Leonard Darwin. Recall that Marie Kopp and Clarence Campbell also floated similar ideas in the pro-eugenic speeches and pamphlets.

This endeavor took the form of encouraging Army Air Corps officers into having more children. How the Pioneer Fund ever checked if these officers were in actuality the direct descendants of the founders of the original colonies, as the charter prescribes, is unknown. The Pioneer Fund would attempt to increase the children of these Army Air Corps families by providing them cash grants. The fund would provide scholarships to families that already had three children and who would have one additional child during the calendar year of 1940. Four thousand dollars would be paid toward "maintenance and educational expenses" as an "outright gift" in installment payments of five hundred dollars per year. The installment payments were spread out over eight years from the child's fourteenth birthday until the age of twenty-one.

Professor Lombardo documents in "The American Breed" that eleven grants were made to nine different Air Force families that met the qualifications. (Pg. 808) Lombardo also points to the Third Reich's *Kinderreich* program, which awarded grants to marriages that met the regime's "racial and social criteria" for having extra children. A *Kinderreich* matron was presented with flowers, money, a special savings account, and given special privileges in the otherwise restricted life in Hitler's Germany during the war. Lothrop Stoddard, the eugenicist that was given nearly unimpeded access to the inner workings of the Third Reich described a *Kinderreich* mother cutting to the front of all lines while doing her grocery shopping.

The Pioneer Fund's second purpose per its charter was to support academic research and the "dissemination of information, into the 'problem of heredity and eugenics'" and "the problems of race betterment." The Fund would fulfill this portion of its charter by distributing the eugenics film *Erbkrank*. ("Hereditary Defective" or "Hereditary Illness") The film was published by Hitler's propaganda machine and will be discussed in the following chapter at greater length. However, it is of note that the Pioneer Fund amended its charter document in 1985 to read "<u>human</u> race betterment," likely because of the onslaught of negative press.

However, the most historically important projects were those personally funded by Draper in secrecy. Draper and the Pioneer Fund are where the international eugenics movement reemerged in order to keep the "races separate" in post-war America. The leaders of racial segregation would leverage and utilize Laughlin, the Pioneer Fund, and Wickliffe Draper's fortunes to bankroll their endeavors.

In the overall analysis of Harry H. Laughlin's history, one could easily argue that the influence of Laughlin grew out of the shadows of Charles B. Davenport with the Racial Integrity Laws. The internal correspondence at the various archives indicates that Laughlin was the primary point of contact between the pro-segregation lobby and the eugenics movement. More importantly, it was Laughlin, not Davenport, which would make key introductions and bring key players together.

From here on Laughlin would be the cog in the eugenic machinery as Davenport yielded his leadership due to old age and health concerns. It is in this May 1929 letter that Plecker first mentions Earnest Sevier Cox and the "Anglo-Saxon Clubs" to Laughlin. This turned out to be a significant introduction, historically speaking, as it would ensure that Cox would have the backing of Wickliffe Draper even after eugenics had fallen into disfavor. Draper also funded the Back to Africa repatriation movement through the connection to Cox. A March 12th, 1936 letter from Laughlin to Draper where Laughlin informs Draper that the Eugenics Research Association would be holding a meeting at the American Museum of Natural History in New York. (Truman) Cox would be presenting a paper on "Repatriation" in that meeting.

Cox's exhaustive work to repatriate African-Americans to Liberia was taken up by Senators Theodore Bilbo of Mississippi, which served from 1938 to 1947, and William Langer of North Dakota, which served from 1949 to 1959. A. Wigfall Green described Bilbo in the biography "The Man Bilbo" as the "Archangel of White Supremacy". Langer pushed the issue of repatriation to Liberia between 1939 and 1959, introducing the so-called Langer Bill in the U.S. Congress a total of five times.

The Truman archives holds a seemingly innocuous letter from Plecker to both Laughlin written on June 8th, 1936. In this letter, Plecker describes the afternoon that he spent with Madison Grant, the eminent eugenicist, and Wickliffe Draper. They discussed an "endowment" which would collect "ten thousand dollars a year" for the cause. This is how the networking of Cox, Draper, and Grant would link one generation of racialists with the next. It would ensure that eugenics would survive the negative taint of The Holocaust as anti-miscegenation and racial segregation laws.

William Tucker documents that in the late 1950s Harry Weyher became the president of the Pioneer Fund. Weyher facilitated the relationship with yet another staunch advocate of racial segregation, Professor Wesley Critz George. Wesley Critz George was a biology professor at the University of North Carolina. Through Weyher, Draper gave $500 to Wesley Critz George, to help distribute a 1961 anti-integration pamphlet. This was in addition to the $1,000 Christmas checks Draper sent George every year until 1972. In his infamous 1962 book, "The Biology of the Race Problem", George identifies himself as a "Professor of Histology and Embryology, Emeritus, formerly head of the Department of Anatomy, University of North Carolina Medical School." Just as was the case with all eugenicists, and as was evident with other figureheads of Jim Crow, George's book is replete with citations from the highest echelons of American and European academia. Some of

the most recognizable names include:
- James F. Bonner, Ph.D.; Professor of Biology, California Institute of Technology
- George F. Carter, Ph.D.; Professor of Geography at Johns Hopkins University
- Henry Pratt Fairchild, Ph.D.; Professor of Sociology, New York University
- Henry E. Garret, Ph.D.; head of the Department of Psychology, Columbia University
- Arnold Gesell, Ph.D., D.Sc., M.D.; Director, Yale University Medical School
- E.A. Hooton, Ph.D.; Professor of Anthropology, Harvard University
- Franz J. Kallmann, M.D.; Professor of Psychiatry, Columbia University
- James G. Needham, Ph.D. Head of the Department of Biology, Cornell University
- Pitrim Sorokin, Ph.D.; Chairman of the Department of Sociology, Harvard University
- Charles Rupert Stockard, Ph.D., D.Sc., M.D.; Head of the Department of Anatomy, Cornell
- Curt Stern, Ph.D., D.Sc.,; Professor of Genetic, Univ. of California at Berkley
- Victor C. Twitty, Ph.D.; Chairman of Dept. of Zoology, Stanford University
- R.M. Yerkes, Ph.D., LL.D., D.Sc.; Professor of Psycho-biology, Yale University

The above names are listed here to demonstrate that these were hardly the Ku Klux Klan types. To the contrary, they were the representatives of the elite institutions from the Northeast and California. In fact, Ernest Sevier Cox publically distanced himself from the KKK. Cox was not engaging in a propaganda move when he distanced himself from the KKK. He was aligning himself precisely with academics like himself. These professors made up the ranks of the American eugenics movement, and which would provide the intellectual foundations and a veil of legitimacy for Jim Crow legislation. Thus, it is unsurprising that George, like Cox, grounded his arguments in the most sacred terrain of science; in the work of Charles Darwin:

> Charles Darwin, one of the most competent and critical observers in the history of science writes, "The races differ . . . in constitution, in acclimatization, and liability to certain diseases. Their mental characteristics are also very distinct." (Chapter 3, "The Biology of the Race Problem", Citing Darwin's "Descent of Man")

Wesley Critz George's 1962 book, like Ernest Sevier Cox's texts, continues the Darwinian thread by citing that second and third generation of Darwinists, namely that of Julian Huxley:

> The enormous phenotypic differences, in individual and social group achievement, are of course obvious. At the moment, it is socially and intellectually fashionable to minimize or even to deny such differences. This is sometimes done in the name of democracy, or because of the hypnotic effects of the ideas of the American and French revolutions concerning the equality of

man, or as misinterpretation of the Christian doctrine, or in natural reaction against the errors of racism, and of eugenic when treated as a dogma and not as an applied science." (Chapter 5, "The Biology of the Race Problem", Citing Huxley's presentation before the Golden Jubilee of Genetics at Ohio State University, September 11-14, 1950)

Chapter six of George's "The Biology of the Race Problem" would quote extensively from Francis Galton's 1869 "Hereditary Genius." Chapter eight would return to cite Julian Huxley's 1950 "Genetics in the 20th Century." The reader should keep the following quote from the chapter entitled "Heredity Versus Environment in Negro History" in mind. It is emblematic of the catastrophic predictions that eugenicists, namely Adolf Hitler's scientists would voice in order to forward their cause. This was the "Precautionary Principle" at work:

> One of the social implications of genetics is all too obvious. The human species is faced in the biologically immediate future with the possibility of genetic degeneration . . . the inevitable result, unless steps are taken to prevent it, will be a gradual lowering of the average level of the genetic basis of all human qualities . . . In the United States one-sixth of the population is producing one-half of the next generation: it is most unlikely that this fact has no differential genetic consequences . . . Those with higher genetic intelligence have, on the whole, a lower reproductive rate than the less intelligent, and this must be dysgenic. The higher reproductive rate of the economically lower levels in many capitalist countries probably means a slight differential multiplication of the more shiftless and less enterprising, and in any case can not possibly be favorable in results . . . The geneticists . . . can point out the present dangers of degeneration as inescapable deductions from the established facts and principles of his science. (Chapter 8, "The Biology of the Race Problem")

The typical apologetic narrative tells us that Darwin was misused by intellectually stunted men like Adolf Hitler in order to justify their political actions. Clearly, there is much evidence that suggests otherwise. It was the heads of American and British academia which forwarded the notion that eugenics was firmly grounded in Darwin's Theory of Evolution. Hitler was only paraphrasing and plagiarizing them. This was especially true for American eugenics, which was headquartered out of the Carnegie Institutions Station for Experimental Evolution by the premiere Darwinist in America, Charles B. Davenport. The names listed as the basis for Wesley Critz George's work are the veritable who-is-who of Darwinism in America. Many corresponded with and were part of the Laughlin-Grant-Draper network that would survive Davenport and the Eugenics Record Office. More to the point, these prominent scientists were the bedrock of the Pioneer Fund's research.

George himself was a Princeton man prior to working at the University of North Carolina. The Wesley Critz George papers held at the University of North Carolina archives document that on May 24th, 1944 George wrote a letter to Howard W. Odum, a sociologist at UNC who bred prized cattle, stating:

You are a breeder of fine cattle, and know something about genetics. And yet according to newspaper accounts and local reports you are promoting public policies the ultimate results of which would be to do to the white race in America the sort of thing that would be done to your Jersey herd if the state were to require you to incorporate into your herd the sorriest scrub bull in North America. I don't understand. (W.C. George Papers, Catalog description of Subseries 1.2. 1944-1954)

The names Cox, George, Plecker, and Bilbo are the infamous names forever tied to the Jim Crow era. Unfortunately, historians have been reluctant to trace the money trail to its source, Draper and the Pioneer Fund. They have inadvertently played along with Wickliffe Draper's wishes to stay anonymous by making the facile and apparently erroneous connection between this trio and the KKK. Paul Lombardo, says there is conclusive evidence that Draper funded a special printing of Earnest Sevier Cox's racist tract "White America" that was sent to every member of the U.S. Congress in 1937. Cox would ride this wave of notoriety to head up the opposition to the desegregation of public schools mandated by the Supreme Court's 1954 decision, <u>Brown v. Board of Education</u>. The U.N.C. catalog also documents that Wesley Critz Geroge's 1961 "Race, Heredity, and Civilization" was published and distributed by Britons Publishing Society of London, England. This is the same publishing house that printed and distributed the infamous "Mankind Quarterly", which was associated with several scientists tied to the Pioneer Fund and Hitler's government. Incidentally, one of the initial supporters for Mankind Quarterly was another relative of Charles Darwin, Charles Galton Darwin.

A small handful of historians have also noted that Draper gave money to the Mississippi Sovereignty Commission in the 1960s. The Sovereignty Commission used the money for a failed effort to stop the passage of the 1964 Civil Rights Act. Doug A. Blackmon of the Wall Street Journal and Prof. William H. Tucker of Rutgers University discovered documents that linked Draper to other episodes of the Civil Rights era. During the 1960s, Draper secretly sent $215,000 to the Mississippi State Sovereignty Commission in 1963 and 1964 to support racial segregation. These financial contributions came to light in the 1990s, when the Sovereignty Commission records were made public. Blackmon interviewed the Morgan Guaranty Trust Co. (J.P. Morgan-Chase today) executive that managed the Draper fund. Blackmon estimates that "Mr. Draper's contributions would be worth more than $1.1 million today." Blackmon continues:

> Morgan did close the asset-management account it maintained for the Pioneer Fund after the furor erupted over "The Bell Curve" in 1994, according to people familiar with the situation. The bank won't give details on why it did so. (D. Blackmon, "Silent Partner: How the South's Fight To Uphold Segregation Was Funded Up North", Wall Street Journal, June 11th, 1999)

Blackmon describes Draper as "a typical Yankee aristocrat" living in a plush East 57th Street penthouse duplex in Manhattan; a description that falls very far from the stereotype of the typical KKK hillbilly. It also seems like Draper missed the intellectual camaraderie of Laughlin once his friend passed, as Draper would spend the rest of his days seeking out scientists that shared his preconceived notions:

> "For $10 an hour, I tutored Draper ... every time I was in New York," says Bruce Wallace, a retired Virginia Polytechnic University professor who adds that he disagreed with Mr. Draper's views. "His contention was that the geneticists had all the figures but they were afraid to add them all up ... He was quite set on the idea that there was superiority and inferiority. I don't think he would have placed blacks among the superior." (D. Blackmon, "Silent Partner: How the South's Fight To Uphold Segregation Was Funded Up North", Wall Street Journal, June 11th, 1999)

Blackmon makes another interesting observation about Draper and the Sovereignty Commission. Blackmon states that the Commission "took steps to discourage violence by the Ku Klux Man [sic.] and other extremist groups." This coincides with the propaganda and marketing efforts of the eugenic leadership. Davenport, Osborn, and Laughlin had made the concerted decision to distance the movement from activists and rabble-rousers precisely because they wanted eugenics to be regarded as a mainstream science, and not a political movement. Blackmon documents that the funds were handled by an ex-president of the American Bar Association, John C. Satterfield of Yazoo City, Mississippi. TIME magazine would label Satterfield as "the most prominent segregationist lawyer in the country" in the 1960s. The campaign of the commission under Satterfield took definitive steps to keep their Yankee benefactor secret, and the executives at Morgan were told to keep the origins of the funds secret. Everything was made to look like a populist movement, as opposed to the project of an Ivy League elitist:

> Over the next year, Mississippi leaders repeatedly claimed that the campaign was being financed by broad grass-roots support in Mississippi and across the U.S. In truth, contributions from Mississippi citizen never topped $30,000. [Of the larger $300,000 budget supplied by Draper] A surviving partner of Mr. Satterfield's law firm says the attorney obliquely referred to the source of the big money simply as "the Wall Street gang." (Blackmon, "Silent Partner: How the South's Fight To Uphold Segregation Was Funded Up North", Wall Street Journal, June 11th, 1999)

Mr. Draper's money buoyed a sweeping attack on the civil-rights bill. The Sovereignty Commission's Washington arm coordinated opposition efforts among less-organized groups, pushed trade associations to fight the bill and lobbied Congress. It sent ghost-written editorials to newspapers around the country and bought ads in 500 daily and weekly papers. By April 1964, the group had distributed 1.4 million pamphlets and mailings, Sovereignty Commission records indicate. (D. Blackmon, "Silent Partner: How the South's Fight To Uphold Segregation Was Funded Up North", Wall Street Journal, June 11th, 1999)

Draper's anonymity only served to further the impression that all these well-funded activities were the product of the KKK. In turn, Draper's efforts through the Sovereignty Commission came to a sudden halt once public opinion turned against the violent acts of the Klan. Blackmon documents that it was the actions of the KKK which would ultimately end the funding, namely the abduction and murders of the three civil rights youths, Michael Schwerner, Andrew Goodman, and James Chaney in the town of Philadelphia, Mississippi. Recall that "poor Southern whites" had always been a target of the Northeast eugenicists. In all likelihood, Draper held no better opinion of poor Southern whites than did Laughlin, Grant, Davenport, or Supreme Court Justice Oliver Wendell Holmes, Jr. To the contrary, Draper wanted his movement to be associated with Ivy League intellectuals, not KKK lowbrows. Staying anonymous however, resulted in the KKK getting credit for his work.

It is interesting to see the conversation between Madison Grant and Ernest Sevier Cox on the various topics including the Racial Integrity Act and how they related to the "Repatriation" project. A letter from Cox to Grant where Laughlin was copied makes an interesting estimation of Jim Crow legislation:

> You are misinformed with regard to Virginia raising the allowance of negro blood in persons deemed white. In 1870 there was a ¾ law. I do not have data as to the change which was made, but in 1924 there was a 15/16 law, which was amended to "no trace whatsoever" in 1924. Prior to 1924, Virginia permitted marriage between whites and Indians. In 1924 a 15/16 law was enacted. ---- Dr. W. A. Plecker will give you reference which will show that certain states abandoned racial integrity legislation. Our small group of conlonizationists were confronted by the legal status of miscegenation. The states which opposed race mixing in theory, possessed laws which in fact permitted it. Negroids, with certain degrees of negro blood, were prohibited from marriage with whites, but negroids of lesser proportion of negro blood were deemed white, and having been legally deemed white were privileged to marry whites and prohibited from marrying colored persons. Prior to 1924 amalgamation was legal if the negroid was 15/16 white. ---- There is a philosophical defect in the advocation of separation when the state provides for miscegenation. This defect has been eliminated. My writing on colonization continues but is delayed by excessive labor in business. I have a manuscript complete on Liberia, in with the methods used by the negro labor group in the South and the negro suffrage group in the North are outlined in the effect upon the break up of the colonization movement. [sic] (Cox to Grant, June 18th, 1931, Laughlin Papers, Truman Univ.)

A discussion about the Pioneer Fund is incomplete without addressing Fredric Osborn. Eugenics is the set of bones that rattles the loudest in the closet of the Progressives and Democrats. The most famous member of the Pioneer Fund is Fredric H. Osborn, whom aside from being a founding member of the American Eugenics Society was part of Margaret Sanger's American Birth Control leadership. In fact, it was Osborn that made the decision to change the name from American Birth Control to Planned Parenthood. Osborne was the grandson of the railroad tycoon, William Henry Osborn, and nephew of Henry Fairfield Osborn, the eugenic-minded director of the American Museum of Natural History in New York. The young Osborn made his money early as part of New York's merchant elite, and later dedicated his life to eugenic causes. He also served as secretary of the Galton Society in 1931 and took over the infamous journal, Eugenics Quarterly. He was an instrumental part of Woodrow Wilson's Office of Population Research, which would infamously generate Dr. Edwin Katzen-Ellenbogen, the Harvard-educated member of Wilson's staff that would work inside of Hitler's death camps. Osborn was a founder of Rockefeller's Population Council, which would later disseminate birth control throughout the Third World.

The Pioneer Fund was also the political crossroads, the political flypaper, where all of the worst representatives from all political factions stick to a common cause. The Draper Immigration Committee members included Representative Francis E. Walter, who would chair of the House Un-American Activities, and Henry E. Garrett, whom like Davenport and Laughlin before him believed that blacks were genetically inferior. Professor Lombardo aptly points out how the Pioneer Fund and Wickliffe Draper became identified with prominent Republicans from the 1960s onwards. As documented earlier, the American eugenicists had a pronounced antipathy towards the egalitarian aspects of the Declaration of Independence and the protections for the individual that the U.S. Constitution provides. However, despite the pronounced Progressive taint to the eugenics cult, Republicans like Rep. Albert Johnson succumbed to base nativist sentiments and aligned themselves with their political rivals:

> This recent attention to Pioneer revives media commentary on the Pioneer Fund that surfaced as early as 1960, when journalists revealed Wickliffe Draper's subsidies to members of the House UnAmerican Activities Committee, and Draper grants to study "genetic and blood-type sciences." Later references to the Pioneer fund were included in accounts of a 1985 lawsuit by CBS, Inc., when Thomas Ellis, a former campaign chair of Senator Jesse Helms (R. N.C.), spearheaded an attempted takeover of that television network along with Pioneer President Harry Weyher. ---- In 1999, a Florida State University psychologists drew attention to the Fund. Glayde Whitney, who has received six-figure grants from Pioneer, wrote the foreword to the autobiography of David Duke, former Ku Klux Klan official and Louisiana political hopeful. (Pg. 752, Lombardo, "The American Breed", Albany Law Review, 2002, Vol. 65, No. 3)

The remaining history of The Pioneer Fund seems to have been to play the role of political crossroads. The Pioneer Fund also attracted support from the likes of Supreme Court Justice John Marshall Harlan, who represented the conservative wing of the Warren Court. Justice Harlan had a career on the bench that would not indicate an ideological alignment with the likes of Draper and Laughlin. Prominent political figures such as Harry F. Byrd of the famous family that produced so many members of the Democratic Party come to mind. Byrd is best known for supporting racial segregation between 1959 and 1964. Byrd was part of the Pioneer Fund along with Eugenie Marry Ladenburg Davie of the Republican National Finance Committee. Other board members and directors of note included Associate Justice of the Supreme Court of Massachusetts, Charles Codman Cabot.

Draper himself opposed Franklin D. Roosevelt's efforts to implement the Social Security Act, expanded child labor laws, and early attempts to pass the equivalent of OSHA-styled regulations. He disliked John F. Kennedy for currying favor with labor unions, for promoting civil rights advances, and for his failure to pass tariff barriers to prevent the import of foreign textiles and cotton. Draper blamed the actions of both of these Democratic Party presidents for the demise of the domestic textile industry that eventually caused the Draper Company to be dissolved by Rockwell International as an insolvent entity.

In academic circles, the Pioneer Fund is best known for funding racially-motivated studies. Professor Lombardo writes in his 2002 Albany Law Review paper, "The American Breed", that Wickliffe Draper financed several studies by Charles B. Davenport. The projects "Negro-White Hybrids in Jamaica: Investigation Made Under the W.P. Draper Fund", and his "Nasal Breadth in Negro x White Crossing" were both financed by the Wickliffe Draper. These studies were published in the Eugenical News of October 1926 and were published as the 1929 book "Race Crossing in Jamaica". (Pg. 766)

However, it is the Pioneer Fund's post-war activities that have caught the eye of investigative journalists. Barry Mehler and Keith Hurt of the Institute for the Study of Academic Racism wrote an article in Searchlight entitled "The Funding of Science". In it they give a brief, albeit somewhat politically myopic summary of the extensive amount of influence the Pioneer Fund has had on through the twenty-first century. They point to Henry Garett, the Chair of Psychology at Columbia University from 1941 to 1955 whose segregationist politics and eugenic science landed him the opportunity to serve as an expert witness in <u>Davis v. County School Board</u> (1952), one of the constituent cases in <u>Brown v. Board of Education</u> in 1954. Garrett helped to distribute grants from the Pioneer Fund and was also one of the founders of the International Association for the Advancement of Eugenics and Ethnology. This organization is best known for bringing together American segregation supporters with the ideological supporters of apartheid in South Africa. By the decade of the eighties Pioneer grants were going to the University of Minnesota, Arthur Jensen's Institute for the Study of Education Differences, the Federation for American Immigration Control, and Roger Pearson's Institute for the Study of Man. Mehler and Hurt continue to detail the influence of the Fund:

> The Pioneer has funded many of the key academic racists in both Right Now! and American Renaissance and the Pioneer was directly involved in funding the parent organization of American Renaissance, the New Century Foundation. Indeed, most of the leading Anglo-American academic race-scientists of the last several decades have been funded by the Pioneer, Including William Shockley,

Hans J. Eysenck, Arthur Jensen, Roger Pearson, Richard Lynn, J. Philippe Rushton, R. Travis Osborne, Linda Gottfredson, Robert A. Gordon, Daniel R. Vining, Jr., Michael Levin, and Seymour Itzkoff – all cited in The Bell Curve. (ISAR, Mehler and Hurt, "Funding of the Science", Searchlight No. 277, Jul. 7th, 1998)

So how did an entity like the Pioneer Fund manage to exist in the immediate shadow of the Holocaust? Draper took extreme steps to conceal his involvement. As Professor Lombardo reports, Weyher has diligently defended the reputation of the Pioneer Fund, not always being forthright about the institution's past. Lombardo quotes Weyher as proclaiming that the Pioneer Fund has "no Nazi connections, no Nazi history," as well as defending Laughlin against a March 9th, 1996 letter to the editor of the Sacramento Bee. Clearly, the vast amount of evidence in the archives, not to mention Laughlin's published work, stands in stark contrasts to Weyher's protestations.

Clearly, its alignment with prominent scientists continues to offer political cover. By far, the most notorious of the Pioneer Fund's activities has to be its involvement in the publishing of the 1994 book "The Bell Curve: Intelligence and Class Structure in American Life." The book was written by American psychologist Richard J. Herrnstein and American political scientist Charles Murray. Hernstein's and Murray's book identified the Pioneer Fund as the source of funding for scientists conducting the research contained in the book. (Pg. 750) The book remains highly controversial, as the authors wrote about racial differences in intelligence. Laughlin is lauded in "The Bell Curve" as "a biologist who was especially concerned about keeping up the American level of intelligence by suitable immigration policies." Professor Lombardo points out that, in addition, Pioneer also had a significant hand in publishing the work of the Canadian psychologist, J. Phillipe Rushton, who is widely cited in "The Bell Curve". Rushton's 1995 book, "Race, Evolution, and Behavior" gives thanks to Pioneer's Harry Weyher for his "unwavering support." Weyher is also acknowledged by Richard Lynn in his 1996 "Dysgenics: Genetic Deterioration in Modern Populations," as well as his 2001 "Eugenics: A Reassessment." The latter links the work documented in "The Bell Curve" with the work of Laughlin's and Davenport's Eugenic Research Association. (Pg. 820) Lynn praises Laughlin in his books.

"The Bell Curve" was not the only racially-provocative study the Pioneer Fund financed in recent history. Professor Lombardo also points out in "The American Breed" that the Pioneer Fund financed the Foundation for Human Understanding of Athens, Georgia. (Pg. 816) The organization received over $150,000 between 1979 and 1992 to research, write, and distribute the book "Testing of Negro Intelligence." The organization also published "America's Bimodal Crisis: Black Intelligence in White Society" by Stanley Burnham in 1985 and its reprinting in 1993.

Equal responsibility has to be given to academia in general. These eugenic-minded scientists emerged from academia, and in turn, remain buried deep in academia's archives. Professor Lombardo points out in his article "The American Breed" the relatively little amount of attention the Pioneer Fund's connection to Hitler's Germany has received.

> Pioneer represents a missing link in the history of eugenics that connects the racial radical branch of American eugenics in the first third of the century, to eugenics in 1930s Germany, and to hereditarian politics of recent years as exemplified in books like *The Bell Curve*. Yet, despite clear connections between Pioneer support and eugenic ideology, a survey of the historical literature on the eugenics movement demonstrates relative neglect on both the Pioneer Fund's genesis and its founders' emulation of Nazi eugenic policy. (Pg. 747, P. Lombardo, "The American Breed", Albany Law Review, 2002, Vol. 65, No. 3)

It is of note that sitting on Pioneer's board was one highly educated individual that was a direct witness to the deeds that resulted from the Third Reich's eugenic programs. One of Pioneer's subsequent directors included John M. Woolsey, Jr., who served as a staff attorney at the Nuremberg Trials. This is certainly a curious member as it was the Nuremberg Trials that made the Nazi eugenicists hang for their implementation of the policies the Pioneer Fund championed.

To return to the core concepts of this book, the Pioneer Fund directly benefitted from the obscurity and opacity provided by sweeping eugenics under the rug. The more America's eugenic bones sat in the closet, the more comfortable political figures have been in associating themselves with what would otherwise be regarded a toxic relationship for any politician. History is not necessarily the arena to speak of hypotheticals. History is better served with a clear outlining of the facts. However, it is tantalizing to wonder how American political history would have developed if the Nazi connection to American eugenics had been more honestly exposed. You do not have to go far to wonder.

The Pioneer Fund is by far the most notorious of eugenic-minded institutions to survive the fallout that rightfully came after The Holocaust. The Pioneer Fund simply could not have the relative success it enjoyed in forming public opinion if there had been a full accounting of the relationships between American academia, American science, and Nazi eugenics. This tacitly agreed to collective amnesia successfully omitted these uncomfortable connections from the version of history that has been communicated to the general public.

The Cold Spring Harbor lab exists to this day with its students and staff mostly oblivious to the lab's history. (Personal conversations) The papers have long since been in the possession of other educational institutions. Nothing but a small fraction of the original research material remains tucked in a small corner of the library. However, some of the scientists associated with the lab have addressed its links to the likes of Davenport and Laughlin. The Cold Spring Harbor Laboratory Press released a short paper entitled "The Banality of Evil: The Careers of Charles Davenport and Harry Laughlin" by Elof Axel Carlson. The article makes a curious speculation that speaks to the lingering influence the American eugenics movement had on the evolving race relations inside of the United States:

> Had the Nazis won the war, I do not doubt that if Davenport and Laughlin had been alive and in good health, they would have played major roles in cleansing the U.S. of its allegedly unfit classes (primarily by sterilization), and they would have cooperated in establishing American race hygiene programs with their German counterparts. (Elof Axel Carlson, "The Banality of Evil", 2006, Cold Spring Harbor Laboratory Press)

Carlson has dedicated as a significant amount of time and effort in studying scientific racism. The opening paragraph of Carlson's paper proclaims Charles Davenport and Laughlin to be "prototypes of Eichmann". This author would say that Laughlin and Davenport were prototypes of Ottmar von Verschuer, the man that Josef Mengele answered to in the Nazi hierarchy.

1937 - ERBKRANK

> *"We all do no end of feeling and we mistake it for thinking.*
> *And out of it we get an aggregation which we consider a boon.*
> *Its name is public opinion. It is held in reverence.*
> *It settles everything. Some think it is the voice of God."*
> *- Mark Twain*

Erbkrank (English: The Hereditary Defective) is a 1936 Nazi propaganda film. *Erbkrank* was produced by National Socialism's *Reichsleitung, Rassenpolitisches Amt* or in English, the "Office of Racial Policy." They were produced to sell the idea to the German public that the "unfit" would cause a serious social catastrophe if left free to reproduce. Directed by Herbert Gerdes, it was one of the six propaganda movies produced by the organization from 1935 to 1937. By 1937, *Erbkrank* was showing in nearly all Berlin film theaters.

The main goal was to gain public support for National Socialism's eugenic policy. The film was made with footage of actual patients in German psychiatric hospitals. *Erbkrank* made unrealistic apocalyptic predictions in the typical fashion of the Precautionary Principle. According to Stefan Kühl, author of the 2002 book "The Nazi Connection," Adolf Hitler saw the movie on February 26th, 1936. Hitler reportedly liked the film so much that he encouraged the production of the full-length film *Opfer der Vergangenheit: Die Sünde wider Blut und Rasse*, or in English, "Victims of the Past: The Sin against Blood and Race." *Erbkrank* portrays "the idiotic black bastard from the Rhineland," which is surely the input from Eugene Fischer's study of the "Rehoboth bastards." The reader will recall that Fischer worked on this study with the help of Davenport.

Stefan Kühl documents that Laughlin brought the film over to be shown to the Carnegie Institution. (Pg. 49, "The Nazi Connection") Laughlin edited the film for his purposes and distributed it in the United States under the title "Eugenics in Germany." However, the Laughlin Papers at Truman University also demonstrates that *Erbkrank* was one of the first projects the Pioneer Fund funded. Laughlin drafted what reads like an executive summary entitled "Motion picture showing how Germany is presenting and attacking her problems in applied eugenics," which was written while at Cold Spring Harbor. In it Laughlin states that the "Eugenics Research Association owns two copies of this two-reel film, and under certain conditions is prepared to lend a copy to responsible schools and societies interested in its use." Laughlin's memo also reports that the film cost "106 RM" at an "exchange value March 12th, 1937 = $43.40". Laughlin describes the specifics of the purchase, which reveal that Hitler's propaganda ministry intended the film to have an international audience:

> The present motion picture entitled "Erbkrank" (The Hereditary Defective) is printed on a standard 16mm. film, prepared in Germany by German eugenists, **with a choice of English, German or French captions.** The whole film (270

meters in length) consists of two reels each of which runs about twenty minutes. (BOX: C-2-3-2-a, "Motion Picture" memo, Truman Univ. – Special Coll., emphasis mine)

The fact that a multiple language subtitle option existed is noteworthy, as it reveals that the Germans were proud of their eugenic policies, and gladly provided the film as a propaganda piece for audiences abroad. Clearly, the Nazis viewed their eugenic program as perfectly in line with the scientific values of the other developed nations, and not just as propaganda the likes a totalitarian regime utilizes to mold the minds of the populace within its walls. Laughlin continues with his description of the film:

> As an introduction the film contrasts the squalid living conditions of normal children in certain German city slums with the finer and costly modern custodial institutions built for the care of handicapped persons produced by the socially inadequate and degenerate family-stocks of that country. ---- If this film reflects accurately the policy of modern Germany, that nation in this particular field of applied negative eugenics has evidently made substantial progress in its intention to act fundamentally, on a long time plan, for the prevention, so far as possible, of hereditary degeneracy. (BOX: C-2-3-2-a, "Motion Picture" memo, Truman Univ.)

The Pioneer Fund financed the printing of 3,000 flyers advertising the film to biology teachers across the United States. The Laughlin Papers at the Truman University archives hold a March 15th, 1937 letter from Laughlin to Draper which reports on the success of the venture. Think about the backdrop upon which Laughlin was openly promoting Nazi films. Note that this is a decade after the publication of "Mein Kampf" and well into the time when Hitler's storm troopers were known for their violence:

> We are making continued use of the German film. I have shown it in Connecticut in connection with this survey to a group of child welfare workers who came to Hartford for a general conference. ---- We have shown it also a number of times at Cold Spring Harbor and a second showing will be made again in Hartford, Conn., on March 22nd at the general conference of welfare workers of the state – workers from the bureaus of the State Department of Welfare – child welfare, institutional management and old age pension. The two main assets in Connecticut which enabled progress up to is present stage are the Governor, Wilber L. Cross and the Commissioner of Welfare, former U.S. Senator F. C. Walcott. Senator Walcott's main interests have been devoted toward the chairman of a recent executive committee which met in St. Louis and formed a permanent association. When he took over the welfare work in Connecticut he saw the task in human conservation in the light of the conservationist. (Laughlin to Draper, March 15th, 1937, Truman Univ.)

The back story of Walcott and Cross are worth delving into. Walcott was a Republican Senator with a scientific background whose most notable accomplishment was working on the Manhattan Project. Governor Cross was a

Democrat. Both were Yale alumni. In fact, Cross was one of the first deans of the Yale graduate program. Laughlin would point out to Draper in an October 6th, 1937 letter held in the Laughlin Papers at the Truman that Walcott was named an honorary member of the Audubon Society in 1929 and had a longstanding reputation for his interests in "conservation of game, animals and fish." Incidentally, Laughlin molded the "Survey of the Human Resources of Connecticut" along these lines as he describes to Draper in a follow-up letter: "We attacked the problem as one interested in the conservation of the natural resources, and made our human study parallel those which have worked out practically in the conservation of plants, animals, and agricultural resources."

The reader will recall that Walcott was also the impetus behind Laughlin's Connecticut Study. Laughlin would also put other environmentalists and conservationists in touch with Draper. Another environmentalist with this curious penchant for likening nature conservation with the eugenic cause was James G. Eddy from Seattle, Washington. The correspondence between Laughlin, Grant, Draper and Eddy touches on this recurring theme. The October 6th, 1937 letter from Laughlin to Draper also introduces Eddy as having an interest extending "from forestry" to the "human tree." The letter documents that Eddy visited Cold Spring Harbor in order to learn how to set up a "clinic" along the eugenic lines that Laughlin prescribed. Being faithful to his penchant for networking like-minded zealots, Laughlin would introduce Eddy to Plecker and Cox, the anti-Civil Rights activists of the 1960s, in an April 19th, 1938 letter.

The conservation of resources theme was at the core of *Erbkrank*'s propaganda message, as it based its political demands upon the assumptions that the "unfit" were consuming the limited resources of the German public. Nor was the link to environmentalism and conservation strange to the German eugenicists. Both Alfred Ploetz and Ernst Rüdin were heavily engaged in these movements as author Paul Weindling fully documents in his 1993 book, "Health, Race and German Politics Between National Unification and Nazism, 1870-1945." Himmler's SS utilized the grounds and forced labor at the Dachau concentration camp to run the single largest organic food gardens in existence at the time. The produce from Himmler's Dachau organic garden would be sold in order to generate funds for the SS. Robert N. Proctor's "Nazi War on Cancer" also delves deeply into the holistic and healthy living aspect of National Socialism. Proctor's book documents the regime's vigorous campaigns against food coloring, alcohol, tobacco, and any other items deemed a danger to their precious Aryan gene pool.

Erbkrank is an onslaught of skewed economic factoids. It is a play on supply and demand of resources available to the community. It portrayed the vast amount of resources being invested in the "socially inadequate" despite the economic suffering of the general German public that resulted from the Great Depression and WWI. The message was that the "useless eaters" were well-fed and housed in lavish institutions with manicured gardens, while every-day Germans suffered and starved. It is of note that the translated version did not edit out the disturbing imagery. Paul Lombardo explains:

> The film portrayed horrible living conditions in the slums of a German city, contrasting those images with lavish pictures of expensive institutions housing disabled residents born to "the socially inadequate and degenerate family-stocks" of the country. It also catalogued the varieties of "human degeneracy" that could be traced to hereditary afflictions. The message was clear: eugenic solutions like sterilization were needed to rid the country of the "socially inadequate." (Pg. 213, "Three Generations, No Imbeciles")

Furthermore, the film drove the theme of "degeneration". Its statistics claimed that the "socially inadequate" were reproducing at an alarming rate. The catastrophic predictions speculated that the German "race" or "nation" would soon be made up of a "feebleminded" and "inadequate" population if sterilization programs were not instituted immediately. Here was the Precautionary Principle at work. William H. Tucker, author of the 2002 book "The Funding of Scientific Racism," describes this aspect of *Erbkrank*:

> In Eugenical News Laughlin described the film's concern with "the problem of hereditary disease and inborn deformity" and its depiction of the enormous expense of these genetic defectives, housed in "costly modern custodial institutions" much finer than "the squalid living conditions of normal children in certain German city slums." The movie indicated, he concluded, that in the "field of applied negative eugenics" Germany had made "substantial progress in its intention to act fundamentally, on a long time plan, for the prevention, so far as possible, of hereditary degeneracy". (Pg. 53, "The Funding of Scientific Racism")

Tucker points out that Laughlin made the curious claim in Eugenical News that there was "no racial propaganda of any sort in the picture." However, the German film did claim "the Jewish people produce an exceptionally high percentage of mentally ill" while showing degrading images of Jews and calling them "deceitful" and "rabble-rousers." (Pg. 53) There would only be one reason for Laughlin to give such aid to Hitler's propaganda machine, and that was because, by 1937, Hitler's domestic policy was coming under international criticism as being anti-Semitic. Its supporters, namely people like Laughlin, would have been specifically sensitive to this criticism as Nazi Germany's domestic policy was in fact Laughlin's "Model Eugenic Law." Michael Burleigh, author of the 1994 book "Death and Deliverance: 'Euthanasia' in Germany 1900-1945" provides the transcripts of the English-language version.

The members of the American eugenics movement clearly knew *Erbkrank* was political propaganda. Professor Lombardo also documents in his 2002 Albany Law Review article "The American Breed," that C.M. Goethe claimed that he had rarely seen "propaganda . . . more convincing than the Nazi pictures of the imbecile, the moron compared with the flower of German youth." (Pg. 790)

Another important aspect of the distribution of *Erbkrank* was that it was part of Laughlin's and Davenport's relentless campaign to indoctrinate America's youth. It was part of their ongoing effort to having their eugenic science taught at all education levels in the United States. Recall that "Hunter's Civic Biology," the textbook that was at the center of the infamous Scopes' Monkey Trial had entire sections about eugenics written by Davenport. These indoctrination efforts would survive the Eugenics Record Office and find a new life through the Pioneer Fund. A 1938 letter from Laughlin to Draper documents the success Laughlin had distributing *Erbkrank* at the high school level even as late as 1938 when Hitler's reputation was already that of a brutal dictator:

> You will be interested to know that the moving picture film "Eugenics in Germany" has proven very popular with senior high school students. Up to date the film has been loaned 28 times. Just now one copy is being used by the Society for the Prevention of Blindness in New York, and the other is in the hands of George Smith in Plainfield, N.J., where his advanced students in high school biology found it very interesting. ---- Most of the high schools now have the projection apparatus so that films of this sort fit well into their program. When education is expected to result in practical long-time race betterment, the moving picture in the school offers a profitable medium for presenting facts. (Laughlin to Draper, Dec. 9th, 1938, Truman Univ.)

Most importantly, *Erbkrank*'s reception by American audiences was used to bolster eugenics back in Hitler's Germany. Stefan Kühl documents that a leading National Socialist newspaper reported on the "exceptionally strong impression" the film had made on American eugenicists. The article was titled "*Rassenpolitische Aufklärung nach deutschem Vorbild: Grosse Beachtung durch die amerikanische Wissenschaft,*" or in English, "Racial Political Propaganda on German Model Receives Great Attention among American Eugenicists" (Pg. 50, "The Nazi Connection") Hitler's government continually had their ear on the ground to gauge interest and response to German internal affairs. Policy was written and revised around international reactions and responses. Thus, the enthusiasm from high profile individuals such as Charles B. Davenport, Harry H. Laughlin, C.M Goethe, Lothrop Stoddard, Fredric Osborn, Madison Grant, Leonard Darwin, and Wickliffe Draper were welcome bolsters to the public image Adolf Hitler tirelessly cultivated.

One point must be clarified. The fact that Laughlin purchased the film from the National Socialists should not be mistaken for Laughlin adopting their propaganda methods. While it is true that Hitler and Goebbels were propaganda fiends, Laughlin and Davenport were employing similar measures a decade earlier. To be precise, point number ten of the "Eugenics Record Office, Report No. 1" released in 1913 was to "publish the results of researches and to aid in the dissemination of eugenical truths." Laughlin and Davenport may not have had highly talented filmmakers at their beckon call like Hitler and Goebbels, but they were certainly employed the same methods. Hassenchal documents in her dissertation, that as early as 1924 the Eugenics Record Office was distributing slide photographs that can be described as mimicking the *Erbkrank* imagery:

> These slides are in the Laughlin Collection and consist of photos taken of materials exhibited at the second and third International Eugenical Congresses, photos of various examples of degeneracy such as mongoloids as feebleminded – a sort of gallery of types – which are accompanied by pictures of the pedigree charts of these "degenerates." The slides appear to be intended to be used as explanatory material as well as to show the seriousness of the problem of permitting various inferior individuals to marry and produce children. (Pg. 81, "Harry H. Laughlin, Expert Eugenics Agent", Hassencahl, University Microfilms, 1970)

Thus, it is important to mention, that the leadership of the I.F.E.O., which included names of international recognition including Leonard Darwin, Charles Davenport, and Alexander Graham Bell, were utilizing similar visual displays in their highly publicized international conferences and world's fairs. While modern viewers of *Erbkrank* would be justified in feeling horrified at its imagery, it is fair to state that those Germans that produced such a horrific film had seen the most famous Americans and Britons indulge in the same type of eugenic propaganda.

NSDAP
SICHERT DIE
VOLKS-
GEMEINSCHAFT

Täglich RM 5.50
kostet den Staat
ein Erbkranker
Für RM 5.50
kann eine erbgesunde Familie
1 Tag leben !
RM
5,50
RM
5,50
48

1938 - THOROUGHBRED STUDY

*"If we knew what it was we were doing,
it would not be called research, would it?"*
- Albert Einstein

Laughlin's equine studies would be uninteresting if their methodology were not so tethered to his eugenics. Laughlin's equine studies were part of his work at Cold Spring Harbor. This work, like all others, had an outside sponsor with the Carnegie Institution managing and contributing to the expenses. The study of race horses at Cold Spring Harbor started in 1923 when Walter J. Salmon, the owner of Mereworth Stud, the horse breeding farm in Lexington, Kentucky, offered to finance a study. The idea was to arrive at a formula for breeding a winner on the race track. The project would produce seven papers that were published by the National Academy of Sciences, Scientific Monthly, and several privately printed compendiums that Laughlin pushed Carnegie into publishing into a book series.

Laughlin's approach to studying animal breeds and that towards humans hardly differed. This was not unusual. Laughlin and Davenport were devoted Darwinists, and as such believed humans were nothing more than animals. Eugenics was, after all, a response to the fear that evolution could work backward, or more precisely "degenerate," through "sexual" selection; the very same forces that were the theoretical impetus behind Darwin's "natural selection." This is how "atavisms" or "throwbacks" came to be. Charles Darwin was an accomplished animal breeder as well, and postulated in his book about the "degeneration" that would occur by allowing the "weakest specimens to breed." ("Descent of Man," 1st ed., Pgs. 168 -169)

There is another reason why Laughlin's equine studies are of historical interest. They serve as a prime example of the fascination eugenicists had with good breeding. It is by no surprise that Hitler's eugenicists entertained similar breeding projects with animal breeds that were of ideological importance to the Third Reich's ideology. National Geographic aired the documentary, "Hitler's Jurassic Monsters" on July 27th, 2014, and the website Metro.co.uk wrote about the documentary in a post titled "Hitler's Jurassic Monsters sheds new light on the Nazis' terrifying vision for the future." The Nazis attempted to recreate the primeval forests of Nordic folklore and embarked in a massive breeding project in order to populate these forests with the ancient beasts of Nordic tales. These scientists were literally attempting to recreate extinct animals so they could later hunt them in the forests of their folklore.

Keep in mind that genetic engineering was still decades away, and that these scientists were not meddling with DNA or anything similar. These scientists were employing the methods of the stockyard in no different way that the other German scientists were trying to breed the characteristics of "Nordic" and "Aryan" men of

Germanic mythology. The two creatures they focused on were "auroch," a super-sized, wild and violent breed of cattle, and a "tarpan," the ancestor of the modern horse.

The brains behind the plan were zoologist brothers Lutz and Heinz Heck. Their plan started as a private project before the Nazis came to power. However, it wasn't long before Lutz embraced the new regime and became good friends with Hermann Göring, Hitler's second in command, and more importantly, the official in charge of all hunting related activities in the Reich.

Perfectly in line with National Socialist ethos, there were two aspects to the scheme: the land and its inhabitants. The National Socialist creed believed in a deep connection between "blood and soil," or in German, *Blut und Boden*. According to Nazi ideology, the land, and its inhabitants could only thrive if the correct inhabitants were joined in existence with the right piece of land. In other words, the Germans were inherently and biologically tied to Germania. The area the Nazis earmarked for this project was the primeval Bialowieza forest in Poland. Hitler's henchmen gained control of the land when they invaded Poland. They cleared 20,000 inhabitants from the desired portion of Poland including a large Jewish population who they either executed on the spot or sent off to concentration camps.

After 14 years of cross-breeding Lutz Heck finally arrived at what looked outwardly like an auroch. While Heck's animals may have resembled the ancient creature superficially, scientists say they were no closer genetically than any other cattle. These animals were released into the Bialowieza forest. Today the forest flourishes as a vast nature reserve between Poland and Belarus. Heck's aurochs were likely slaughtered by Soviet officials once Poland was consumed by the USSR.

Laughlin's horse breeding project was no more sophisticated than Hitler's. The lustful desire to alter the trajectory of evolution was hardly different between the gambler and the political zealot. Laughlin's horse study only reveals the vast amount of similarities between those desiring a formula for breeding winners at the race track and those stubbornly intent in designing and orchestrating society. Frances Janet Hassencahl is of the opinion that the notoriety of arriving at a scientific formula for breeding a winning race horse aroused more interest and publicity than Laughlin's work on humans. (Pg. 83) This was the original impetus behind the thoroughbred study as pitched by Laughlin to Dr. Merriam:

> The Pattern Formula is a new genetics tool with the use of which we can readily compute the correct **specific formula of heredity for any quality, functional or structural, in plants, animals or man**, which is definitely measurable in an individual and which in any manner tends to run-in-the-family. (Laughlin files, Carnegie Inst., April 13th, 1934, Laughlin to Merriam, emphasis mine)

Hassencahl documents that even the scientists who were helping Laughlin with the study had a pretty negative opinion of the work. She describes how Dr.

Clyde Keeler felt about the study that he helped carry out from 1924 to 1925,:
> Keeler did not have a great deal of faith in the study and recognized that some of the factors going into the calculations were guesses, but Laughlin refused to discuss such matters with him. He soon discovered after a conversation with Salmon's head trainer at the Belmont Race Track that the data they were using was contaminated. ---- A colt that looked good and performed well, but was born of lowly parents, might magically aquire a new pedigree of distinction as the offspring of a famous line. Another factor, which Laughlin could not and did not take into consideration was cheating. Jockies were paid to win or lose. ---- Thus, even if Laughlin had been able to work out a formula, he would never have been able to know whether a winner won because of blood, drugs, or luck. [sic.] (Pg. 85, "Harry H. Laughlin, Expert Eugenics Agent," Hassencahl, University Microfilms, 1970)

Hassencahl points out that despite the impressive volume of statistics, charts, and pedigrees accumulated, "Laughlin's research in genetics consisted primarily of formulating theoretical mathematical formulas of heredity without ever testing the hypothesis by experimentation". (Pg. 86) That is as stunning, but accurate assessment of the man whom so many governments would rely on in order to decide the fate of tens of thousands if not millions, of individuals. Curiously enough, Hassencahl found a quote by Lord Kelvin that Laughlin had in a folder full of favorite quotations. The quote serves to illuminate Laughlin's approach, albeit an oversimplification of Lord Kelvin's contribution to science:
> When you can measure what you are speaking about and express it in numbers, you know something about it, but when you cannot measure it, when you cannot express it in numbers your knowledge is a meager and unsatisfactory kind; it may be the beginning of knowledge, but you have scarcely in your thoughts advanced to the stage of science. (Pg. 86, "Harry H. Laughlin, Expert Eugenics Agent," Hassencahl, University Microfilms)

Of course, there is a more probable explanation than just believing Laughlin was careless. The historical record tends to indicate that Laughlin and his cohorts were interested in social engineering as much or more than they were in testing the scientific validity of eugenics. This was the case from the onset. They crossed the line from breeding animals, human or not, to controlling the future of humanity. In other words, the conclusion came before the science. Laughlin's tireless accumulation of data was but a way of reassuring himself and the rest of the world as to the rigorousness and validity of his political views.

Therefore, Laughlin's thoroughbred study is also important as it is a prime example of how Laughlin manipulated data and how he often made assumptions that demonstrated a naiveté of the facts of life. To make a long story short, Laughlin's study of the race horses demonstrates obliviousness to the fact that the competitors often cheated any way they could where large sums of money were on the line.

Unfortunately, some of the early leadership at the Carnegie Institution was reluctant to believe the work was as deficient as it truly was, even after experts within the organization pointed this out. A memorandum written for Dr. Merriam by Dr. Frank F. Bunker of the institution's Office of Publications could have, in hindsight, been an accurate opinion of the bulk of the work Laughlin produced at Cold Spring Harbor:

> Inasmuch as the tables, formulas, etc. in these two manuscripts are not supported by basic analyses of original data . . . these books, in my opinion, will be of (little or) no value to geneticists or to other groups of scientists. [sic.](Laughlin files, Carnegie Inst., Dec. 29th, 1937, "Memorandum on Manuscript Submitted by Dr. H.H. Laughlin")

Dr. Bunker was in essence stating what Laughlin's critics had stated about his immigration studies. The data collected did not support Laughlin's conclusions, and that the data itself had dubious inconsistencies that made it of little value to those interested in a truly scientific inspection of the work. Yet, the desire to print the two-volume work entailing "The Measure of Racing Capacity" and "The Inheritance of Racing Capacity" seemed to stay afloat at the Carnegie Institution even after Laughlin died. Some of the correspondence reads like the leadership was reluctant to face the reality that they had spent an obscene amount of money on the type of laboratory theatrics that could be only be described as smoke and mirrors.

Pieces of correspondence from Dr. Merriam indicate that he held out hope that the study would come together once fully completed. It is interesting to see that as late as 1941, years after Laughlin had already been forced to retire by Dr. Merriam's successor, the project still seemed to be afloat. However, Dr. Vannevar Bush was much more skeptical of Laughlin and proceeded more cautiously. When Walter J. Salmon, the horse breeder that initiated the study, approached the Carnegie Institution to complete the study, Dr. Bush was savvy enough to enlist Dr. John W. Gowen of Iowa State College. It is interesting to see that the allure of having a "Pattern Formula" for heredity was still of interest to the institution:

> Inasmuch as these cooperative studies of Dr. Laughlin were carried on largely while he was a staff member of the Carnegie Institution, I am interested in obtaining a review of his present reports by a competent authority, and your name has been suggested to me in this connection. Assuming that Dr. Laughlin's method of procedure in analyzing his material is sound, **it is possible that his reports will prove of value and service in a more general manner in genetics than simply in connection with the horse**. It is, however, our general policy to make competent review, with particular attention to scientific validity, before publication or distribution in the name of the Institution. (Laughlin files, Carnegie Inst., July 14th, 1941, Bush to Gowen, emphasis mine)

Dr. Gowen's response is interesting, as he points to the same disconnect between Laughlin's conclusions and the very large amount of data collected:

> Our interest lies in the scientific contributions the two papers make. Dr.

Laughlin's papers in the Proceedings of the National Academy of Sciences and in the Scientific Monthly presumably lay the basis for this work. I had expected that the manuscripts would give us a really adequate presentation of the whole analysis. This would be a thoroughly worth while contribution but the manuscripts do not do this. **The bulk of the manuscripts is detailed calculation, the logic of which cannot be traced.** The tabular matter could equally well be represented by charts or nomographs at greatly reduced expense. Publication of the material as it stands would not meet the scientific need. [sic.](Laughlin files, Carnegie Inst., Aug. 7th, 1941, Gowen to Bush, emphasis mine)

It is hard to discern whether Dr. Gowen was being diplomatic, insulting, or still somewhat hopeful when he closes this letter by suggesting that someone with "a good and sympathetic biological training should at least edit the material for him." In other words, the Carnegie Institution should employ a 'real scientist' to salvage whatever it could from the very large amount of data collected by Laughlin.

The last piece of correspondence on the subject of Laughlin's thoroughbred horse study is dated as late as February of 1956. It is from a Jerry Holtzman from the Sports Department at the Chicago Sun-Times. By this time, the Carnegie Institution had already handed off all of Laughlin work to archives and libraries and otherwise forgotten about him. Yet, Laughlin's Thoroughbred Study, remains a perfect example of how even the most questionable work in science can continue to be sought after even after being exposed as fraudulent. Such has been the case with the many eugenic studies on humans as well. They are cited in journals and books to this day. Alas, the infamous book, "The Bell Curve," was citing Laughlin as late as 2002. Hassencahl offers an interesting opinion in the opening pages of her thesis on Laughlin:

> As is shown in his post-Immigration Act activities, Dr. Laughlin could not adjust to a changing situation. Like many inflexible advocates of holy causes he continued to say essentially the same thing in 1939 that he had said in 1920. (Pg. iii, "Harry H. Laughlin: 'Expert Eugenics Agent'" Hassencahl, 1970, University Microfilms)

The above quote is a succinct way of describing the eugenics movement in general. Laughlin was hardly alone. C.M. Goethe was unrepentant and unapologetic about his support for Hitler's National Socialists for the remainder of his life. Charles Galton Darwin, the famous biologist's grandson, would continue the eugenic cause along with the Nazi scientists that escaped being hung at Nuremberg. He would collaborate with Ottmar von Verschuer, the man that Mengele answered to in the Nazi hierarchy, in the now infamous journal Mankind Quarterly. The work in Mankind Quarterly, in turn, was funded by the equally unrepentant Wickliffe Draper. Julian Huxley used his position at UNESCO to publish several pro-eugenics papers the years immediately following the Nuremberg trials. Huxley would be removed from his position at UNESCO prematurely, likely because of these documents, as UNESCO would follow-up his dismissal with publications that directly contradicted and corrected for the record UNESCO's position on eugenics. Even to this day, Laughlin is positively cited by scientists that believe in the eugenic cause, namely Seymour Itzkoff. Itzkoff, incidentally, is funded by Laughlin's and Draper's Pioneer Fund.

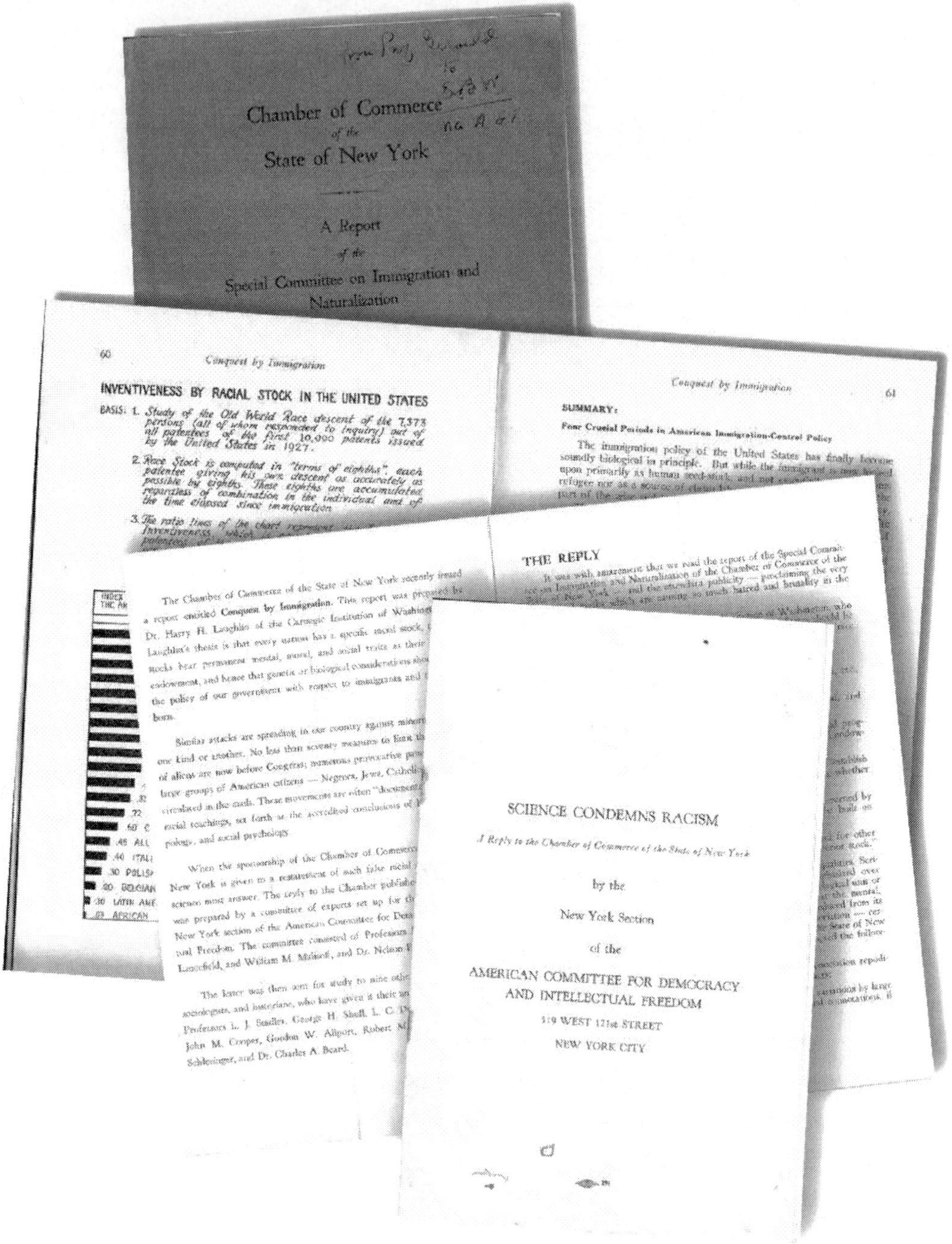
Chamber of Commerce
of the
State of New York
A Report
of the
Special Committee on Immigration and Naturalization
60
Conquest by Immigration
INVENTIVENESS BY RACIAL STOCK IN THE UNITED STATES
Conquest by Immigration
61
SUMMARY:
THE REPLY
SCIENCE CONDEMNS RACISM
A Reply to the Chamber of Commerce of the State of New York
by the
New York Section
of the
AMERICAN COMMITTEE FOR DEMOCRACY AND INTELLECTUAL FREEDOM
519 WEST 121st STREET
NEW YORK CITY

1938 - CONQUEST BY IMMIGRATION

> "Dr. Laughlin's 'purification of race theory,' - is as dangerous and as spurious as the purified Aryan race theories advanced by the Nazis, to which it bears suspicious resemblance."
> – New York Times, May 7th, 1934

Hitler had assumed unchecked power in Germany by 1933, and by 1934 the German-Jewish population had come to understand that the aggression voiced in his speeches was more than just old "Jew-hating" rhetoric. Many fled to New York to become part of a prominent Jewish-American community. It is by no surprise that one of the loudest reactions to Laughlin's work came when the New York Chamber of Commerce commissioned a study by Laughlin. The Chamber took an interest in Laughlin's work, and as early as 1934, the Chamber published a fifty-one page report by Laughlin entitled "Immigration Control". The preface to the report is signed by John B. Trevor, Edward L. Beck, Francis K. Stevens, Henry R. Sutphen of the Special Committee on Immigration and Naturalization of the New York Chamber of Commerce. The work was first delivered in report form to the Chamber on April 16th, 1934 but subsequently published for public consumption on May 3rd, 1939 as "Conquest by Immigration".

Frances Janet Hassencahl takes note of Laughlin's careful posturing. Laughlin's report made direct allusions to the flight of German-Jews towards American shores. It contested the notion that the United States had always been an asylum for victims of religious persecution by stating that persecution by itself was not a measure of personal worth. The report callously dismissed the cries for special legislation that would allow German-Jews to immigrate to the United States:

> Almost as though he wished to ward off charges of anti-Semitism Laughlin added that there were inferior and superior Jews and if any could meet "our standards of physical stamina, mental quality and moral fibre" that they should be admitted under the quota just like the immigrants from other European countries. Laughlin continually used the approach that Jews were welcome, adding that the condition of their welcome was contingent upon their personal qualities. He assumed that such qualities were not present in the Jewish people in sufficient quantity to make them desirable immigrants. (Pg. 235, "Harry H. Laughlin, Expert Eugenics Agent", Hassencahl, University Microfilms, 1970)

The official version of "Conquest by Immigration" has a publication date of May 15th, 1939. The title mimics the title of Madison Grant's second book, "Conquest of a Continent: The Expansion of Races in America." According to Professor Lombardo, Grant had conferred with Laughlin prior to publication. Laughlin's suggested title was "The American Breed: The Differential Expansion of Races in America". Laughlin even wrote a promotional letter for Grant's book in 1933. The letter was targeted at high school teachers throughout the United States. Although not part of "Conquest by Immigration," the content of that promotional piece is worth recounting here as it foreshadows the spirit of the work:

> TO THOSE INTERESTED IN THE FUTURE OF AMERICA: We have just published a provocative book for a day when national consciousness is awakening throughout the world – THE CONQUEST OF A CONTINTNET by Madison Grant. National problems today are, at bottom, race problems. **Herr Hitler has stated that problem for Germany – and is working out his own solution.** We in America have our own problem – but we do not seem to recognize the seriousness. In this new book Mr. Grant explodes the "Melting Pot" fallacy with cold figures. He calls our attention to the fact that because we have always considered America the refuge of the oppressed, we have let ourselves in for grave difficulties. (Pg. 794, Lombardo, "The American Breed", Albany Law Review, Vol. 65, No. 3, 2002, emphasis mine)

Professor Lombardo quotes "Conquest of a Continent" in order to illustrate exactly what Laughlin and Grant meant by "We in America have our own problem":

> The salvation of the country rested on enforcement of the National Origins restrictions written into the 1924 Immigration Restriction Act. "No one should be allowed to enter the United States . . . except white men of superior intellectual capacity." We should also "sympathize with the firm resolve of the handful of white men in South Africa . . . to control and regulate the Negro population there," as we sympathize with "[t]he struggle for the maintenance of the supremacy fo the white man over the native" in other parts of the world. (Pgs. 795-796, Lombardo, "The American Breed", Albany Law Review, Vol. 65, No. 3, 2002)

In many ways Laughlin's work for the New York Chamber of Commerce reads like his *magnum opus*. The 1939 book incorporates a full list of Laughlin's legislative dreams, including legislative recommendations for sterilization, segregation, immigration control, and international treaties all based on eugenics. However, the tone is not as dispassionate as his "expert" testimony before the United States Congress. The blurb on the cover page sets the tone:

> A study of the United States as the receiver of Old World emigrants who become the parents of future-born Americans; a research on the essential long-time **parallel between conquest following successful military invasion and enforced settlement on the one hand and legalized, peaceful immigration and settlement on the other**; and an investigation into those forces by which a sovereign nation can, to its own benefit, control immigrant-additions to its own reproductive stocks in number, geographic distribution, race-descent and inborn quality. (emphasis mine)

It is important to explain that at this point in history the New York Chamber of Commerce led the way in lobbying for further restriction of immigration. They desired a further tightening of the already highly restrictive quotas written into the 1924 Immigration Restriction Act. The chamber took great pride in boasting this position of leadership:

The Chamber of Commerce of the State of New York was the first great commercial body to advocate restriction upon immigration into the United States. (Pg. 1, N.Y. Chamber of Commerce Immigration Report)

The report leverages Laughlin's position an "authority on genetics" working for the Carnegie Institution and appointed as an "expert" for the United States Congress. The preface cites an August 4th, 1934 article by the Saturday Evening Post which plays into this aura of scientific legitimacy:

> We have long needed just such a handbook, written by a scientist abreast of modern thought, to supersede some of the out-of-date books from the pens of sentimentalists who were avowed adherents of the now-discredited melting-pot theory. (Pg. 1, N.Y. Chamber of Commerce Immigration Report)

"Conquest by Immigration" presents its position by framing the arguments using textbook Darwinism as its bedrock:

> Human history is basically a biological record – the account of a species of animal – homo sapiens – and his spread, in many varieties over the earth. If the details be left out, the skeleton outline of human history reads very much like that of the natural history of many other kind of successful animal. It tells of the origin, development and decline of new human varieties, races and family-stocks. (Pg. 6, "Conquest by Immigration", N.Y. Chamber of Commerce)

Note how Laughlin makes immigration policy appear to be the rational thought process of a horse breeder purchasing new studs:

> If the American people hold their basic racial inheritance too valuable for experimental purposes they can, by sound methods, build up the purity and capacity of their own racial inheritance. If a race is to conserve its own basic, hereditary qualities, without racial change, it can receive into its mate-selection circles only persons closely related by blood to themselves. Racially the American people, if they are to remain American, are to purge their existing family-stocks of degeneracy, and are to encourage a high rate of reproduction by the best-endowed portions of their population, can successfully assimilate in the future many thousands of northwestern European immigrants, but only such of these as are carefully inspected and selected in search of inborn family qualities superior to the average of our own people. But we can assimilate only a small fraction of this number of other white races; and of the colored races practically none. (Pg. 22, N.Y. Chamber of Commerce Immigration Report)

Laughlin explicitly states and restates this position throughout his presentation. The "eugenical" and "race-betterment" basis for immigration control is at all times expressed as the "dominant factor" amongst all economic, cultural, and political considerations:

> Immigration into a relatively young and still immigrant-receiving country must be looked upon as essentially an addition to the human reproductive stock of the nation. (Pg. 48, N.Y. Chamber of Commerce Immigration Report)

Laughlin describes the process by which one "race" displaced another, whether peacefully or by force. This was a concept proposed by Charles Darwin in Volume 1 of "Descent of Man" (Pgs. 200-201):

> In successful self-directed efforts to guide the evolution or development of a nation or a race, it is necessary to establish racial standards, to hold the country against all alien would-be invaders, whether they come as enemies in battle or as friendly immigrants, and to set up standards for the admission of outside reproductive stocks into the mate-selection circle of the established race. (Pg. 6, N.Y. Chamber of Commerce Immigration Report)

In Chapter 1, subsection 2, entitled "Migration Conquests: Examples in the Plant and Animal World", Laughlin continues the evolutionary theme:

> Any kind of plant or animal which enters the territory of a related variety, establishes itself, reproduces abundantly, lives successfully therein, and replaces the native stock, thus makes the conquest of the invaded country. If the operation concerns races or family-stocks of men, the invasion may have come as a consequence of formal battle, arranged with as much ceremony as a professional bull-fight, following the "rules of war" as indeed many human conquests did. Or the invasion may have come insidiously as a quiet immigration, a few individuals at a time. But in the long run the result is the same – practical conquest – if the invader or immigrant of new or alien stock finally succeeds in establishing himself in the new country. (Pg. 10, N.Y. Chamber of Commerce Immigration Report)

Laughlin, like his Nazi counterparts linked "race" and "geography", "blood and soil", ethnicity and statehood:

> Conquest by immigration is basically the turning point between the two policies of marking political territorial boundaries. One policy is based upon natural geographic region and physiographical boundary. It gives civil government to whomsoever happens to live within the particular natural geographic region. The second policy makes race the main basis of territorial ownership, so that when one race expands into the territory of another the invader proceeds to annex the invaded territory politically. ---- If the territory into which the alien immigrates, settles and becomes the majority and dominating race is adjacent to the country from which the immigrant came, then, in due season, the demand for political annexation of the territory newly conquered by alien settlement to the nation from which he emigrated becomes a vital political issue, more definite and incurable than if the conquest were made by military invasion only. (Pg. 10, N.Y. Chamber of Commerce Immigration Report)

In subsection 3, entitled "Immigration vs. Warfare: Germany Won the World War", Laughlin enters deeper into the realm of Hitlerisms. Laughlin extrapolates his eugenic thinking into what is a barely disguised version of Nazism's *Lebensraum* policy:

> The first "World War" was, by test, not so effective in attaining conquest, with its racial and populational results, as were old-fashioned wars in which one tribe

or province raided another, killed the men, married the women and settled on the land. In the World War modern machinery and invention wrought terrible destruction at tremendous cost of life and treasure – all on a world-wide scale. But we find among its results none of those basic conquests which ancient warfare, according to history, provided for the military winner. Now, less than a generation after the World War, the "defeated" German nation, because she is still in possession of her own lands and natural resources, and because her population was left essentially intact, and because she is now producing another generation ... she is now a relatively stronger nation than ever, and maybe feels able to reverse her technical military defeat. ---- If the Allies had followed the rules which governed old-fashioned tribal conquests, told of in past history, they, logically enough in their next step, following their military victory, would have moved into Germany, enslaved the people, destroyed the surplus population and settled upon the German land. That would have been real conquest.[sic] (Pgs. 10-11, N.Y. Chamber of Commerce Immigration Report)

Laughlin goes on to explain that a real war is a war that is a "struggle for existence" which results in the "survival of the fittest." He bemoans that World War I did not accomplish the traditional ends of war in a Darwinian sense. Anyone that is vaguely familiar with Adolf Hitler's speeches would have recognized this trend of thought. These were the same justifications for war that Hitler's zealots were utilizing. As for Laughlin, the lessons that both he and the Germans gleaned from history seemed to apply to the United States:

Races and cultures have been highly specialized, as indeed they must continue to be if mankind is to make great progress in the world of culture and civilization. Such progress cannot be built on mongrel melting-pots, but it is based on organized diversity of relatively pure racial types. In the past that racial group which maintained its own integrity and improved the hereditary endowments of its own family-stocks, made progress, added to human culture, and increased its own success and happiness. The failure of the superior-endowed stocks to reproduce, whether such failure was caused by decimating warfare, infertility of the sounder stocks, or an inferior immigrant invasion, the result is the same – failure to advance culture – and the particular nation and stock became extinct, or at least declined. (Pg. 18, N.Y. Chamber of Commerce Immigration Report)

Laughlin dissects the history of immigrant populations from the Orient, Mexico, France, Italy, Spain, Ireland and weighs the value of "racial mixing" with the American Indian and the "imported Negro slave." Here was the influence of Harvard's Professor Shaler apparent in the ethos of the eugenicists. He identifies the American "race" as predominantly British. However, it is curious that he singles out a religion, despite his allusions to "biological" differences in the subsection entitled "The Jew as an Immigrant Into the United States." Clearly he was echoing Nazi propaganda by proposing that the Jewish community was a "race". Laughlin leads up to this subsection with the following thought:

But besides many of our best families who came as such refugees, also many present day American degenerates – persons who failed to make good here – came from the Old World in the same migrant waves which were generated by European oppression. Biologically these facts mean that whenever population pressure is exerted on the borders of an immigrant-receiving nation, the time is ripe for the receiving nation to set still higher admission standards and to sort all the more alertly, to select from would-be immigrants only individuals who personally and their near-blood-kin represent the most energetic, capable and moral personalities as additions to the population of the receiving country. (Pg. 20, N.Y. Chamber of Commerce Immigration Report)

Laughlin recognizes the many accomplishments of the Jewish community and praises them, albeit in a somewhat dismissive fashion. This is where Laughlin returns to his "biological" requirements for acceptable immigrants. He does not dismiss the Jewish immigrants as incompatible because of their religion. He questions if they meet the biological standards. Again, this mirrors the standard objection that Hitler makes to the German-Jewish population; that their inclusion will lead to a biological degeneration of the "superior stock". This is, after all, the core concept of eugenics, that humans allowed to breed without the traditional geographical or political boundaries are in danger of reversing evolution, of "degenerating." This was the "race suicide" Theodore Roosevelt warned against:

> The immigrant Jew who enters this country legally is welcome on terms of equality with all other white immigrants. This means that he must meet American immigrant-standards of physical soundness, mental capacity and moral attitude. Both personally and in family-stock the immigrant Jew, like every other immigrant, is expected to carry inherent qualities which will improve the hereditary basis of American family stocks. (Pg. 21, N.Y. Chamber of Commerce Immigration Report)

Of course, the above quote makes Laughlin's immigration criterion sound even-handed. This is the game he played when he utilized an outdated Census as the basis for the 1924 Immigration Restriction Act. The amount of European Jews allowed in was reduced practically to zero since the quotas of the 1924 Act were based on Jewish population of 1890, a Census year when the Jewish-American population was at its lowest.

The section entitled "Specific Recommendations" is a list of 38 legislative, and procedural recommendations intended to control the "biological" and "eugenic" aspect of population. Much of it calls for "legal definitions" of ethnic terms in order to make it legally expedient to carry out his recommendations. For example, point #5 states:

> That for the purpose of American immigration laws, a white person be defined as one all whose ancestors were members of the white or Caucasian race. (Pg. 91, N.Y. Chamber of Commerce Immigration Report)

The above point was indicative of the work Laughlin was conducting with the leaders of the pro-segregation lobby, namely the infamous "one-drop rule" used to define what made a person legally black in some States. Many of the other recommendations call for the typical "standardized testing" that was the stock-in-trade of the eugenics movement. Some are overtly bigoted and prejudiced. For example, point #4 states

> That no immigrant be admitted, whether by quota or otherwise, who is not – First, a member of the white race; Second, the possessor of inherent personal qualities – physical, mental and moral. . . (Pg. 91, N.Y. Chamber of Commerce Immigration Report)

The Legislative mechanisms Laughlin proposed are worth dissecting if only to understand how to prevent future zealots from implementing them. As was the case with Laughlin's other legislative recommendations, it is clear that Laughlin had a pronounced disdain for the Federalist form of representative government that the United States operates as. More specifically, Laughlin and his cohorts had a distrust or dislike of the "separation of powers" doctrine. This is apparent in some recommendations where he proposes the Executive Branch have the power to override all other branches of government. For example, Laughlin would give the Executive the power to suspend all immigration without laws having been passed by the Congress. Furthermore, Laughlin flirts with the mechanisms of a totalitarian form of government by recommending that the U.S. Government have the power to revoke citizenship if someone merely engaged in "political propaganda." Laughlin neither defines what type of "propaganda" is punishable by deportation nor does he address the obvious conflicts with the First Amendment to the United States Constitution.

One curious aspect of Laughlin's report is how it transitions from immigration controls to domestic policy. Laughlin uses his study of the amount of foreign-born in mental or correctional institutions. "Conquest by Immigration" also contains the results of the "Survey of the Human Resources of Connecticut." The study claims to analyze the costs to the State of harboring or caring for the "inadequate", "feeble-minded", and "degenerates" linking them to the foreign-born:

> In this particular field Connecticut is the first one of the United States to organize a survey of its human resources on the biological basis. ---- The Connecticut survey is unique in that most previous analyses which sought the key-basis for population policy and welfare were based primarily upon public health or employment. Connecticut went forward with biology as its key-basis .... The country has learned how to locate and treat parallel problems connected with the plant industry, the animal industry, the soil, the forests and the wild life. Connecticut initiated the similar study of its human resources as one of its basic natural resources. [sic.] (Pgs. 66-67, N.Y. Chamber of Commerce Immigration Report)

The mission statement in the subsection entitled "Purpose of this Particular Research: The Survey of the Human Resources of Connecticut" reads like the justification provided for eugenic legislation in Hitler's Germany. These were neither immigration measures nor an initiative for the well-being of Connecticut's populace. It was a breeding project that looked at the population as a stockyard full of animals. The State would selectively breed, segregate and sterilize in order to continually improve its "human resources":

> In the turnover of its population from the present generation to the next, the State may develop a policy which will have for its purpose the improvement of the hereditary physical, mental and spiritual endowment of the succeeding generation. In its negative aspect, i.e., in the lessening of inherited degeneracy, such a policy, in its practical application, seeks first to prevent the immigration into the state of persons – regardless of race – who are defective in their hereditary endowments, as shown by their own case histories and **by the qualities of their near-blood kin**. Secondly, it seeks the location of the prevention of reproduction by its residents – **regardless of race or citizenship** – who are definitely shown to be defective or degenerate in some seriously handicapping manner on account, primarily, of some defect in hereditary endowment. (Pg. 67, N.Y. Chamber of Commerce Immigration Report, emphasis mine)

The reader should note that these proposals called for controls of both foreign and domestic migration, "regardless of race or citizenship." Laughlin was not only looking to control foreign migration, but migration between the States as well. The policy, as recommended, was an insidious attack on the individual rights of Connecticut citizens.

The genealogical and eugenic data of "near-blood kin" collected was intended for precisely the same purposes as it was in Hitler's Germany. Anyone whose ancestors or relatives were found to have racial or eugenic defects was fair game for deportation, segregation, or sterilization. This is how the German census and IBM tabulation machinery became the tools of ethnic cleansing in Hitler's Germany. This is how many Germans, many who had no idea of their ancestry showed signs of "hereditary degeneracy" became victims to an ever-enlarging dragnet by the authorities. This aspect of Nazi Germany would no longer be conjecture in 1939. The world had seen the violence of November 1938, infamously remembered as *Kristallnacht*, the night when Hitler's henchmen wreaked havoc on the German-Jewish community.

"Conquest by Immigration" demonstrated the unwavering resolve of the American eugenics lobby. At the time this report was written, total immigration into the United States was at the lowest level since reliable immigration statistics were first collected in 1820. The 1924 Immigration Act would be a horrifying success, and the harshness of the 1924 Act was prominent in the minds of the immigrant community. The immigrant community in New York would take notice of the first report and later of the 1939 publication. The major newspapers covered the publications and the reaction of the local immigrant community as well. The New York Times made the report public knowledge in a May 4th, 1934 article titled

"Relaxing Quotas for Exiles Fought". The article lauds Laughlin as the premiere "expert" on the matters:

> He is beyond doubt the foremost authority in the United States today on the subject, and his previous researches along similar lines for the Committee on Immigration and Naturalization of the House of Representatives peculiarly fitted him for the task. (NYT, May 4th, 1934, "Relaxing Quotas For Exiles Fought: Eugenist in Report to State Chamber Says Desirability Should Be Only Test")

The article continues under the subheadings of "Would Bar Non-Whites" and "Committee to Offer Resolutions Later After Studying Views of Dr. Laughlin". It quotes Laughlin extensively:

> No exceptional admission for Jews who are refugees from persecution in Germany. No admission for any immigrant "unless he has a definite country to which he may be deported, if occasion demands." No immigrant to be admitted whose ancestors were not "all members of the white or Caucasian race." (NYT, May 4th, 1934, "Relaxing Quotas For Exiles Fought: Eugenist in Report to State Chamber Says Desirability Should Be Only Test")

It is clear from these quotes that Laughlin fully understood that there was more at stake than an issue of immigration under normal circumstances. Laughlin was aware that what was being debated was a lifeline to a population with a justified fear for their lives:

> "There is a movement now to make special legislative provisions for the Jews persecuted in Germany. If, as a result of persecution or expulsion by any foreign country, men of real hereditary capacity, sound in physical stamina and of outstanding personal qualities, honesty, decency, common sense, altruism, patriotism and initiative, can be found, they should, because of such qualities, and not because of persecution, win individual preference within our quotas and be welcomed as desirable human seed-stock of future American citizens. If any would-be immigrant cannot meet these standards, he should, of course, be excluded. The Jews are no exception to races which are widely variable in family-stock quality within their own race. There are superior Jews, and there are inferior Jews." (NYT, May 4th, 1934, "Relaxing Quotas For Exiles Fought: Eugenist in Report to State Chamber Says Desirability Should Be Only Test")

The article continues by quoting Laughlin in a stance that could easily be confused as outright cooperation with the stated aims and policies of the Third Reich:

> Dr. Laughlin characterized the problem of alien propaganda "a side issue to immigration-control," but declared that even naturalized citizen and certainly alien must "abstain from foreign, group, or racial propaganda within the United States." He advocated punishment and deportation whether the propaganda was, for instance, in support of the Nazi government, or an attempt to destroy the Nazi government. (NYT, May 4th, 1934, "Relaxing Quotas For Exiles Fought: Eugenist in Report to State Chamber Says Desirability Should Be Only Test")

The article closes by documenting that Laughlin called for further tightening of the 1924 Immigration Restriction Act quota system. Laughlin wanted to reduce the quotas further by 60 percent, calling the American "melting pot" motto a fallacy:

> "Let the metaphor of the melting pot go and come back to the real thing. The great nations of the past have been both made and destroyed by immigration, mate selection and difference in size of family in reference to inborn capacity. These nation-making forces can be substantially controlled by living nations." (NYT, May 4th, 1934, "Relaxing Quotas For Exiles Fought: Eugenist in Report to State Chamber Says Desirability Should Be Only Test")

The report hardly went without notice or rebuttal. A New York Times article documents how prominent leaders of the American Jewish community took note of Laughlin's claims and spoke out against it. None other than Rabbi Stephen S. Wise and Bernard S. Deutsch of the American Jewish Congress called a meeting for the specific purpose of discussing Laughlin's report with other Jewish organizations in which 1,500 attendees heard them speak:

> Dr. Laughlin had pointed out that "there is a movement now ot make special legislative provision for the Jews persecuted in Germany" and asserted that if any would-be immigrant could not meet certain standards he should be excluded. (NYT, May 7th, 1934, "State Chamber Assailed by Jews")

This turned out to be a major tipping point for the American eugenics movement. The article goes on under the subtitle "Proposals Bear a 'Suspicious Resemblance' to Nazi System, Says Aldermanic Head" and it continues under the subheading "Likened to Nazi Stand" quoting Bernard S. Deutsch:

> "Dr. Laughlin's 'purification of race theory,'" Mr. Deutsch said in opening the conference, "is as dangerous and as spurious as the purified Aryan race theories advanced by the Nazis, to which it bears suspicious resemblance. His singling out of the Jews for mention as a particular race group to be barred from general admission to the United States, despite the condescending tribute to so-called 'superior' Jews, is a knavish, deliberate slur upon the whole Jewish people, which differs only from the Nazi brand in that it is couched in more polite language. Dr. Laughlin's report carried all the earmarks of an attempt to introduce a racial passport system in the United States, based on the Nazi model. Inherent in his proposal is a threat as formidable as that of Hitlerism in Germany." (The New York Times, May 7th, 1934, "State Chamber Assailed by Jews", emphasis mine)

It is unknown if the New York Chamber of Commerce was aware of Laughlin's relationship with Hitler's eugenicists, or if the Chamber delved into how much Laughlin's proposals actually resembled the eugenics of the Third Reich. The relationship between Laughlin and the New York Chamber of Commerce would continue for some years. As late as June of 1939 Laughlin would speak before the Chamber with "Conquest" finalized:

Dr. Laughlin recommends that the census of 1940 "should revise its enumeration items so as to provide definitely and clearly the following items for each person listed: Personal identification, place of birth, race descent, citizenship and legal residence and family connections – identification of father and mother, husband or wife, sons and daughters." (NYT, June 8th, 1939, "Immigration Curb is Urged in Survey")

Laughlin did not feel hindered in demanding "racial qualities" when reading "Conquest by Immigration." To the contrary, Laughlin and his fellow eugenicists would campaign to have the standards of the 1924 Immigration Restriction Act further stiffened as a response to all those racial minorities escaping Europe:

"In each case of application for admission as an immigrant," Dr. Laughlin says, "the test should ask: 'Is the applicant a potential parent or desirable future Americans?'" (NYT, June 8th, 1939, "Immigration Curb is Urged in Survey")

The opposition would generate its own literature. It published "Science Condemns Racism: A Reply to the Chamber of Commerce of the State of New York, by the New York Section of the American Committee for Democracy and Intellectual Freedom, 519 West 121st Street, New York City." The chairman of the committee was none other than Franz Boaz, the famous enemy of the eugenics movement, but most importantly, it included L.C. Dunn. The importance of including L.C. Dunn cannot be overemphasized. Recall that Dunn had already warned the Carnegie leadership of the parallels to National Socialist eugenics. The small pamphlet was published on July 18th, 1939 and undoubtedly Dunn made sure it made its way into the hands of the higher-ups at the Carnegie Institution.

Furthermore, the preface indicates that their formal reply was signed by a group of respected scientists within and without the American Committee for Democracy. These signatories included L.C. Dunn, L.J. Stadler, George H. Shull, Th. Dobzhansky, John M. Cooper, Gordon w. Allport, Robert M. Maciver, and A.M. Schlesinger, and Dr. Charles A Beard. The preface opens up as follows:

The Chamber of Commerce of the State of New York recently issued a report entitled Conquest by Immigration. This report was prepared by Dr. Harry H. Laughlin of the Carnegie Institution of Washington. Dr. Laughlin's thesis is that every nation has a specific racial stock, that such stocks bear permanent mental, moral, and social traits as their biological endowment, and hence that genetic or biological considerations should govern the policy of our government with respect to immigrants and the foreign born. Similar attacks are spreading in our country against minority groups of one kind or another. No less than seventy measures to limit the civil right of aliens are now before Congress; numerous provocative pamphlets against large groups of American citizens – Negroes, Jews, Catholics – are being circulated in the mails. These movements are often "documented" by spurious racial teachings, set forth as the accredited conclusions of biology, anthropology, and social psychology. When the sponsorship of the Chamber of Commerce of the State of New York is given to a restatement of such false doctrines, men of science must answer.

Interestingly enough, Laughlin is mentioned more often than the New York Chamber throughout the pamphlet. This official "REPLY" to the New York Chamber tears into the foundations upon which Laughlin's report was based:

> Mr. Harry H. Laughlin of the Carnegie Institution of Washington, who wrote this report, asserts that immigration into the United States should be cut down to the vanishing point in the interests of "race integrity" and "race improvement". The underlying principles on which the report is based are that:
> 1.) Every nationality – English, French, Irish, Italian, Spanish, etc., is a "race".
> 2.) Every "race" has its inherent, unalterable physical, mental and moral qualities.
> 3.) Some of these "races" are superior and others inferior, and progress in human society and culture is primarily due to the biological endowment of "racial purity".
> 4.) The successful development of a nation requires it to "establish racial standards, to hold the country against all would-be invaders, whether they come as enemies in battle or as friendly immigrants..."
> 5.) The immigrant policy of the United States should be governed by biological or "racial" considerations because "progress cannot be built on mongrel melting pots."
> 6.) The cost of public institutions for the mentally ill and for other public charges is largely due to the immigration of "racially inferior stock."
> 7.) The entire argument follows the theory of innate racial qualities. Serious psychologists, anthropologists, and sociologists have emphasized over and over again that it is absurd to speak of any nation as a biological unit or "race," and that no proof has ever been given to show that the mental, cultural, or moral characteristics of a so-called race can be deduced from its descent.

The pamphlet goes on to directly attack the "107 pages" of statistics that made up the bulk of Laughlin's report, citing competing works by fellow scientists. These 107 pages of statistics extrapolated Laughlin's theory that immigrants were not only inferior, but endangered the State and Federally run institutions. As this book has previously documented, Laughlin manipulated the numbers by using Census figures that did not correlate to the generation he was analyzing, but which bolstered his desired goals. The scientist that prepared the "REPLY" also took noticed that Laughlin had not only cooked the numbers but also arrived at conclusions that even the data published in the report did not support. The "REPLY" concludes:

> We view with alarm the rapid spread in our own country of the hysterical cry that the alien or the Jew or the Catholic, or some other scapegoat, is responsible for all the ills of society. The report of the Chamber of Commerce of the State of New York seeks to lend scientific support to such demagoguery. We would not be true citizens of democracy if we did not enter our vigorous protest against any such abuse of science. The scientist has an ethical obligation to avoid conclusions that are not warranted by the evidence. What can we say of the ethics of Mr. Laughlin when he makes a report which so patently violates all the

rules of scientific method and procedure, or of the Chamber of Commerce when it publishes such a report without ascertaining whether Mr. Laughlin's views are supported by reputable scientists?

The unfortunate answer to this poignant question is that Laughlin was surrounded and supported by "reputable scientists". His mentor, Charles B. Davenport, was the most famous and reputable of scientists of the era. History has eschewed Davenport, but Laughlin's ilk included the scientific men of the Darwin clique, namely Galton, and Julian Huxley, who is still regarded as "reputable" by scientists of the 21st century. The eugenics movement leading up to this controversial report was headed up by institutions like Harvard, Yale, Stanford, Cal. Berkley and Johns Hopkins in addition to the Rockefeller and Carnegie Institutions. More to the point, none of the conclusions in the report were new by any stretch of the imagination. The six fundamental notions that the "REPLY" enumerates had been the basis for the science of eugenics for decades going back to the 1860s.

L.C. Dunn's efforts to warn the Carnegie leadership succeeded. The Laughlin files at the Carnegie Institution evidence that its leadership received a copy of Laughlin's "Conquest by Immigration" on May 27th, 1939. A one page memo was written that date for Dr. Vannevar Bush. It gives a brief description of the publication, and maybe a hint as to the work's volatility, as in it Laughlin describes immigrants as invaders:

> A study of the United States as the receivers of Old World emigrants who become the parents of future-born Americans; a research on the essential long-time parallel between conquest following successful military invasion and enforced settlement on the one hand and legalized, peaceful immigration and settlement on the other. (Laughlin files, May 27th, 1939 MEMORANDUM FOR DR. BUSH, CHAMBER OF COMMERCE of the STATE OF NEW YORK – A Report of the Special Committee on Immigration and Naturalization Submitting a Research on CONQUEST BY IMMIGRATION)

It is also clear that the Carnegie leadership was significantly influenced by the correspondence resulting from "Conquest by Immigration." They apparently not only kept a file, but also made it a point to hand a copy of the letters to Laughlin. The handwritten note makes reference to the "report prepared for the N.Y. Chamber of Commerce" and labels it "subj. controversial". (Carnegie files) It also asks that Laughlin take a look at another file entitled "N.Y. Times 1939", which indicates that Carnegie also kept a file on the onslaught of negative press that the report instigated.

The correspondence at Carnegie reveals that the institution received an onslaught of mail communicating anger and disapproval. The hate mail arrived in quantities significant enough to make it all but impossible for Dr. Vannevar Bush to ignore. The institution had previously voiced his disapproval of Laughlin crossing the line between scientific research and direct application. The response to "Conquest by Immigration" made it clear to Dr. Bush that Laughlin's work crossed this line and that the institution was now being perceived as being aligned with Hitler's government. Dr. Bush made his displeasure clear in a May 1939 letter quoted at length here as it is one of the strongest rebukes of both Laughlin and the eugenics movement:

> You have as I see it two major present activities, one the administration of the Record Office, and the second the production of material of the general type represented by this present report. You and I have agreed throughout, I believe, that a normal program for this Institution involves the establishment of scientific facts and relationships, and the rendering of these available, but that it does not include properly activities in support of various objectives by influencing public opinion and the like. This conclusion has nothing to do whatever with the evaluation of such activities themselves, and I would come to the same conclusion no matter how valuable the objectives might be, and no matter how much it appeared that public opinion needed to be influenced. Rather it was our feeling as we conferred that a scientific institution ought to stick to its primary tasks and leave the application of its results in the hands of others. (Laughlin files, Carnegie Inst., May 4th, 1939, Merriam to Laughlin)

Of course, what Dr. Bush was stating was justified, but it was also the direct opposite of what the institution's policy towards Laughlin's work had been throughout the duration of Dr. Merriam's tenure. Merriam had routinely agreed to have Laughlin directly influence public policy in the most visible of ways, by acting as an "expert" for the United States Congress, the State Department, and the Labor Department. Dr. Bush continues with the reasons for his displeasure:

> Now I think the difficulty with your position in the Institution has been quite clearly the fact that you have wished to carry on this second type of activity, whereas it has not been a normal activity for the Institution in which you are placed. I sympathize greatly with your point of view, and I admire the courage and persistence which you have shown in the matter. The situation, however, remains anomalous, and it appears to me that we ought to arrive at some solution which would as far as possible leave the Institution in a clear-cut position before the public as a scientific organization and at the same time interfere as little as possible with your own personal objectives. (Laughlin files, Carnegie Inst., May 4th, 1939, Merriam to Laughlin)

Dr. Bush understood the restlessness of zealots like Laughlin. He also understood that Laughlin's political sympathies would be attributed to the institution for as long as he remained employed by it. Dr. Bush's "solution" therefore involved creating a chasm of separation between Laughlin and the Carnegie Institution:

> This, it seems to me, necessarily involves your dropping out of one of the two branches of your present effort. I do not think you could drop out of the second aspect and remain content; in fact, constituted as you are, I am inclined to believe that it is just impossible for you to leave off all activity in the second

category and remain satisfied that you are contributing your best efforts to progress along the lines in which you are intimately interested. I have been led, therefore, since our last conference to ponder the problem from another point of view. A solution would be arrived at if you dropped off the first activity and now retired definitely from connection with the Record Office. This would involve your going onto the retired list before your normal time of retirement. You would then have no formal connection with the Institution, but would be a free citizen, and there would be no reason whatever that I could see why your activities and efforts should then conform in any way to a pattern of effort which would be reasonable and normal for the Institution itself. (Laughlin files, Carnegie Inst., May 4th, 1939, Merriam to Laughlin)

Ironically, Laughlin would have been justified in pointing out that Dr. Bush's criticism was in direct contradiction to the policy Carnegie had adopted decades prior to his arrival. Laughlin was correct in perceiving that Dr. Bush's reaction was politically motivated, as it appeared when Dr. Bush reversed the error in Dr. Merriam's blind support for Laughlin. Officially, Laughlin was asked to retire for health reasons. All the evidence certainly indicates that his premature retirement was instigated by the very negative press that followed "Conquest by Immigration." This becomes amply clear in a December 5th, 1939 memorandum prepared for Dr. Bush, which details a date by date extrapolation of the events that led up to Laughlin being forced to retire. The memo reads like notes prepared for an attorney, and it was revised and edited several times in order to get the facts and wording right. The correctness and completeness of the memo was clearly of importance to the leadership of the Carnegie Institution. The first date enumerated in the seven-page memo is October 26th, 1937 and the last is December 1st, 1939 with the most revealing part coming in the last paragraph and the hand written notes:

> During July and August 1939, during DR. Bush's absence from the office, several letters were received expressing disagreement with Dr. Laughlin's statements in "Conquest by Immigration," published by the New York Chamber of Commerce. Mr. Gilbert advised Dr. Bush by telephone of the receipt of these, and this was the first knowledge by Dr. Bush of any protest concerning Laughlin's statements as there expressed. Dr. Bush instructed Mr. Gilbert that any such protest could be answered by stating that Dr. Laughlin had an entire right to express [in a reasonable manner] his personal opinion on a matter of public interest, but that the Institution as such had expressed no opinions on the matter in controversy. (Laughlin files, Carnegie Inst., Dec. 5th, 1939, MEMORANDUM RE RETIREMENT OF H.H. LAUGHLIN)

There is no indication in the correspondence made available to this author that Dr. Bush was aware of the fact that Laughlin had already started upon another avenue by creating the Pioneer Fund. It is also important to note that there is nothing in the correspondence that indicates that Dr. Bush personally had any objections to the science of eugenics itself. While Dr. Bush was not as enthusiastic as Dr. Merriam, the correspondence between Dr. Bush and Laughlin demonstrates a generally supportive language. Even the letter above opens up with Dr. Bush diplomatically praising Laughlin for completing "Conquest by Immigration", although this may be interpreted as cordial diplomacy. However, there is a written letter prior to the onslaught of negative press where it is clear that Dr. Bush had voiced a disdain for Laughlin involving himself in the practical application of eugenics:

> In New York yesterday the matter of your proposal in regard to a clinic for advice on eugenic matters came up for informal discussion. I have already indicated to you in a previous letter my feeling in regard to this matter. It seems to me that the primary function of the Carnegie Institution of Washington must always be to establish scientific facts and relationships in any such field, and that this is a matter of such importance and scope that the application of those facts in specific instances and for practical purposes must be largely left to other organizations. I feel quite definitely, therefore, that activity along the line that you have suggested in this particular instance would be unwise. I found that this was the general sentiment in the group which discussed your proposal in New York. (Laughlin files, Carnegie Inst., April 21st, 1939, Bush to Laughlin)

It is also interesting to see a concurrent internal memo dated May 1939 listing candidates to conduct a survey "concerning the soundness and effectiveness" of the Eugenics Record Office. The names listed either demonstrate a continuing support for eugenics or an ignorance of the eugenic network by the upper management at the Carnegie Institution. The names include Dr. Domingo Ramos of the Pan American project, Major Leonard Darwin, John B. Trevor of the New York Chamber of Commerce immigration committee, Clarence Campbell, C.M. Goethe, and Dr. W.A. Plecker. Dr. Bush closes the April 21st, 1939 letter by proposing that Laughlin refer all requests for practical application of eugenic principles to the "Institute of Family Relations," which the famous eugenicist Paul Popenoe operated out of Los Angeles. This list would indicate that Dr. Bush was completely unacquainted with the relevant players of the international eugenics movement. Anyone vaguely familiar with the political activism of these doctors and scientists would have known that they were hardly adequate as candidates for a sober-minded appraisal of the work of the Eugenics Record Office.

The public's reaction to "Conquest by Immigration" had effectively sounded the alarm of the volatility of eugenics during the era of Nazism. The Carnegie leadership clearly wanted to create separation not just with Laughlin, but with the eugenics movement, in general. This was made plain when the institution also demanded that Laughlin change the name of the Eugenics Record Office to "Genetics Record Office" no later than July 1st, 1939. The instructions came in a May 16th, 1939 letter from Administrative Secretary, W.M. Gilbert. The date of this letter to Laughlin immediately follows the span of time when the institution received the most negative responses to "Conquest by Immigration".

RELAXING QUOTAS FOR EXILES FOUGHT

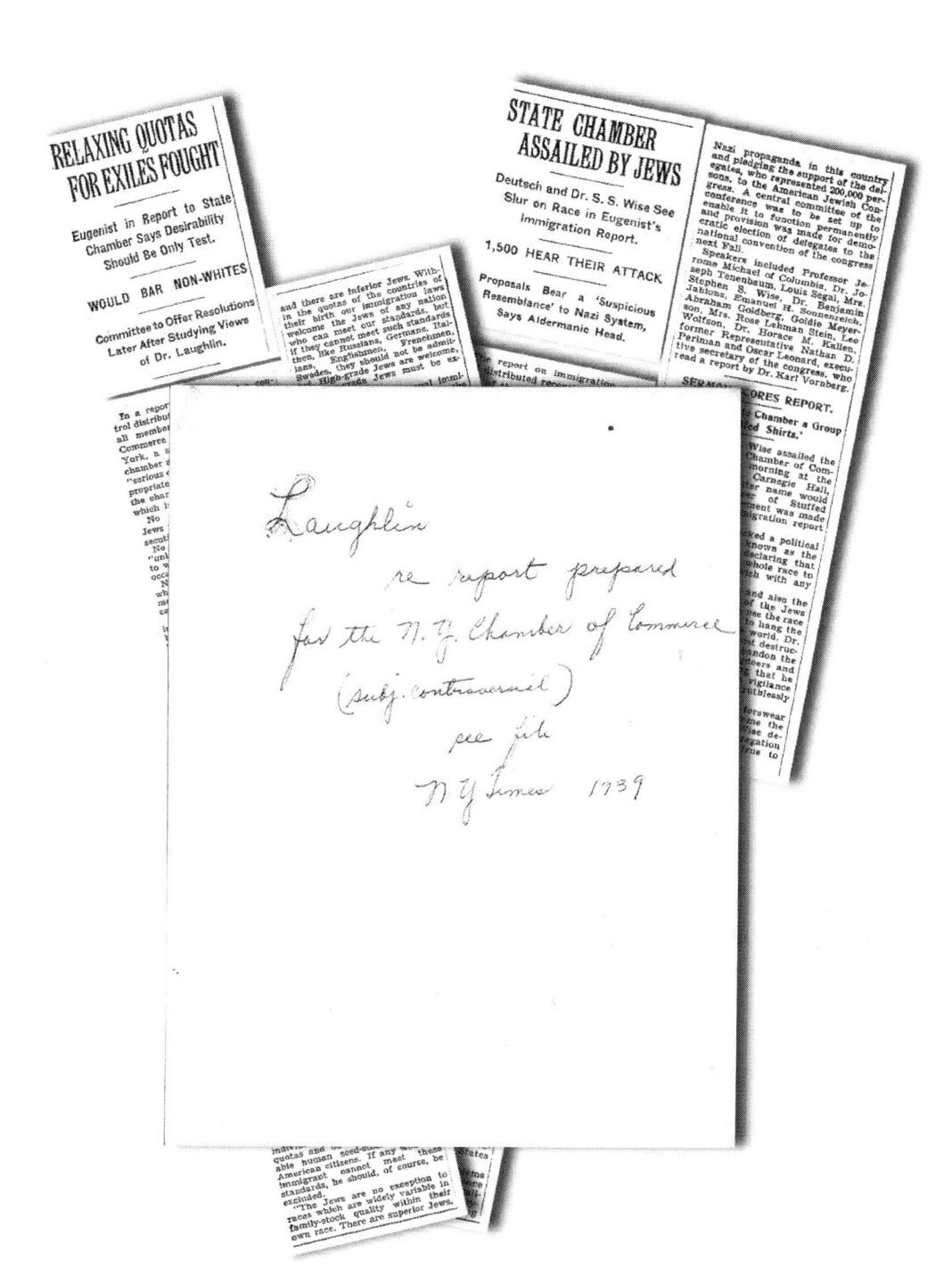

Eugenist in Report to State Chamber Says Desirability Should Be Only Test.

WOULD BAR NON-WHITES

Committee to Offer Resolutions Later After Studying Views of Dr. Laughlin.

STATE CHAMBER ASSAILED BY JEWS

Deutsch and Dr. S. S. Wise See Slur on Race in Eugenist's Immigration Report.

1,500 HEAR THEIR ATTACK

Proposals Bear a 'Suspicious Resemblance' to Nazi System, Says Aldermanic Head.

Laughlin

re report prepared
for the N.Y. Chamber of Commerce
(subj. controversial)

see file
N.Y. Times 1939

1939 - CARNEGIE'S PATIENCE RUNS OUT

> *"Doubt everything or believe everything:*
> *these are two equally convenient strategies.*
> *With either we dispense with the need for reflection."*
> *- Henri Poincare*

Ironically, Laughlin's social habits and health played a role in Carnegie finally pulling the plug. Frances Janet Hassencahl's dissertation documents that Laughlin suffered from epileptic seizures, a condition that did not manifest itself until after a severe tooth infection that occurred during his trip to Europe in 1923. Historians point to Laughlin's epilepsy and speculate that the Laughlin marriage stayed childless because of his epilepsy. Hassencahl disagrees with this assessment. (Pg. 66) However, the combination of Laughlin's *grand mal* seizures and alcoholism became a liability the Carnegie leadership could no longer ignore. They also offered a convenient justification for Laughlin's forced retirement. The correspondence still held at the institution demonstrates that concern over Laughlin's health resurfaced in 1937:

> We have been receiving indirect reports for some time regarding Dr. Laughlin's health and his being subject to attacks that appear to be epileptic in nature. It has come to our attention that this has resulted in automobile accidents, which might have had serious consequences. One of these occurred but a few weeks ago. Also these attacks are said to have occurred in the office in the presence of the staff and in the presence of visitors, for example Frederick Osborn. (Laughlin files, Carnegie Inst., Oct. 26th, 1937, Streeter to Merriam)

Laughlin's drinking problem and epilepsy are ironic as they were amongst the ailments listed by eugenicists as "degenerate" traits. In fact, Laughlin and his eugenic counterparts would list ailments as benign as speech impediments as reasons for forcible sterilization or segregation. In Laughlin's case, they were a legal liability. The Carnegie leadership seems to have been concerned about the liability of having an executive with a drinking problem driving around town:

> It has been reported to me that Dr. Laughlin is continuing to drive his car alone. A week or so ago Climenko, of the L.I.B.A., was driving through Cold Spring Harbor toward Huntington and, without interference from another car, ran into a fence, somewhat seriously banging himself as well as his car. The report is that he occasionally gets drunk and that undoubtedly this was one of the occasions. However, the report came to us indirectly from someone in Cold Spring Harbor village that an accident had happened to one of the Carnegie workers who was subject to fits and probably had an attack at the time of the accident. (Laughlin files, Carnegie Inst., Nov. 3rd, 1937, Albert F. Blakeslee to Streeter)

The Carnegie leadership asked Laughlin to get a medical examination. Laughlin likely attempted to conceal the seriousness of his illness by going to a doctor from his hometown. A 1938 letter from Dr. Merriam demonstrates that the leadership at Carnegie simply didn't find the medical results Laughlin turned in as credible:

> Examination of the statement from your physician has brought out a number of serious questions, one of which involves the competence of the physician, so that I have not been able to make use of this statement to the extent which I had hoped would be possible. (Laughlin files, Carnegie Inst., December 31st, 1938, Merriam to Laughlin)

Laughlin's health kept being an issue as late as October of 1939, when the decision to force Laughlin to retire was already a foregone conclusion. A letter from A.F. Blakeslee to W.M. Gilbert, the Administrative Secretary at Carnegie, describes the how even Charles Davenport was no longer able to ignore Laughlin's ill health:

> In conversation with Dr. Davenport today he raised the question of Laughlin's attacks. This was especially in his mind on account of the recent rather severe attack that Laughlin had a week ago Monday, In which he ran around the laboratories. Someone got Davenport to come down and Laughlin started to attack him before he came out of his spell. (Laughlin files, Carnegie Inst., October 10th, 1939 Blakeslee to Gilbert)

However, the internal correspondence held at the Carnegie Institution leaves very little doubt that the most pressing reason for forcing Laughlin to retire was the uproar caused by "Conquest by Immigration". This becomes amply clear in that December 5th, 1939 memorandum prepared for Dr. Bush that detail the events that led up to Laughlin forced to retirement. On one of the many drafts there is a handwritten note that states "Laughlin's acceptance of the blame of retirement" just under the section that recounts the onslaught of negative press between July and August of 1939.

Laughlin also tried to defend the continuation of the eugenics work at the Carnegie owned and funded Cold Spring Harbor facilities. Laughlin answered by drafting his "Proposed Clinic of Human Heredity." (Item Id.: 11710 Eugenics Records). The proposal was addressed to Vannevar Bush. C.M. Goethe stepped in to support Laughlin in a letter to James G. Eddy of the Carnegie Foundation in an October 27th, 1937. C.M. Goethe expresses concern that the Germans would steal the credit away from the American eugenicists, precisely the very juxtaposition that the Carnegie Foundation now sought to avoid:

> The Germans are forging far ahead of us in this matter of accumulated data. They say they have already 4 Nobel prizes to 1 of ours, population considered, and that if we do not accept their methods, they will run away from us with world leaders. (Item No.: 1035, "Harry Laughlin Papers," Truman University)

It also seems that Laughlin attempted to put the full might of his political networking into defending his position at the Eugenics Record Office. The Laughlin files at Carnegie have correspondence from no less than Herbert Hoover, Frederick A. Delano of the State Department, and a Senator from North Carolina named Robert R. Reynolds, who made the most noise. Reynolds served in the Senate's Committee on Immigration and was seeking to reenlist Laughlin's efforts for future legislation. Reynolds contacted and conscripted anyone that may have been interested in keeping Laughlin in order to put political pressure on the Carnegie leadership. It seems that Senator Reynolds insisted that Laughlin be allowed to appear as an expert before the United States Congress again. Dr. Bush responded by insisting that Laughlin would have to "appear as an individual." The memo documents that Dr. Bush also wrote to Laughlin on the same day to reiterate the message that if the Senator wished him to appear before Congress, Laughlin would have to "appear as an individual."

Dr. Bush distributed Senator Reynolds' letters to various key members of the Carnegie team. A response by an Hon. W. Cameron Forbes indicates that those at the Carnegie Institution were keen on the fact that Laughlin had orchestrated the faux outrage that had allegedly ensued due to his forced retirement:

> I have your letter of December 5th, with appropriate information in regard to Senator Reynolds' rather fulminating document. It sounded almost as though he thought he were in position to give orders to the Carnegie Institution. His letter, I should think, might have been written by Laughlin. I was almost tempted to reply to Senator Reynolds that I had just read Mr. Laughlin's letter, to which he had attached his signature . . . (Laughlin files, Carnegie Inst., Dec. 7th, 1939, Forbes to Bush)

Dr. Bush's December 11th, 1939 response to Forbes indicates they were poised to do battle with Laughlin. The letter alludes to "investigations" and utilizes the terminology of legal posturing such as "subjected to an attack" and "strong position". The letter makes clear that Dr. Bush felt they had gathered enough medical evidence to prove that Laughlin was "incapable of directing an office." It also indicates that Dr. Bush suspected Charles B. Davenport had a hand in writing the forceful letters that Senator Reynolds signed as his own.

Most importantly Dr. Bush voices that "an investigation of his scientific standing would be equally conclusive." Dr. Bush made direct reference to damage Laughlin had done to his reputation by taking such an unpalatable political stance based premises not supported by the research. This specific December 11th, 1939 letter from Dr. Bush to Forbes makes it amply clear that it was Laughlin's politics that had become the real liability for the Carnegie Institution. While Laughlin's health was inconvenient and maybe even precarious, its use as justification for a premature retirement was but pretext and legal cover.

Laughlin was keen enough to understand the Carnegie Institution responsibilities in managing the original charter of the ERO, and therefore leveraged it to help his dilemma. Laughlin also understood that he was being forced to retire because of his application of eugenics into practical legislation. It had proven to be politically inconvenient for the Institution. More so, Laughlin was aware that under Merriam his approach had been supported and encouraged. Dr.

Vannevar Bush had reversed this policy, and rightfully so. However, Laughlin also understood that this was a contradiction to the stated scope and purpose of the Eugenics Record Office under the original charter. A letter accompanied by a memo entitled "Studies on the Archives of the Eugenics Record Office" reminds W.M. Gilbert, Carnegie's Administrative Secretary of a paragraph in the Articles of Incorporation that declared the scope of the ERO:

> A paragraph in the Articles of Incorporation of the Institution which declares, in general, "that the objects of the Corporation shall be to encourage, in the broadest and most liberal manner, investigation, research and discovery and the application of knowledge to the improvement of mankind." (Laughlin files, Carnegie Inst., Sep. 16th, 1939, Memo Laughlin to Gilbert, emphasis his)

Laughlin's posturing was insufficient. It is fitting that Charles B. Davenport prepared a statement for Carnegie to publish in the journal SCIENCE. A January 16th, 1940 letter from Streeter to Gilbert of Carnegie insists that any press release make it clear that Laughlin ran the ERO "under the directorship of Dr. C.B. Davenport". The insistence to "bring in the name of Davenport" seems to suggest that the Carnegie leadership wanted it known that Laughlin had conducted all of that now controversial work under one of the most respected scientists of the era.

The Carnegie leadership was also leery of the fiasco getting out of control. A June 15th, 1939 memorandum prepared by W.M. Gilbert for Dr. Bush makes it clear that they were relieved by Laughlin's "voluntary" retirement:

> In Laughlin's telegram to me of June twelfth, in regard to the amount of return on his annuity policy, he uses the word "voluntarily" in referring to retirement. I hope this means that he will act in such a spirit and not broadcast to the world that he has been fired. (Laughlin files, Carnegie Inst. June 15th, 1939, MEMORANDUM FOR DR. BUSH)

In 1939, Dr. Bush officially asked Laughlin to follow his mentor Davenport into retirement. Lombardo tells the story in the context of Laughlin's own ailing health:

> In January 1940, Laughlin was forced into premature retirement. He returned to his boyhood home of Kirksville, Missouri, and spent his last three years studying hereditary qualities of thoroughbred horses. There is no record of how reacted to his own diagnosis of epilepsy, which under his Model Law would have marked him for sterilization. Laughlin died without children on January 23, 1943. (Pgs. 213-214, "Three Generations No Imbeciles")

Thus, in nothing more than the quiet internal politics and deliberations of an institution, the doors were shut on one of the most influential offices in the history of the United States. Professor Garland Allen explains how Laughlin's papers came to be in the possession of Truman University, which was known as Northeast Missouri State University prior to 1995:

> Laughlin and his wife retired to Kirksville in December 1939, bringing with them his many reprints, records kept while he was Superintendent of the ERO, books,

and both professional and personal correspondence. Shortly after his death in 1943, Laughlin's widow gave her husband's papers to the Pickler Memorial Library of Northeast Missouri State. (Pg. 341, "The J.H.B. Archive Report: The Papers of Harry Hamilton Laughlin, Eugenicist", by Randall D. Bird and Garland Allen, Annals of the History of Biology, Vol. 14, no. 2, Fall 1981)

Harry H. Laughlin had significantly altered the course of history by cloaking himself in the objectivity of science and using the political and academic credentials of his supporters to enact sterilization laws in 30 of the States in the Union. He had influenced the creation of major immigration acts in the United States Congress, provided expert testimony for landmark cases before the U.S. Supreme Court, and in turn directly influence the decision makers in Hitler's National Socialist government. Hitler's government bestowed a medal on this relatively obscure American for all these accomplishments. This goes unmentioned to this day even when the plight of all those Americans, Germans, and European Jews is recounted by mainstream historians.

Laughlin's legacy, along with his endless stacks of papers, was swept under the rug. Professor Garland Allen documents in the 1986 paper, "The ERO at Cold Spring Harbor", that Milislav Demerec, the director of the organization that supplanted the ERO at Cold Spring Harbor, had the unfortunate task to clear out the old ERO building. Demerec was confronted with a dilemma since practically no one wanted the millions of index card records, back issues of "Eugenical News", or eugenical pedigree studies. The only institute to voice interest was the Dight Institute. (Pg. 242, Allen) All that work, those hundreds of thousands of dollars invested by the Harriman family, Carnegie, and Rockefeller in the end amounted to be only of a historical value. The money invested literally translates to millions in today's currency value. Ironically, the collections only worth is that of a paper trail for the human-made catastrophe that was the eugenics movement.

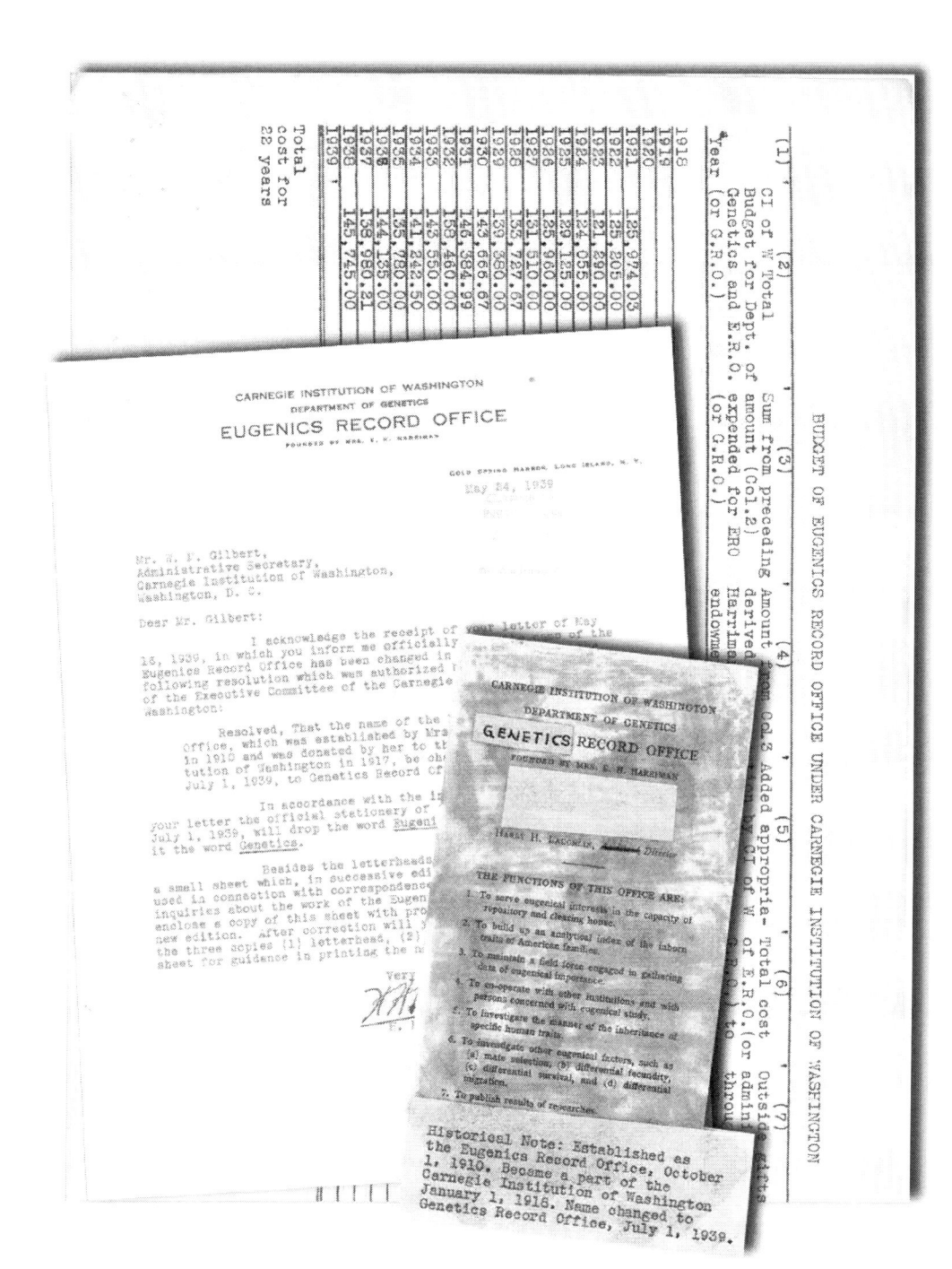

BUDGET OF EUGENICS RECORD OFFICE UNDER CARNEGIE INSTITUTION OF WASHINGTON

(1) Year (or G.R.O.)	(2) CI of W Total Budget for Dept. of Genetics and E.R.O. (or G.R.O.)	(3) Sum from preceding amount (Col.2) expended for ERO (or G.R.O.)	(4) Amount derived from Harriman endowment	(5) Added appropriation by CI of W	(6) Total cost of E.R.O. (or G.R.O.)	(7) Outside gifts to admin through
1918	125,974.03					
1919	125,205.00					
1920	121,290.00					
1921	124,055.00					
1922	121,890.00					
1923	124,055.00					
1924	125,960.00					
1925	123,125.00					
1926	125,960.00					
1927	131,520.00					
1928	135,510.00					
1929	139,360.00					
1930	143,666.67					
1931	146,384.99					
1932	158,460.00					
1933	143,550.00					
1934	141,242.50					
1935	135,780.00					
1936	135,135.00					
1937	138,980.00					
1938	145,745.00					
1939						
Total cost for 22 years						

CARNEGIE INSTITUTION OF WASHINGTON
DEPARTMENT OF GENETICS

EUGENICS RECORD OFFICE

FOUNDED BY MRS. E. H. HARRIMAN

COLD SPRING HARBOR, LONG ISLAND, N.Y.

May 24, 1939

Mr. W. M. Gilbert,
Administrative Secretary,
Carnegie Institution of Washington,
Washington, D. C.

Dear Mr. Gilbert:

I acknowledge the receipt of your letter of May 18, 1939, in which you inform me officially that the Eugenics Record Office has been changed in ___ following resolution which was authorized ___ of the Executive Committee of the Carnegie ___ Washington:

Resolved, That the name of the ___ Office, which was established by Mrs. ___ in 1910 and was donated by her to the ___ tution of Washington in 1917, be changed ___ July 1, 1939, to Genetics Record Office ___

In accordance with the ___ your letter the official stationery of ___ July 1, 1939, will drop the word *Eugenics* ___ it the word *Genetics*.

Besides the letterhead ___ a small sheet which, in successive edi___ used in connection with correspondence ___ inquiries about the work of the Eugen___ enclose a copy of this sheet with pro___ new edition. After correction will ___ the three copies (1) letterhead, (2) ___ sheet for guidance in printing the n___

Very ___

CARNEGIE INSTITUTION OF WASHINGTON
DEPARTMENT OF GENETICS

GENETICS RECORD OFFICE

FOUNDED BY MRS. E. H. HARRIMAN

HARRY H. LAUGHLIN, Director

THE FUNCTIONS OF THIS OFFICE ARE:

1. To serve eugenical interests in the capacity of repository and clearing house.
2. To build up an analytical index of the inborn traits of American families.
3. To maintain a field force engaged in gathering data of eugenical importance.
4. To co-operate with other institutions and with persons concerned with eugenical study.
5. To investigate the manner of the inheritance of specific human traits.
6. To investigate other eugenical factors, such as (a) mate selection, (b) differential fecundity, (c) differential survival, and (d) differential migration.
7. To publish results of researches.

Historical Note: Established as the Eugenics Record Office, October 1, 1910. Became a part of the Carnegie Institution of Washington January 1, 1918. Name changed to Genetics Record Office, July 1, 1939.

CARNEGIE INSTITUTION OF WASHINGTON
DEPARTMENT OF GENETICS
GENETICS RECORD OFFICE
FOUNDED BY MRS. E. H. HARRIMAN

COLD SPRING HARBOR, LONG ISLAND, N. Y.

June 22, 1939.

Dr. Vannevar Bush,
President of the Carnegie Institution of Washington,
Washington, D.C.

Mr. President:—

In response to your letter of June 21, I hereby express my willingness to retire from active duty on January 1, 1940, provided, as you offer, I am allotted a life annuity of $3,000.

Very Sincerely
Harry H. Laughlin

In Laughlin's telegram to me of June twelfth, in regard to the amount of return on his annuity policy, he uses the word "voluntarily" in referring to retirement. I hope this means that he will act in such a spirit and not broadcast to the world that he has been fired.

W. M. Gilbert

1944 - "IN PARI DELICTO"

> "Where all are guilty, no one is; confessions of collective guilt are the best possible safeguard against the discovery of culprits, and the very magnitude of the crime the best excuse for doing nothing."
> - Hannah Arendt

One of the most unfortunate aspects of United States history is the fact that entire boatloads of refugees escaping Hitler's henchmen were turned away. Films like the 1976 "Voyage of the Damned" revisited the history that otherwise played out in the headlines of newspapers. However, seldom have historians extrapolated upon the legislative mechanisms that made it so difficult for refugees to reach the safety of U.S. shores. The consequences of the 1924 Immigration Restriction Act can only be appreciated in the context of its proximate results. Laughlin and his eugenic cohorts would expend a significant amount of effort lobbying to make sure the 1924 Act was both followed, and if possible, expanded. Recall that Laughlin's "Conquest by Immigration" called for a 60% reduction on the already paltry 1924 quotas.

Historians have since documented how F.D.R's administration actively blocked the use of the already limited 25,000 slots available to German Jews per year. The result was an average of 2,000 immigration slots used per year during The Holocaust. Jewish Historians have also documented President Franklin D. Roosevelt's ardently anti-Semitic views. The reader will recognize the eugenic taint of the President's decision-making. Rafael Medoff, author of the 2013 book "FDR and the Holocaust: A Breach of Faith" is but one of the many authors that have revisited this aspect of the Roosevelt Administration. Medoff recalls what those closest to the President wrote in their memoirs about "The Unmentionable Jew", a term referring to the precariousness that prominent cabinet members used to broach the subject.

Yet, the history commonly told blames the American public in general. The commonplace history claims that American bigotry prevented those refugees from reaching the safety of U.S. shores. One of the most important facts documented by Medoff is the April 1944 Gallup poll commissioned by FDR's White House. This crucial poll revealed that 70% of Americans favored the creation of emergency shelters for Jewish refugees, thus disproving that anti-Semitism was either a general or widespread hurdle. Medoff furthermore documents bi-partisan support in the Congress, as well as support from prominent Protestants and Catholics. The Pope himself was also at this moment in history threatening to excommunicate participants in the atrocities. They were joined by outspoken public figures such as Fiorello La Guardia and the famous baseball player, Babe Ruth, speaking out on behalf of the victims. In other words, the world had become aware of the extent of Hitler's crimes, and amidst the outrage, the administration only hunkered down and stiffened their resolution.

Medoff brings up another interesting fact. We know that the 1924 Immigration Restriction Act's core mechanism was to restrict by quotas based on national origins. As discussed in previous chapters, the quota system drastically reduced the amount of those admitted. We also know the unreasonable amount of bureaucratic hoops potential candidates had to jump through just to be considered. Recall that these bureaucratic hoops were largely set up at the consulates abroad in order to whittle away at the potential immigrants at the source. Clearly the "restriction" aspect of the 1924 Act worked as planned. Medoff reports that only 27,408 of the 129,795 slots for German nationals were filled between 1933 to 1937, a meager 21% of an already drastically limited quantity. (Pg. 46)

What is most important about books like "FDR and The Holocaust" is the documentation of FDR's views. While Medoff does not define FDR's views as eugenic, the quotes he does provide can hardly be understood as anything else. The reader will recognize the eugenic flavor to the President's views. The President informed his position on immigration by surrounding himself with Ivy League eugenicists cut of the same cloth as Davenport, Grant, and Laughlin. Medoff documents that Isiah Bowman was placed in charge of the "M [for Migration] Project" in November 1938, in the wake of the *Kristallnacht* pogrom against German Jews. Incidentally, both the FDR and Bowman were products of a Harvard education. Bowman had studied under William Morris Davis, whom predictably, had himself been a product of Nathaniel Shaler. Medoff cites the President's instructions to Bowman. Note the eugenic assumptions:

> The President specifically asked [Bowman's] committee to consider such questions as the following: Is the South Italian stock – say, Sicilian – as good as the North Italian stock – say, Milanese – if given equal social and economic opportunity? (Pg. 30, Rafael Medoff, "FDR and The Holocaust")

In fact, FDR's "M Project" can be said to have been explicitly eugenic as Bowman said so in no uncertain terms. Medoff quotes Bowman:

> Our civilization will decline unless we improve our human breed. To support the genetically unfit and also allow them to breed is to degrade our society. ----
> A people having staked out a territory as we have done in America certainly has the right to look after itself from the **eugenic standpoint**. (Pg. 30, Rafael Medoff, "FDR and The Holocaust", emphasis mine)

Nor can it be said that eugenic thinking was solely attributable to Bowman's influence on the President. Medoff documents an incident that took place in 1923 when Roosevelt was a member of Harvard's Board of Overseers. FDR himself recalled the idea of imposing quotas on Jews serving as Federal employees in Oregon in a November 1941 cabinet meeting. Medoff cites the President:

> Some years ago a third of the entering class at Harvard were Jews and the question came up as to how it should be handled....I asked [a fellow-board

member] whether we should discuss it with the Board of Overseers and it was decided that we should....It was decided that over a period of years the number of Jews should be reduced one or two per cent a year until it was down to 15%....I treat the Catholic situation just the same....I appointed three men in Nebraska – all Catholics – and they wanted me to appoint another Catholic, and I said that I wouldn't do it....You can't get a disproportionate amount of any one religion. (Pg. 19, Rafael Medoff, "FDR and The Holocaust")

The most disgruntled cabinet members were Henry Morgenthau, Jr., the Secretary of the Treasury, and one of his other deputies, Randolph Paul. Medoff cites Morgenthau as privately commenting that the "attitude" from the administration was "no different than Hitler's attitude" in its cold-hearted indifference. (Pg. 100) He quotes Randolph Paul as coming to the conclusion that the administration was in *"para-delicto"*, or of "equal guilt", and "aiding and abetting Hitler." (Pg. 96)

The administration's inaction became too much for either Morgenthau or Paul to bear. They took the growing support for the refugees in Congress as a bolster to their position. On January 16th, 1944, Morgenthau and Paul personally visited the President Roosevelt in order to coerce him to finally act. More diplomatic efforts had failed, so Morgenthau's approach strengthened. The report Morgenthau brought to F.D.R. was, if not a desperate, then a necessary act. It was desperatly needed in order to coerce a response from an administration that was systematically and overtly preventing both private and official help for the victims escaping Hitler. The report documents a pattern of attempts by the State Department to obstruct rescue opportunities and block the flow of intelligence to the United States. Morgenthau warned the President that the refugee issue had become "a boiling pot on [Capitol] Hill," and Congress was likely to pass the rescue resolution if faced with a White House unwilling to act. Roosevelt understood the deep implications and pre-empted Congress. The result was the January 22nd, 1944 "Executive Order 9417" that created the War Refugee Board.

The report Morgenthau and Paul had delivered was titled, "Report to the Secretary on the Acquiescence of this Government in the Murder of the Jews." Josiah DuBois wrote the report, and it was an all-out indictment of the U.S. State Department's diplomatic, military and immigration policies. The Jewish Virtual Library website by the American-Israeli Cooperative Enterprise has a copy of the report posted, reprinted here at length:

> I am convinced on the basis of the information which is available to me that certain officials in our State Department, which – have been guilty not only of gross procrastination and willful failure to act, but even of willful attempts to prevent action from being taken to rescue Jews from Hitler.

The catalyst for the Report was an incident involving 70,000 Jews whose evacuation from Romania could have been procured with a relatively meager

$170,000 bribe. The Foreign Funds Control unit of the U.S. Treasury, which was within Randolph Paul's jurisdiction, had already authorized the payment of the funds. From mid-July 1943, when the proposal was made, through December 1943, the State Department and the British Ministry of Economic Warfare interposed various obstacles. The report continues:

> Unless remedial steps of a drastic nature are taken, and taken immediately, I am certain that no effective action will be taken by this government to prevent the complete extermination of the Jews in German controlled Europe, and that this Government will have to share for all time responsibility for this extermination. (January 13th, 1944, "Report to the Secretary on the Acquiescence of this Government in the Murder of the Jews")

The report enumerates the pattern of delay tactics intended to prevent the immigration of Jewish refugees:

> (1) They have not only failed to use the Governmental machinery at their disposal to rescue Jews from Hitler, but have even gone so far as to use this Government machinery to prevent the rescue of these Jews.
> (2) They have not only failed to cooperate with private organizations in the efforts of these organizations to work out individual programs of their own, but have taken steps designed to prevent these programs from being put into effect.
> (3) They not only have failed to facilitate the obtaining of information concerning Hitler's plans to exterminate the Jews of Europe but in their official capacity have gone so far as to surreptitiously attempt to stop the obtaining of information concerning the murder of the Jewish population of Europe.
> (January 13, 1944, "Report to the Secretary on the Acquiescence of this Government in the Murder of the Jews")

Keep in mind that this incredibly harsh report came from within the President's Cabinet. The report accuses the heads of the U.S. State Department as actively trying to "cover up their guilt by" acts of "concealment and misrepresentation," the "giving of false and misleading explanations" for their "failures to act", as well as their willful "attempts to prevent action." The implications were clearly detrimental to the administration.

Prior to the State Department, Hull had been a congressman from the Fourth Tennessee District from 1907 for the Democratic National Party, and served as a U.S. Representative until 1931, interrupted only by two years as Chairman of the Democratic National Committee. In his career in Congress, Hull was a member of the House Ways and Means Committee for eighteen years as well as the author of Progressive legislation such as the first Federal Income Tax Bill of 1913. Hull is also recognized as the "Father of the United Nations." Together with Alger Hiss, who would later be exposed as a Communist spy, Hull headed the creation of the United Nations in 1941. Hull and his staff drafted the original charter in 1943, and as Julian Huxley's eugenic work while at UNESCO evidences the United Nations eugenic mindset at the time.

In order to comprehend how so many Europeans, Jewish and non-Jewish alike, were turned away by the U.S. State Department, one must first understand that this level of micro-management by a single agency of the U.S. government was not possible before 1924. While the State Department has always been in charge of immigration and naturalization in some capacity, the Secretary of State is not consulted on a case by case basis on the entry of foreign individuals. The position Secretary of State is part of the President's Cabinet, and otherwise too important, especially during a world war, to preoccupy itself with the job that is otherwise relegated to lower level immigration officials. Secretary of State Cordell Hull was given this inordinate amount of power precisely because the acceptance of Jews, along with many other ethnicities, was made illegal by the 1924 Immigration Restriction Act of 1924. This level of centralized control had been the intent of the 1924 Act, after all. Laughlin would boast about his contribution towards passing the 1924 Act in a January 3rd, 1925 letter to E.S. Gosney, one of the heads of California's highly touted eugenics movement:

> The report on immigration has been printed and I have sent you a copy. I have had the pleasure of seeing this study bear some fruit in connection with the work of the House Committee on Immigration and Naturalization. I shall try to keep up these studies for the purpose of doing what I can to insure the biological or racial basis for developing our immigration policy. This policy ultimately is bound to take the place of our primary economic viewpoint, and the sooner our national immigration laws and their administration are supported by the biological or family-stock viewpoint, the more surely will eugenics be serving the nation. (E.S. Gosney Papers, Caltech Univ. Archives, Folder 7.2 – Box 7)

The true intent behind the 1924 Act is evidenced by the internal correspondence of the Immigration Restriction League. The report entitled "The New Immigration Act of 1924" was authored by a "Committee on Selective Immigration", which included Madison I, Chairman, Robert DeC. Ward, Vice-Chairman and Acting Chairman, H.H. Laughlin, Secretary, Charles W. Gould, Lucien Howe, Roswell H. Johnson, Francis H. Kinnicutt, John B. Trevor. The above list mirrors the membership of the Immigration Restriction League. The report reveals the impetus behind the legislative effort to cut off immigrants at the source nation:

> Although the Immigration Act of 1924 contains no specific provisions looking towards a more rigid exclusion of eugenically undesirable aliens, it is accomplishing a better selection than has hitherto been possible. It embodies the first real attempt which the United States has ever made to conduct a preliminary selection abroad. Under the new law, a consular officer may refuse to issue an immigration visa, "if he knows or has reason to believe that the immigrant is inadmissible to the United States under the immigration laws." While the new plan involves a large amount of paper work, and while there will surely be many cases of perjury and of fraud, **many aliens who have been declared excludable for eugenical or other reasons can be headed off by our consuls** when application is made. (Pg. 2, THE NEW IMMIGRATION ACT OF

1924 - Second report of the Sub-Committee on Selective Immigration of the Eugenics Committee of the United States of America, E.S. Gosney Papers, Caltech Univ. Archives, Folder 7.2 – Box 7, emphasis mine)

In effect, what Morgenthau was asking for FDR's State Department to do was to waive the 1924 Act in the face of an unprecedented emergency. More poignantly, any competent politician or legislator that remembered the controversy during the passing of the 1924 Act knew perfectly well that it was wholeheartedly the product of eugenic racial policies. All of this would inevitably create a serious problem for the F.D.R. administration, as mounting criticism came from the American Jewish community. As discussed throughout the book, eugenics was also recognized as being part of the Progressive political platform, and F.D.R.'s administration was regarded as synonymous with Progressivism. Bowman was one of the many members of the administration that was publically recognized as aligned with the eugenics of the Progressive movement. Supreme Court Justice Robert H. Jackson had been one of the leaders of F.D.R.'s election committee and recognized as an F.D.R. man by the time he wrote the <u>Skinner v. Oklahoma</u> opinion which upheld sterilization for eugenic reasons. The Robert H. Jackson Papers held at the Library of Congress contain several boxes dedicated to his work as part of the leadership of F.D.R.'s campaign staff. There are many letters from prominent politicians, fellow judges, attorneys, and the general public congratulating him for his hand in winning the presidential campaigns he helped FDR win. In other words, Morgenthau's report revealed the eugenic wing of the Progressives was woven into the fabric of F.D.R's administration.

To make matters worse, the administration had gone out of its way to not just uphold the 1924 Act, but to go beyond its already stringent measures. It was actively preventing those attempting to flee Europe from using the few slots available in the quotas. Newspaper articles from the era reveal that it was public knowledge that even the unreasonably restricted quotas had gone unused. Here is a sample of the newspaper coverage as the events unfolded:

> Far from being a human rubble heap, displaced Jewish populations would soon become economic assets to Europe as well as to this country and others through a limited immigration and resettlement program, speakers asserted. ---- Mr. Johnson urged strong support for the bill introduced in Congress by Representative William G. Strantton, Republican, of Illinois, calling for admittance of 100,000 DP's a year for four years. He said that this would recapture 40 percent of the unused quotas of the war period. (NYT, June 5th, 1947, "Jewish Group Asks Aid for Displaced")

This New York Times article is indicative of the political debate that arose from the refugee problem. It documents how some Republicans, Roosevelt's political enemies, would introduce legislation to bring DP's (Displaced Persons) to the United States by using the unfilled quotas from the last five years of the war.

Elections have serious implications for how the United States conducts itself abroad. Foreign policy in the United States is often a reflection of domestic political battles. One can easily argue that FDR reacted out of political calculation, not empathy for the victims, as a result of Paul's and Morgenthau's report and the political pressure coming from the Republican Congressmen.

TIME
THE WEEKLY NEWSMAGAZINE

SCIENCE

Eugenics for Democracy

Many a sociologist and historian used to agree with Paleontologist Henry Fairfield Osborn that Anglo-Saxons were God's special gift to earth. Osborn was a leading eugenist in the days when many believed that the "unfit" should be weeded out rather than cared for under public health measures which coddled weaklings, allowed them to reproduce, ultimately lead to an inferior stock. While these ideas have occasionally furnished fodder for opponents of public housing, relief, the New Deal, the only places where they are still flourishing today are Nazi Germany and Italy. Long before Henry Osborn died in 1935, a new generation was hard knocking them down.

Among the leaders of the new, mental-eugenics is Frederick Osborn of Manhattan, sixty-odd nephew of the late Henry Fairfield. A sometime railroad executive (president of Tosch), and Ironton R. R., Frederick Osborn in 1928 decided to devote his energies to something he liked, discussed many times the problem of heredity with his uncle. He took seriously, is now a director of the American Eugenics Society. Last week, in *Preface to Eugenics* (Harper), Mr. Osborn presented the scientific evidence to demolish the last remnants of his uncle's fancy.

Heredity & Environment. There is evidence that any racial group or class has more native intelligence than another. There are more variations in ability among individuals of a group than among any social or racial groups. Children tend to be like their parents in hereditary capacity; if their endowments are weak, not even a college education can make them bright. "In the limiting circumstances of isolated and marginal people," said Mr. Osborn, "good hereditary capacities do not have a chance to develop as they would in a better environment... environment equalized at a higher level would show up a superior heredity in numbers, of persons now at a low level of development."

Genetic Inheritance. In the U. S. it is estimated three to five million persons suffer from serious incapacities (feeblemindedness, mental disease, blindness, deafness, etc.) for which their heredity is in part responsible. Voluntary sterilization...

August 12, 1939.

Prof. Dr. Ernst Rudin, President,
Fourth International Congress for Eugenics,
Einemstrasse 11,
Berlin W 62, Germany.

Dear Professor Rudin,

    We have just received announcement of the Fourth International Congress of Eugenics. Workers in this field in all of the countries of Pan America congratulate the International Committee on its selection of Rudin as President, of Vienna for the site, and 1940 for the date. The whole setting presages a successful meeting.

    In order to hold the advances thus far made in building the science of Eugenics and to plan the next steps in research and trial, it is necessary that a new congress assembles soon; that its business be to take stock of the world's knowledge of human heredity; to evaluate the technique of practical population-control; and to exchange experiences and plans among leaders in the biological betterment of mankind.

    I am taking the pleasure in sending by today's parcel post to your laboratory, addressed to the President of the Fourth International Congress of Eugenics, a package of books ... some records of the past ... on the subject of eugenics ...

Truly yours,

Harry H. Laughlin
Secretary of the
...onal Congress of Eugenics.

AMNESIA OR DÉJÃ VU...?

> *"History, despite its wrenching pain,*
> *Cannot be unlived, but if faced*
> *With courage, need not be lived again."*
> *- Maya Angelou, On the Pulse of Morning*

Some that read this book will find its Libertarian and Constitutionalist slant a bit obtuse and maybe even off-putting. This author makes no appologies for viewing the history of the eugenics movement from this political perspective. It is the ethical and legal underpinnings of the American Revolution that remain as a guiding light while the eugenics movement continues to reemerge long after its alleged demise. Limited, or rather minimal government, goes a long way to curtail the disconnect that emerges when government grows so large that it no longer feels compelled to heed to the dictates of the governed.

The giving of care to the needy is where government's alleged benevolence can be best judged. Historically there has been a slide from private to public institutions in the caretaking of the needy. The Veteran's Administration scandal of 2014 is a prime case of the emotional indifference found in government-run institutions. Those made physically or mentally "defective" due to the ravages of war were treated in not a dissimilar way from the lists of the "hereditary defective" during the eugenics era. Government employees must be lauded for their devotion to service, but their motivations differ from the emotional investment inherent in religious charities, by contrast. Government jobs are a career, and as we have seen, budgets create competition between caretaker and the cared for. Salaries compete with benefits. Job security competes with inmate population. The ward's interests often compete with the warden's political calculations. More specifically, the centrally-planned economics of the "welfare state" are specifically vulnerable to unproductive and over-abundant populations that draw from their carefully allocated and limited resources.

Case in point, whenever eugenics has reemerged in a post-Holocaust world, it is has been the very large footprint of a government that is to blame. It is, therefore, refreshing to see L.C. Dunn include in his June 1951 UNESCO "Statement" the notions enshrined in the Declaration of Independence. Point number eight states:

> We now have to consider the bearing of these statements on the problem of human equality. We wish to emphasize that equality of opportunity and equality in law in no way depend, as ethical principles, upon the assertion that human beings are in fact equal in endowment. (June 1951, "Statement on the Nature of Race and Race Differences", UNESCO)

The consequence of an incomplete telling of this history is that the allure of eugenics, that desire to jettison society's dead weight, to breed humans free of the undesirable traits, would inevitably endure. The pattern of paternalism in eugenics is nowhere clearer than in the history of Native Americans. The consequences of paternalism have been dire since the Native American population was deemed as "domestic dependent nations" and as "wards of the state" by the Supreme Court in 1831. Sally J. Torpy of the California Department of Parks and Recreation's Indian Museum wrote a piece entitled "Native American Women and Coerced Sterilization: On the Trail of Tears in the 1970s." It was published by the American Indian Culture and Research Journal. In it she recounts how Native Americans as "wards of the state" became the victims of eugenic-minded doctors and social planners in the decades after The Holocaust:

> Thousands of poor women and women of color, including Puerto Ricans, Blacks, and Chicanos, were sterilized in the 1970s, often without full knowledge of the surgical procedure performed on them or its physical and psychological ramifications. Native American women represented a unique class of victims among the larger population that faced sterilization and abuses of reproductive rights. These women were especially accessible victims due to several unique cultural and societal realities setting them apart from other minorities. Tribal dependence on the federal government through the Indian Health Service (HIS), the Department of Health, Education, and Welfare (HEW), and the Bureau of Indian Affairs (BIA) robbed them of their children and jeopardized their future as sovereign nations. Native women's struggle to obtain control over reproductive rights has provided them with a sense of empowerment consistent with larger Native American efforts to be free of institutional control. (Pg. 1, S.J. Torpy, "Native American Women and Coerced Sterilization: On the Trail of Tears in the 1970s", Am. Indian Culture and Research Journal, 24:2, 2000, 1-22)

Torpy recounts the plight of the women that had the courage to speak up. She laments the fact that there are many more victims to the "paternalistic and racist beliefs" of government institutions. We simply do not know about them precisely because many of these women were coerced with threats of losing their children or having their welfare benefits taken away. In many cases, namely that of Norma Jean Serena, the Armstrong County Child Welfare Service acted on its threats and took her children away. (Pg. 2) A jury would later determine that she was subjected to a tubal ligation and her children placed in foster homes under false pretenses.

The reader will recall that many of these victims of eugenical sterilization in the early 20th Century were told they were undergoing an appendectomy only to find out years later that they had been sterilized. In the case of welfare women, the consent forms were also obtained after the operations had already been carried out or while under sedation in the tense moments just prior to a caesarean birth. Torpy traces the impetus behind the dubious practices to the advent of the welfare state, or in other words, Progressivism:

> Other significant influences in the late 1960s, such as government concern over the growing population, prompted President Richard M. Nixon's appointment of John D. Rockefeller III as chairman of the new Commission on Population and the American Future. President Lyndon B. Johnson's previous War on Poverty reflected fear that world resources would not be able to provide for the future

population. Political and social pressures to limit family size and push sterilization helped lead to the new Office of Economic Opportunity, an organization that sought federal funds to provide not only education and training to the poor, but also a less well-known service: contraception. The Family Planning Act of 1970 passed the Senate by an overwhelming vote of 298 to thirty-two. Statistics reflect the combined impact that this new legislation and medical practices had on minority women. During the 1970s, HEW funded 90 percent of the annual sterilization costs for poor people. Sterilization for women increased 350 percent between 1970 and 1975 and approximately one million American women were sterilized each year. Physicians and social workers found themselves in a potent situation in which they could use, but in reality abuse, their authority in dealing with poor and minority families and their reproductive rights. The conflicting needs and rights between women of different economic background and color coinciding with new fertility laws, medical advancement, and tenacious eugenic lore, culminated in disaster for many women. Inevitably, examples of blatant and subtle coercion became public. (Pg. 3, S.J. Torpy, "Native American Women and Coerced Sterilization", Am. Indian Culture and Research Journal, 24:2, 2000, 1-22)

Torpy documents that the growing outrage inspired the creation of several groups, namely the Committee to End Sterilization Abuse and the Committee for Abortion Rights and Against Sterilization Abuse. She documents the various lawsuits that inevitably resulted. Most importantly, she documents how close the measures came to eradicating an already miniscule Native American population. Ironically enough, the social planners focused their fears of "overpopulation" on a culture whose numbers were already decimated. Of the 800,000 Native Americans living during the 1970s, the sterilization measures brought the number of women of a reproductive age below 100,000. A General Accounting Office did a study involving Albuquerque, Phoenix, Oklahoma City, and Aberdeen, South Dakota. They found that between 1973 and 1976 HIS facilities sterilized 3,406 Native American women. (Pg. 7) Torpy points out that these 3,406 women were the equivalent of 452,000 of the general American population being sterilized under dubious or false circumstances. Torpy also makes it a point to emphasize that these acts had repeated themselves because the paternalistic attitudes towards ethnic minorities that were seen as "over-breeders" or as a dependents:

> Physicians were convinced that welfare patients were unreliable and not intelligent enough to properly use other methods of birth control such as contraceptive devices or pills. Physicians played God, deciding for the poor or minority member what they felt would provide a higher standard of living by limiting the size of families. Many physicians, government administrators, and health corporation planners felt that sterilization provided an inexpensive and permanent method of controlling population, reducing poverty, and insuring who could reproduce. (Pg. 12, S.J. Torpy, "Native American Women and Coerced Sterilization: On the Trail of Tears in the 1970s", Am. Indian Culture and Research Journal, 24:2, 2000, 1-22)

A series of more recent events also prove L.C. Dunn's foresight right. This became amply clear the summer of 2013 when 148 female inmates at the Valley State Prison in California were sterilized against their will. The event was an eerily parallel practice of the eugenics from one-hundred years prior. The Center for Investigative Reporting found that these 148 sterilizations were conducted between the years of 2006 and 2010, mostly without the consent or knowledge of the women. The women were heavily sedated and strapped to an operating table in preparation for a C-section when consent was allegedly obtained. The excuse given by OG-GYN that conducted these operations, Dr. James Heinrich, reveals the eugenic nature of his sterilization campaign. A July 10th, 2013 letter from California State Senator Ted W. Lieu to Dr. Sharon Levine of the California Medical Board cites the doctor's reasoning. Dr. Heinrich, an apt name for one practicing eugenics, claimed the reason for the sterilizations was as a measure to "save in welfare paying for these unwanted children – as they procreated more."

Patrick McGreevy and Phil Willon wrote an article about the incident in the July 13th, 2013 Los Angeles Times. They give an account of how consent was obtained by fraudulent means:

> Kelli Thomas of Los Angeles was an inmate in Chowchilla when she went into surgery for a biopsy and to have two cysts removed. She gave the doctor permission to remove her ovaries if cancer was found, she said, but she told him she hoped it wouldn't be necessary. Thomas said she told the doctor she wanted to have children when she left prison, where she served a sentence for voluntary manslaughter of a domestic partner she said was abusive. Her medical records show that no cancer was found but her ovaries were removed, according to Cynthia Chandler, co-founder of Justice Now and a law professor at Golden Gate University, who reviewed the records. (July 13th, 2013, "California Prisons Sterilized 148 Women", Los Angeles Times)

Here were the most educated representatives of the State of California, its doctors, concluding that the undesireable would only produce equally unwanted children. These doctors utilized their position of power to violate the bodily integrity of these women at the moment when they were the most vulnerable.

Nor can it be said that these 148 women were the unfortunate victims of an anomalous chapter in contemporary medicine. This has repeated itself over and over again in the decades after The Holocaust. To the contrary, there is a discernible pattern of eugenic activism by the medical profession. Anne-Emmanuelle Birn, ScD, MA and Natalia Molina, Ph.D., MA wrote the editorial entitled "In the Name of Public Health" for the July 2006 American Journal of Public Health. The editorial documents the modern age of California eugenics where doctors exercised their eugenic beliefs by sterilizing ethnic minorities. They expose how after WWII the movement became part of the "cost saving" measures of the welfare state:

> Although many accounts portray eugenics as a unitary movement informed by conservative ideas and supported by political counterparts, it was above all a

technocratic development that could be and was appropriated and refashioned by utopians, social progressives, nativists, and Nazis. ---- In linking eugenics to right-wing political agendas, some scholars have inaccurately pointed to the end of World War II and the discrediting of "Nazi science" at the Nuremberg Trials as the demise of eugenics. Yet, as Stern shows for California, eugenics did not disappear then; support for eugenic sterilization merged with growing concerns about over-population and family planning. Birth control, at bottom a technocratic measure, was also appropriated differentially by various actors. Seized upon as a means of freedom for elite and middle-class women, birth control has had more conflicted meanings and consequences for poor and working-class women around the world. (Pg. 1096, "In the Name of Public Health", Am. Journal of Public Health, July 2005, Vol. 95, No. 7)

Dr. Birn's and Dr. Molina's editorial was a review of Alexandra Minna Stern's paper entitled "Sterilized in the Name of Public Health: Race, Immigration, and Reproductive Control in Modern California." Stern also clarifies the fact that the reemergence of eugenics occurred in 1964when federal agencies began their family planning measures as part of the Lyndon B. Johnson's War on Poverty. (Pg. 1128) Stern recounts how the Progressive politics of the era became the impetus behind the measures:

> A series of overlapping factors created the milieu for widespread sterilization abuse in the United States from the late 1960s to the mid-1970s. This period saw the confluence of the gains of mainstream feminism with regard to reproductive rights, an unprecedented federal commitment to family planning and community health, and the popularity of the platform of zero population growth, which was endorsed by immigration restrictionists and environmentalists and put into practice on the operating table by some zealous physicians. (Pg. 1132, A.M. Stern, "Sterilized in the Name of Public Health: Race, Immigration, and Reproductive Control in Modern California", Am. Journal of Public Health, July 2005, Vol. 95, No. 7)

Stern retraces the transition from the eugenics of the 1930s to the eugenics emerging from the activist environmentalist, reproductive rights, and zero population growth crowd, again, the strongholds of Progressive politics:

> [A]n emphasis on parenting skills and welfare dependency began to supplant hereditary fitness and putative innate mental capacity as the determinants of an individual's social and biological drain on society. By this time, many eugenicists had conceded that earlier attempts to stamp out hereditary traits defined as recessive or latent, including alcoholism, immorality, and the catchall "feeblemindedness," had been proven futile by the Hardy-Weinberg equilibrium principle. ---- Accompanying this realignment was a heightened interest in the manipulation and management of human heredity through population control, which postwar eugenicists and their allies pursued through groups such as the Population Council, Population Reference Bureau, and Planned Parenthood. ON the basis of a revamped rationale of bad parenthood and population burden, sterilizations increased in the 1950s and 1960s in southern states such as North Carolina and Virginia. Concurrently, sterilization often regained a punitive edge

and, preponderantly aimed at African American and poor women, began to be wielded by state courts and legislatures as a punishment for bearing illegitimate children or as extortion to ensure ongoing receipt of family assistance. By the 1960s, the protracted history of state sterilization programs in the United States, and the consolidation of a rationale for reproductive surgery that was linked to fears of overpopulation, welfare dependency, and illegitimacy, set the state for a new era of sterilization abuse. (Pg. 1132, A.M. Stern, "Sterilized in the Name of Public Health: Race, Immigration, and Reproductive Control in Modern California", Am. Journal of Public Health, July 2005, Vol. 95, No. 7)

Stern makes it a point to emphasize how the goals and values of Progressive-minded activists drastically contrasted those of ethnic minorities that viewed childbearing in more traditional ways:

While many minority and working-class women also clamored for greater reproductive control, they often found themselves combating the reverse equation, namely, that they were destructive overbreeders whose procreative tendencies needed to be managed. Given that the family planning model was underpinned by the principle of population control and the idea of 2 to 3 children per couple, a substantial influx of resources into birth control services and the absence of standardized consent protocols made the environment ripe for coercion. (Pg. 1133, A.M. Stern, "Sterilized in the Name of Public Health: Race, Immigration, and Reproductive Control in Modern California", Am. Journal of Public Health, July 2005, Vol. 95, No. 7)

Stern documents cases such as <u>Madrigal v. Quilligan</u> and <u>Relf v. Weinberger</u> where obstetrics departments in family planning clinics and delivery rooms were "meeting quotas." Young residents took advantage of a sector of the female population lacking the wherewithal to defend their rights in order to gain surgical experience. Karen Benker worked at one of these hospitals and appeared as a witness in <u>Madrigal v. Quilligan</u>. Her testimony echoes so many of the cases documented in this book:

She recalled conversations in which Dr. Edward James Quilligan, the lead defendant and head of Obstetrics and Gynecology at County General since 1969, stated, "poor minority women in L.A. County were having too many babies; that it was a strain on society; and that it was good that they be sterilized." She also testified that he boasted about a federal grant for over $2 billion dollars he intended to use to show, in his words, "how low we can cut the birth rate of the Negro and Mexican populations in Los Angeles County." (Pg. 1135, A.M. Stern, "Sterilized in the Name of Public Health", Am. Journal of Public Health, July 2005, Vol. 95, No. 7)

It would be a mistake to dismiss these examples as mismanagement of otherwise well-intended government agencies. This pattern always includes the heavy hand of government acting on a misguided sense of paternalism. These eugenic endeavors are always the product of the individual being subsumed under the prerogative of the collective, and by extension, individual rights trampled in the name of the social good. The ideological father of Progressivism, the economist Keynes, was a devoted eugenicist before and after WWII. He understood that the Achilles heel of a centrally-planned economy was an out of control population or a disbalance between the productive and dependent sectors. The 'plans' for the centrally-planned society are easily upturned if the population itself is not also meticulously planned. "Total" control is a necessity of the "Total State," after all.

Nor can it be said that these were the rumblings of 20th Century ideologues and zealots. Stern aptly pointed out that it was those ideologically committed toward planning for a more environmentally sound society, or for a welfare state, that focused on "zero population growth" and "reproductive rights." This is a trend that has not changed. Unsurprisingly, Jonathan Gruber, one of the mastermind's behind the Affordable Care Act (Obamacare) has written favorably of the eugenic aspects of abortion. His aptly titled 2007 paper, "Abortion and Selection," throws around terminology that would make Laughlin and Osborn proud. (Pgs. 124-136, The Review of Economics and Statistics, Feb. 2009) Gruber's paper attempts to find a correlation between the 1973 Roe v. Wade decision, "positive selection," and the "quality" of the population. The 2014 headlines evidence Gruber's paternalistic thinking, as he became infamous for claiming that the "stupidity" of the American voter was a necessity in passing the Affordable Care Act.

We can also begin to conclude this book as it began. The elite students of the 21st Century are being taught by eugenically-minded ideologues as they were at the beginning of the 20th Century. Recall the pivotal role schools like Harvard had in the creation of the American eugenics movement. The online journal, Edge.org published a series of articles on the topic of "What should we be worried about?" The entry by Geoffrey Miller, an evolutionary psychologist at NYU, discusses Chinese Eugenics as a long-term threat to the West. The following quote will ring similar to those found on previous pages:

> Many scientists and reformers of Republican China (1912-1949) were ardent Darwinians and Galtonians. They worried about racial extinction (miezhong) and "the science of deformed fetuses" (jitaixue), and saw eugenics as a way to restore China's rightful place as the world's leading civilization after a century of humiliation by European colonialism. (Edge.org, 2013, Geoffrey Miller, "What should we be worried about?")

On January 16th, 2013 Kevin MacDonald of the Occidental Observer reviewed Miller's paper in an article titled "The Big Questions: Eugenics and Ethno-States." It would be difficult to contain one's laughter if the topic were not so dire. The Occidental Observer's full name is "Occidental Observer: **White Identity**, Interests, and Culture." (emphasis mine) History certainly has a strange way of repeating itself. Can we really continue to feign surprise to find a Progressive eugenicist, from a prestigious educational institution like NYU, in ideological alignment with white supremacists?

Page 2

the Legislature with recommendations to ensure unauthorized surgical procedures on patients never happen...

Sincerely,

TED W. L...
Chair, Sen...

HANNA...
Vice-Cha...

NOREE...
Chair, S...
Former...

California State Senate

STATE CAPITOL, ROOM 4061
SACRAMENTO, CA 95814
TEL (916) 651-4028
FAX (916) 323-9058

DISTRICT OFFICE
2512 ARTESIA BLVD., SUITE 320
REDONDO BEACH, CA 90278
TEL (310) 318-6994
FAX (310) 318-6733

WWW.SEN.CA.GOV/LIEU
SENATOR.LIEU@SEN.CA.GOV

SENATOR
TED W. LIEU
TWENTY-EIGHTH SENATE DISTRICT

CHAIR
BUSINESS, PROFESSIONS AND
ECONOMIC DEVELOPMENT

MEMBER
AGRICULTURE
GOVERNMENTAL ORGANIZATION
INSURANCE
VETERANS AFFAIRS

July 10, 2013

Sharon Levine, M.D.
President, Medical Board of California
2005 Evergreen Street, Suite 1200
Sacramento, CA 95815

Dear Dr. Levine:

An investigation by the Center for Investigative Reporting (CIR) found 148 female inmates were sterilized without state approval between 2006 and 2010. The CIR story also describes incidents in which inmates were forced or coerced into "consenting" for tubal ligations. One situation occurred when a doctor asked his patient to agree to a tubal ligation when she was sedated and strapped to an operating table for a C-section. Other incidents involved doctors repeatedly harassing and pressuring inmates to get tubal ligations. Particularly troubling was a statement by Dr. James Heinrich, OG-GYN at Valley State Prison, who made a reference that tubal ligations on inmates "save in welfare paying for these unwanted children – as they procreated more."

We are writing to request the Medical Board to investigate the practices and conduct of the physicians involved in tubal ligations at California state prisons. A physician's sole and only concern should be that of the patient. Whether a surgical procedure would have any hypothetical effect on welfare rolls should never, ever play a part in a doctor's decision. Physicians are also expected to "First, do no harm" to their patients. Physicians are required to get actual consent--not a coerced agreement--before performing a surgical procedure on a patient, especially in the case of a tubal ligation, which can have life altering effects and is largely irreversible.

The CIR story raises troubling allegations that doctors violated state law, disregarded ethical guidelines, and fell well below the standard of care. Physicians licensed in California are required to follow California laws and regulations, and are subject to the regulatory authority of the Medical Board. We ask that you investigate the physicians involved in unapproved female inmate sterilizations at California state prisons and determine whether any disciplinary actions or license revocations are warranted. We also request that you provide

FORGETTING OR FOREBODING...?

> *"Hitler should be made honorary member of the E.R.O.!!"*
> – Harry H. Laughlin

Why does The Holocaust persist in haunting our conscience? Why does it dominate the introspection of philosophers and historians alike? By the numbers alone, the murders were not unprecedented. At that juncture of 20th Century history, Stalin and Lenin had already brutally murdered tens of millions. The Holocaust fascinates not because of its numbers, but because of the means employed. At no point in time had an entire society dedicated its full might to the perpetual elimination of those unwanted elements of the population. Every aspect of Hitler's National Socialism was geared towards cleansing and improving the breeding stock of *Germania*. Hitler's National Socialist government was focused on the breeding, education, and training of a "master race." The social, cultural, legislative, and industrial mechanisms of Hitler's National Socialism were designed to perpetually "select" its populace. The central planners of National Socialism would "select" those that would live, those that would die, and those that would be sterilized slave labor. National Socialism was intended to have the "total" control to decide who would be allowed to procreate, and as a result, those that would be allowed to contribute to Hitler's ideal society.

There are nuances that must not escape us. Hitler's greatest savagery was not focused on outsiders, but on the insiders. The German Jews were not foes from a foreign nation. They were patriotic Germans, many who had fought bravely in the Great War and which contributed positively to German society. We must also recall that Hitler's first 400,000 victims were of "Aryan" ethnicity with birth defects, diseases, or psychological ailments as mild as alcoholism and depression. The first victim of Hitler's euthanasia campaign was an infant of "Aryan" parenthood. The infant had the misfortune of coming into the world with birth defects, and at the unfortunate time when Hitler's government was looking for a precedent upon which to legalize their eugenic policies.

The personality profile of the perpetrators certainly contributes to our continued awe and disbelief. However, it seems that historians have spent too much time obsessing over Hitler's street thugs, the Brown Shirts. They have spent a disproportionately small amount of time on the industrial, scientific, and legislative might that was necessary for the scale of the murder machine that Nazi Germany became. The Brown Shirts, brutal as they may have been, murdered in the thousands, while their counterparts in lab coats and tailored suits murdered in the millions. Hitler's policies were drafted and carried out by highly educated professionals. Thus, we are horrified that it was the scientists, the engineers, the judges and doctors who were Hitler's "willing executioners." Therefore, in order to truly understand The Holocaust, it is these doctors, these judges, these scientists and legislators that must become the focus of our inquiry.

So how did society's most revered members become its greatest menace? L.C. Dunn became president of the American Society for Human Genetics in 1961. In his presidential address that year, Dunn noted that in the early decades of the twentieth century, the excitement that surrounded scientific discoveries fed the eugenics movement.

> "Rapid translation of new knowledge into terms applicable to improvements of man's lot is at such time," Dunn warned, "likely to take precedence over objective and skeptical evaluation of the facts." Dunn was concerned that this tendency, like other "defects in adolescent period of human genetics," had not disappeared, even late in his own career. (Pg. 279, "Three Generations No Imbeciles")

We must also recall that some of these prominent intellectuals did not recant their eugenic views after The Holocaust. John Maynard Keynes, after all, remained part of the British eugenics movement for the rest of his life. Darwin's grandson, Charles Galton Darwin, would help commence Mankind Quarterly, the infamous journal which became a megaphone for the scientists Wycliffe Draper funded.

Nor has the support for eugenics hurt some of the most prominent scientists of the 20th Century. Julian Huxley used his position at the United Nations (UNESCO) to publish pro-eugenics documents. Huxley did so only three to four years removed from the Nuremberg Trials, with the embers at the extermination camp ovens still burning. Huxley had been the face of British eugenics for decades. He had taken every opportunity to market the beliefs of the movement in all of the leading newspapers around the world, granting interviews and offering pro-eugenic quotes on a consistent basis. Yet, when it came time to write his memoirs, Huxley would completely leave out mention of the decades of work he did for the cause. Yet, Huxley remains as one of the most respected individuals in the history of science.

It would be left to scientists like L.C. Dunn to clean up the public relations disaster left in the wake of the eugenic-minded papers Huxley published under the UNESCO banner. L.C. Dunn and other scientists would publish a retraction in the June 1951 "Statement on the Nature of Race and Race Differences":

> There was no delay or hesitation or lack of unanimity in reaching the primary conclusion that there were no scientific grounds whatever for the racialist position regarding purity of race and the hierarchy of inferior and superior races to which this leads. (June 1951, "Statement on the Nature of Race and Race Differences", UNESCO)

Half a century after Dunn, Professor Garland Allen made a similar observation in his 2011 paper, "Eugenics and Modern Biology." Evidently, what Dunn forecasted has been proven largely true:

> We have been treated for several decades at the end of the 20th century to a barrage of claims about the genetic basis of a multitude of human complex behaviors, from I.Q. to criminality, aggressiveness, alcoholism, shyness, sexual

orientation, manic depression, bipolar disorder and attention-deficit hyperactive-disorder – even "religiosity." Many of these claims have not held up to careful scrutiny, and all have been criticized for the same faults for which the older eugenic studies were found guilty. (Pg. 324, "Eugenics and Modern Biology")

Dunn and Allen are perfectly correct that the lessons of history have not been absorbed. This criticism directly applies equally to academia. It seems that there was a rush to erase the memory of American eugenics once historians began to link the movement to the crimes of The Holocaust. We know that the Carnegie Institution made it a point to "drop the word <u>Eugenics</u> and substitute it for the word <u>Genetics</u>" in May of 1939. In 1954, the publication Laughlin had started as the organ for the international eugenics movement, the Eugenical News, was renamed first to Eugenics Quarterly and then to Social Biology in 1969.

Studies have shown that Holocaust historians did not begin to publish in any significant numbers until the 1960s and 1970s. (See "From a 'Race of Masters'") It seems that this was when the myth of eugenics as the "discredited science" began to emerge. A mad dash to change the names of institutions and publications to erase any link back to a eugenic past coincided. This pattern of evasion seems to have begun as public knowledge of Nazi aggression became impossible for these intellectuals to ignore. On October 25th, 1938, the leadership of the Eugenics Research Association called a "special meeting" to change name to "Association for Research in Human Heredity." The Eugenics Research Association was headed up by Frederic Osborn. The reader will recall that Osborn was not just part of the A.E.S. leadership, but also one of the men responsible for creating the Pioneer Fund. Osborn would proclaim at the A.E.S. Conference on Eugenics in Relation to Nursing that the Nazi Law for the Prevention of Hereditarily Diseased Offspring was "the most exciting experiment that had ever been tried." ("Summary of the Proceedings," Feb. 24th, 1937, A.E.S. Archives) This proclamation coincided as the violence on German streets was coming to a boiling point. It was also Osborn that took over Eugenics Quarterly after Laughlin, whose name he would change to Social Biology in 1969. Osborn also dropped the subtitle "Current Record of Human Genetics and Race Hygiene" when he took over the publication of Eugenical News in 1939 after Carnegie forcibly retired Laughlin.

There is a discernible pattern of evasion that follows Osborn. Osborn was also part of the leadership of Margaret Sanger's Birth Control organization. As late as 1973, and in the immediate wake of the <u>Roe v. Wade</u>, Osborn made it a point to drop the name American Birth Control League for Planned Parenthood. He knew how closely American Birth Control had worked with the Harry H. Laughlin and Leon Whitney. Just after the <u>Roe v. Wade</u> victory, Osborn was quoted as stating that "Birth Control and abortion are turning out to be the great eugenic advances of our time." More importantly he was well aware of his own ties to eugenics. Most revealing was the hiring of Hans Harmsen for *Pro Familia*, the European arm of Planned Parenthood. Hans Harmsen was one of Nazi Germany's population policy architects.

Of note is that Osborn is frequently described as the less radical and more respectable face of the American eugenics movement. Professor Lombardo cites Daniel Kelves characterization of Osborn as a "reform" eugenicist:

> Such an assessment does not, however, explain sentiments such as the excitement Osborn expressed over the Nazi sterilization program. Osborn, in the same year the Pioneer Fund was initiated, praised it as "the most important social experiment . . . ever tried." Osborn's deliberate down-playing of the human tragedies arising from Nazi "Population policies," and his positive judgment of Wilhelm Frick's role in them, suggests a need for further scrutiny of his "reform" stance. While Osborn's brand of eugenics eschewed both totalitarian ideology and overt racism, his regular commerce with the most malignant of old-line eugenicists and his seeming embrace of government coercion as a legitimate means to effect eugenic goals leave him, at best, an ambiguous figure in the history of eugenics. (Pg. 813, Paul Lombardo, "The American Breed", Albany Law Review, 2002, Vol. 65, No. 3)

An honest reading of the evidence, namely Osborn's private correspondence reveals that Lombardo is correct. Totalitarianism is a horrid form of government precisely because it employs "government coercion" and unchecked power. Thus, Osborn's politically crafted words about the Third Reich are of dubious honesty. Osborn feigned outrage about Nazism's "racial hygiene" in the Eugenical News issues published after 1939. However, Professor Lombardo accurately points out that he continued to publish the work of Hitler's eugenicists even after the revelations of The Holocaust. Osborn gleefully cooperated with Laughlin and Draper whenever it suited him. Therefore we can conclude that the criticism Osborn lays on the likes of Laughlin was only calculated posturing.

Another prominent eugenicist to change the name of the organization they headed up was Marion S. Norton. Norton was the founder of the Sterilization League of New Jersey that helped Woodrow Wilson pass eugenic laws while he was governor of the State. The organization has been working in sexual and reproductive health since 1937 under various names and with shifting goals. The reader will remember Norton as one of those that used their positions to provide favorable coverage for Hitler's Nuremberg Laws. After The Holocaust, the organization came under pressure to change its name once again. Internally, the organization was nearly torn apart by debates, pitting eugenics-minded members against those who believed sterilization should be voluntary and available to anyone who wanted it, for personal or socioeconomic reasons. The latter philosophy prevailed, and in 1962, the organization's name was changed to the Human Betterment Association for Voluntary Sterilization (HBAVS). In the early 1970s, AVS and its allies in the family planning movement launched an intensive campaign to promote sterilization, right around the time when so many ethnic minorities were sterilized against their will or without their knowledge. AVS together with the ACLU and Zero Population Growth launched "Operation Lawsuit," a series of successful lawsuits against various U.S. hospitals for refusing to comply with patients' requests for sterilization. The current name, EngenderHealth, was introduced in 2001. Objections from relatives of Ezra Gosney, founder of the Human Betterment Foundation of California, forced the organization to formally change its name to Birthright, Inc., a national, nonprofit organization with the aim of promoting "all reliable and scientific means for improving the biological stock of the human race."

In one telling instance, there was even the intentional destruction of documentation. C.M. Goethe, Laughlin's financial supporter while in the Eugenics Records Office and on through to the Pioneer Fund, would outlive most of his eugenic cohorts. Goethe passed away in 1966, still unrepentant and distinctly committed to the eugenic cause. He left California State, Sacramento University a generous endowment meant to fund the continued study of eugenics.

Tony Platt, a professor at the Center for the Study of Law & Society of the University of California, Berkeley, endeavored to bring Goethe's story to the surface. Goethe's appreciation for racialist ideology was well known in Sacramento, especially to those in charge of the university he founded. It had always been and continues to be a point of contention for the University of California, Sacramento. Goethe's research endowment has grown to $1.8 million dollars according to Eric Stern, who wrote about the uncomfortable situation for the Sacramento Bee on March 1st, 2007. The article entitled "The Ugly Side of Philanthropist Divides CSUS" recounts what Professor Platt encountered. Platt was warned that he would find that Goethe's papers "had a bit of an Aryan feel." Goethe, after all, had often and vociferously defended Nazi Germany's "honest yearnings for a better population." This was common knowledge to anyone who cared to know in the local community. Goethe's formidable assets had gone towards directly tying him to the eugenics movement. According to Platt, Goethe had spent over a million dollars of his own money publicizing and promoting eugenics. Like Laughlin, Goethe was an avid letter writer with the added benefit of being able to afford a secretarial staff towards those efforts.

The forewarning of the racialist content of Goethe's papers was not the worst news. In 2005, Platt requested funds from the endowment to research Goethe. Platt found that he was not the first to look into Goethe's past. A CSUS Professor and personal friend of Goethe's had looked into the collection of documents left behind by the philanthropist. The Professor, Rodger Bishton, had been the recipient of thousands of dollars of gifts and grants from Goethe. (Platt 2004) Bishton had been a primary beneficiary of Goethe's philanthropy, aside from the university as an institution as a whole. Bishton was endeared and indebted to Goethe. Despite knowing Goethe's ideological leanings, Bishton apparently did not like what he found. According to Professor Platt, the collection contained back-and-forth correspondence with Nazi officials. Bishton betrayed the trust given to him due to his position at the university, and allowed all those boxes of historically important documents to rot in a backyard shed. Platt is of the opinion that CSUS to this day is practicing a "calculated amnesia." Platt recounts his experience in a 2004 article he wrote for the Sacramento Bee:

> Why would my university, with its strong commitment to multicultural values, pay homage to somebody devoted to breeding a master race? I decided to do my own investigation of Goethe's relationship to his adopted alma mater. What I discovered was that in the 1950s and early 1960s, when Sacramento State College, as it was then known, was courting Goethe for his money and prestige, the university turned a blind eye to his widely known racist views. (Feb. 29th, 2004, Sacramento Bee, "Sacramento: Curious historical bedfellows: Sac State and its racist benefactor")

The response Platt received from the administration demonstrates the discomfort the university feels about one of its major benefactors:

> The use of funds from the C.M. Goethe Bequest to expose or undermine the donor himself – no matter how abhorrent his views seem to educated people today – is inappropriate. (Stern, March 1st, 2007, Sacramento Bee, "The Ugly Side of Philanthropist")

CSUS had lauded and celebrated its benefactor until the late sixties and early seventies, coinciding with the time when the tie between eugenics and The Holocaust began to be revisited by historians. CSUS had to back down from its reluctant support for its benefactor in April 1965. CSUS students protested in 1965 after the plan was announced to name a new building after Goethe. The decision was lambasted as a "blasphemy against science." (Platt 2004) Two years later, the faculty quietly voted to remove Goethe's name from the building. Goethe's plush residence was part of the initial endowment. Later on September of 2000, the administration also removed his name from the residence in what was, again, a deliberately tactful and intentionally quiet fashion.

Just around the same time, CSUS had another uncomfortable reminder about their founder. The arboretum on campus was also named after Goethe. As the reader will recall, Goethe was equally dedicated towards environmental activism. According to Professor Platt, the University of the Pacific awarded him an honorary doctorate for the research projects involving plant biology and genetics. The National Park Service made him an "honorary chief naturalist" and the Save-the-Redwoods League posthumously named a grove after him in the Prairie Creek Redwoods State Park. (Platt 2004) However, the local community and university could not escape the local chatter about Goethe's ideology. The university quietly changed the name of the arboretum in 2005. The remaining $85,000 from Goethe's endowment to the arboretum was used to clean up the unkempt thicket and to rededicate the grove. The old sign is now part of the university's archival collection; a collection which only recently the CSUS current administration has begun in earnest to rebuild and reconstitute.

Why is recounting this name changing important? Because it reveals, at least in part, how these institutions prevented their collaboration with Hitler's henchmen from being traced back to them. This epidemic of changed-names reveals how the pro-segregation lobby of the American Civil Rights era eluded being traced back to its links to Nazism. It also reveals, at least in part, why such a pivotal figure as Harry H. Laughlin have largely escaped the infamy of others like Madison Grant, Joseph Mengele, or Karl Brandt. American academia begot Laughlin, and American academia has largely contained his story. The "calculated amnesia" Professor Platt gleaned from his studies of California eugenics is more than palatable to anyone that has dedicated any serious research and contemplation on the subject.

All of this changing of names certainly coincided with the decision by the Carnegie Institution to drop funding for the Eugenics Record Office and the demand that Laughlin retire prematurely. As such, it also coincides with the creation of the Pioneer Fund as the replacement for Carnegie. Paul Lombardo documents in his 2002 Albany Law Review paper, "The American Breed", that Fredric Osborn and Laughlin had agreed that the term "eugenics" should not be part of the Pioneer Fund. According to Professor Lombardo, both Laughlin and Osborn agreed that "'eugenics' must be strengthened until it takes the high place in the public mind . . . it might be a dangerous name for the Fund." (Pg. 788) This was a February, 24th, 1937 letter that Lombardo is quoting. Therefore, placing this strategic move to disguise the eugenic backbone of the Pioneer Fund at least two years prior to Hitler's invasion of Poland. It is revealing to see that even a zealot like Laughlin understood the dangers of his utopian proposals and thus acted duplicitously about revealing the true nature of his organization.

A January 29th, 1943 letter from W.M. Gilbert to Dr. M. Demerec of the Carnegie Institution documents that Laughlin died as a result of a "coronary thrombosis" while retired in Kirksville, Missouri. Laughlin's international fame was quickly forgotten, as very likely was intended. Laughlin's vision of the future did not reflect well on those associates that survived him.

There is a curious newspaper clipping held at the Truman State University archives that has become somewhat of a factoid about Laughlin amongst those that are aware of his role in history. It seems that Laughlin took the time to cut out a 1933 New York Tribune article entitled "Nazis Open Race Bureau For Eugenic Segregation: Aim is 'Pure' German Stock Free of Semitic Influence". The title itself captures the inescapable relationship between eugenics as a science, the law, and The Holocaust. The article prophetically documents that the upcoming "laws will be passed providing for 'segregation and improvement of races'." Laughlin pasted it on a letter-sized piece of paper and inscribed it with the statement: **"Hitler should be made honorary member of the E.R.O. !!"**

In hindsight, the suggestion was certainly appropriate. All available evidence points to the fact that Hitler's infamous Nuremberg Decrees were intended to create a eugenic utopia. Hitler was faithfully implementing the key points of the eugenic doctrine. Hitler himself described the Third Reich as a "Total State." His deputies described its form of government as "applied biology". Hitler knew the eugenic utopia described in "Mein Kampf" could only be sustained by a hyper-socialized and centrally-planned society. In order to create a "race of masters", the state had to be imbued with the "total" control a horse breeder has over the horses; namely the power to decide which horses to put down, to sterilize, or elevate to the rank of "thoroughbreds."

"There is not a truth existing which I fear, or would wish unknown to the whole world."

- Thomas Jefferson -

United States Senate
COMMITTEE ON
INTERSTATE AND FOREIGN COMMERCE

11 March 1957

Mr. C. M. Goethe
Crocker-Anglo Bank Building
Seventh and J Streets
Sacramento, California

Dear Mr. Goethe:

Thank you for your letter of March 6 regarding the McCarran Walter Act. I appreciate your comments, as I am also opposed to opening up our immigration flood gates. I am sure that as a result of your Southern ancestry, you can understand our problem in the South.

With best wishes,

Sincerely,

Strom Thurmond
Strom

ST:das

ROBERT F. KENNEDY
NEW YORK

United States Senate
WASHINGTON, D.C.

July 23, 1965

Mr. C. M. Goethe
3731 Tea Street
Sacramento, California

Dear Mr. Goethe:

Thank you for your letter regarding immigration reform.

The aims of the immigration bill now before the Congress are not to increase immigration sharply but to allocate existing quota numbers fairly -- on the basis of individual merit and relationship to United States citizens and residents, rather than on the outmoded standards of an immigrant's place of birth. Under present law, a laborer from many countries can enter this country long before a scientist or doctor from others -- or long before the mother or sister of a United States citizen. This the bill would change.

Further, the bill would result in a maximum increase of less than 50,000 immigrants each year -- of whom less than 25,000 would be entering the work force. Since our labor force is now nearly 70,000,000, this increase would be less than 1/2800 of our present labor force. In fact, immigrants admitted by the bill would probably increase employment in the long run -- because the skills and capital they bring with them result in the creation of new businesses and the hiring of citizen workers.

Because the bill would eliminate unwarranted discrimination without adverse effects on the United States, I support it. I hope the foregoing answers your questions, and I look forward to hearing your views on other issues in the future.

Sincerely,

Robert F. Kennedy

Africans, the, 94
Alexander, Leo, 218
Allen, Garland, 4, 5, 8, 19, 20, 45, 46, 47, 49, 64, 65, 106, 109, 110, 112, 113, 173, 245, 307, 308, 328, 329
American Breeders' Association, 32, 33, 36, 37, 39, 40, 43, 45, 46, 60, 72
American Civil Rights, 125, 129, 240, 242, 265, 275, 333
American Civil War, 72
American Consulates, 95
Aryans, the, 122, 137, 138, 161, 189, 193, 212, 213, 218, 230, 241, 242, 275, 280, 287, 296, 327
atavism, 11, 57
Baur-Fischer-Lenz, 15
Beer-Hall Putsch, 135
Bellamy, Edward, 114, 171
bigotry, 23, 76
birth control, 241, 268, 321, 323, 324
Black, Edwin, 68, 125, 268
Blakeslee, Dr. Albert F., 191, 244, 304, 305
Bolshevik, 132, 176, 189
Bowman, Isiah, 312
Brown Shirts (Nazi), 138
Buck v. Bell, 1927, 36, 145, 148, 149, 150, 151, 155, 156, 200, 215
Buck, Carrie, 146, 150
Bush, Dr. Vannevar, 283, 284, 299, 300, 301, 302, 305, 306, 307
California, State of, 26, 41, 74, 91, 92, 96, 115, 138, 164, 200, 201, 202, 203, 207, 210, 260, 263, 315, 320, 322, 323, 324, 331
Carnegie Institution of Wash. D.C., 5, 15, 20, 21, 22, 23, 27, 45, 46, 47, 48, 77, 94, 97, 98, 99, 104, 106, 107, 109, 115, 120, 139, 166, 169, 185, 191, 192, 196, 218, 219, 222, 224, 225, 226, 227, 228, 229, 230, 236, 241, 244, 245, 246, 247, 248, 249, 250, 251, 255, 257, 259, 260, 264, 273, 280, 281, 283, 284, 289, 297, 298, 299, 300, 301, 302, 304, 305, 306, 307, 308, 329, 333
Carrel, Alexis, 54

Catholic Church, 221
caucasian, 7, 68, 69, 74, 76, 104, 127, 165, 292, 295
Celler, Emmanuel, 103, 110, 111
Census, 60, 61, 66, 67, 71, 102, 104, 106, 121, 124, 248, 292, 298
centrally planned society, 179, 233, 325
Chase, Allan, 27, 105, 106, 208
Chicago Tribune, 112, 136, 161, 179, 180, 196, 333
Churchill, Winston, 247
Cold Spring Harbor, 11, 22, 27, 28, 45, 46, 47, 49, 106, 109, 139, 142, 164, 169, 175, 225, 228, 244, 245, 246, 250, 257, 260, 271, 272, 273, 274, 275, 280, 283, 304, 305, 308
compulsory sterilization, 83, 148, 153, 195, 218
Connecticut, State of, 248, 249, 250, 251, 260, 274, 275, 293, 294
Conquest by Immigration, 104, 287, 288, 289, 290, 293, 294, 296, 297, 299, 300, 301, 302, 305, 311
Constitution (U.S.), 148, 177, 179
D'Antonio, Michael, 158, 159
Darrow, Clarence, 120
Darwin, Charles, 7, 8, 11, 12, 13, 16, 24, 37, 38, 46, 67, 70, 104, 118, 126, 157, 188, 228, 263, 265, 280, 290
Darwin, Leonard, 4, 14, 15, 16, 23, 26, 37, 39, 46, 84, 90, 96, 132, 133, 135, 137, 179, 201, 207, 216, 226, 228, 229, 235, 247, 261, 277, 278, 302
Darwinian, 26, 27, 41, 119, 153, 186, 263, 291
Declaration of Independence, 41, 142, 169, 252, 268, 319
degeneration, 11, 15, 36, 57, 61, 118, 121, 195, 264, 276, 280, 292
DeJarnette, Joseph S., 41, 92, 133, 153, 199, 202
Draper, Wickliffe, 23, 129, 207, 240, 259, 260, 261, 262, 264, 265, 266, 267, 268, 269, 270, 274, 275, 277, 284, 285, 328, 330
due process, 83, 145, 148, 149, 150, 153,

200
Dunn, L.C., 245, 246, 247, 248, 249, 297, 299, 319, 322, 328, 329
dysgenic, 21, 135, 238, 239, 264
Eastern Europeans, the, 75, 87, 112, 161
Eddy, James G., 275, 305
enumerated powers, 152
eugenic courts, 153, 214, 215
Eugenical News, 47, 191, 192, 194, 196, 230, 232, 241, 246, 269, 276, 308, 329, 330
Eugenics Record Office, 3, 5, 23, 27, 29, 33, 50, 53, 60, 61, 77, 85, 96, 142, 166, 183, 185, 191, 210, 222, 225, 227, 244, 245, 249, 264, 277, 302, 305, 333
Evolution, Theory of, 8, 57, 264
evolutionary ladder, 11, 12, 118
F.D.R.. *See* Franklin D. Roosevelt
Fascist, 132, 165
FDR. *See* Franklin D. Roosevelt
feeble minds, 39, 62, 63, 64, 110, 119, 138, 173, 205, 233, 251, 293
fittest, survival of, 13, 291
Foreign Affairs, 180, 256, 257
foreign policy, 256
founding documents, 79, 179, 216, 238
Founding Fathers, 41, 80, 179, 221
Galton, Francis, 8, 10, 12, 13, 16, 19, 22, 26, 27, 34, 38, 46, 70, 77, 126, 135, 138, 157, 171, 176, 188, 192, 207, 219, 228, 247, 248, 261, 264, 265, 268, 284, 299, 328
gene pool, 8, 10, 11, 35, 76, 137, 153, 161, 193, 216, 275
Genetic Health Courts, 200
Germ Plasm, 72, 110
Gilbert, W.M., 20, 48, 98, 225, 226, 244, 301, 302, 305, 307, 333
Gilman, Joseph, 112, 113
Goebbels, Josef, 138, 193, 195, 206, 214, 277
Goethe, C.M., 26, 61, 67, 68, 74, 75, 76, 94, 103, 115, 122, 127, 161, 164, 165, 167, 173, 179, 203, 205, 260, 276, 277, 284, 302, 305
Gosney, E.S., 77, 96, 203, 204, 205, 206, 207, 208, 210, 260, 315, 316, 331
Grant, Madison, 25, 34, 67, 70, 74, 76, 77, 103, 105, 106, 107, 121, 122, 124, 127, 128, 153, 167, 175, 176, 179, 186, 196, 214, 262, 267, 277, 287, 288, 315, 333
Great Depression, 132
Great War, 14, 61, 88, 106, 132, 133, 140, 200, 291, 327
Gruber, Jonathan, 325
Günther, Hans, 128
Haeckel, Ernst, 12
Handlin, Oscar, 108
Hardy, G.H., 15, 16, 17, 323
Hardy-Wineberg Principle, 17
Harry Olson (Judge), 77
Harvard, 21, 25, 26, 27, 33, 34, 36, 40, 42, 43, 72, 87, 105, 111, 118, 127, 145, 158, 214, 215, 260, 263, 268, 291, 299, 312, 325
Hassencahl, Frances Janet, 4, 5, 11, 13, 16, 19, 20, 21, 22, 33, 37, 38, 39, 40, 41, 46, 48, 71, 88, 89, 94, 95, 96, 97, 99, 104, 106, 107, 108, 110, 111, 112, 113, 114, 115, 116, 148, 169, 175, 180, 181, 278, 281, 282, 284, 287, 304
hearings (Congressional), 42, 87, 88, 94, 99, 105, 108, 109, 110, 114, 165
Heidelberg Degree, 254
Heidelberg University, 254
Hereditary Genius, 188
Holmes, Jr., Oliver Wendell, 145, 146, 151
Holocaust denial, 3
Holocaust, The, 3, 4, 5, 8, 9, 11, 39, 52, 88, 105, 129, 133, 136, 138, 153, 160, 193, 196, 203, 204, 207, 213, 250, 262, 271, 311, 312, 313, 320, 322, 327, 328, 329, 330, 333
Hottentot Venus, 188
House Committee (U.S. Cong.), 71, 72, 73, 74, 96, 99, 104, 107, 108, 109, 110, 115, 165, 315
Hudlow, Raymond, 156, 157, 158, 162
Hull, Cordell, 181, 257, 315
Human Betterment Foundation, 208
Huxley, Julian, 314

IBM, 68, 124, 248, 294
IFEO (Itl. Fed. of Eugenic Org.), 56, 84, 85, 96, 133, 134, 135, 139, 152, 159, 191, 192, 196, 201, 202, 234, 260
Immigration Restriction Act (1924), 76, 94, 102, 105, 113, 115, 121, 123, 165, 214, 292, 294, 311, 312, 315, 316
Immigration Restriction League, 25, 39, 40, 42, 72, 74, 89, 95, 105, 106, 112, 114, 315
inalienable rights, 221
income redistribution, 137, 194, 207, 260
International Federation of Eugenic Organizations, 139
Irish, the, 11, 19, 24, 69, 72, 87, 112, 161, 298
Italians, the, 24, 72, 75, 76, 87, 112, 115, 161, 165, 298, 312
Ivy League, 14, 16, 21, 23, 25, 26, 27, 33, 36, 74, 127, 145, 203, 228, 247, 266, 267, 312
Jennings, Herbert Spencer, 36, 65, 89, 111, 112, 120
Jews, the, 3, 4, 9, 11, 39, 54, 68, 69, 74, 75, 84, 85, 87, 88, 92, 93, 102, 103, 104, 106, 109, 110, 112, 113, 116, 122, 124, 161, 189, 193, 194, 204, 209, 211, 212, 215, 216, 236, 240, 242, 254, 256, 276, 281, 287, 291, 292, 294, 295, 296, 297, 308, 311, 312, 313, 314, 315, 316, 327
Johnson, Albert, 72, 75, 76, 88, 89, 96, 102, 103, 105, 106, 107, 108, 109, 110, 111, 112, 114, 115, 165, 166, 167, 168, 173, 214, 268, 315, 316, 320, 323Journal of Heredity, 32, 60, 113, 184, 201, 211
Jukes, 220
jurisdiction, 7, 8, 83, 84, 97, 192, 232, 314
Kaiser Wilhelm Inst., 84, 161, 205, 211, 257, 259
Kantsaywhere, 171
Kelves, Daniel, 15, 330
Keynes, John Maynard, 26, 28, 209, 247, 325, 328

Kidder, A.V., 227, 228, 229, 245, 246, 247, 248, 249
Kinderreich, 260, 261
KKK, 127, 129, 263, 265, 266, 267
Knauer Baby, 153
Kopp, Dr. Marie, 205, 206, 207, 208, 232, 261
Kühl, Stefan, 128
Labor Department, 236, 300
laissez-faire, 19, 20, 41, 107
Law for the Prevention of Genetically Diseased Offspring, 29, 195
Lehmann, J.F., 128
limited government, 41, 80, 83, 149, 151, 179, 199
Lincoln, Abraham, 60, 129, 255, 256
Lombardo, Paul, 245, 246, 254
Los Angeles, CA, 302, 322, 324
Lundborg, Herman, 9
lynching, 69
Malthus, 27, 105, 176, 208, 209
Marshall, Louis, 54, 55, 56, 57, 58, 79, 80, 208, 260, 268
Master Race, 3, 14, 29, 69, 118, 158, 159, 240
Mediterranean (people), 75, 104, 105, 107, 108, 113
Medoff, Rafael, 311, 312, 313
Melting Pot, 87, 88, 89, 94, 95, 99, 108, 110, 166, 254, 288
Mendel, Gregor, 16, 219
Mendelian, 16, 47, 48, 65, 219, 220
Mengele, Josef, 4, 5, 7, 9, 272, 284, 333
Merchants of Light, 132
Mereworth Stud. *See* Salmon, Walter
Merriam, John Campbell, 22, 23, 48, 94, 98, 99, 225, 226, 227, 228, 229, 230, 244, 245, 246, 247, 248, 249, 250, 281, 283, 300, 301, 304, 305, 306
Mexicans, the, 75, 94, 164, 324
Meyerson, Abraham, 218
military tribunal, 7
Miscegenation, 134, 137, 195
Model Eugenic Law, 53, 54, 56, 57, 78, 80, 81, 83, 85, 133, 137, 139, 142, 145, 153, 155, 200, 202, 205, 226, 233,

249, 276, 307, *See* Model Law
Morgenthau, Henry, 313, 316, 317
N.Y. Chamber of Commerce, 104, 287, 288, 289, 290, 291, 292, 293, 294, 296, 297, 298, 299, 301, 302
National Socialism, 1, 4, 7, 9, 11, 14, 25, 41, 90, 104, 127, 128, 133, 137, 138, 139, 155, 161, 162, 176, 191, 194, 197, 199, 201, 202, 203, 204, 206, 208, 211, 212, 214, 215, 216, 218, 220, 230, 232, 233, 234, 235, 236, 237, 240, 241, 245, 247, 255, 259, 260, 270, 271, 272, 273, 274, 275, 276, 277, 281, 284, 290, 291, 294, 295, 296, 323, 327, 329, 330
Native American, 84, 121, 320, 321
Naturalization, and Immigration, 42, 74, 88, 94, 99, 102, 105, 108, 109, 110, 115, 125, 165, 166, 181, 235, 287, 295, 299, 315
Nazi. *See* National Socialism
Nazism, 128, 155, 188, 205, 242, 275, 290, 302, 330, 333
negro, the, 34, 126, 129, 264, 269, 270, 288, 291, 324
New Deal, 96, 152
New York Times, 57, 87, 112, 136, 137, 138, 151, 196, 199, 207, 213, 241, 287, 294, 296, 316
newspaper (media), 5, 26, 111, 136, 196, 209, 228, 265, 277, 316, 333
Nordic, the, 40, 74, 75, 93, 105, 107, 108, 111, 127, 128, 137, 189, 193, 212, 218, 241, 247, 256, 280
Northeast (U.S.A.), 25, 35, 87, 113, 161, 263, 267, 307, 308
Nuremberg decrees, 5, 137, 193, 240, 330
Nuremberg Trials, 5, 7, 136, 149, 155, 192, 232, 271, 323, 328
Oberlander Trust, 205
Occidental Observer, 325
one-world government, 171
Osborn, Fredric, 135, 260, 267, 277, 333
Osborn, Henry Fairfield, 34, 87, 111, 225, 268

Paul, Randolph, 63, 313, 314
Pearson, Karl, 4, 16, 27, 70, 96, 137
pedigrees, 16, 23, 25, 37, 46, 47, 48, 96, 126, 184, 185, 186, 219, 282
phrenology, 135
Planned Parenthood, 156
Plecker, Dr. Walter Ashby, 120, 121, 122, 123, 124, 125, 262, 265, 267, 275, 302
Ploetz, Alfred, 4, 9, 29, 85, 128, 134, 135, 139, 152, 171, 179, 201, 275
Population Congress (1935), 236, 240, 259
population control, 179
pre-Adamite, 67
precautionary principle, 90
Precautionary Principle, 89, 90, 112, 264, 273, 276
Progressivism, 1, 19, 20, 26, 28, 60, 96, 103, 106, 107, 113, 114, 130, 151, 171, 177, 179, 194, 268, 314, 316, 323, 324, 325
Prohibition. *See* Volstead Act
Prolegomena, 171
Protestants, 19, 67
racial state, 38, 214, 254
Ramos, Dr. Domingo, 225, 226, 227, 302
Rassenhygiene, 14, 128
religion, 93, 211, 212, 221, 238, 248, 291, 292, 313
restrictionist, 113
Revolutions of 1848, 106
Roe v. Wade, 156
Roosevelt, Franklin D., 23, 103, 179, 185, 224, 269, 311
Roosevelt, Theodore, 25, 33, 34, 35, 36, 186
Rüdin, Ernst, 4, 29, 85, 134, 136, 139, 153, 179, 195, 196, 201, 220, 275
Sabath, Adolph, 110
Salmon, Walter J., 169, 280, 282, 283
Sanger, Margaret, 156
Savo, Welling, 158, 159
Schallmayer, Wilhelm, 171
Schmidt, Ulf, 218
Scientific Racism, 27, 208, 276

separation of powers, 52, 216, 293
Seven Devils, 64
Shaler, Nathaniel Southgate, 34, 35, 36, 72, 87, 118, 291, 312
single-origin (theory), 67
Skinner v. Oklahoma, 155
social body, 153
State Department, 97, 98, 99, 102, 236, 257, 274, 300, 305, 313, 314, 315, 316
Stoddard, Lothrop, 25, 34, 49, 69, 85, 127, 128, 214, 215, 232, 261, 277
Supreme Court, 36, 79, 83, 145, 146, 148, 149, 151, 155, 200, 215, 308
T4 Euthanasia, 153
Taft, William Howard, 78
The Bell Curve, 265, 270, 271, 284
Third Reich, 7, 9, 10, 29, 58, 78, 90, 116, 120, 122, 124, 127, 134, 135, 138, 139, 146, 153, 155, 160, 161, 171, 189, 191, 192, 193, 194, 201, 202, 203, 205, 206, 207, 208, 209, 210, 211, 215, 216, 221, 235, 250, 254, 255, 261, 271, 280, 295, 296, 330, 334
thoroughbred horses, 134, 284
Total State (Hitler), 194, 202, 325, 334
totalitarian, 10, 132, 151, 274, 293, 330
Trevor, John B., 105, 106, 287, 302, 315
Truman University, 128, 175, 305
UNESCO, 314
unfit, the, 13, 35, 36, 37, 38, 41, 54, 126, 142, 146, 147, 152, 153, 158, 166, 179, 184, 189, 202, 209, 236, 238, 247, 272, 273, 275, 312
United Nations, 314
Utopia, 132, 172, 173
Virginia (State), 26, 81, 120, 121, 122, 123, 124, 125, 127, 129, 138, 142, 143, 144, 145, 147, 148, 149, 150, 155, 156, 157, 202, 237, 238, 266, 267, 323
Volstead Act, 92, 110, 167
Vorsorgeprinzip, 90, 91
Wagner, Richard, 25
Weindling, Paul, 128
Whitney, Leon, 159, 167, 179, 208, 209, 210, 212, 216, 220, 232, 237, 268, 329
Wilson, Woodrow, 22, 201, 203, 268, 330
WWII, 3, 7, 128, 136, 156, 160, 164, 203, 212, 213, 322, 325
zeitgeist, 136, 138, 201
Zero Population Growth, 323, 325

Made in the USA
Charleston, SC
04 June 2015